2ND EDITION

UK Government & Politics

Mark Garnett & Philip Lynch

Editor: Eric Magee

Philip Allan Updates
Market Place
Deddington
Oxfordshire
OX15 0SE

tel: 01869 338652
fax: 01869 337590
e-mail: sales@philipallan.co.uk
www.philipallan.co.uk

ISBN-13: 978-1-84489-416-1
ISBN-10: 1-84489-416-9

Design and illustrations by Neil Fozzard
Printed by Ian Allan Printing Ltd, Hersham, Surrey

P00530

Contents

Chapter 4 The UK party system

Chapter 5 Voting behaviour

Chapter 6 UK political parties

Chapter 7 Party ideologies

Chapter 8   Pressure groups

Chapter 9   The constitution and constitutional reform

Chapter 10   Parliament and parliamentary reform

Chapter 11   The executive

Chapter 12 Rights, the judiciary and the law

Chapter 13 Devolution

Chapter 14 The United Kingdom and the European Union

Index

Introduction

This textbook has been written specifically to meet the needs of AS students of Government and Politics. It provides comprehensive, accessible and up-to-date coverage of all the key topics on the Edexcel, AQA and OCR specifications. Our aim is to ensure that you need few other resources during your AS course but, by its very nature, politics is changing all the time and you should keep completely up-to-date by following events in the media and reading magazines such as *Politics Review*.

Each chapter provides comprehensive coverage of the topic under consideration which enables you to start reading wherever you or your teacher decide to begin the course. To enable you to relate one topic to another, there are references within the chapters to the other chapters where an issue is discussed in more detail. In addition, you can use the detailed contents pages and the index at the back of the book to lead you to the section containing the information you require.

Although everything you need to achieve a high grade is provided between these covers, you may choose to read more widely beyond the information provided in each chapter. This will obviously help you to do well in your examinations. You will get more out of this book if it is used in conjunction with the *AS/A-Level UK Government and Politics Essential Word Dictionary* written by A. J. Turner and published by Philip Allan Updates.

Assessment objectives

There are three assessment objectives:

➤ AO1 — knowledge and understanding
➤ AO2 — analysis and evaluation
➤ AO3 — communication

About half of all AS marks are for AO1, your knowledge and understanding of the key topics on the specification, but you will not achieve the highest marks and therefore the top grades if you do not also score highly on AO2, which focuses on analysis and evaluation.

Command words

The key to maximising marks for both AO1 and AO2 is to obey the command words in the questions.

➤ Words which are wholly or predominantly AO1 include: 'outline', 'describe', 'what', 'define', 'name' and 'explain the term...'.

➤ Those that are wholly or predominantly AO2 include: 'explain', 'analyse', 'discuss', 'assess', 'why', 'in what ways' and 'to what extent'.

You need to know the difference between, for example, outlining or describing and discussing or assessing. To outline or describe involves using your knowledge and understanding, which is essentially AO1. To explain or analyse involves looking at a range of arguments, weighing up the strengths and weaknesses of each and reaching a conclusion, which is essentially AO2.

Revision and exam technique

The most difficult thing about revision is getting started. Once you have taken the first step, the rest is pretty straightforward. You will need to:

➤ **Organise your notes**. AS examinations are in units, so make sure your notes, handouts, press cuttings and reference material are filed under the appropriate unit headings. Use coloured file dividers for this.

➤ **Familiarise yourself with the specification**. If you don't have your own copy, get one from your teacher or the library. Use it to check that you have notes on all the topics and that you have your notes in the right part of your file.

➤ **Study past papers, mark schemes and examiners' reports**. These are a guide to the types of questions asked and the approach you are likely to encounter when you sit the unit tests. Mark schemes reveal what the examiners are looking for in your answers, and examiners' reports make clear what has been good about students' answers and also what has gone wrong.

➤ **Draw up a revision plan**. Outline the units to be revised with a time scale. Work out how much time there is before the dates of your exams by numbering the days downwards from, say, day 60 to zero, the day of the relevant unit test. You should also be clear about what you are going to revise on a particular day. Electoral reform on Day 10 is not enough. You need to know exactly what has to be covered under this heading by looking at the specification and past papers.

➤ **Write timed answers under examination conditions**. In each unit test you have quite a lot to do in a relatively short time. If you have not practised answering questions in the required time, you could get your timing wrong, not complete all of your answers, lose valuable marks and therefore get a poor grade.

➤ **Know topics thoroughly**. A frequent complaint of examiners is that students do not answer the question on the paper but produce prepared answers. This is a disastrous approach because examiners are unlikely to use a question this time round worded exactly as it was in previous unit tests. It is therefore vital that you know each topic thoroughly to enable you to answer any question you are likely to be asked.

Finally, some do's and don'ts for exam success.

Do:

➤ get your timing right
➤ use up-to-date and relevant examples
➤ obey command words
➤ study past papers, mark schemes and examiners' reports
➤ practise answering questions under examination conditions
➤ answer the question on the paper, not the one you hoped would be there

Don't:

➤ use out-of-date examples when more recent ones are available
➤ copy out large chunks of any stimulus material provided
➤ write down all you know about a topic — instead, apply what you know to answer the question you have been asked
➤ use prepared answers

We hope you enjoy your course and wish you success in your AS units.

Acknowledgements

The authors would like to thank everyone at Philip Allan Updates who helped so efficiently in the production of this book, particularly David Cross and Penny Fisher. They are also grateful to their colleagues and students in the Department of Politics and International Relations at the University of Leicester. Their greatest debt is to Eric Magee, who has been a rigorous and supportive editor.

Accreditations

We are grateful to the following for permission to reproduce copyright material:

- Tables 2.2, 2.6, 5.2, 5.3, 5.5, 5.6 and 14.6, Figures 5.1, 5.2 and 5.3, and Boxes 2.2 and 2.4 are based on data from www.mori.com, reproduced with permission of MORI.
- Material in Tables 11.2, 11.5 and 11.6, and Box 11.2 is Crown Copyright, reproduced with permission.
- Tables 2.1, 3.3, 3.4, 3.5, 3.6, 13.2, 13.3 and 13.6 use data from the Electoral Commission, www.electoralcommission.gov.uk, reproduced with permission.
- Table 13.1 is from Curtice, J. and Seyd, B., 'Is devolution strengthening or weakening the UK?', in Park, A. et al. (eds), *British Social Attitudes: the 18th Report* (Sage, 2001).
- Table 13.4 is from the 'Northern Ireland Life and Times Survey 2004', www.ark.ac.uk/nilt/2004/Political_Attitudes/NIRELAND.html

In a few cases it has been impossible to trace the owners of copyright material. We apologise to any copyright holders whose rights have been unwittingly infringed.

Chapter 1

Democracy and participation

The political system known as 'democracy' is common to all Western states, which are usually described as conforming to the principles of 'liberal democracy'. In the UK, the system is so familiar that at times we seem in danger of taking it for granted, along with associated principles such as the right to free speech. Yet the UK has only been fully democratic since 1928, when women were given voting rights on the same basis as men. As we shall see in Chapter 3, arguments persist over the most appropriate type of voting system. Critics argue that the UK could be made still more democratic, by allowing people to participate in key decisions between general elections. Some go even further, claiming that the UK is not really democratic at all because, like other Western states, it has a system of representative rather than direct democracy. We need to start a thorough discussion of these questions with a look at the nature of politics itself, and to appreciate that there are several contrasting ways of understanding the subject.

Key questions answered in this chapter

➢ What is politics?
➢ What is meant by the term 'democracy'?
➢ How democratic is the UK?
➢ Do referendums improve or endanger democracy?
➢ What are the future prospects for democracy in the UK?

What is politics?

We are all used to seeing politicians arguing with each other — some people think they do little else. Even people who write about politics manage to disagree about the nature of their subject. But this is not simply because people who like politics enjoy a good argument — although free debate is the essence of democratic politics. There is a wide range of plausible answers to the question 'What is politics?' and our choice among these will give a clear hint of our approach to the other key political issues.

Definitions of politics

The most common definitions are as follows.

Politics is about government

This is closest to the 'everyday' definition of politics. It concentrates on specific people and institutions, such as MPs, parliament and the civil service. On this view, political decisions are those that are taken and implemented by people holding positions of authority, whether they hold them as a result of free elections or by appointment. Political institutions such as parliament are where those decisions are taken.

Politics is about public affairs

The first definition has the advantage of being straightforward and restricted in its scope. But does it cover all activities that are distinctively political? Political decisions in the first sense — those taken by MPs and implemented by government officials — affect all of us. Some people disagree with these decisions so deeply that they demonstrate against them. Even though the people in the demonstrations may be butchers and bakers, when they take action of this kind they are clearly *participating* in politics. Voting is also a political act, so that in representative democracies like the UK, it is expected that ordinary people will take part in politics on a regular basis.

We can clarify this definition by arguing that the key distinction lies between *public* and *private* life, and that politics is about public affairs of all kinds. We are constantly dealing with other people, which means that most of our activities are 'public'. If this is accepted, all sorts of decisions might be brought under the umbrella term of 'politics'. For example, we often talk about such things as 'office politics', even when the office in question has nothing at all to do with politics as understood in the first definition. People often use this phrase in a negative sense, suggesting that 'office politics' is a distraction from the important business of a workplace. But in an office, decisions have to be taken which affect everyone working there. The same is true of voluntary bodies, such as clubs and even churches.

Politics is about reaching compromises, in private and in public

This definition takes the second one still further. It is based on a particular understanding of human nature, best illustrated in the work of the Greek philosopher Aristotle (see Box 1.1). According to this view, human beings are sociable creatures. When they live or work together, they all influence each other to some extent, and they all have personal interests that tend to conflict. To be effective, decisions that affect everyone should take account of the widest possible range of views and feelings, in the hope of striking a fair balance between the different interests. It is very unlikely that every decision will satisfy everyone, but there is a good chance of reaching a workable compromise if everyone at least feels that they have been consulted.

Box 1.1 Is man a 'political animal'?

The Greek philosopher Aristotle (384–322 BC) famously wrote that 'man is a political animal.' He did not mean that people had a constant urge to vote or to deliver speeches. What he really meant was that it is *natural* for human beings to live in association with each other. They have needs that they cannot satisfy themselves, and they can communicate with each other. Any being who can live without others, Aristotle thought, is either 'a beast or a god'.

Although we should be careful not to mistranslate Aristotle, his views chime in with definitions 2 and 3. If it is natural for people to live together, it is also natural for them to make decisions that affect their relationships. The ability to think things through, and to communicate, means that these decisions can be discussed in advance. Decisions that affect how people live together seem to be distinctively 'political', whether taken in a formal setting or not.

According to this third definition, then, politics is about finding a way to satisfy, as far as possible, everyone affected, through formal or informal discussions. It includes what we would normally describe as 'private' life as well as public affairs. For example, some people, particularly feminists, argue that decisions about the division of responsibility within a family should be seen as 'political'.

An important aspect of this definition is that, although it is far broader in scope than the first one, it rules out some decisions that we would normally consider to be 'political'. For example, if a government imposes a tax without consulting the public at all, it is not acting 'politically' in terms of this definition. Equally, if a manager in an office imposes a decision without consulting anyone, he or she has failed to act politically.

Furthermore, the use of *force* is excluded from the definition. As soon as a government tries to impose a decision in this way, it has abandoned politics. Thus, for example, people often draw a clear distinction between a 'military' (i.e. imposed) and a 'political' (i.e. negotiated) solution in a country affected by civil war.

Politics is about power

This final definition is the most far-reaching. Those who accept it tend to see 'politics' everywhere — in the home as well as in the public sphere, and in decisions that are imposed without discussion as well as those that are reached through debate (see Box 1.2). This definition rests on a view of human relations that contrasts strongly with Aristotle's definition. On this interpretation, wherever we look, and whatever the procedure, conflict is unavoidable if people associate with each other — and someone always wins. People who take this view usually argue that one group of people tend to get their way again and again. For feminists, the 'winners' in every important conflict are men. For Marxists, the social group (or class) which has the most economic power will always get its way.

Importantly, this definition includes the use of force within the sphere of politics. Indeed, people who adopt this fourth definition tend to think that *every* decision ultimately rests on force, and that the outcome of peaceful negotiations always reflects the balance of power between the various parties rather than any 'fair' assessment of the issues.

Box 1.2 Are consumer choices 'political'?

People who accept the fourth definition of politics often argue that, whether consciously or not, we take political decisions even when we are out shopping. Pressure groups object to the business practices of certain firms, and urge other consumers to boycott their products. The reason may be environmental damage caused by the firms, or the poor conditions for their workers. But some companies today are so large that their decisions can affect governments across the globe. Trying to change the policy of a firm through demonstrations and boycotts can therefore affect politics even on the narrow first definition. Oil companies, banks, sportswear manufacturers and fast-food outlets have all been targeted by campaigners in recent years.

Activists of this kind often argue that people should be more aware of the real scope of politics, and realise that their political power is not restricted to the right to vote. Apparently the message is getting through: research published in 2003 suggested that 17 million people in the UK had made at least one purchase for political reasons.

Which definition do we choose?

In identifying the proper subject-matter of politics, we can take something from all of these different approaches. On reflection, we might think that the first one is too restrictive. For example, it would exclude from the definition of politics much of the everyday activities of *pressure groups*, which obviously affect important decisions even though they are not normally official members of the UK government or parliament (see Chapter 8). For example, the nationwide protests against the high level of fuel tax in September 2000 persuaded the UK government to revise its plans for future increases, and although mass demonstrations in March 2003 did not prevent the war on Iraq, they encouraged Labour MPs to vote against the policy of their government. At the same time, it is obviously true that there are some people who are constantly engaged in decision making by virtue of the offices they hold, and it is reasonable that students of politics should devote much of their attention to them.

However, it is also true that ordinary people participate in politics. Where they are not allowed to vote, they may demonstrate and even remove governments in a revolution. Moreover, the distinction between decisions taken by the people we recognise as professional politicians, and those taken in other public places like the working environment, does not seem as clear as we might have thought when we come to examine the matter in detail. This suggests that our second definition is more satisfactory than the first. Nevertheless, it runs the opposite risk, of making the definition too 'inclusive' and making it hard to distinguish politics from other forms of social activity.

You might have noticed that the third and fourth definitions shift the focus, away from *who* participates in politics, towards *how* political decisions are taken. To be complete, a definition of politics seems to require a discussion of 'how' as well as 'who'. Without embracing the fourth definition fully we might agree that some groups tend to get their way more than others. The generally accepted definition of a *state* (see p. 6) implies that government *ultimately* rests on force.

People who accept the fourth definition usually argue that their view of human nature is based on realistic observation of the facts of political life. They believe that those who accept the third definition are wrong because they are too optimistic in their assessment of human behaviour. For those who hold this view, the idea that politics is about compromise is a piece of wishful thinking.

Box 1.3 Approaches to the study of politics

Academic political writing is usually divided into two broad categories.

Political science is concerned with existing facts. Typically, a political scientist will investigate phenomena such as governments, parties and voters, describing their activities without saying what they *ought* to do.

Political theory, by contrast, is about *values*. Instead of merely describing existing systems of government, political theorists often put forward their own view of what *could be*.

In practice, the division between these two branches of the subject is more difficult to establish than the 'scientists' and 'theorists' would like to think. It is hard to keep our own values out of our 'factual' judgements, however objective we try to be. Equally, our thinking is bound to be affected to some extent by our experiences. This means that even theorists who put forward the case for an 'ideal state' which is completely different from anything in existence base their thinking on their own interpretation of 'reality'.

This introduces us to what is probably the most important underlying cause of all disputes about politics. People who disagree about human nature tend to interpret things in very different ways. These disputes about human nature lie at the root of *ideological* disagreements (see Chapter 7), and different ways of studying politics (see Box 1.3).

Those who prefer the third definition might argue that, whatever their opponents might think, many decisions are in fact taken after wide-ranging discussions. This understanding of politics as a means of reaching compromises between everyone affected — or at least a majority of them — might be idealistic. But it is an ideal reflected in the decision-making procedures of a *liberal* or *representative democracy* — the type of political system normally associated with the UK and other Western states. For this reason, most people in the UK find it the most appealing of all our definitions.

Key terms

> **Civil society.** This refers to voluntary organisations within a state, such as political parties, pressure groups, charities and clubs. Within the general boundaries of the law, they establish their own rules and conventions. In liberal democracies they are seen as an essential element of a free society.
> **State.** Like most important political concepts, the definition of a state is still hotly contested. But it can be seen as 'an association that holds a monopoly of power within a given territory'. It should be distinguished from a *government*, which refers more explicitly to the political arrangements within a state. So systems of government can change while the state remains the same; and citizens or subjects belong to a state whether or not they are members of a government.

Summary

What is politics?

> There are many competing definitions of politics. Four common ones are:
> – Politics is about government.
> – Politics is about public affairs.
> – Politics is about compromising.
> – Politics is about force.
> The third and fourth definitions take account of *how* decisions are taken, rather than just *who* does the deciding. To be complete, a definition has to include both of these factors.
> Our personal definition will depend on our understanding of human nature, and this is open to endless debate. The important thing is to show that we are aware of the different definitions, and appreciate that all of them are at least *partially* true, even if we decide that not one of them is *completely* true.

What is democracy?

'Democracy' is one of the most familiar words in the political vocabulary. Even if we are hard pressed to give a definition of democracy, we regard it as a very good thing. Equally, calling something 'undemocratic' is one of the most reliable ways of making people dislike it. Throughout this book, we will be examining UK political institutions and asking questions like 'are political parties good for democracy?'

The word 'democracy' originated in ancient Greece, along with political terms like 'monarchy' and 'aristocracy' that identified different types of system and the various ways in which power was exercised. Monarchy meant the rule of the single best person, while aristocracy was the rule of the few best people. Democracy meant the rule of the many, or rule by the people as a whole.

Despite our own strong preference for democracy, it is important to note that the Greeks had mixed feelings about it. Writers such as Plato (427–347 BC) and Aristotle studied existing forms of government and were troubled by their apparent tendency to become corrupt. Thus monarchy could turn into 'tyranny' — that is, the single ruler could abuse his or her power (see Box 1.4). Aristocratic government could turn into 'oligarchy' — instead of the few best people governing, power could be monopolised by a group which ruled in its own interests. In fact, Aristotle equated 'democracy' with rule by the many in their own interests — at the expense of the minority.

Box 1.4	Lord Acton on power (1887)

'Power tends to corrupt and absolute power corrupts absolutely.'

Types of democracy

The continuing influence of classical writers such as Plato and Aristotle helped to ensure that the principle of democracy was accepted very slowly in most European states, and although the USA prides itself on its democratic institutions, even the US constitution reflects lingering suspicions of majority rule. Nevertheless, most states nowadays claim to be fully democratic. They only disagree about the best form that democracy should take. There are two main forms: *direct* and *representative* (or *liberal*) democracy.

Direct democracy

When Plato and Aristotle wrote about democracy, they had in mind a system that allowed the many to rule *directly*. In some of the relatively small city-states of ancient Greece, citizens were allowed to take decisions in public meetings, rather than relying on representatives to discuss and decide on their behalf. In the Greek democracies, ordinary citizens did not stand for election as they do in the UK today. Even posts that we would regard as specialised, like that of a judge, were filled by rotation, or by the ancient equivalent of pulling names out of a hat. Women and slaves were not allowed any political voice, however; they were denied the status of *citizenship* in 'democratic' Athens.

Representative (or liberal) democracy

Representative democracies are systems in which citizens elect people to take political decisions on their behalf, on the basis of one person, one vote (see Box 1.5). Thus in these systems the form of participation for all but a small minority of citizens is *indirect*. To safeguard against abuses, the representative must be *accountable* to the electorate — that is, citizens have the right at regular intervals to make an alternative choice if they are not satisfied with the performance of their representatives. Those who are qualified to vote in elections can also stand as candidates themselves, subject to minimal requirements such as the ability to persuade fellow citizens to nominate them, and to pay a small deposit.

Box 1.5　Representatives or delegates?

One of the key questions for supporters of representative democracy is the distinction between *delegates* and *representatives*. A delegate is someone who is instructed to vote in a certain way, while a representative is entrusted with the authority to make up his or her mind having examined all of the arguments. MPs tend to regard themselves as representatives, exercising independent judgement and then submitting their records to the verdict of their constituents when their term of office is over. In practice, though, the normal working procedures of the House of Commons make most of them into delegates for their parties.

Some of the loudest criticisms of UK democracy have come from people who would prefer their MPs to act as delegates on behalf of the majority of their constituents. But although this is clearly preferable to MPs obeying party orders without question, it still seems to be an unsatisfactory halfway house towards direct democracy:

➤ MPs cannot be expected to consult their constituents on every issue, however trivial.

➤ People with independent judgement would be deterred from standing for parliament.

➤ Constituents who support unfashionable, minority causes would lose an important chance to have their views raised in parliament.

The term 'liberal democracy' (not to be confused with the UK's Liberal Democrats) is often used to denote a system of representative government. A liberal democracy is governed by a framework of publicised laws and accepted conventions, which apply equally to everyone. For example, while in some other states the government changes the rules of voting to suit itself, in liberal democracies electoral fraud is against the law. Among other things, liberal democracy depends on a free press, freedom of speech and the right to cast a vote in secret.

Closely associated with liberal democracies is the concept of *pluralism*. Some theorists believe that democracy is meaningless without competition, and a pluralist system is one in which any candidate who wishes to stand for election is free to do so. Pluralists accept that people have different interests, so they expect that freedom to stand for election will normally result in a range of competing candidates.

Criticisms of direct democracy

Direct democracy remains an ideal for some. Indeed, purists refuse to accept that the representative model is 'democratic' at all. As we shall see, the debate on this subject in the UK is far from over. Most supporters of representative democracy argue as follows:

➤ Direct democracy is only suitable for very small states, where all the citizens can gather together to hear the debates and vote for their favoured policy.

➤ In modern states, vital decisions often have to be taken rapidly. Even if it were possible to gather all the people together, it would take far too long.

➤ Professional representatives can devote most of their time to political issues, while people generally have many other distractions. On this view, representatives can usually be trusted to make better decisions than the people as a whole.

> A mass audience is swayed more easily by passionate speeches, even if these distort the issues.

Criticisms of representative or liberal democracy

Even the admirers of representative democracy tend to admit that it is an imperfect system — the least bad option, as it were (see Box 1.6). Its opponents can argue:

> Representative democracy encourages people to think less about politics than they *could* do, even allowing for their busy lives. Many people take an interest only at election time — and a growing number do not even do that.

> Representatives are not truly *accountable*. If they vote against the clear wishes of the electorate on crucial issues, citizens have to wait until the next general election to remove them. Even if they consistently vote against the will of the electorate on minor issues, they might continue to win elections because many ordinary voters take insufficient interest in political events.

> Representative government seems to be inseparable from political parties, which impose their views on their members. People tend to vote for party labels rather than on the merits of individual candidates. The system encourages people to conform to the opinions of others, rather than speaking up for themselves.

> Regardless of their backgrounds, representatives tend to lose touch with voters as soon as they are elected. Spending more time with other representatives than with ordinary people, they begin to see the world differently and follow interests of their own. They also develop powers of persuasion that can cover up their failures.

Box 1.6 Winston Churchill on democracy

'Democracy is the worst form of government except all the other forms which have been tried from time to time.'   Winston Churchill, 1947.

Totalitarian democracy

A good way of appreciating the ideals of liberal democracy is to contrast it with its most common alternative. A *totalitarian* state is one in which the government controls (or tries to control) every meaningful aspect of people's lives, and allows no political opposition. It seems contradictory to talk of 'totalitarian democracy', but many totalitarian states (e.g. the former Soviet Union) have claimed that they are actually *more* democratic than their Western counterparts. The ruling party always wins the elections or referendums, but totalitarian governments seem to find them worthwhile as a way of claiming *legitimacy* (see Box 1.7). In October 2002, for example, President Saddam Hussein of Iraq claimed to have received nearly 100% of the votes in a poll on his continued leadership. He was the only candidate, and the 'election' took place without independent observers to ensure that the process was free and fair. Thus for supporters of liberal democracy the 'contest' was utterly meaningless.

Box 1.7 Power, legitimacy and authority

It might be thought that power, legitimacy and authority are different words for the same thing. But there are some subtle differences, which underline the importance of choosing words carefully when writing or speaking about politics.

➤ *Power* is the ability to make people do what they would not otherwise have done. It is best seen as a 'neutral' or purely descriptive term, because we speak of a party being 'in power' whether we approve of it or not, and even if it has won its position unfairly. We also speak of 'the power of persuasion', which means the ability to bring someone round to a different way of thinking without using force.

➤ *Legitimacy*, on the other hand, has a strongly positive flavour. When we say that a government is legitimate, we mean that its right to govern is generally accepted. In a liberal democracy, legitimacy arises from victory in a free and fair election.

➤ When speaking of a government that we believe to be legitimate, we often refer to its *authority*. In a healthy liberal democracy, people accept a government's authority even if they have not voted for it. On the other hand, governments that deny freedom to their citizens are often described as 'authoritarian' regimes.

Key terms

➤ **Citizenship.** A status that recognises a person's rights and responsibilities as a full member of a particular state, including the right to play some role in politics. By contrast, to be a *subject* of a state implies something less than full membership and (at best) a passive role in political decisions.

➤ **Liberal democracies.** Countries that are governed in accordance with certain 'core' liberal principles, such as the right to free and fair elections, freedom of expression at all times, and the impartial administration of justice. The UK is generally regarded as a liberal democracy, even if it is an unusual one because it lacks a written constitution (see Chapter 9).

Summary

What is democracy?

➤ Under direct democracy, every citizen has the right to an important role in decision making.

➤ Under indirect democracy (e.g. representative government), everyone has the right to have a say in choosing the people who take decisions.

➤ Liberal democracies are indirect democracies in which governments are chosen through free and fair elections, and people have the right to make a public protest if they object to policies implemented between elections. The UK is usually seen as a liberal democracy.

➤ In 'totalitarian democracies', polls are held which do not satisfy the principles of liberal pluralism, and which the ruling party always wins. Without a guarantee of free speech, or even of the personal safety of the government's critics, no democratic validity can be attached to the results.

Democracy in the UK

Representative democracy in the UK has come about gradually, and only quite recently. Before 1832, the right to vote was generally connected to the ownership of property, which excluded the majority of the population. But the system was haphazard because constituencies were created at different times and the extent of voting rights depended on the prevailing local conditions. In a few constituencies, every resident had the right to vote; in others, hardly anyone did. The only constant factors were that women could not vote anywhere and the electors had to make an open declaration of their choices (secret ballots were not introduced until 1872).

The constituencies themselves had no rational basis because they reflected historical developments rather than the principles of liberal democracy. Before 1832, the deserted village of Old Sarum in Wiltshire had the right to send two representatives to parliament, while the thriving industrial town of Manchester had no MPs of its own! In 1819 a large but peaceful crowd protesting against this state of affairs was attacked by mounted soldiers. Eleven protesters were killed and 400 were wounded in what became known as the 'Peterloo Massacre'. This was only the most dramatic of many violent incidents on the road to liberal democracy in the UK.

Even in 1900, the UK electorate was only around 400,000 out of a population of 16 million. After a long struggle by the Suffragettes, involving direct action by them and severe repression by the authorities, women over 30 won the right to vote in 1918. The same legislation included all men over 21 in the electorate, with a few trivial exceptions. It was not until 1928 that the sexes were allowed to vote on an equal basis. Only after this could it be said that the UK had a system of *universal suffrage* — one of the most important features of a liberal democracy.

In 1969 the voting age was lowered to 18. Since an act of 1885, steps have also been taken to ensure that the size of constituencies remains roughly equal. The Boundary Commission regularly assesses the effects of population movements and adjusts the shape of UK seats accordingly. In an era of rapid social mobility, its work is more important today than ever before.

Criticisms of UK democracy

The UK has a 'first-past-the-post' (FPTP) electoral system, meaning that in each constituency the winner is the person who receives the most votes. The main criticism is that under this system votes are not of equal value, as the strict principles of liberal democracy demand. The people who vote for losing candidates in a seat might just as well have stayed at home — whether their candidate loses by 20,000 votes or by one, the outcome is the same. Similarly, if a candidate wins by 20,000 votes, 19,999 of his or her votes are technically 'wasted'!

The main proposed remedy is to replace FPTP with one of the available systems of *proportional representation* (PR), to make sure (as far as possible) that everyone's vote has roughly equal value. There may also be a case for *fixed-term* parliaments, with elections held only at intervals laid down by law. At present, a prime minister can call an election at a time which suits the governing party (within the 5-year period laid down by law as the maximum duration between general elections).

We look at this debate in more detail in Chapters 2 and 3. For now, we are addressing the question of whether or not the UK should be regarded as a liberal democracy, which is best answered by comparing the ideals of liberal democracy with the conduct of UK politics in general.

Those who argue that the UK is a liberal democracy can point to a good deal of concrete evidence. British elections are conducted according to rules that are the same for everyone. Candidates and voters alike have the right to free speech, and the state provides money to ensure that a message from every person standing in an election reaches the electorate before polling day. Ballot slips are numbered, which means that it is possible to find out how individuals voted. But this is considered to be a necessary safeguard against electoral fraud, and at least voters do not have to make an open declaration as they used to do. Fraud is punished: for example, the Labour MP Mohammed Sarwar almost lost his seat at Glasgow Govan because of alleged irregularities at the 1997 general election. Once MPs have been legally elected, their right to free speech is protected. No one can be prosecuted for statements made in parliament, even if MPs make remarks about individuals which would lay them open to charges of slander if they said the same things in any other place.

In addition, we saw earlier that definitions of politics that restrict the role of ordinary people to the occasional casting of a vote are too narrow. While the eighteenth-century French philosopher Jean-Jacques Rousseau jeered that the British were only free at election time, even then there were other means by which disgruntled voters could pressurise governments to change their minds. Recent mass demonstrations over the poll tax (1990), fuel taxes (2000), hunting (2002) and the war with Iraq (2003) are only the most spectacular examples of the British using their right to free speech. There are many other avenues available for people who wish to influence policy, such as joining a political party and writing to the newspapers or to MPs.

Protesters voice their anger at the government's decision to go to war with Iraq, 2003

Another common objection to the UK system is that, although most politicians are elected, many powerful people hold their positions without having to face the voters. Over the years criticism has focused on the House of Lords, the civil service and judges. Recently, many civil service functions have been given to so-called quangos — 'quasi-autonomous non-governmental organisations', such as National Health Trusts and the BBC — which are often headed by unelected people who are highly sympathetic to the government of the day.

A reform of the House of Lords has been under way since 1997. Although the final shape of the second chamber is still uncertain, the demand for at least partial election of its members is unlikely to be resisted for much longer (see Chapter 10). In the other cases, change is unlikely to be so dramatic. The most common general response to criticism of unelected officials is that certain offices must be filled by people with relevant expertise. Judges, for example, have to be experienced in the legal profession. Even in the USA, where many law officers are elected, the most senior judges are appointed by the president (with the Senate's approval). Similarly, the fact that civil servants are not elected ensures continuity. Even when governments change, the new ministers can ask for advice from people who understand the issues from the inside. Quangos are far more difficult to defend on democratic grounds but, if pressed, ministers can argue that it makes sense to appoint people who can be trusted to implement the government's policies.

In view of the evidence, it can be argued that the UK does not have a system that satisfies all the conditions laid down by the principles of liberal democracy. On balance, however, its institutions and conventions are a close enough match to justify the label, and there are reasonable explanations for its failure to live up to the ideals in every respect.

The Marxist approach

Finally, some people (particularly Marxists) argue that any form of democracy in a capitalist system is completely irrelevant (see Box 1.8). However 'fair' the procedures might be in the abstract, the result can only be a victory for those who hold the dominant economic power in society — and these people are not democratically accountable to anyone. This is a reflection of the fourth definition of politics that we looked at earlier: politics as the exercise of power.

Box 1.8 Ken Livingstone on democracy

'If voting changed anything, they'd abolish it.'

Title of a book by Ken Livingstone, former Labour MP and current Mayor of London, 1988.

Although Marxism is widely assumed to have been discredited by the practice of the Soviet Union and other countries, Marxist objections must be taken seriously. It is not enough to reply that liberal democracies have institutions like a free press, which should ensure that the real motives of decision-makers are open to constructive criticism (or worse!). Much of the media is in the hands of private companies, which are unlikely to give positive publicity to people who favour alternatives to capitalism.

By contrast, some people argue that true democracy is impossible without a 'free market' economic system, and that, instead of representing a threat to liberal democracy, the private ownership of newspapers and television channels is its best guarantee. This may or may not be true, but there have always been examples of countries in which a free market has existed *without* liberal democracy. China appears to be conforming to this model, as did the UK itself before 1918.

Ultimately, our attitude to this problem depends on our own ideological viewpoint — a question examined in Chapter 7. Marxism depends upon a particular view of human nature, which portrays the institution of private property as inherently corrupting. At present, we should merely note the possibility that people continue to vote for UK parties that support capitalism because they genuinely reject other possible social and economic arrangements. We might, for example, say that capitalism is open to serious abuses, but that democratic institutions still offer the best defence of the public interest, and a chance of peaceful change if voters grow tired of the existing system.

In recent years, political scandals have been unearthed by the media and investigated by parliament. It may be the case that these are only the tip of an iceberg. The point is that democracy as practised in the UK does provide the opportunity to expose corruption, and the system can only be as effective as the people who operate it. So we can conclude that, despite its faults, the UK does fulfil the general criteria of a liberal democracy.

Summary

Democracy in the UK

The UK has the following democratic features:

➢ free and fair elections — all adults over the age of 18 may vote in a secret ballot
➢ representative institutions such as parliament
➢ free press and media — no government control
➢ the rule of law
➢ freely operating parties and pressure groups
➢ little political corruption
➢ an impartial, anonymous and permanent civil service

The UK has the following undemocratic features:

➢ a first-past-the-post electoral system for Westminster elections, which is unfair
➢ many powerful people who hold their positions without having to be elected
➢ executive domination of parliament
➢ no entrenched Bill of Rights
➢ government secrecy
➢ a capitalist system in which power resides with those in a dominant economic position
➢ the prime minister's extensive powers of patronage

Do referendums improve or endanger liberal democracy?

There is, though, another device that could be used to make the UK more democratic. The use of *referendums* — votes of the whole electorate on specific issues — has been urged as a way of re-introducing an element of direct democracy in a representative system. In the specific circumstances of the UK, referendums seem to infringe the constitutional principle of parliamentary sovereignty (see Chapter 9). However, critics argue that this would be no bad thing, since parliament is supposed to be the representative voice of the people, and it should be overridden if it is failing in this task.

Those who favour the regular use of referendums argue that:

➢ Certain issues, notably on constitutional questions, are so important that they cannot be settled by votes in parliament.

➢ Other issues, such as moral questions, cut across party lines, and governments cannot reasonably claim that election victories give them a mandate to enforce all of their policies.

➢ An element of direct democracy will 'reconnect' ordinary people with politics. Having actively participated in a referendum, people will take far more notice of the real issues at election time, rather than deciding on the basis of superficial factors like the image of the party leaders.

➢ Although the outcome of a referendum is not necessarily decisive for all time, a direct vote of the people on a specific issue can be said to carry more authority than a parliamentary decision.

➢ Although the procedures of ancient Greece are impractical in a country as large as the UK, advances in the electronic media mean that everyone can be well informed, and even take part in a national debate.

Arguments against referendums

Those who dislike referendums are often accused of being unimaginative and simply opposed to change of all kinds. However, there are some powerful arguments against the device:

➢ It is associated with totalitarian rule. Dictators find it attractive as a way of claiming democratic legitimacy, even when the vote has taken place without free speech or safeguards against fraud.

➢ The frequent use of referendums in the UK would undermine the traditional constitutional principle that parliament is the sovereign lawmaking body.

➢ The questions can be phrased in a way that influences the choice of voters. However careful

THEY SHOULD ASK THE PEOPLE IF THEY WANT A REFERENDUM.

DAVID AUSTIN

the wording, it may exclude certain options that could actually prove very popular. To be fair, the words of the question should themselves be chosen by a referendum, but this would make things impossibly complicated.

➤ People who do not normally take an active interest in politics can be swayed by emotional rhetoric, rather than deciding on the real issues.

➤ Even if all the campaigning groups are given equal funding and equal access to the media, people tend to vote for the side that is supported by the best-trusted politicians, regardless of the arguments.

➤ Referendums can be held at a time that suits the ruling party. So, despite all the outward trappings of direct democracy, elected representatives retain the most powerful influence over the eventual decision.

➤ In other European states, a vote that does not suit the ruling party tends to be followed by another poll so that the public gets the 'right result' in the end.

➤ On a more practical level, referendums are expensive and disrupt other government business.

Referendums in the UK
Membership of the Common Market

All of these arguments were expressed before the first UK-wide referendum, held in 1975, on the question of continued membership of what was then the European Community (EC). Before the contest was held, the arguments against the use of referendums tended to be used by people who wanted the UK to stay in the Community. With justification, they claimed that the then prime minister, Labour's Harold Wilson, only favoured a referendum because it allowed him to avoid personal responsibility for a decision that was bound to split his party.

As it turned out, the supporters of EC membership had reason to be thankful for Wilson's decision. The result of the poll, held on 5 June 1975, was almost two-thirds in favour of continued membership. The turnout was high — also around two-thirds — and almost every area of the UK said 'yes'. The pro-EC group could thus claim that 'the people had spoken', and that the issue of EC membership was now settled for ever.

However, the defeated opponents of membership had plenty of counter-arguments. The question presented to voters was: 'Do you think that the United Kingdom should stay in the European Community (the Common Market)?' Voting to stay in was very different from voting to join in the first place — but the electorate had not been allowed a direct vote when the initial decision was taken. So, opponents argued, the outcome was a foregone conclusion. In addition, the pro-EC campaign was much better funded than the opposing side — and when the UK had joined, people had been bombarded with favourable government propaganda, funded by the taxpayer.

The EU constitution

Eurosceptics oppose what has since 1993 been the European Union, and have repeatedly urged that further referendums be held on the UK's membership. They believe that important changes have been introduced since 1975 without public consent. The Referendum Party contested 547 seats at the 1997 general election; it failed to win any of them but caused considerable discomfort to the Conservatives, who were seriously divided over the necessity for a referendum. Successive governments have been reluctant to call referendums on European questions, not just because they fear exposing divisions within their own party ranks, but because public opinion in the UK has almost invariably been hostile towards the EU.

After some hesitation, the Labour government agreed that there should be a referendum on the new EU constitution. The necessary legislation was introduced before the 2005 general election, including the proposed question: 'Should the United Kingdom approve the Treaty establishing a Constitution for the European Union?' The wording was endorsed by the independent Electoral Commission. At first the government had resisted demands for a referendum on this subject on the grounds that the constitution would introduce only minor changes to existing practices within the EU. It had already accepted that a referendum would be held if and when it proposed to join the European single currency.

Other UK referendums

One reason for the lack of debate over the principle of referendums is that several more have been held in the UK since 1975, although not across the whole nation (see Box 1.9). The basic idea seems to be that major constitutional changes should not take place without a vote of those who will be most affected. The first of these referendums, in Northern Ireland, took place 2 years before the 1975 poll. Although this vote received relatively little attention in other parts of the UK, for the inhabitants of Northern Ireland it concerned the most vital question of all — whether governments based in Westminster or Dublin would have the ultimate authority over them.

The problem is that, although it seems agreed universally that referendums should be held on important constitutional issues, people continue to differ in their view of what is important. Thus in June 2003 the Labour government promised referendums on regional government in the north east, the north west and Yorkshire and Humberside. In the end, only one was held (in the northeast — see Box 1.9). Ironically, at the same time the government was opposing the idea of a referendum on a European constitution, arguing that this would not make a significant difference to the way in which the UK was governed.

Box 1.9 UK referendums

1973: Northern Ireland's membership of the UK

A vote on the continued existence of Northern Ireland as a part of the UK was held shortly after the abolition of the devolved Stormont government. The result was an overwhelming majority in favour, but most opponents boycotted the referendum, so the outcome was of limited significance.

1975: UK membership of the European Community

(See p.16 for details.)

1979: devolution for Scotland and Wales

Scotland voted 'yes' to the Labour government's proposal for a devolved assembly with legislative powers in areas such as health and education. However, the result of the referendum was very close — 1.23 million to 1.15 million, on a turnout of less than 64%. The opponents of devolution had inserted a clause in the legislation ensuring that devolution would not come into effect unless the proportion of those who voted in favour exceeded 40%. Since the relevant figure was only 32.9%, the referendum vote was nullified. As a direct result, Labour lost the support of Scottish Nationalists in the House of Commons and the government was defeated on a vote of confidence, leading to the 1979 general election.

The proposed devolved assembly for Wales would have had no independent legislative powers, being concerned more with the implementation of measures laid down at Westminster. In fact, an overwhelming majority of Welsh voters rejected devolution. Less than a quarter of a million — only 20% of those who cast a vote — endorsed the proposal. The turnout was less than 59%.

1997: devolution for Scotland and Wales

After Labour's landslide election victory in 1997, both the Scots and the Welsh approved of devolution. In Scotland, voters were given the option of a parliament with wide-ranging legislative authority and limited tax-raising powers. This was approved by 63.5% of those who voted. (The turnout was 60.2% — below that of 1979.)

For Wales, Labour proposed an assembly without tax-raising powers. The result of the referendum in Wales was even closer than that for Scotland in 1979, with the important difference that the turnout was much lower — only 50.1%. The 'yes' vote was 50.3%. Since the anti-devolution Conservative Party no longer had a single Welsh MP, the result mainly reflected continuing divisions among local Labour Party supporters.

1998: devolution for Northern Ireland

A poll was held after the 'Good Friday Agreement' to restore the Stormont government on a reformed basis (see Chapter 13). The result was 71% in favour, on a turnout of 80%. The agreement was also endorsed by a vote in the Republic of Ireland. However, some groups remained adamantly opposed and the new institutions have been suspended on two occasions.

1998 onwards: elected mayors

A London-wide election was held to decide whether the UK should have its first directly elected mayor and a separate assembly. The proposal was accepted by almost three-quarters of those who voted, but the turnout was very low (only 34%).

Since 1998 there have been other local polls on the subject of elected mayors, in which the turnout has usually been very low. In Sunderland in October 2001, it was a miserable 10%. The results have varied too. By the summer of 2005, 20 out of 31 referendums (including Tony Blair's constituency base at Sedgefield) had rejected the idea of an elected mayor.

2004: regional assembly for northeast England

Although the Labour government re-elected in 2001 had ambitious plans for devolution to specific regions of England, it only held one referendum — in the northeast, where opinion was presumed to be strongly favourable. However, in November 2004 voters rejected the proposal in an all-postal ballot. On a turnout of around 48%, less than a quarter of voters were in favour. The government immediately abandoned plans to hold polls in the northwest and in Yorkshire and the Humber.

Local referendums

Recently many local councils have held referendums, most frequently in an attempt to win backing for their policies on taxation and spending. In February 2005 Edinburgh's citizens voted to reject a plan to reduce traffic congestion, which was based on the scheme introduced by London's elected mayor, Ken Livingstone. However, campaigners for direct democracy have noted that the 1972 Local Government Act provided for referendums to be held on the initiative of ordinary residents, rather than the councils themselves. This has given voters the opportunity to pronounce on matters of national as well as local significance. For example, opponents of UK membership of the euro have tried to use local referendums to stop their councils from spending money to prepare for the introduction of a single European currency.

Major referendums in the UK, 1975-2005

Year	Issue	Electorate	'Yes' vote (%)	'No' vote (%)	Turnout (%)
1973	Constitutional status of Northern Ireland	Northern Ireland	98.9	1.1	58.6
1975	Continued UK membership of EEC	UK	67.2	32.8	64.5
1979	Devolution for Scotland	Scotland	51.6	48.4	63.8
1979	Devolution for Wales	Wales	20.2	79.8	58.3
1997	Devolution for Scotland	Scotland	74.3 for parliament; 63.5 for tax-raising powers	25.7 against parliament; 36.5 against tax-raising powers	60.4
1997	Devolution for Wales	Wales	50.3	49.7	50.1
1998	Approval of Good Friday agreement for Northern Ireland	Northern Ireland (poll also held south of the border)	71.7	28.9	80
2004	Elected assembly for northeast England	Northeast England	22.1	77.9	47.7

In theory, regular referendums on key political questions are an important asset to any liberal democracy. Yet the original objections still have some force. On the basis of UK practice, another oddity can be identified. One would expect that people would regard the results of referendums as being more conclusive than parliamentary votes, since everyone in the country has a direct voice. Yet this has not been the case. Apart from the local referendums on elected mayors, the only UK referendums that have apparently laid a controversy to rest are the 1997 polls on devolution to Scotland and Wales. Even these decisions might be revised if demands grow for complete independence. Despite the overwhelming defeat of plans for regional government in the northeast of England, the question could easily be revived in the future as part of a more systematic reshaping of local institutions.

There is actually a good reason for this phenomenon. Reserving the referendum for really 'big' questions seems, in theory, to be a fair compromise between direct and indirect democracy. However, these are precisely the issues about which passions are least likely to die away, even after 'the people have spoken'.

Despite these remaining questions, it is fair to conclude that, in principle, the referendum can be an asset for a liberal democracy. Even if UK-wide referendums remain infrequent, it seems that local polls will be a regular feature, at least in part because of an increasing awareness that they are often used in the US (even on divisive issues like abortion). There are now several pressure groups, such as the Direct Democracy Campaign (DDC), that advocate an increased use of referendums.

Summary

Do referendums improve or endanger liberal democracy?
Arguments for:
➤ a form of direct democracy
➤ encourages political participation
➤ provides a clear answer to a specific question
➤ unites divided parties
➤ provides a mandate for controversial issues
➤ a device for resolving controversial moral issues
➤ a form of entrenchment
➤ legitimises important decisions affecting the constitution

Arguments against:
➤ inconsistent with the doctrine of parliamentary sovereignty
➤ issues may be too complex to be resolved in simple yes/no terms
➤ regular use could result in voter apathy and low turnouts
➤ effective alternatives to test public opinion already exist
➤ low turnouts may distort the result
➤ results may not be decisive
➤ funding differences may affect the result

➤ possible bias in the questions asked
➤ used for the 'wrong' reasons
➤ could result in the 'tyranny of the majority'

The future of democracy in the UK

Democracy by email?

The most radical ideas for the reform of democracy concern the internet. In theory, at least, this would allow ordinary people to vote on every conceivable issue. Perhaps parliament would not be abolished entirely, but elected politicians would merely express their views in each debate. The actual decisions would be left to the people as a whole, and would be implemented by a bureaucracy whose leaders would be subject to regular elections.

While this proposition is highly attractive to some idealists, in practice the general objections to referendums apply with even greater force. Lacking specialist knowledge, people might vote for frivolous reasons on issues that do not affect them personally, even though they might be of considerable importance to other groups. Furthermore, public opinion can change almost overnight depending on recent events.

It can be argued, in fact, that public opinion already has more impact on political decisions than ever before. The major parties all consult 'focus groups', which give them an idea of the likely response to a policy (see Box 1.10). In addition, opinion polls on specific issues are published frequently. The Labour government under Tony Blair is keen to make voting in elections easier (and more attractive) by using the internet. On balance, this looks a safer option than using new technology to give the general public a direct influence on a wide range of controversial issues.

Box 1.10 **'Deliberative democracy'**

There is a more modest way in which governments can find out what well-informed members of the public think about specific issues. Researchers can recruit a group of people who constitute a broadly representative sample of the general public. They can be asked for their views at the outset, then provided with information and competing arguments on the subject in question. At the end of the session, they can be asked whether or not their views have changed.

This approach is particularly useful to governments, opposition parties and media organisations as a way of gauging public opinion and testing the likely reaction to specific policies. Before the 1997 general election, 'New Labour' certainly benefited from the 'focus groups' that are now a key feature of political strategy for all the main UK parties. A similar idea, that of small 'citizen's juries' paid to deliberate on specific issues, has been championed by the think-tank the Institute for Public Policy Research (IPPR). However, such bodies can be seriously misleading. Can any group of people really be 'representative' of the whole population? Do people gathered together to consider one specific topic think and decide like the increasingly isolated and distracted individuals of 'real life'?

The rise of apathy

Most political participants and commentators are seriously worried about the apparent rise of *apathy* in the UK. The turnout in some recent polls, such as European and local elections, has been extremely low. The situation has traditionally been much better in general elections, where the outcome is recognised to have a significant impact on everyone's lives. Yet even here the turnout has fallen steeply, from 77.7% in 1992 to 71.5% in 1997 and down to a fraction below 60% in 2001. In the election of May 2005 turnout rose to 61.2%, but if anything this was even more troubling because there had been a national campaign to encourage voting and an unprecedented number of people (almost 6 million) had taken the easier option of voting by post. In these circumstances, a much greater increase could have been anticipated.

In itself, low turnout need not be a very bad thing. For example, it might reflect a high level of satisfaction with the existing government — or, indeed, a widespread belief that the government is so bad that its defeat is inevitable anyway. At the same time, though, it might signify a loss of interest in politics and a disdain for the people who stand for parliament. The evidence suggests strongly that this was the case in the UK in 2001 and 2005. The development raises serious questions about the democratic credibility of the UK's political system.

One likely reason for the disappointing turnout is the influence of the media. More than ever before, general election coverage focuses on party leaders and the question of who will govern the UK. While ordinary voters might be able to convince themselves that their support could tip the balance in their own constituencies, they are very unlikely to think that a single vote will do anything to change the overall national outcome. This is far from being the only respect in which the media, which could have done so much to inform and enthuse the electorate, seems to have worked the other way.

Although healthy liberal democracies depend on significant levels of electoral participation, we should remember that politics is not just about elections. Research published in 2003 showed that in other respects UK citizens are showing their interest in public affairs. For example, 22 million people had signed at least one petition, and 2.5 million had taken part in a demonstration (the research was conducted before the anti-war demonstrations of February and March 2003, which involved many people who had never been active before). This evidence supports the view that the problems of democracy in the UK lie with politicians, rather than an 'apathetic' public.

Compulsory voting

One way of halting the slide in turnout might be the introduction of compulsory voting. Unless they had a reasonable excuse, under this system voters would be punished with a small fine if they refused to register their choices. Every ballot paper would include a separate section, labelled something like 'none of the above', to allow voters to express an opinion even when they dislike all of the candidates. A nationwide figure that tallied up all of these disgruntled voters might give politicians more of a shock than any fall in turnout! A more positive reason for compulsory voting is that when people have been forced to vote on one occasion they might get into the habit, and even pay more attention to the issues discussed in future campaigns.

The idea has been implemented in several countries, including Australia, and the evidence suggests that it does make a difference. In 1998 the Home Affairs Select Committee of the UK Parliament considered it too, and expressed a desire for a wider public debate. At present, though, compulsory voting seems unlikely to be introduced.

One obvious problem with compulsory voting is that it infringes long-established civil liberties. If people think that they have better things to do, why should they be dragged into polling stations? But this seems a rather trivial point. Voting really ought to be regarded as a duty, rather than as a right. People have suffered in the fight for the vote, and abstention seems like an insult to their memories at a time when polling stations are within easy reach for most people. If turnout continues to fall, far more serious liberties might come into question. Politicians will become ever more distant from ordinary people, and extremist parties of all kinds have a better chance of winning power when the majority stays at home.

But there are other serious problems with the idea of compulsory voting:

➤ If people have to vote even if they have paid no attention to the campaign, their choices are likely to be bad ones.

➤ The system would be very difficult to administer. People who have recently moved house, are on holiday or are genuinely ill would have to be relieved of their fines. Those who cannot afford to pay would also have to be excused.

➤ The fall in turnout may be a symptom of deeper problems, and not just a problem in itself. Some of these problems may well be the fault of our existing politicians, but it is unlikely that others (such as the negative influence of the media) will go away just because people are forced to express an opinion. Even a high 'none of the above' vote might obscure the real difficulties.

Rather than taking the drastic option of making voting compulsory, the UK could increase turnout at elections by making it easier to vote. In July 2002 the Cabinet Office published a consultation paper, *In the Service of Democracy*, which invited the public to offer opinions on various ideas, including more accessible polling stations, voting via the internet, postal-only elections and voting by telephone. There had already been some experiments with these methods in the local elections of May 2002, author-ised by the 2000 Representation of the People Act and funded by the government. Turnout increased in 14 of the 16 council wards that held all-postal ballots. However, after widespread allegations of fraud in the 2004 local and European elections, the Electoral Commission argued that rather than helping matters the experiment was actually bringing democracy into disrepute. The government's response to this report showed that its enthusiasm for democracy by post had rapidly diminished. Before the 2005 general election there was speculation that some results would be subject to legal challenges.

Some councils have been experimenting with voting via the internet and text messaging, with encouraging results. However, the government is well aware of practical problems for general elections. One obvious difficulty is that stringent rules would be needed to prevent people voting more than once, as they do when participating in television programmes such as *Big Brother*. As a result it is envisaged that the first 'e-enabled' nationwide contest will not take place until 'sometime after 2006'. By the time these changes are agreed, it might also be possible to hold general elections on a Sunday, instead of the traditional Thursday.

Although these ideas may make it less likely that people who are inclined to vote will miss the opportunity of doing so, the underlying problem should not be overlooked. Even the most voter-friendly system will make little difference, if people are not sufficiently inspired by the alternatives on offer.

The limitations of democracy

The system of government that has developed in the UK undoubtedly has a strong element of representative democracy, and whatever the defects of the system it does satisfy most of the key principles of liberal democracy. But while liberal institutions and practices should always be maintained and reformed if necessary, we should not accept without question ideas that are designed to make the system 'more democratic'. Standing for election nowadays is a draining (and sometimes demeaning) process. We need to strike an appropriate balance that allows ordinary people to hold decision-makers to account without making the constant threat of re-election a serious distraction from the work they were chosen to carry out. Equally, while referendums clearly have a part to play, there is a danger of overusing a device which is still open to serious objections and may quickly induce 'voter fatigue', producing results which are discredited by derisory turnout figures.

Elected politicians are currently very unpopular in the UK, which helps to explain why people are taking an interest in alternative systems. But if the criticisms are justified, it seems too simplistic to grasp at radical changes in the system of representative government. After all, if we cannot be trusted to elect honest representatives, will our direct decisions on important issues be any better?

Summary

The future of democracy in the UK

➤ Opinions differ about the quality of UK democracy, and it would be a mistake to think that it was incapable of improvement. However, it does clearly satisfy the basic criteria of a representative system, and institutions such as free speech make it reasonable to describe the UK as a liberal democracy.

➤ Referendums are a way of incorporating an element of direct democracy in a system of representative government. They can be an important asset to any system of liberal democracy. However, there are serious, unresolved problems about the use of this device, and proposals to bypass elected representatives entirely are potentially dangerous.

➤ Since the 2000 Representation of the People Act, the government has encouraged electoral turnout by permitting new voting methods. The early results have been encouraging, but this should not be allowed to obscure the fact that public discontent with politicians has deep roots.

Suggested reading

Arblaster, A., *Democracy* (Open University Press, 1994).

Batchelor, A., 'Democratic triumph or flawed reform? The growth of direct democracy in the UK since 1975', *Politics Review*, vol. 15, no. 1, September 2005.

Broughton, D., 'Political participation in Britain', *Politics Review*, vol. 9, no. 4, April 2000.

Dahl, R., *Democracy and its Critics* (Yale University Press, 1989).

Faulks, K., 'Should voting be made compulsory?', *Politics Review*, vol. 10, no. 3, February 2001.

Held, D., *Models of Democracy* (Polity Press, 1996).

Heywood, A., 'What is politics?', *Politics Review*, vol. 11, no. 2, November 2001.

Hoffman, J., 'Political violence', *Politics Review*, vol. 7, no. 2, November 1997.

Hoffman, J., 'Representation', *Politics Review*, vol. 10, no. 4, April 2001.

Horrocks, I. and Wring, D., 'The myth of e-thenian democracy', *Politics Review*, vol. 10, no. 4, April 2001.

Jones, B. 'Apathy: why don't people want to vote?', *Politics Review*, vol. 12, no. 4, April 2003.

Magee, E. and Outhwaite, D., 'Referendums and initiatives', *Politics Review*, vol. 10, no. 3, February 2001.

Pyper, R., 'Redress of grievances', *Politics Review*, vol. 7, no. 3, February 1998.

Pyper, R., 'Making government accountable', *Politics Review*, vol. 11, no. 4, April 2002.

Wilson, D., 'Quangos in British politics', *Politics Review*, vol. 6, no. 1, September 1996.

Websites

www.edemocracy.gov.uk

www.electoralcommission.org.uk

www.yourparty.org

Exam focus

Using this chapter and other resources available to you, answer the following questions:

1 'Politics is about reaching compromises, in private and in public.' Why might people in the UK find this an appealing definition of politics?
2 What is democracy?
3 What is direct democracy?
4 Outline the main criticisms of direct democracy.
5 What is representative democracy?
6 Outline the main criticisms of representative democracy.
7 Distinguish between the concepts of power, legitimacy and authority.
8 Present the case for the UK being a democracy.
9 Outline the main criticisms of democracy in the UK.
10 What is a referendum?
11 Present the arguments for and against the use of referendums.
12 In what circumstances have referendums been held in the UK?
13 To what extent do referendums widen democracy?
14 What other devices might be used to widen democracy?
15 Present the case for and against compulsory voting.

Chapter 2

Elections

Elections are at the heart of the democratic process. For many citizens, voting in an election is their main form of political activity. Through the electoral process, governments are held accountable for their record in office: voters can remove unpopular governments. During election campaigns, political parties issue manifestos that outline the policies they would introduce if they gained power. Victorious parties are then expected to deliver on those pledges in government.

 Key questions answered in this chapter
- ➢ What are the functions of elections?
- ➢ What types of election take place in the UK?
- ➢ What impact do funding, manifestos and campaigns have?
- ➢ How significant are the media and opinion polls?
- ➢ Do elections guarantee democracy?

Functions of elections

In a liberal democracy, elections should be competitive, free and fair. A competitive election requires that voters have a meaningful choice between different political parties. Free elections require basic civil liberties, such as freedom of speech and association, the right to join and stand for a party of one's choice and a free press. The maxim 'one person, one vote, one value' is a key criterion for a fair election: all citizens should each have one vote that is of the same worth. Electoral law should be free from bias and overseen by an impartial judiciary. The electoral system should also translate votes cast into seats won in the legislature in a reasonably accurate manner.

Elections have a number of functions, including the following:

➤ **Representation.** In a representative democracy, elections are a means by which a large group (the electorate) selects a smaller number of people (representatives) to act on its behalf. As we will see later, however, the issue of who should be represented and how is disputed. By contrast, in a direct democracy such as the ancient Greek city-states, all eligible citizens would themselves take part in political decisions. Most political theorists believe that direct democracy is impractical in large modern states.

➤ **Choosing a government.** In the UK parliamentary system, general elections determine the composition of the legislature (albeit one chamber of it) rather than the executive. However, as the majority party in the House of Commons forms the government, most general elections effectively decide which party will take power. Exceptions occur in the case of a *hung parliament*, where no single party has an overall majority. Then, as in proportional representation systems where elections rarely produce a decisive majority, deals between political parties determine the composition of the government.

➤ **Participation.** For most citizens, voting in a general election is their key act of political participation. Turnout in general elections is significantly higher than for other contests, but fell dramatically in 2001. At the ballot box, the voter expresses a political preference by voting for the candidate of a particular political party. However, citizens require a real choice between alternative positions and must have some understanding of the options available if their choice is to be meaningful.

➤ **Influence over policy.** Elections allow ordinary citizens to have their policy preferences heard and to influence the political agenda. Voters can choose the party offering a package of policies that best meet their interests or values, but have only limited scope to influence individual decisions. Election defeat can, however, force a party to rethink policies that proved unpopular at the polls (e.g. Labour's 1983 policy of unilateral nuclear disarmament). The doctrine of the mandate gives the winning party authority to press ahead with the programme that it presented successfully to the electorate, but it also suggests that radical initiatives should not be introduced without prior approval from voters. Even though elections are a rather ineffectual means of influencing, they do at least reacquaint MPs with the concerns of those voters whom they meet on the campaign trail.

➤ **Government accountability.** Facing the electorate every 5 years is one of the ways in which the government is held accountable for its performance in office. The record of the governing party is often a crucial factor in determining how people vote. Individually, Members of Parliament (MPs) may be held accountable for their efforts in their constituency too. However, this is unlikely to be a major consideration for voters unless the MP in question has an unusually good or bad reputation.

➤ **Citizen education.** Election campaigns provide citizens with information on major political issues, the policies of the main political parties, the government's record, etc.

In theory, this enables citizens to make an informed decision about how to vote, but in practice, the information provided in an election campaign is imperfect.

➢ **Legitimacy.** Free and fair elections provide legitimacy for the political system as a whole. By the act of voting, even for a losing party, citizens give their consent to the workings of the system. Voters accept implicitly that elections are free and fair. The government also gains legitimacy, as by winning an election it can claim to be both representative of, and responsible to, the people.

➢ **Elite recruitment.** Finally, elections are a means of recruitment to the governing elite. Political parties are the key agents of recruitment, as they nominate candidates for election, provide them with the resources to conduct a successful campaign and then expect loyalty to the party line once those candidates become MPs.

'Top-down' and 'bottom-up' functions

The above list contains purposes that can be considered as 'top-down' functions of elections or 'bottom-up' functions or both. The distinction between top-down and bottom-up functions reflects the differing interpretations of the role of elections offered by *elitist* and *democratic* theories of the state.

For elite theorists, the primary purpose of elections is to provide authority and stability for the political system, allowing elites to get on with the task of governing, with only limited recourse to the expressed wishes of the people. They highlight 'top-down' functions such as legitimacy and elite recruitment. Representation allows an elite to decide what is in the best interests of the people.

By contrast, democratic theorists prioritise the role of the people in the political process. They focus on 'bottom-up' functions such as policy influence, participation and accountability. For them, representation requires the government to respect and act in accordance with the wishes of the people.

Summary

Functions of elections

➢ representation   ➢ choosing a government

➢ participation   ➢ influence over policy

➢ government accountability   ➢ citizen education

➢ legitimacy   ➢ elite recruitment

Types of election in the UK

General elections

Elections take place at different levels in UK politics. The most significant are general elections, in which the entire House of Commons is elected. The 646 MPs are elected in single-member constituencies that average some 70,000 voters (see Chapter 3).

The timing of general elections in the UK is not fixed. A number of circumstances might lead to parliament being dissolved and an election being called. A general election must be held if the parliament has run its full 5-year term. However, the prime minister is free (subject to the consent of the monarch) to call a general election at a time of his or her choosing and in practice often goes to the polls in the fourth year of a parliament.

This freedom of manoeuvre gives the governing party a distinct advantage over its rivals, as the prime minister can call an election at a favourable moment or make policy (for example, introduce a tax-cutting budget) with the timing of the election in mind. The government is expected to resign and call a general election if it is defeated on a motion of censure or loses a critical vote. The only postwar instance of this occurring came in 1979 when James Callaghan's Labour government lost a vote of confidence on devolution. Labour lost the ensuing election.

European Parliament elections

Elections to the European Parliament (EP) are the other nationwide elections of representatives that are held in the UK. The EP has been directly elected since 1979. It is the only directly elected institution of the European Union (EU). The UK elects 78 out of a total of 732 Members of the European Parliament (MEPs). Elections to the EP are held at fixed intervals of 5 years. Turnout in these elections is significantly lower than for general elections. It rose from 24% in 1999 to 38.5% in 2004, in part because of the use of all-postal ballots in four regions. The regional list system of proportional representation is used for elections to the European Parliament (see Chapter 3).

Elections to devolved assemblies

The devolved assemblies in Scotland, Wales and Northern Ireland are all directly elected. The Scottish Parliament and National Assembly for Wales are elected using the additional member system, while the Northern Ireland Assembly elections are conducted under the single transferable vote system (see Chapter 3). The Scottish Parliament has a 4-year term, but the Scottish first minister can request that it be dissolved and an election called at any time. This is not the case with the National Assembly for Wales. Elections to this body must be held at a date fixed in advance; the assembly cannot be dissolved if the executive no longer enjoys its support.

Local elections

Local councillors are elected for fixed 4-year terms. In some local authorities, all councillors face the electorate at the same time; in others, only a proportion of members (normally a quarter) are elected each year. Although many candidates stand on behalf of a political party, independent candidates have fared better historically at local elections than at general elections. Turnout at local elections is much lower than for general elections. Under changes introduced by the Blair government, some towns and cities in the UK now have directly elected mayors.

Ken Livingstone, standing as an independent, became the first elected mayor of London in 2000.

By-elections

If a constituency seat becomes vacant due to the death or resignation of an elected member of one of these bodies, a by-election is held to choose a new representative. These are one-off events, but in the case of by-elections to the House of Commons they can attract considerable publicity and produce shock results. The party that the departed MP belonged to decides the date of the by-election, though it must be called within a specified time.

Significant parts of the UK polity are not elected. These include the head of state (the hereditary monarch), the second chamber of the legislature (the House of Lords) and the judiciary. Parts of the executive are also unelected: some government ministers are members of the House of Lords while, in common with other liberal democracies, civil servants are appointed.

The mechanics of voting

Competitive elections were a feature of UK politics long before the democratic era. Before the Reform Act of 1832, voting was largely restricted to some 400,000 aristocratic men who made up around 2.5% of the population. The franchise was gradually extended (see Box 2.1) to wealthy middle-class property owners (1832), skilled working-class men (1867) and rural workers (1884). In 1919 all men over 21 and women over 30 got the vote. The year 1928, when the age restriction for women was reduced to 21, was in effect the first time that the UK had mass suffrage. The age restriction for voting was reduced from 21 to 18 in 1969.

Box 2.1 Milestones in UK democracy

1832: 'Great' Reform Act. This extended the franchise to urban and rural middle-class property owners, ended many antiquated practices and redistributed parliamentary seats. The electorate rose to just 700,000 people or about 5% of the adult population.

1867: Parliamentary Reform Act. This extended the franchise to urban householders. The electorate reached 2.2 million.

1872: Ballot Act. This introduced voting by secret ballot.

1883: Corrupt and Illegal Practices Prevention Act. This set a maximum limit on candidates' election expenses and restricted bribery.

1884: Franchise Act. This extended the franchise to rural labourers. The electorate reached almost 5 million.

1911: Parliament Act. This reduced the maximum life of a parliament from 7 to 5 years.

1918: Representation of the People Act. This abolished the property qualification and extended the franchise to women aged 30 and over, and all men aged 21 and over. Women were permitted to stand for election to the House of Commons.

1928: Representation of the People Act. This extended the franchise to all women aged 21 and over. Universal adult suffrage was achieved.

1949: Representation of the People Act. This abolished plural voting (e.g. university seats) and introduced single-member constituencies for all MPs.

1969: Representation of the People Act. This reduced the voting age to 18.

1985: Representation of the People Act. British citizens living abroad or on holiday could apply for a postal vote.

2000: Representation of the People Act. Residency requirements were relaxed. The homeless, remand prisoners and people in mental institutions could register through a 'declaration of local connection'.

2000: Political Parties, Elections and Referendum Act. This set a maximum limit on election campaign spending by parties. Large donations to parties had to be reported. An Electoral Commission was established.

Who votes

Nowadays, the vast majority of UK citizens over the age of 18 are entitled to vote in general elections, but their names have to appear on the electoral register. More than 44 million names appeared on the register in 2005. Electoral registration officers send forms to every household on an annual basis and it is compulsory for citizens to register. The register is made available for public scrutiny. 'Rolling registration' allows names to be added throughout the year. Some people (e.g. students) may be registered in two different constituencies, but they are only permitted to vote once. In Northern Ireland, individuals are required to provide additional information when registering and to produce evidence of their identity at the polling station.

There are still some exceptions to 'universal' suffrage in the UK. Members of the House of Lords, prisoners detained at the time of the election, people convicted of electoral fraud within the last 5 years and those deemed incapable of reasoned judgement because of mental illness are not entitled to vote. The Representation of the People Act (2000) made it easier for the homeless, remand prisoners and people in mental institutions to register through a 'declaration of local connection'. The European Court of Human Rights ruled in 2004 that prisoners should not be denied the right to vote, but the government indicated that it would not change the law.

Citizens of Commonwealth countries and citizens of the Irish Republic who are resident in the UK are permitted to vote in British general elections. Some 10,000 UK citizens living abroad can apply for a postal vote. The 1993 Treaty on European Union (the Maastricht Treaty) granted citizens of EU member states who are resident in the UK the right to vote in local elections and elections to the European Parliament in the UK, but not general elections.

How to vote

Elections are traditionally held on a Thursday, with voting taking place from 7 a.m. to 10 p.m. Schools and colleges are used as polling stations, although in remote areas, pubs and private homes are used occasionally. On entering the polling station, the voter identifies himself or herself to the officials and is given a ballot paper bearing an official stamp. Candidates are listed in alphabetical order (according to their surname) on the ballot paper and a brief party identification is included. Ballot papers for general and local elections are relatively simple in design, but those for other elections held in the UK can be more complicated.

Voting has been a private act since the 1872 Ballot Act. The voter places a cross (X) in the box next to the name of the candidate of his or her choice. Failure to do this clearly may mean that the ballot paper is 'spoiled', in which case the vote will not be counted. The manual voting machines that were used in the USA — and which caused so much controversy in Florida during the 2000 presidential election — are not used in the UK.

The Department for Constitutional Affairs has overall responsibility for the conduct of elections. An independent Electoral Commission with the power to investigate and make recommendations on the administration of elections and referendums was established in 2001. It maintains a Register of Parties, scrutinises party funding and reviews electoral law.

Alternative voting methods

There has been a marked decline in turnout in local, European and general elections in recent years. The government responded by setting up a number of pilot schemes to test alternative methods of voting (see Box 2.2). These were conducted at local elections between 2000 and 2004. The pilots experimented with extended voting hours, all-postal ballots and electronic voting (e-voting), e.g. via the internet and text messaging. The largest trial was that of all-postal ballots in four English regions in the 2004 European Parliament elections.

All-postal voting trials brought the largest increases in turnout. In some local elections, turnout doubled; it increased by 20% in the four regions using all postal-ballots in the 2004 European Parliament elections. Trials of e-voting had little impact on turnout.

Box 2.2 Alternative forms of voting (2000–05)

Postal voting
- At the 2001 and 2005 general elections, postal votes were available to all citizens who requested them.
- Postal ballots were issued to 6.8 million people (15% of the electorate) in 2005, compared to 0.7 million people (2% of the electorate) in 1997.
- Concerns about electoral fraud were raised by the Electoral Commission.
- The government proposed new regulations to improve the security of postal voting.

All-postal ballots

➢ These were piloted in over 50 local elections between 2000 and 2005.

➢ Turnout increased, doubling in some areas.

➢ All-postal ballots were used in four regions, comprising 14 million eligible voters, in the 2004 European Parliament elections.

➢ Turnout increased by 22% in the four regions, compared to a rise of 12% in regions using traditional voting methods.

➢ Concerns about electoral fraud were raised, notably in a court case on vote rigging in a Birmingham ward.

➢ The Electoral Commission recommended subsequently that all-postal ballots should not be used again.

E-voting

➢ This has been piloted in more than 20 local elections since 2002.

➢ Methods of e-voting include: touch-screen voting in a polling station or kiosk; remote internet voting using PCs; voting by telephone; voting by text message.

➢ It had only a limited impact on turnout (up slightly in most areas).

➢ The Electoral Commission recommends that e-voting should not be used more widely until concerns about security and secrecy have been addressed.

➢ Electronic counting of votes was piloted in the 2004 Greater London Assembly elections.

Advanced voting and extended polling hours

➢ Pilot schemes have been conducted in over 20 local elections since 2000.

➢ There was limited impact on turnout.

➢ Few voters took advantage of the additional time available.

➢ Mobile polling stations and weekend voting involved extra costs.

Intention to vote

A June 2001 MORI poll asked people who had not voted in that month's general election if suggested methods for improving turnout would have made them more likely to vote.

	More likely (%)	Less likely (%)	No difference (%)
Weekend voting	36	3	61
Polling in supermarkets	49	3	46
24-hour polling stations	42	2	55
Internet	40	4	55
Telephone/mobile phone	66	3	30
Postal voting	51	7	40
'None of the above' on the ballot paper	12	2	86

Source: MORI, www.mori.com

Postal votes were available on demand for all citizens at the 2001 and 2005 general elections. Previously, requests for a postal vote had to state a reason and be approved by electoral registration officers. In 2005, 6.5 million people requested postal ballots (15% of the electorate) compared to 1.7 million in 2001 and 0.7 million in 1997.

Although new voting methods have helped to improve voter turnout, their use has also prompted concerns about electoral fraud. Greater use of e-voting is unlikely until doubts about its security and secrecy can be allayed. Fraudulent practices involving all-postal ballots (e.g. multiple voting, intimidation and vote stealing) came to light at the 2004 European Parliament elections. A High Court judge, presiding over a case of vote rigging in Birmingham, described the system as 'an open invitation to fraud'. The Electoral Commission argued that all-postal ballots should not be held again. Concerns about the security of postal voting were raised at the 2005 general election, prompting the government to propose tighter regulations (e.g. preventing political parties from handling postal ballot papers). Voting is compulsory in states such as Australia, Belgium and the Netherlands, but the Electoral Commission has not (yet) recommended that this be introduced in the UK.

Funding and funding reform

Running a general election campaign is an expensive business for political parties. Advertising, manifestos, press conferences, polling, transport and rallies are all costly (see Table 2.1). For the 1997 general election, the Conservatives spent £28.3 million, Labour £25.7 million and the Liberal Democrats £3.5 million. The figures fell in 2001 as spending limits were enforced (see p. 36).

The two main parties raise large sums of money ahead of general election campaigns. But they also face routine running costs averaging over £20 million per year. Both parties experienced a funding crisis in the 1990s. At one stage, the Conservatives had a £20 million deficit. Labour has traditionally enjoyed financial backing from the trade unions, but has actively (and successfully) sought backing from private business under Tony Blair. The Conservatives gained large sums of money from companies and wealthy individuals, but as their popularity waned and they lost office, they found themselves heavily indebted. Party members also provide money through membership subscriptions and local fundraising activities.

'Sleaze'

Declining party membership has meant that both main parties have had to rely increasingly on wealthy donors for funding. A number of cases in the 1990s raised concerns about the influence or 'favours' that people making large donations to a party might expect in return. In the mid-1990s, the Conservatives accepted large donations from overseas. One example among many was a £450,000 donation from Asil Nadir, who had fled the UK when accused of fraud. The problem did not disappear when the Tories left office, as the Blair government too became embroiled in 'sleaze' allegations. In 1997, the Labour Party accepted a £1 million donation from Formula One owner Bernie Ecclestone shortly before the Blair government took the decision to exempt the sport from a ban on tobacco advertising. These cases damaged the public standing of politicians and brought demands for a more transparent system of party funding.

Standards in public life

Following well-publicised cases of 'sleaze', the Committee on Standards in Public Life, then chaired by Lord Neill, launched an inquiry into party funding in 1997. The Fifth Report of the Committee on Standards in Public Life duly made a number of recommendations, most of which were put into effect by the Political Parties, Elections and Referendum Act (2000). The key elements of the act are as follows:

- ➤ A ceiling on national campaign expenditure was established. The ceiling was initially set at £30,000 per constituency.
- ➤ Parties must produce quarterly reports that detail donors and donations (in cash or in kind) of £5,000 or more made to the central party organisation, and of £1,000 or more made to regional or local party bodies.
- ➤ Weekly donation reports must be submitted during election campaigns.
- ➤ Foreign donations to UK parties are banned.
- ➤ Party accounts and donation reports are overseen by the Electoral Commission.

The maximum spending limit for parties contesting every constituency in Great Britain was £18.84 million in 2005 (Labour, the Conservatives and the Liberal Democrats do not contest seats in Northern Ireland). Table 2.1 details spending by the main parties at the 2001 general election — the spending cap has forced the main parties to give more thought to how money is spent. Limits on constituency spending by candidates pre-dated the Neill Report. The maximum limits on spending by candidates in 2005 were £7,150 plus 7 pence per elector in county constituencies, and £7,150 plus 5 pence per elector in borough constituencies.

Donations

In the first quarter of 2005, the Conservatives received donations totalling £8.1 million, Labour £9.1 million and the Liberal Democrats £4.2 million. The Conservatives rely heavily on individual donations. Donations from companies fell dramatically when they lost office, but began to recover when Michael Howard became leader. Labour still receives significant funds from trade unions, but also enjoys financial support from businesses and individuals. Former supermarket supremo Lord Sainsbury has donated more than £13 million to Labour since 1996. The Liberal Democrats received their biggest ever donation — £2.4 million from finance company Fifth Avenue Partners — in 2005.

Despite the 2000 act, questionable donations have continued to come to light. These included a £100,000 donation to the Labour Party from Richard Desmond in 2002, after his takeover of Express Newspapers, which had not been contested by the Department of Trade and Industry.

State funding

The Neill Report and the two main political parties rejected state funding for the extra-parliamentary organisation of political parties. Parties already receive significant sums from the state. Since 1975, opposition parties have received a state subsidy (known as 'Short money') to help them carry out their parliamentary duties. This was increased after the Neill Report. A new Policy Development Fund was established to distribute some £2 million among the parties.

The issue of state funding returned to the agenda in 2002 when the Blair government signalled its support. It argued that additional state funding would ensure greater equality in election spending and erode the reliance on (occasionally dubious) private donations. However, opponents such as the Conservative Party argue that state funding is a misuse of taxpayers' money and establishes an unhealthy link between political parties and the state.

Table 2.1 Spending during the 2001 general election campaign (£)

	Con	Lab	Lib Dem
Party political broadcasts	568,423	241,755	57,619
Advertising	4,479,117	5,049,205	199,188
Unsolicited material to electors	1,255,341	1,565,447	54,345
Manifesto and party documents	1,098,861	539,806	49,673
Market research and canvassing	1,695,754	931,889	55,719
Media	459,597	760,086	245,629
Transport	1,471,596	786,926	672,736
Rallies & events	1,740,340	1,264,905	30,085
Total	12,769,029	11,140,019	1,364,994

Source: Electoral Commission, www.electoralcommission.gov.uk

Summary

The debate on state funding of parties

Arguments for:

➤ Parties already receive some funding from the state.
➤ It would ensure greater equality of resources for parties at election time.
➤ It would end over-reliance on private donations.
➤ It would increase public confidence in parties.

Arguments against:

➤ It would extend an unhealthy link between parties and the state.
➤ Equality in funding is not sufficient to improve the performance of small parties.
➤ It would not end questionable donations.
➤ It is a misuse of taxpayers' money.

Manifestos and mandates

The doctrine of the *mandate* has an important place in UK politics. The key idea here is that the winning party in an election gains an authoritative instruction (mandate) from the electorate to implement the programme it put forward during the election campaign. Parties thus issue manifestos setting out their main priorities and policies should they enter government. An election *manifesto* is seen as a promise of future legislative action or a contract between a party and those who voted for it. In office, the winning party can claim that it has been granted the authority to put its proposals into practice. However, the mandate idea can also be interpreted to mean that a government should not introduce a major policy change (particularly a constitutional change) unless it has been presented to the electorate.

The doctrine of the mandate is, however, rather slippery. Governments often treat it not as an instruction to fulfil a detailed legislative programme, but as a general mandate to govern. The doctrine is also based on questionable assumptions and reality does not always accord with the theory. It assumes that voters are well informed and rational, deciding which party to support on the basis of its policies. Although manifestos do provide substantial information on a party's core policy proposals, few voters will be fully aware of their content and fewer still will actively agree with every proposal.

Furthermore, as we will see in Chapter 5, it is far from certain that people decide how to vote solely or mainly on the basis of the policies offered by political parties. Social background, traditional allegiances and perceptions of the main parties and their leaders are all significant factors in voting behaviour. Nonetheless, the idea that the winning party has a mandate to pursue its broad policy goals (e.g. lower taxes or better public services) is of value, particularly if the election campaign revealed significant differences in the aspirations of the main parties.

Labour and the mandate

A further question concerning the mandate relates to the extent to which governments succeed in meeting the policy commitments made in their manifestos. Generally, the record here is good. The Labour government claimed in 2001 to have fulfilled a substantial majority of the policy commitments it outlined in its 1997 election manifesto. However, the decision to give the Bank of England's Monetary Policy Committee the authority to set interest rate levels was probably the single most important macroeconomic decision taken by the government. Yet this policy, announced just days after the party's election victory, was not foreshadowed in Labour's 1997 election manifesto.

In fact, a number of major decisions taken by the Labour government elected in 2001 were not flagged in Labour's manifesto. Differential university tuition fees were introduced even though the manifesto had declared that Labour 'will not introduce top-up fees'. The Conservatives pledged to cut taxes in their 1992 manifesto, but increased indirect taxes (though not income tax) once in office. The perception that the Conservatives had reneged on their promises contributed to their defeat in 1997.

Labour's election pledges

Labour challenged the traditional view of the mandate in 1997 and 2001 when it issued five headline pledges. These included specific targets. In 1997, for example, Labour promised to cut class sizes to 30 for 5–7 year olds and to cut NHS waiting lists by 100,000. In 2001, it promised 10,000 extra secondary school teachers, 20,000 extra nurses and 10,000 additional doctors. This simplified the idea of a mandate and, in theory, made it easier for voters to judge whether the party had met its commitments. Labour duly claimed to have met its commitments, although commentators detected some fudging. The Conservatives set out five 'guarantees' in 1999, but had retreated from some of these by the 2001 general election.

Both Labour and the Conservatives issued six key pledges in 2005 (see Box 2.3). These were couched in general terms, although more detailed commitments were included in their manifestos.

Box 2.3 **Labour and Conservative general election pledges, 2005**

Labour	Conservatives
➤ Your family better off	➤ More police
➤ Your child achieving more	➤ Cleaner hospitals
➤ Your children with the best start	➤ Lower taxes
➤ Your family treated better and faster	➤ School discipline
➤ Your community safer	➤ Controlled immigration
➤ Your country's borders protected	➤ Accountability

Key terms

➤ **Mandate.** An authoritative instruction or command.

➤ **Mandate theory.** The doctrine that the winning party at a general election receives an instruction from the electorate to implement its policy programme.

➤ **Manifesto.** A document in which a political party sets out the policies it plans to pursue if it wins office.

Election campaigns

The main political parties run professional, choreographed general election campaigns. Many of the new campaign techniques have been learned from the USA, where some of the trends we have seen in recent UK campaigns are well established, notably the prominence of spin doctors, the use of focus groups, the significance of television and the emphasis on personality. Advertising agencies and opinion pollsters are brought in to offer their expertise.

Agenda setting

Agenda setting is the key goal for election campaign managers. They promote issues that show their party in a good light and reflect badly on their rivals. Successful agenda setting requires a skilful, carefully organised campaign, good links with the media and an element of luck. The election campaigns of the main parties are managed from 'war rooms' at party headquarters. Here, senior politicians and strategists map out their plan of action. Most days begin with an early morning press briefing where each party promotes its theme for the day, linking it to a policy announcement, keynote speech or pre-arranged campaign visit by the party leader.

So, on a typical day in 2005 Labour focused on the economy, talking up its record and warning about a return to economic instability under the Conservatives, as well as highlighting a visit by Tony Blair and Gordon Brown to a successful business. The Conservatives would then aim to set the agenda by focusing on immigration, criticising the increase in illegal immigration under Labour, promising tougher action and highlighting Michael Howard's visit to Kent.

Even the best-planned campaigns can go awry. Labour was thought to have run the best campaign in 1992 and the opinion polls suggested that victory was possible. However, the tax increases suggested by Labour's 'shadow budget' fostered unease and in the final week of the campaign the party managed to appear both nervous (talking about electoral reform) and over-confident (at a 'triumphalist' rally in Sheffield). Despite running a lacklustre campaign in which John Major took to his soapbox to rally support, the Conservatives were returned to power.

The 2001 campaign was dull until Labour endured a nightmare day on 16 May. The launch of its manifesto was overshadowed by the barracking of Jack Straw at a Police Federation conference, the haranguing of Tony Blair by the partner of a patient at a Birmingham hospital, and John Prescott punching an egg-throwing protestor in north Wales. Fortunately for Labour, the following day's tabloid press treated the Prescott punch with more humour than disdain and the opinion polls barely moved.

Although the result was not the foregone conclusion it had been 4 years earlier, the 2005 campaign provided little excitement. The two main parties adopted a negative tone. Labour looked to persuade its wavering supporters by warning of a Conservative victory if too many of them abstained or switched to the Liberal Democrats. Michael Howard branded Blair a 'liar' and invited voters to 'send him a message' by voting Conservative.

Communications

Posters and newspaper advertisements are mainstays of election campaigning, although few of them have a significant impact. Those that did included a 1979 Conservative poster showing a long dole queue under the caption 'Labour isn't working' and a 1992 Conservative poster that used the phrase 'Labour's double whammy' to allude to tax and interest rate rises.

Political parties have embraced new technology to get their message across. Both parties use sophisticated computer programmes to identify target voters, particularly those in marginal seats. Voters may then be contacted by telephone, e-mail or text message, or even sent a message on DVD. Labour sent thousands of text messages on the night before the 2001 election in which they implied that opening hours for pubs would be extended. Direct contact can be crucial in converting voters, but people's dislike of cold calls and spam e-mail means that it can be counterproductive too.

Parties also used the internet to relay information to activists, journalists and voters. The number of hits recorded by these websites, and those of news organisations such as the BBC, increased dramatically. In 2005 other popular sites included one that offered voters advice on who to vote for based on an interactive quiz, and one advocating tactical voting. A large number of election 'blogs' also appeared, written by politicians, commentators and ordinary voters. The impact of the internet in 2001 was minimal as only one in three homes had internet access. It figured more prominently in 2005, but its impact on the election outcome appears to have been limited.

A Labour election poster from the 2005 campaign, featuring Thatcher, Major and Howard

Target seats

Parties focus their resources on a relatively small number of target seats — close contests that could be crucial in deciding if they gain or retain power. In 2005, the Conservatives and Labour directed much of their campaigning towards 800,000 voters in crucial marginal seats. The centralisation of campaign organisation has undermined some of the time-honoured features of the campaign at local level. Fewer people display election posters in their windows, and public debates between candidates are less frequent. Nonetheless, local activists continue to deliver leaflets, knock on doors, transport supporters to the polling station and (importantly) organise postal votes, in an effort to maximise their support. However, strict limits on spending by candidates apply. In close-run contests, constituency activism can produce several hundred crucial extra votes.

National issues

National rather than local issues dominate general election campaigns — and European Parliament and local council election campaigns as well. As in England, health and education were key issues in the 2005 campaign in Scotland, even though these policy areas were the responsibility of the Scottish Parliament rather than Westminster. Local issues are rarely decisive, but an independent candidate, Dr Richard Taylor, won the seat of Wyre Forest in 2001 and 2005 having campaigned against the closure of units at a local hospital.

Evidence on the significance of the national campaign is patchy. Most voters will have made their minds up on how they will vote before the campaign even gets under way. However, there is usually some movement in the opinion polls during the campaign as undecided voters make their choice and wavering voters change their allegiance. But this 'churning' will not be decisive unless most of those who switch camp move in the same direction. Opinion poll support for Labour fell slightly in the course of the last three general election campaigns. The Liberal Democrats were the main beneficiaries. They may have benefited from their additional media exposure at election time.

The media and elections

Election campaigns invariably bring complaints of bias from all political parties. Strict guidelines are in place to ensure that television news programmes afford equal treatment to the main parties. Yet as we will see later, tabloid newspapers have few qualms about slanting their news coverage to favour the party they support. The relationship between the media and politicians is a complex one. Both sides need each other, but the relationship is unequal and produces occasional spats. The parties' communications strategists want television news programmes to feature their message and newspapers to give their policy pronouncements a favourable spin. Television and newspaper journalists want inside information, access to politicians and 'scoops' to entice their viewers and readers.

Interdependence

This interdependence is most apparent during election campaigns, when politicians need favourable coverage and the media need a frequent supply of good stories. The 2005 election featured heavily in the press and on television news bulletins, but reader-ship and viewing figures fell during the campaign. The relationship is also sustained by the networks of contacts established by former media figures working for the parties. In 2001, for example, Alastair Campbell, Labour's press secretary, was formerly political editor of the *Daily Mirror* while his Conservative counterpart, Amanda Platell, had been editor of the *Sunday Express*.

Despite this interdependence, the relationship between the media and politicians is sometimes a troubled one. Each side is suspicious of the perceived power and influence of the other. Politicians are concerned that media owners (such as Rupert Murdoch, who owns Sky, the *Sun* and *The Times*) exercise too much power and distort the news agenda. By contrast, journalists and newspaper proprietors believe that government spin doctors are overly concerned with presenting a favourable message and obstructing their search for the 'truth'. The government can also make ominous noises about tightening the regulation of a troublesome media.

Key terms

➤ **Focus group.** A small sample group of people asked to voice their opinions in an open discussion.

➤ **Opinion poll.** A survey of voters designed to discover their political attitudes and voting intentions.

➤ **Soundbite.** A short, easily remembered phrase that is included in a speech by a politician and repeated by the media.

➤ **Spin doctor.** A political aide who seeks favourable media coverage and tries to prevent negative publicity.

Television

Television is a crucial medium for election campaigns and one that has had an important impact on the way in which campaigns are conducted. News bulletins feature soundbites (short, snappy phrases) rather than lengthy extracts from speeches. Their coverage concentrates on party leaders, thus encouraging, according to some commentators, the 'presidentialisation' of UK election campaigns. Party leaders receive far more television coverage than other senior politicians. Decisions made by television news executives and journalists about their lead stories can alter the tenor of the election campaign. However, during election campaigns they have to work within guidelines designed to ensure balanced coverage over the course of a week's news.

Party managers recognise the importance of television coverage and gear their campaigns in order to get their message across. Their involvement ranges from the trivial — selecting the colour of the party leader's tie — to the serious, such as concerted efforts to shape the agenda or demands about the format of programmes involving the party leaders. Both Blair and Howard faced some awkward moments when they took part in television programmes in which they were questioned by political interviewers and/or a studio audience. However, the live 'head-to-head' debates that play a crucial part in the US presidential election campaign have not featured in UK elections. At different times, Labour and Conservative leaders have refused to take part in a UK version.

Election broadcasts

Political parties are allocated election broadcasts (a version of the party political broadcast) based on the number of candidates they put forward. These tend to be rather dull and do not attract large audiences, although some have proved memorable or controversial. In 1987, a Labour broadcast sought to counter the negative image of party leader Neil Kinnock in a film (dubbed 'Kinnock: the Movie') focusing on his life and values.

Broadcasts focusing on the character of the party leader have since been a staple part of election campaigns. Labour's 1992 'Jennifer's ear' broadcast was criticised for featuring the case of a child waiting for medical treatment. The broadcasts of fringe parties such as the British National Party tend to be the most controversial.

Newspapers

Questions about the impact of the media on voting behaviour are hardy perennials for students of UK elections. In 1992, Conservative Party chairman Michael Ancram suggested that front-page attacks on Neil Kinnock in the *Sun* newspaper had been crucial to the Tories' victory. Kinnock agreed. In typical fashion, the paper congratulated itself by running the headline 'It's The *Sun* Wot Won It'. However, the political influence of the press is, in reality, far from clear-cut.

Do newspapers influence their readers?

The impact of newspapers' coverage of politics on the attitudes and voting intentions of their readers has been widely examined by political scientists but no definitive answers have emerged. It is difficult to establish cause and effect: that is, whether people read a newspaper that reflects their existing political views or, instead, form their opinions based on what they have read. There are three broad perspectives on the impact of the media:

> **Reinforces existing perceptions.** This view argues that media coverage tends to reinforce the views already held by voters rather than creating opinions. Most people read a newspaper that reflects their own political views (see Table 2.2). But they are selective in the way they obtain, perceive and absorb political news. A tabloid reader might ignore most political stories, accepting only those views that he or she already holds and relying on television for non-partisan news. Voters filter out those stories they disagree with and are swayed only by hard-hitting items that accord with their own perceptions of the world.

> **Direct influence.** This perspective holds that the media do directly influence attitudes and voting behaviour. People's opinions on high-profile issues such as asylum and 'sleaze' are formed by media coverage. There is evidence to suggest that, allowing for class and existing attitudes, readers of Labour-supporting newspapers are more likely to vote Labour than are readers of pro-Conservative newspapers. This view claims that the *Sun*'s conversion to New Labour caused some of its readers to change their political allegiance.

> **Shapes the agenda.** This view claims that although the media are unlikely to have a direct influence over people's opinions, they do shape the agenda. Newspapers decide which political issues are significant and, as importantly, which are not. The interpretations that newspapers place on issues often frame the political debate. Asylum seekers, for example, are presented as a threat to public order. Complex issues such as UK membership of the European single currency are presented in simplistic terms that rely on stereotypes. The media also encourage

Table 2.2 Party supported by daily newspaper readers, 2005, 2001 and 1997 (%)

Newspaper	Election year	Con	Lab	Lib Dem
Sun	2005	35	44	10
	2001	29	52	11
	1997	30	52	12
Daily Mirror	2005	13	66	15
	2001	11	71	13
	1997	14	72	11
Daily Mail	2005	57	24	14
	2001	55	24	17
	1997	49	29	14
Daily Express	2005	44	29	20
	2001	43	33	19
	1997	49	29	16
Daily Star	2005	17	53	13
	2001	21	56	17
	1997	17	66	12
Daily Telegraph	2005	64	14	18
	2001	65	16	14
	1997	57	20	17
The Times	2005	44	27	24
	2001	40	28	26
	1997	42	28	25
Guardian	2005	7	48	34
	2001	6	52	34
	1997	8	67	22
Independent	2005	11	38	43
	2001	12	38	44
	1997	16	47	30
Financial Times	2005	36	34	23
	2001	48	30	21
	1997	48	29	19

Source: MORI, www.mori.com

a focus on the personality of party leaders. Radical opinions are marginalised and rarely given press coverage.

Support for Labour

The most interesting development in the last 20 years has been the defection of much of the traditional 'Tory press' to New Labour (see Table 2.3). At the 1992 election, only the *Daily Mirror* and the *Guardian* were staunch Labour supporters. Five years later, the *Daily Star*, the *Independent* and (most significantly) the *Sun* switched their support to Labour. Twice as many people read a Labour-supporting paper in 1997 than in 1992. The inadequacies of the Major government, along with the emergence of New Labour (and its opinion poll leads), contributed to this shift of allegiance. In 2005, only three daily newspapers endorsed the Conservatives. *The Times*, *Financial Times* and the *Sun* — firm Tory supporters in the 1980s — backed Labour.

More than half of the press coverage of the 2005 election focused on Labour. This is unsurprising given that it was the party in power. Labour was the party most mentioned in stories on the economy, health and education. Coverage of Labour's record and manifesto proposals on these areas was largely positive in the Labour-supporting press. But Labour suffered negative coverage on Iraq and 'trust' in the final week of the campaign.

Labour strategists invested considerable energy in courting and then retaining the support of the *Sun*. Owned by billionaire media mogul Rupert Murdoch, the *Sun* is the UK's biggest selling newspaper and its readership includes many of the southern English skilled working-class voters whose support was crucial for Labour's victory. Whether the *Sun* played a crucial role in converting former Conservative voters to the New Labour

Table 2.3 Partisanship and circulation of national daily newspapers at general elections in 2005, 2001 and 1997

Newspaper	Preferred winner 2005	Circulation 2005 (000s)	Preferred winner 2001	Circulation 2001 (000s)	Preferred winner 1997	Circulation 1997 (000s)
Sun	Lab	3,098	Lab	3,288	Lab	3,842
Daily Mirror	Lab	2,059	Lab	2,056	Lab	3,084
Daily Mail	Con	2,278	Con	2,337	Con	2,151
Daily Express	Con	883	Lab	929	Con	1,220
Daily Star	No endorsement	735	Lab	585	Lab	648
Daily Telegraph	Con	868	Con	989	Con	1,134
The Times	Lab, but smaller majority	654	Lab	667	More Eurosceptic MPs	719
Guardian	Lab, plus increase in Lib Dem MPs	327	Lab, plus increase in Lib Dem MPs	362	Lab	401
Independent	More Lib Dem MPs	226	Not Con, plus more Lib Dem MPs	197	Lab	251
Financial Times	Lab	131	Lab	176	Lab	307
Total Con circulation		4,029		3,326		4,504
Total Lab circulation		6,269		8,063		8,533

Note: Circulation figures from Audit Bureau of Circulation

cause, or skilfully recognised that its readership was fed up with the Tories and liked Blair, is a moot point. Even when backing the pro-European Labour government, it has retained the brash Euroscepticism favoured by many of its readers.

Opinion polls

Newspapers regularly publish opinion polls indicating how a sample of the electorate would vote in a general election. During the campaign, the publication of such polls reaches a frenzy as politicians and commentators look for changes in the mood of the electorate. A dramatic shift in the predictions can make headline news, although such swings might be the result of a rogue poll. In France, opinion poll findings cannot be published in the final days of the campaign, but it seems unlikely that this practice will extend to the UK.

The following are key characteristics of opinion polls:

➤ They are surveys of the political behaviour and attitudes of a sample group of the population at a particular moment.
➤ They are conducted by professional organisations (e.g. MORI, NOP) for newspapers, political parties, private companies, etc.
➤ They are based on a sample of between 1,000 and 2,000 people, chosen as being representative of the electorate.
➤ People are invited to respond to fixed questions in face-to-face interviews, telephone interviews or, in the case of YouGov, online polls.
➤ They usually have a margin of error of ±3%.

Opinion poll accuracy

Doubts about the reliability of the polls reached a crescendo in 1992, when virtually all the polls conducted during the election campaign failed to predict a Conservative victory. By predicting a hung parliament, the opinion poll forecasts were more than eight points off the real result. The polling organisations had systematically underestimated support for the Conservatives. A post-election review conducted by the pollsters claimed that this was because Conservative voters were more reluctant to reveal their intentions than supporters of other parties. The pollsters subsequently adjusted their calculations to take account of this.

Predicting Labour's landslide victories in 1997 and 2001 proved less taxing, but the opinion polls again exaggerated support for Labour and underestimated Conservative support. Every poll conducted in the 2001 campaign overestimated Labour's lead. In the 2005 election, Labour's lead in the final opinion polls was marginally higher than the actual result (see Table 2.4). But the MORI/NOP exit poll, based on a survey of 20,000 actual voters, correctly predicted a 66-seat Labour majority. The greater accuracy of the polls resulted from the sophisticated techniques used to measure turnout and support for the parties among different social groups.

Table 2.4 Final opinion polls, 2005

Polling organisation	Fieldwork	Con (%)	Lab (%)	Lib Dem (%)	Other (%)	Labour lead (%)
ICM	1–3 May	32	38	22	8	+6
MORI	3–4 May	33	38	23	6	+5
NOP	1–3 May	33	36	23	8	+3
Populus	2–3 May	32	38	21	9	+6
YouGov	3–4 May	32	37	24	7	+5
MORI/NOP exit poll	5 May	33	37	22	8	+4
Actual result (GB)		33	36	23	8	+3

Source: adapted from British Policy Council, **www.britishpolicycouncil.org/press.html**

Summary

Features of general election campaigns

➤ Parties publish manifestos.

➤ They run organised, choreographed campaigns to set the agenda.

➤ The focus is on a small number of national issues.

➤ Spin doctors and soundbites are very important.

➤ Party leaders have a high profile.

➤ Parties use advertisements, election broadcasts and the internet.

➤ They focus their efforts on key target seats.

➤ Television plays a prominent role.

➤ Newspapers declare a party allegiance, which often colours their coverage.

➤ A large number of opinion polls are published.

MPs as representatives

One of the main functions of elections is to choose representatives. However, there is no single theory of representation. For our purposes, five different views on representation are important.

The delegate model

A delegate is an individual who is selected to act on behalf of others on the basis of clear instructions. Delegates are duty-bound to relay the views of those whom they represent without deviation. They should not alter their instructions on the basis of their own judgement or personal preferences. Examples of this model include trade union delegates, who cast the votes of the union according to an earlier decision of the union leaders or membership. However, MPs are not expected to act as delegates, slavishly bound to the instructions of their voters. There is unlikely to be a consensus among the 65,000 voters in a constituency on complex issues, while ascertaining the views of the majority on every issue would be time-consuming. The position of an MP would also be less attractive if politicians were unable to exercise their own judgement or display leadership.

The trustee model
Rejecting the delegate model, Edmund Burke MP (1729–97) put forward the trustee model in the 1770s. MPs are responsible for representing the interests of their constituents in parliament. Once elected, they are free to decide how to vote based on their own independent judgement of the merits of an issue. Unsurprisingly for a conservative thinker of the eighteenth century, Burke's model has a strong elitist undercurrent. It assumes that MPs know better than their constituents, as they have greater and more specialised knowledge of affairs of state. Rational voters will therefore bow to the better judgement of their elected representative. In its original form, the trustee model was associated with an elitist rather than a democratic view of society. However, the view that MPs should have some freedom to exercise their own judgement remains, although they are expected to pay serious attention to the (sometimes competing) demands of their constituency and party.

Constituency representation
MPs are elected in single-member geographical constituencies and are expected to maintain links with their constituency when in parliament. In particular, MPs might be expected to protect and advance the interests of individual constituents and the collective interests of the area. On the former, MPs receive numerous requests for help from constituents, through either indirect contact (usually mail) or direct contact at regular constituency surgeries. MPs may then raise these problems with the relevant government department in an attempt to resolve them or speed up their solution. On the latter, local MPs may lobby the government about developments in the constituency (e.g. the future of a threatened coal mine or factory, or the proposed site of a reception centre for asylum seekers or a trial for genetically modified crops).

This relationship between an MP and a constituency is often seen as important for a healthy democracy. It may also bring locally active MPs a 'personal vote' (perhaps numbering several hundred votes) that might tip the scales in their favour in a close election. However, when it comes to the crunch, few MPs are prepared to side with the interests of their constituency to the extent that they vote against their own party.

The party model
This model recognises that political parties are the dominant actors in modern elections. Almost all successful candidates in UK general elections are elected not for their

personal beliefs and qualities, but because they stand for a political party. MPs owe a duty of loyalty to their party. This model sees parties as the main agents of representation — they represent the interests of particular groups in society. The doctrine of the mandate supports this model further. It claims that because citizens vote for the party whose policies they most support, the winning party is granted authority to put its policies into practice.

Resemblance

A final view of representation suggests that parliament should mirror the society it represents. Representation is equated with resemblance. Parliament should be a microcosm of the larger body: all major social groups should be present in numbers roughly proportional to the size of the groups in the electorate as a whole. The underlying assumption is that only people with similar social characteristics (gender, ethnicity, class, etc.) can properly identify with and represent the interests of particular groups. So, it might be argued that women understand motherhood better and members of ethnic minorities have more experience of institutional racism.

MPs' backgrounds

If resemblance were a crucial test of representation, the House of Commons would score poorly. The social background of MPs is very different from that of the electorate

Tony Blair surrounded by his female Labour MPs, 1997. Women still make up only 20% of MPs

as a whole. Most MPs are middle class. The largest occupational groups among Labour MPs are public sector professionals, white-collar workers and political organisers. Business and private sector professions were prominent in Conservative ranks. Recent years have seen an increase in 'career politicians'. These are MPs who previously worked as an official or researcher for the party they represent and have little or no work experience outside politics.

As well as the working class, two other key social groups are under-represented at Westminster: women and ethnic minorities. A record 128 women MPs were elected in 2005 (see Table 2.5). This is a major improvement on the situation in 1983, when there were 23 women MPs. But only 20% of MPs are women, compared to more than 50% of the UK population. Only 15 MPs elected in 2005 were members of minority ethnic groups, 13 Labour and 2 Conservative.

Problems of the resemblance model

There are problems with the resemblance model. The narrow assumption that only people drawn from a group can faithfully represent its interests is disputed. Critics argue that individuals need not have suffered disadvantage or discrimination themselves to regard these as reprehensible and to press for social reform. The model is also flawed as it wrongly assumes that people belong to only one social group, and that groups are homogeneous. Furthermore, it is divisive, emphasising (and freezing) differences rather than fostering common interests and shared values.

Achieving a legislature that accurately mirrors society as a whole may require, in the short term at least, a system of quotas under which a certain percentage of seats are reserved for women or ethnic minorities. This would undermine the selection of candidates by local parties and would narrow the choice presented to voters.

All-women shortlists

The main political parties are, however, committed to increasing the number of women and ethnic minority candidates they put forward in winnable seats. In 1993, the Labour Party introduced all-women shortlists in some seats. This policy was dropped briefly after an employment tribunal in 1996, but those already selected stayed in place and helped produce a near threefold increase in women Labour MPs. By 2005, 28% of Labour MPs were women.

The 2002 Sex Discrimination (Election Candidates) Act now permits political parties to adopt positive action — such as quotas or all-women shortlists — in selecting candidates for public office. However, parties are not obliged to take such measures. The Conservatives have traditionally opposed positive action but have encouraged local associations to select female candidates. The number of female Conservative candidates almost doubled between 1997 and 2005. But claims of bias remained because relatively few women secured the nomination in winnable seats, and the number of women Conservative MPs only increased from 13 to 17.

Table 2.5 Women candidates and MPs, 1983–2005

	Conservative		Labour		Liberal Democrat		
	Candidates	MPs	Candidates	MPs	Candidates	MPs	Total women MPs
1983	40	13	79	10	75	0	23
1987	46	17	92	21	105	2	41
1992	59	20	138	37	144	2	60
1997	66	13	155	102	139	3	120
2001	93	14	148	95	140	5	118
2005	123	17	166	98	145	10	128

Note: total includes MPs from other parties.

Summary

Five accounts of representation

➤ delegate model
➤ constituency representation
➤ resemblance
➤ trustee model
➤ party representation

Key terms

➤ **Delegate.** An individual who is authorised to act on behalf of others, but who is bound by clear instructions.
➤ **Positive action.** The use of different selection criteria for representatives of some groups as a way of tackling existing social inequality.
➤ **Representation.** The process by which an individual or individuals act on behalf of a larger group.
➤ **Representative.** (a) *noun* — an individual acting on behalf of a larger group; (b) *adjective* — exhibiting a likeness, typical.

Elections and democracy

Regular, competitive, free and fair elections are necessary but not sufficient conditions for a healthy liberal democracy. The list of functions presented at the start of this chapter offers an idealised view of elections, but helps us to reach an informed judgement about the vitality of electoral democracy in the UK. General elections score well against many of the criteria. Virtually all citizens have the right to vote; elections are contested by a range of parties from across the political spectrum, while electoral law ensures that they are free and fair. Governments have a good record in putting their manifesto commitments into practice and most MPs carry out their constituency duties diligently.

Criticisms of elections

Nonetheless, critics have drawn attention to a number of concerns about elections in the UK. This chapter has already noted that general elections provide only a blunt tool for policy influence, while there are marked differences between the social composition of parliament and the electorate as a whole. One of the most persistent criticisms of elections and democracy in the UK is that the simple plurality electoral system is 'unfair'. This is explored in Chapter 3. Before then, two further issues are mentioned briefly: participation and a democratic political culture.

Low turnout

Low turnout weakens the legitimacy of elections and the political system, undermines representation and the doctrine of the mandate, and calls into question the educative function of elections. The 2001 general election produced a turnout of just 59.4%, the lowest ever under the full franchise (see Box 2.4 overleaf). More than 5 million people fewer voted than in 1997. Turnout rose in 2005 to 61.3%, still a long way short of the postwar average of 78.3% (see Table 2.6).

A number of explanations have been offered for the decline in election turnout:

➤ **Rational choice.** Rational choice theory suggests that individuals will be unlikely to vote if the costs of doing so outweigh the likely benefits. Survey evidence indicates that non-voters often cite practical reasons (e.g. being away from home) for their abstention. People are more likely to vote in a close contest because their vote is more likely to make a difference to the result: turnout was generally higher in marginal seats than in safe seats in 2001 and 2005. But most people do not make a decision on whether to vote on purely instrumental grounds: two-thirds of people feel that voting is a civic duty.

➤ **Partisan dealignment.** People who feel a strong attachment to a political party are more likely to vote than those who do not identify with a party. Only around one in six people now have a

Table 2.6 Turnout at the 2005 general election

Category	Turnout (%)	Change since 2001 (%)
Gender		
Male	62	+1
Female	61	+3
Age		
18–24	37	-2
25–34	49	+3
35–44	61	+2
45–54	65	+0
55–64	71	+2
65+	75	+5
Social class		
AB	71	+3
C1	62	+2
C2	58	+2
DE	54	+1
All voters (GB)	61	+2

Source: MORI, www.mori.com

'very strong' attachment to a party. Non-voters often feel that they have been let down by a party they used to support. Turnout among Labour supporters was lower than that among Conservative supporters in 2001 and 2005, in part because former

---

Box 2.4 Reasons for low turnout at the 2001 general election

Short-term factors

➢ Personal circumstances (illness, holiday etc.).

➢ The election campaign inspired little interest.

➢ The outcome was predictable — Labour was expected to win comfortably.

➢ Discontent with leaders — Blair and Hague were not very popular with voters.

➢ Discontent with parties — the Labour government's record in office had disappointed many of its supporters; the Conservatives were widely viewed as unelectable and did not attract 'floating voters'.

➢ Discontent with policy — voters were dissatisfied with the policy record and policy proposals put forward by the main parties.

➢ A decline in partisanship — fewer people felt a strong attachment to a political party.

Long-term factors

➢ Public disaffection with politics and the political system.

20% of people surveyed by MORI in June 2001 had not voted in the general election. They offered a variety of reasons for not voting, including:

Reason	%
Inconvenient	21
Away	16
No polling card/postal vote	11
Not interested in politics	10
Not registered to vote	6
Didn't know enough about parties/candidates	6
Too busy	6
Didn't like parties	5
Didn't like candidates	4
Vote wouldn't have made a difference	2
No point/parties the same	2
Favoured party had no chance	2
None of parties worth voting for	2
Don't think voting is important	1

Source: MORI, www.mori.com

Labour voters were disillusioned with Tony Blair. People who do not vote are more likely to feel that the two main parties offer the same sort of policies.

➤ **Disinterest in politics**. Some commentators suggest that low turnout is a reflection of growing apathy in the political process. Opinion polls show that trust in politicians has waned. Recent election campaigns have failed to mobilise large numbers of potential voters. However, it should not be assumed automatically that dissatisfaction with Westminster politics equates to a general disinterest in politics. Surveys suggest that most people are interested in (broadly defined) politics and participation in other forms of political activity (e.g. demonstrations and consumer boycotts) has increased.

➤ **Social groups**. Levels of turnout vary across social groups. In 2001 and 2005, turnout was greatest in constituencies with high proportions of elderly, university-educated and middle-class voters. Groups least likely to vote were the working class and young people (see Table 2.6). The 18–24 age group was the only major social group in which turnout fell in 2005. People aged over 65 were almost twice as likely to vote as those aged 18–24. Research conducted by MORI and the Electoral Commission after the 2001 election suggested that young people were:

➤ less likely to be registered to vote
➤ most likely to say that 'no one party stands for me'
➤ more likely to complain about the lack of campaign information
➤ increasingly negative about politics and elections

Whereas older electors tended to mention civic duty as a reason for voting, young voters cited 'having a say'. However, suggestions that young people are uninterested in political issues (rather than in the 'ya-boo' politics of Westminster) may be overstated, given the real interest many young people have in issues such as university tuition fees and the war on Iraq. The student vote was a factor in Liberal Democrat victories in at least four seats in 2005.

The four interpretations of declining turnout presented above offer different perspectives on how participation might be increased. The rational choice view implies that making the act of voting easier (e.g. by postal voting or e-voting) will improve turnout. Interpretations focusing on dealignment and disinterest in politics argue that politicians must engage people in the political process more effectively. The final interpretation suggests that efforts must be targeted at certain groups, particularly young people. An Electoral Commission study (2004) rejected a proposal that the voting age be reduced to 16. Such a move would not increase turnout and was supported by only a third of people under the age of 25.

A democratic political culture
Democracy requires active citizens and a supportive political culture. Political parties, the media and citizens share the blame for the failings of UK democracy. Parties are often more interested in winning than in explaining complex political questions

effectively. Opinion polls on the European single currency, for example, consistently show that citizens do not feel they have enough quality information to make an informed judgement. Parties often present one-sided information, misrepresent the views of their opponents and avoid tricky issues such as the decriminalisation of drugs. The media are guilty of promoting style over substance, focusing on personalities rather than policies and offering trite soundbites rather than reasoned analysis. Apathetic and uninformed citizens must, however, also bear some of the responsibility for the shortcomings of UK democracy.

Suggested reading

Butler, D. and Kavanagh, D., *The British General Election of 2005* (Palgrave, 2005).

Curtice, J., 'Historic truimph or rebuff? 2005 UK general election', *Politics Review*, vol. 15, no. 1, September 2005.

The Electoral Commission, *Age of Electoral Majority*, 2004.

The Electoral Commission, *Voter Engagement and Young People*, 2004.

Fisher, J., 'Party finance: new rules, same old story?', *Politics Review*, vol. 12, no. 4, April 2003.

Jones, B., 'Apathy: why don't people want to vote?', *Politics Review*, vol. 12, no. 4, April 2003.

Norris, P. and Wlezien, C. (eds), *Britain Votes 2005* (Oxford University Press, 2005).

Websites

BBC 2005 general election site (information on results, the campaign and how to vote): http://news.bbc.co.uk/nol/ukfs_news/hi/uk_politics/vote_2005/default.stm

Department for Constitutional Affairs (responsible for legislation on election administration): www.dca.gov.uk/elections/index.htm

The Electoral Commission (responsible for reviewing the conduct of elections): http://www.electoralcommission.gov.uk

The Fawcett Society (campaigns for improved representation of women): www.fawcettsociety.org.uk

Operation Black Vote (campaigns for improved representation of ethnic minorities): www.obv.org.uk

Richard Kimber's 2005 general election site (gateway to hundreds of election-related sites): www.psr.keele.ac.uk/area/uk/ge05.htm

Votes at Sixteen (campaigns for a reduction in the voting age): www.votesat16.org.uk

Exam focus

Using this chapter and other resources available to you, answer the following questions:

1 What are the key functions of elections?
2 Outline the different types of election that take place in the UK.
3 Why has there been a decline in turnout in elections in recent years?
4 How likely to work are the various schemes and proposals suggested to improve voter turnout?
5 Why has the funding of political parties become a controversial issue?
6 Discuss the arguments for and against the state funding of political parties.
7 'The doctrine of the mandate is rather slippery.' Discuss.
8 How important is the campaign in determining the outcome of general elections?
9 Discuss the impact of the media on general elections.
10 Discuss the impact of opinion polls on the outcome of general elections.
11 Which model of representation best fits British MPs, and why?
12 What are the main criticisms of elections in the UK?
13 'Elections promote democracy.' Discuss.

Chapter 3

Electoral reform

Electoral systems provide the means by which votes cast by citizens are translated into political outcomes — either seats in a legislative assembly or a victorious candidate for office. Electoral systems have a number of functions (see Chapter 2), but the relative importance of these is disputed. For some, the most important tasks of an electoral system are to produce a clear winner and a strong government, and to maintain a link between MPs and geographical constituencies. Majoritarian systems are appropriate in this case. Others argue that an electoral system should provide maximum choice for voters and reflect accurately the diversity of opinion among the electorate. Proportional representation (PR) systems fit the bill here.

Key questions answered in this chapter
➤ What are the key features of the first-past-the-post electoral system?
➤ What are the advantages and disadvantages of FPTP?
➤ What are the main alternatives to FPTP?
➤ Which electoral systems are used in the UK?
➤ How has the electoral reform debate developed in the UK?

Characteristics of first-past-the-post (FPTP)

The FPTP system is used for general elections and local elections in the UK. Some claims made frequently about the outcomes of FPTP elections should be treated with caution. FPTP tends to benefit both main political parties, but does not always do so. It normally produces a decisive outcome, too — but not always. Several broad characteristics of the first-past-the-post system can, however, be identified.

Simple plurality

The first-past-the-post electoral system is a simple plurality system. In order to win a contest conducted under FPTP, a candidate has only to score the highest number of votes. There is no requirement to obtain a majority of the votes cast (i.e. 50% + 1 vote). The winner need only gain a *plurality*: that is, one more vote than the second-placed candidate.

In contests involving three or more candidates, the winner may fall well short of an overall majority. An extreme example occurred at the 1992 general election when Sir Russell Johnston won Inverness, Nairn and Lochaber for the Liberal Democrats with only 26% of the vote. Johnston had a lead of just 696 votes (1.4% of the total vote) over the third-placed candidate.

Single-member constituencies

Elections to legislative assemblies conducted under FPTP usually take place in single-member constituencies (Japan is an exception). The UK is divided into 646 constituencies of roughly equal size for general elections. Each constituency elects one, and only one, representative (MP) to the House of Commons.

The size of these constituencies and their boundaries are determined by the independent Boundary Commissions, one for each of the UK's component nations. The commissions review the size of the electorate in each constituency every 8 to 12 years. They make recommendations on revisions of boundaries based on projected population movements. The aim is to have constituencies that are as equal 'as is practicable' in terms of the size of their electorate.

UK constituencies

Geographical considerations can be responsible for significant differences in the size of constituencies. The Isle of Wight has an electorate of 108,000 while, at the other extreme, Na h-Eileanan An Iar (the Western Isles) has fewer than 22,000 voters. The nature of the union between the different nations of the UK also produced inequity. In 2001, Scottish and Welsh constituencies averaged 55,000 voters; English constituencies averaged 69,000. This over-representation reflected historic concerns that Scottish and Welsh interests would not have sufficient voice in a union with England.

Devolution weakened the case for over-representation. The Scotland Act (1998) stated that the number of Westminster constituencies in Scotland would be reduced. For the 2005 general election, the number of Scottish constituencies duly fell from 72 to 59.

Two-party system

FPTP tends to foster a two-party system, as it advantages major parties with strong nationwide support while placing at a disadvantage smaller parties whose support is spread thinly. A small swing in the popular vote can lead to a large number of seats changing hands, transforming a party's fortunes.

There is little electoral incentive for a faction within one of the main parties to break away and form a new party. Small parties, both old and new, have found it difficult to loosen the main parties' stranglehold on seats at Westminster. A case in point is the Social Democratic Party (SDP), which was formed by disaffected MPs from the Labour right in 1981. In an alliance with the Liberals, the new party won a quarter of the vote in the 1983 general election. This was a creditable performance so soon after its creation. But the SDP/Liberal Alliance had failed to translate broad support into constituency victories, winning only 23 seats. Without a major breakthrough at Westminster, the SDP's fortunes waned rapidly.

For much of the last 60 years, the UK electoral system has offered the Labour and Conservative parties a good chance of winning power with a comfortable parliamentary majority. They have been the major postwar beneficiaries of FPTP. However, the FPTP system does not automatically reward both main parties simultaneously. Instead, it often gives the party securing the largest vote a 'bonus' in seats, at the expense of its main rival.

Winner's bonus

FPTP tends to exaggerate the performance of the most popular party. It produces a 'winner's bonus' or 'landslide effect'. This means that a small increase in the share of the vote is translated into a substantial net gain in seats and a working majority in parliament. This was most apparent in the election victories won by Labour in 1945, 1966, 1997, 2001 and 2005 (see Figure 3.1), and by the Conservatives in 1983 and 1987 (see Table 3.1). In 1983 and 1987, the Conservatives won majorities of over a hundred seats on just over 42% of the popular vote. Labour's 43.4% of the vote in 1997 and 40.7% in 2001 produced parliamentary majorities of 179 and 167 respectively. At the 1992 general election, the Conservatives' 41.8% of the popular vote translated into a 51.6% share of seats in the Commons. They had secured a 'winner's bonus', but Labour also won significantly more seats than it merited. Tories feel aggrieved that the record-breaking 14 million votes they accrued brought them only a 21-seat parliamentary majority.

Figure 3.1 Percentage of seats won and votes cast in 2005

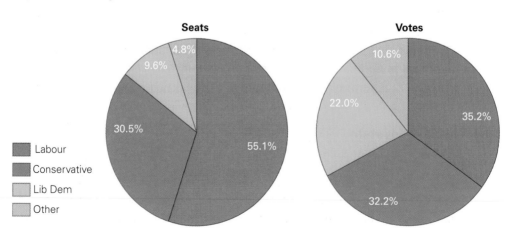

Table 3.1 UK general election results: votes and seats

	Conservative			Labour			Liberal		
	Vote (%)	Seats (%)	Diff	Vote (%)	Seats (%)	Diff	Vote (%)	Seats (%)	Diff
1945	39.6	31.1	−8.5	48.0	61.4	+13.4	9.0	1.9	−7.1
1950	43.4	47.7	+4.3	46.1	50.4	+4.3	9.1	1.4	−7.7
1951	48.0	51.4	+3.4	48.8	47.2	−1.6	2.6	1.0	−1.6
1955	49.7	54.8	+5.1	46.4	44.0	−2.4	2.7	1.0	−1.7
1959	49.4	57.9	+8.5	43.8	41.0	−2.8	5.9	1.0	−4.9
1964	43.4	48.3	+4.9	44.1	50.3	+6.2	11.2	1.4	−9.8
1966	41.9	40.2	−1.7	48.0	57.8	+9.8	8.5	1.9	−6.6
1970	46.4	52.4	+6.0	43.1	45.7	+2.6	7.5	1.0	−6.5
1974 Feb	37.9	46.8	+8.9	37.2	47.4	+10.2	19.3	2.2	−17.1
1974 Oct	35.8	43.6	+7.8	39.2	50.2	+11.0	18.3	2.0	−16.3
1979	43.9	53.4	+9.5	36.9	42.4	+5.5	13.8	1.7	−12.1
1983	42.4	61.1	+18.7	27.6	32.2	+4.6	25.4	3.5	−21.9
1987	42.3	57.8	+15.5	30.8	35.2	+4.4	22.5	3.4	−19.1
1992	41.8	51.6	+9.8	34.4	41.6	+7.2	17.9	3.1	−14.8
1997	30.7	25.0	−5.7	43.4	63.4	+20.0	16.8	7.0	−9.8
2001	31.7	25.2	−6.5	40.7	62.7	+22.0	18.3	7.9	−10.4
2005	32.3	30.5	−1.8	35.2	55.1	+19.9	22.0	9.6	−12.4

Notes: Liberal includes the SDP/Liberal Alliance (1983 and 1987) and the Liberal Democrats (1992–2005).

Bias to Labour

John Curtice notes that, rather than simply favouring the winning party, the electoral system has become biased in favour of Labour. Labour won a 167-seat majority in 2001 on a smaller share of the vote than the Conservatives had managed in 1992. Then in 2005, Labour won 55.1% of seats on 35.2% of the vote. There are a number of reasons for the bias towards Labour:

➤ Labour benefits from differences in constituency size. The average electorate in Labour-held seats in 2005 numbered 67,000; in Conservative-held seats it was 73,000. This is largely a result of population movement from urban constituencies to suburban and rural constituencies since the pre-1997 revision of boundaries.

➤ Turnout is lower in Labour-held seats. In 2005, turnout was 58% in Labour seats compared to 65.5% in seats won by the Conservatives.

➤ In 1997, Labour secured its largest vote swings in constituencies where it mattered most, winning a series of Conservative-held seats. It held on to many of these in 2001 when the swing to the Tories in these seats was less than the national average. The Conservatives won some back (especially in Greater London) in 2005.

➤ Anti-Conservative tactical voting helped Labour win additional seats in 1997 and 2001.

➤ Labour benefited from the over-representation of Scotland at Westminster in 1997 and 2001. For the 2005 election, the number of Scottish constituencies was reduced from 72 to 59.

Labour's vote is thus more efficiently distributed — Labour has needed fewer votes because of its seats' smaller population size and lower turnout. In 2005, Labour won one MP for every 26,900 votes it secured, the Conservatives one MP for every 44,500 votes and the Liberal Democrats one MP for every 96,400 votes. But effective local campaigns also boosted Labour's seats total. Constituency boundaries are likely to be redrawn before the next election, following Boundary Commission reviews. This will reduce, but not eliminate, the pro-Labour bias in the electoral system.

To win the 2005 general election, the Conservatives required a uniform swing of 11.5% from Labour. Even if the two parties secured the same number of votes, Labour would have won a comfortable parliamentary majority. The Conservatives' share of the vote (32.3%) was only 0.6% higher than in 2001. But they made a net gain of 33 seats thanks to their concentration of resources in marginal seats, a higher than average swing in Greater London and the fragmentation of the Labour vote in some constituencies.

Discrimination against third parties

The FPTP electoral system discriminates against minority parties whose support is not concentrated in particular regions. A third party whose support is spread thinly across the country will fare especially badly. There are no rewards for coming second or third — gaining a plurality of votes in single-member constituencies is what counts.

In the period of two-party dominance between 1945 and 1970, on average only ten MPs per parliament represented third or minor parties. That figure has since risen: the average between 1974 and 2005 was 53 MPs. The 93 MPs from third and minor parties elected in 2001 made up close to one-fifth of the total membership of the House of Commons. This suggests that the electoral system has become less effective in keeping minor parties out of the Commons and/or that smaller parties are addressing some of the obstacles the FPTP system puts in their way rather better than they did in the past.

Third and minor parties in the UK

The Liberal Democrats (and their predecessors) have been consistent and heavy losers under the FPTP system. In 1983 the SDP/Liberal Alliance scooped 25.4% of the vote but won only 23 seats (3.5%). The Alliance trailed Labour by just 2.2% of the vote, but by a massive 186 seats. The Liberal Democrats won fewer seats than their vote merited in 1997, 2001 and 2005. Nonetheless, they improved their performance in terms of seats in each contest. The 62 seats won by the Liberal Democrats in 2005 was the highest third-party total since 1923. Tactical voting and effective campaigning in their target seats, particularly in southwest England where they are the second party, accounted for this increase.

Minor parties whose support is concentrated in particular regions fare better. The Scottish Nationalist Party (SNP) and Plaid Cymru have consistently won seats at

Westminster since 1970. They do not contest seats across the UK, but focus their resources in their own nations. Plaid Cymru gained a greater voice at Westminster than its share of the UK (and Welsh) vote merited, as its support was, for much of this period, concentrated in a small number of Welsh-speaking constituencies.

Summary

Characteristics of FPTP

- simple plurality
- two-party system
- discrimination against third parties
- single-member constituencies
- winner's bonus

Key terms

- **Representative.** An elected person (e.g. an MP in the House of Commons), who speaks or acts on behalf of those who elected him or her.
- **Simple plurality system.** The first-past-the-post electoral system. The winning candidate need only secure a plurality of votes (one more than his or her nearest rival) to win in a single-member constituency.
- **Single-member constituency.** A geographical area represented by one elected Member of Parliament.

Advantages of FPTP

Supporters of the first-past-the-post system point to a number of advantages.

Simplicity

FPTP is easy to understand and to operate. The ballot paper is simple, electors only vote once and counting the votes is a relatively straightforward matter. Voters are familiar with the current system and, for the most part, view it as legitimate and effective. Popular demand for electoral reform is limited: few voters identify electoral reform as a major issue facing the country.

Clear outcome

Elections conducted under FPTP normally (but not always) produce a clear winner. Even if no party secures a majority of the votes cast, the party securing the largest number of votes (a *plurality*) often achieves a majority of seats in the House of Commons. This means that an election determining the composition of the Commons will also usually establish which party will form the government. This avoids the lengthy and secretive brokering by party leaders that precedes the formation of coalition governments in proportional representation systems.

Strong and responsible government

Supporters of FPTP argue that, by favouring the two main parties and giving the winning party an additional 'bonus' of seats, the UK electoral system produces strong government. As we have seen, governing parties regularly secure parliamentary majorities even though they invariably fail to achieve a majority of the popular vote. Single-party governments with working majorities exercise significant control over the legislative process. This, it is said, produces more effective policies, as the government is able to develop a sustained position. Furthermore, a government that is sure of its parliamentary majority can act swiftly and decisively when unforeseen problems emerge.

Supporters of FPTP are often wary of *coalition governments* (i.e. governments made up of more than one political party). Coalitions are said to be unstable and less accountable. Third parties or minor parties often achieve undue influence as, with a small number of MPs, they can make or break coalitions. The terms by which a coalition government is formed are negotiated in secret and may require a party to abandon some of the policy commitments it made during the election campaign.

Exponents of the 'Westminster model' also claim that the simple plurality electoral system helps to ensure that the government is responsible and accountable. The doctrine of the *mandate* (see Chapter 2) has practical application in a system that produces single-party government. Political parties present the electorate with their policy programmes at a general election, with the winning party then obliged to put its proposals into practice. Elections conducted under FPTP provide voters with a clear choice between alternative governments and also give the winning party an artificial majority that enables it to implement its commitments. The government is held accountable to the electorate in a direct manner: in a contest between two main parties, voters can either reward or penalise the government for its record in office.

Effective representation

The single-member constituencies used for UK general elections are said by supporters of FPTP to improve representation. One Member of Parliament is responsible for representing the interests of a constituency area and all citizens living within its boundaries. This can produce a closer bond between MPs and their constituencies than exists in multi-member seats where a blurring of responsibilities may occur. It also encourages sitting MPs to work on behalf of all their constituents rather than act on narrow party lines. Their reward may be a small, but potentially significant, 'personal vote'.

Disadvantages of FPTP

Critics of FPTP respond by noting its disadvantages.

Unfairness

The principal argument made by critics of the first-past-the-post system is that it is unfair in the way it distributes seats. The system is disproportionate — the number of parliamentary seats won by political parties at a general election does not reflect accurately the share of the vote they achieved. There are three main criticisms relating to this mismatch between votes and seats:

> One party can win more votes than its nearest rival, but receive fewer seats.
> FPTP gives an unfair advantage to the two main parties, and an additional bonus to the election 'winner'.
> Small parties with national support are disadvantaged.

Twice in postwar UK politics, the party coming second in the popular vote has 'won' a general election by securing more seats in the House of Commons than its main opponent. In 1951, Labour won 48.8% of the popular vote, but the Conservatives on 48.0% won 26 more seats. In February 1974 the Conservatives scored more votes (37.9%), but Labour (37.2%) won 4 more seats.

Electoral bias

The Conservative and Labour parties have both benefited from FPTP in the postwar period, winning parliamentary majorities that their popular support did not merit (see Table 3.1). Shifts in public opinion have also been exaggerated, producing parliamentary landslides. Recently, the electoral system has exhibited a bias towards Labour that gave it very large majorities in 1997 and 2001.

Small parties with thinly spread national support fare particularly badly. The Liberal Democrats have won fewer seats than their vote merited. Critics of FPTP argue that proportional representation would produce a 'fairer' distribution of seats. From being a party permanently out of office, PR might transform the Liberal Democrats into an omnipresent party in government. If PR were introduced for general elections, the most likely outcome would be a Labour/Liberal Democrat coalition, for in the current political climate the Liberal Democrats are Labour's 'natural' coalition partner. Labour/Liberal Democrat coalitions have held office in Scotland and Wales. Supporters of FPTP argue that PR would thus produce 'unfair' outcomes. A minority party would have more power (either as a member of the governing coalition, or as a maker and breaker of coalition deals) than its limited support in the country merited.

Plurality, not majority

FPTP does not require either winning candidates in parliamentary constituencies or the governing party to secure a majority of the votes cast. Two thirds of MPs elected in 2005 (426 MPs or 66%) did not secure a majority of the vote in their constituency. This is the highest proportion in UK electoral history. Fifty-five MPs were elected on less than 40% of the vote: Gordon Banks won Ochill and South Perthshire on just 31.4%. The low turnout also meant that a substantial majority of MPs were supported by less than one in three of the eligible electorate.

The last time a UK political party won a majority of the vote at a general election was in 1935. Labour's 35.2 % of the vote in 2005 was the lowest ever recorded by a winning party. Only 21.6% of the electorate (9.6 million people) voted for the Labour Party.

Votes are of unequal value

The FPTP system does not meet squarely the 'one person, one vote, one value' principle of representative democracy. Disparities in constituency size mean that votes are of different value. A vote cast by a person resident in a relatively small constituency is more likely to influence the outcome of that contest than is a vote cast in a larger constituency.

Wasted votes

Critics of FPTP argue that a substantial number of votes cast in UK general elections are 'wasted'. A 'wasted vote' is usually defined as a vote for a losing candidate in a single-member constituency. These votes do not help elect a candidate and are of no importance in the electoral process. In 2005, 52% of votes in the UK were 'wasted' in this sense, according to the Electoral Reform Society. The definition of a 'wasted vote' can be stretched further to include those votes cast for a winning candidate that were not required for him or her to win. The size of the winner's lead over his or her nearest rival does not matter under first-past-the-post. In 2005, 18% of the votes cast in the UK fell into this category.

Safe seats

Furthermore, a large number of seats can be classified as 'safe seats'. Here, one party has a substantial lead over its nearest rival that is unlikely to be overturned at the next election. Supporters of other parties have very little chance of seeing their favoured party win: their votes are effectively 'wasted'. Curtice calculated that only 114 seats were marginal 'two-way' fights between Labour and the Conservatives in 2001.

Many UK voters have a constituency MP who is not a member of their chosen political party. This raises questions about the representation of the views of these voters both at constituency level and in the House of Commons.

Limited choice

Critics of FPTP claim that many voters are denied an effective choice in UK general elections. In single-member constituencies, only one official candidate stands on behalf of each political party. Voters cannot choose between different candidates from the same party. Labour voters can only register support for their party by voting for the official Labour Party candidate. In a multi-member constituency, they would in theory be able to express a preference between Labour candidates from the left and right of the party, or choose between male and female candidates. The use of single-member constituencies places significant power in the hands of party officials. In safe seats, local or national party officials effectively decide who will represent that constituency at Westminster.

The discrimination against small parties that occurs under FPTP persuades some electors to cast their vote tactically. Here a voter whose first choice party has no realistic prospect of winning the seat in question, votes instead for the candidate who is best placed to prevent their least-favoured party from winning. Rather than making a positive choice, the voter makes a tactical decision.

FPTP is divisive

Opponents of FPTP argue that it is a divisive system that encourages political conflict rather than cooperation. The electoral map of the UK illustrates one aspect of these divisions. Many of the seats held by the Conservatives are in southern and rural England, while Labour is dominant in Scotland, Wales, the north of England and most big cities. The Conservatives won 24% of the vote in the six English metropolitan counties outside London in 2005, but only 5 out of 124 seats. Large parts of urban Britain are 'electoral deserts' for the Tories.

Critics of the UK electoral system have questioned its legitimacy. In the 1960s and 1970s, it was argued that FPTP had fostered a period of *adversary politics*. Small shifts in voting behaviour were producing frequent changes of government. Once in power, ideologically motivated parties were overturning the key legislation introduced by their predecessors at the expense of political and economic stability.

By the late 1980s, critics of FPTP claimed that the electoral system had contributed to a period of one-party rule. The Conservatives won four successive general election victories without winning more than 44% of the vote. Critics claimed that the Conservatives ignored the views of a majority of the electorate.

Summary

First-past-the-post

Advantages:

➢ simplicity

➢ clear outcome

➢ strong and stable government

➢ effective representation

Disadvantages:

➢ unfairness

➢ plurality, not majority

➢ votes are of unequal value

➢ limited choice

➢ FPTP is divisive

Key terms

➢ **Coalition government.** Governments made up of more than one political party.

➢ **Safe seat.** A constituency that normally elects an MP from the same political party at every election.

➢ **Tactical voting.** Voting for the candidate most likely to defeat the voter's least favoured candidate.

➢ **'Wasted vote'.** A vote for a losing candidate in a single-member constituency.

Alternative electoral systems

A variety of electoral systems are used in liberal democracies. Electoral systems can be divided into three main types:

> majoritarian
> proportional
> mixed

In majoritarian systems, candidates are usually elected in single-member constituencies. The winner is the candidate who secures the most votes. FPTP is a simple plurality system in which the winning candidate requires only one more vote than the second-placed candidate. However, it is often classified as a majoritarian system. In other majoritarian systems (e.g. the alternative vote system), a candidate must secure a majority of the votes cast to win. These systems often exhibit a sharp gap between votes for parties and the seats they win: they are not proportional.

Proportional systems produce an accurate fit between the votes cast in an election and the seats allocated to political parties in the legislative assembly. They use multi-member constituencies. Examples of PR systems include the single transferable vote (STV) and regional list systems.

Mixed systems, such as the additional member system (AMS), combine elements of the plurality or majoritarian systems and proportional representation. Some MPs are elected in single-member constituencies. The remainder are elected by proportional representation in multi-member constituencies. These 'top-up' seats produce 'additional members', who are allocated to parties on corrective lines. Parties winning fewer single-member constituencies than their share of the vote merits gain the most 'top-up' seats.

Majoritarian systems

Alternative vote (AV)

In the alternative vote system, the winning candidate has to achieve an overall majority of the votes cast. Instead of voting for a single candidate, electors indicate their preferences by writing '1' beside the name of their first choice, '2' next to the name of their second choice, '3' for their third choice and so on. If no candidate secures an absolute majority of the first preferences, the lowest-placed candidate is eliminated and the second preferences of his or her voters are transferred to the remaining candidates. This process continues until one candidate reaches the 50% + 1 vote threshold. AV is used in elections in Australia.

Advantages of AV

> MPs are elected by majorities in their constituencies.
> A link between MPs and constituencies is retained.

Disadvantages of AV

> It is even less proportional than FPTP.
> It exaggerates swings in public opinion.

Supplementary vote (SV)

The supplementary vote is a variant of AV, designed for use in the election of the Mayor of London. The elector has one vote and records only his or her first and second preferences on the ballot paper. If no candidate in a single-member constituency wins a majority of first preferences, all but the top two candidates are eliminated. Second preferences for the remaining two eligible candidates are then added to their first preference votes. The candidate with the highest total is elected. SV is used to elect mayors in a number of UK towns and cities.

Advantages of SV
➢ It is a simple system.
➢ Second preferences of voters who supported minor parties are not counted.

Disadvantages of SV
➢ It is not a proportional system.
➢ The winning candidate need not get a majority of the votes cast.

Proportional representation systems

List system

Electors choose from a list of candidates in large multi-member constituencies. Seats are allocated according to the proportion of votes won by each political party. In *open list* systems, voters select from a list of individual candidates representing political parties and independent candidates without a party affiliation. In *closed list* systems, electors can only vote for a party slate or for an independent candidate. They cannot choose between candidates representing the same political party. The closed list thus gives party managers greater control over the electoral process, as they can put their favoured candidates at the top of the list. Their least favoured candidates would be placed at the bottom of the list, giving them little realistic chance of being elected. A closed list system is used in Great Britain for elections to the European Parliament.

Advantages of the list system
➢ There is a high degree of proportionality.
➢ Each vote has the same value.

Disadvantages of the list system
➢ In closed list systems, voters have little or no choice between candidates.
➢ By determining the order in which candidates are placed on the list, party officials can stifle minority views.

Single transferable vote (STV)

The single transferable vote system uses multi-member constituencies only. Voting is preferential: that is, electors indicate their preferences among a potentially large number of candidates by writing '1' beside the name of their first preference, '2' next to the name of their second choice and so on. Voting is also ordinal: electors can vote for as many or as few candidates as they like. A candidate must achieve a quota, known as the *Droop quota*, in order to be elected. Any votes in excess of this quota are redistributed on the basis of second preferences. The quota is calculated as follows:

$$\text{Droop quota} = \left(\frac{\text{total valid votes}}{\text{total number of seats} + 1} \right) + 1$$

If no candidate successfully reaches the quota on the first count of the votes, the lowest-placed candidate is eliminated and their second preferences are transferred. This process of elimination and redistribution of preferences continues until the requisite number of seats is filled by candidates meeting the quota. STV is used in local and European Parliament elections in Northern Ireland. It is also used for general elections in the Republic of Ireland.

Advantages of STV

> It is broadly proportional and ensures that votes are largely of equal value.
> Only a party or coalition of parties that wins more than 50% of the popular vote can form a government.
> Voters can choose from a range of candidates, including different candidates from the same party.

Disadvantages of STV

> The system is less accurate in translating votes into seats than list systems or some versions of AMS.
> It uses large multi-member constituencies that break the link between individual MPs and their constituency.
> It produces coalition governments. This can give disproportional power to minor parties that hold the 'balance of power'.

Mixed systems

Additional member system (AMS)

The additional member system is a mixed system. A proportion of seats in the legislative assembly are elected using the first-past-the-post system in single-member constituencies. The remaining seats are *additional members* allocated to a political party on the basis of a party list of candidates. At a general election, electors cast two votes: one for their favoured candidate in a single-member constituency and one for their favoured party in a multi-member constituency.

Additional members are allocated to political parties on a corrective basis to ensure that the total number of seats they have in the legislative assembly is proportional to the number of votes they won. Parties winning a share of the popular vote that is not reflected in the number of single-member constituency seats won have their total number of seats 'topped up' by additional members. The d'Hondt formula is used to allocate these 'top-up' seats (see Box 3.1).

Box 3.1 The d'Hondt formula

The d'Hondt formula is a mathematical formula for allocating seats proportionally. It was invented by the nineteenth-century Belgian academic Victor d'Hondt. It is known as the Jefferson method in the USA. The d'Hondt formula is a 'highest average' system that uses a divisor method rather than a quota. It does not deliver strict proportionality, slightly favouring large parties over smaller parties.

In the UK, the d'Hondt formula is used to allocate seats in the AMS elections in Scotland, Wales and Greater London as well as in the closed list elections to the European Parliament. The formula is also used to appoint members of the Northern Ireland Executive.

Under d'Hondt, the total votes of each party are divided by the number of seats it already has, plus the next seat to be allocated. The following example is taken from the list election in Mid and West Wales, the second part of the AMS election of the National Assembly of Wales in May 1999:

	Con	Lab	Lib Dem	Plaid Cymru	Winner
Constituency seats won	0	2	2	4	
List votes	36,622	53,842	31,683	84,544	
First divisor	1	3	3	5	
First seat	**36,622**	17,947	10,561	16,910	**Con**
Second divisor	2	3	3	5	
Second seat	**18,311**	17,947	10,561	16,910	**Con**
Third divisor	3	3	3	5	
Third seat	12,207	**17,947**	10,561	16,910	**Lab**
Fourth divisor	3	4	3	5	
Fourth seat	12,207	13,460	10,561	**16,910**	**Plaid Cymru**

List seats were allocated according to the calculation of the number of votes for each party divided by the number of seats won by the party plus 1. The party with the highest score after this calculation wins the list seat. For the first seat, the calculation was based only on the number of constituency seats (decided by FPTP) won by each party in the region. The calculations for the second, third and fourth list seats then took the new total of seats (constituency and list) into account.

Adapted from: J. Bradbury, 'Labour's bloody nose', *Politics Review*, vol. 9, no. 2, November 1999, p. 7.

In Germany, 50% of seats in the Bundestag (lower house) are allocated to additional members. However, a political party must reach a threshold requirement of 5% of the nationwide popular vote to be eligible for additional members. This provision in the German constitution was designed to prevent extremist parties from gaining a foothold in the legislative assembly. In the UK, versions of AMS are used to elect the Scottish

Parliament, the National Assembly for Wales and the Greater London Assembly (see Table 3.2). None replicates the German 50:50 split between constituency MPs and additional members.

Table 3.2 Additional member systems in Great Britain

	Size of assembly	Constituency: top-up seats ratio (%)	Top-up areas	Top-up seats per area
Scottish Parliament	129	57:43	8 European constituencies	7
Welsh Assembly	60	67:33	5 European constituencies	4
Greater London Assembly	25	57:43	Greater London	11
Jenkins Report AV+ system	659	83:17	80 counties, parts of metropolitan counties, European constituencies	1 or 2

Advantages of AMS

➢ The results are broadly proportional and votes are less likely to be 'wasted'.
➢ A number of single-member constituencies are used, ensuring a link between geographical areas and their parliamentary representatives.
➢ Electors have two votes — the first can be used to support a particular candidate and the second a political party.

Disadvantages of AMS

➢ It creates two categories of representative in the legislative assembly — one with constituency duties and one without a distinct base.
➢ Parties can have significant control over the party lists used to elect additional members.
➢ Small parties may still be under-represented, especially if they must reach a threshold of support.

Summary

Types of electoral system

Majoritarian:
➢ first-past-the-post (FPTP)
➢ alternative vote (AV)
➢ supplementary vote (SV)

Proportional:
➢ list system
➢ single transferable vote (STV)

Mixed:
➢ additional member system (AMS)

Key terms

➢ **Alternative vote.** A majoritarian system: a candidate must win an overall majority of votes to be elected. Voting is preferential: electors indicate their preferences among candidates by writing 1, 2, 3, etc. beside the name of their first, second and third choice candidates on the ballot paper. If no candidate achieves an absolute majority of first preferences, the

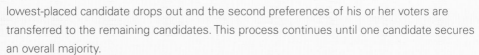

lowest-placed candidate drops out and the second preferences of his or her voters are transferred to the remaining candidates. This process continues until one candidate secures an overall majority.

➤ **List system.** A proportional representation system. Votes are cast for a party list of candidates in large multi-member constituencies. Seats are allocated proportionally according to the proportion of votes secured by each party. In 'open list' systems, voters choose from a list of individual candidates representing political parties and independent candidates. In 'closed list' systems, electors can only vote for a party or for independent candidates. The size of the multi-member constituencies can range from large regions to the entire country. Electoral formulas (e.g. the d'Hondt formula) are used to determine the allocation of seats.

➤ **Majoritarian system.** An electoral system in which the candidate with the most votes in a single-member constituency wins the election.

➤ **Mixed system.** An electoral system where a proportion of MPs are elected under a majoritarian system in single-member constituencies and the others are elected as 'additional members' using a proportional system in multi-member constituencies.

➤ **Preferential voting.** Voters record their preferences among candidates by writing 1, 2, 3, etc. on the ballot paper.

➤ **Proportional representation system.** An electoral system using multi-member constituencies in which an electoral formula is used to match the percentage of seats won by each party to the percentage of votes it won.

➤ **Second ballot.** If no candidate achieves a majority of the votes cast, a second ballot is held some days later. Candidates who scored poorly on the first ballot are often eliminated.

➤ **Single transferable vote.** Voters indicate their preferences among a range of candidates contesting multi-member constituencies. A candidate must achieve a quota of votes (the 'Droop quota') in order to be elected. Any votes that a candidate achieves in excess of this quota are redistributed according to second preferences. If no candidate reaches the quota, the lowest-placed candidate is eliminated and the second preferences of his or her voters are transferred. This process of elimination and distribution of second preferences continues until the required number of candidates meets the quota.

➤ **Supplementary vote.** A variant of the alternative vote system. Voters indicate their first and second preferences only. If no candidate wins a majority of first preferences, all but the top two candidates are eliminated. Second preferences for the remaining candidates are then added to their first preference totals. The candidate with the most votes is elected.

The UK's multiple electoral systems

Since the Labour government came to power in 1997, a number of new electoral systems have been introduced for a series of elections. Devolution saw elected assemblies created in Scotland, Wales and Northern Ireland. A number of cities have also adopted directly elected mayors. None of these new bodies is elected by the first-past-the-post system used for general elections. The system used for electing the UK's representatives in the European Parliament was changed from FPTP to a closed list PR system too.

Scottish Parliament

In Scotland, 73 out of a total of 129 Members of the Scottish Parliament (MSPs) (i.e. 57%) are elected in single-member constituencies using FPTP. The remaining 56 MSPs (43%) are 'top-up' members drawn from lists of candidates put forward by the parties. These 'additional members' are elected using the d'Hondt method of proportional representation in eight regions. The regions are based on existing European Parliament constituencies. Each sends seven MSPs to the Scottish Parliament.

Electors have two votes: one for the FPTP constituency MSP and one for a party list 'additional member' MSP in a multi-member region. In the elections to the Scottish parliament held in 1999 and 2003, almost all electors used both votes. Most voters chose the same party in both the constituency and regional list contests, but a significant number used their list vote to support a minor party.

Minor parties were the main beneficiaries in the 2003 election. The Scottish Green Party did not put up candidates in the FPTP constituency contests but won seven MSPs in the regional lists. The Scottish Socialist Party saw six MSPs elected from the regional list section but none in the FPTP constituencies. Four independent candidates were also elected, two in each section.

Labour was the largest party in both the 1999 and 2003 elections, but on neither occasion did it win a majority of seats (see Table 3.3). In 1999, Labour won 53 of the 73 FPTP contests (72.6% of the FPTP seats) on 38.8% of the vote. The better a party does in the constituency contests, the fewer 'top up' seats it gets. Labour thus won only three 'additional members', all in the Highlands and Islands region. In 2003, Labour lost seven constituency seats but gained a further list seat.

Table 3.3 Elections to the Scottish Parliament, 2003

	Constituency contests		Regional lists		
	Share of vote (%)	Seats won	Share of vote (%)	Seats won	Total seats
Conservative	16.6 (+1.1)	3 (+3)	15.5 (+0.1)	15 (−3)	18 (+0)
Labour	34.6 (−4.1)	46 (−7)	29.3 (−4.3)	4 (+1)	50 (−6)
Lib Dem	15.4 (+1.2)	13 (+1)	11.8 (−0.6)	4 (−1)	17 (+0)
SNP	23.8 (−5.1)	9 (+2)	20.9 (−6.5)	18 (−10)	27 (−8)
Green	0.0 (+0.0)	0 (+0)	6.9 (+3.3)	7 (+6)	7 (+6)
Scottish Socialist	6.2 (+5.2)	0 (+0)	6.7 (+4.7)	6 (+5)	6 (+5)
Others	3.4 (+1.7)	2 (+1)	8.9 (+3.3)	2 (+0)	4 (+3)

Turnout: constituency seats: 49.4% (−8.8), regional list: 49.4% (−8.7).   Note: figures in brackets refer to change since 1999.

Source: the Electoral Commission, www.electoralcommission.gov.uk

Following each election, Labour formed a coalition with the Liberal Democrats. The Liberal Democrats' period in government did not have a pronounced impact on their electoral performance — they again won a total of 17 seats and were fourth in the 2003 election. The Scottish National Party finished second in both 1999 and 2003, though it suffered a net loss of eight seats in the later contest. The Conservatives failed to win any FPTP constituencies in 1999 despite scoring 15.5% of the vote. Having opposed proportional representation, the Tories were then rescued by the regional list system under which they secured 18 'additional member' seats, so ensuring that their support was reflected in the parliament more accurately. The Conservatives won three FPTP seats in 2003 but again relied heavily on 'top up' seats.

National Assembly for Wales

The additional member system is used in elections for the National Assembly for Wales too. Forty of the 60 members of the assembly (AMs) (i.e. two-thirds of the total) are elected in single-member constituencies using FPTP. The other 20 AMs are elected in five multi-member constituencies, with each area sending four top-up members to Cardiff. The d'Hondt rule is used to allocate top-up seats. Neither the Scottish nor the Welsh system sets a threshold of votes needed to win seats.

Labour emerged as the largest party in the 1999 and 2003 assembly elections. Labour initially formed a minority administration, having fallen short of a majority in the assembly in 1999. After the downfall of its leader Alun Michael the following year, the new first minister Rhodri Morgan negotiated a Labour–Liberal Democrat coalition. Labour won 30 seats in 2003 — one short of an overall majority — and formed the assembly government in its own right.

Labour's dominance of the constituency contests means that it has secured only one regional list 'top up' seat since the assembly was formed — that won by Alun Michael in Mid and West Wales in 1999. Plaid Cymru and the Conservatives have been the main beneficiaries of the top-up system. Plaid Cymru has established itself as the second party in Wales, though it suffered the largest fall in seats and share of the vote in 2003.

Table 3.4 Elections to the National Assembly for Wales, 2003

	Constituency contests		Regional lists		
	Share of vote (%)	Seats won	Share of vote (%)	Seats won	Total seats
Conservative	20.4 (+4.5)	1 (+0)	19.2 (+2.9)	10 (+2)	11 (+2)
Labour	39.5 (+1.9)	30 (+3)	36.6 (+1.2)	0 (−1)	30 (+2)
Lib Dem	14.1 (+0.7)	3 (+0)	12.7 (+0.3)	3 (+0)	6 (+0)
Plaid Cymru	21.2 (−7.2)	5 (−4)	19.7 (−10.6)	7 (−1)	12 (−5)
Others	4.8 (+0.1)	1 (+1)	11.8 (+3.3)	0 (+0)	1 (+1)

Turnout: constituency seats: 38.2% (−7.7), regional list: 38.1% (−7.8). Note: figures in brackets refer to change since 1999.

Source: the Electoral Commission, www.electoralcommission.gov.uk

Greater London Assembly

The Greater London Assembly (GLA) is also elected by a variant of the AMS. Here, 14 of the 25 members of the assembly (57%) are elected by FPTP in constituencies merging two or three London boroughs. The remaining 11 are additional members elected from Greater London as a whole using the d'Hondt formula. A party must reach a threshold of 5% of the London-wide vote to be entitled to representation in the GLA. This makes it more difficult for extremist parties such as the British National Party to win seats. In the 2004 election, the Conservatives won nine seats, all of them constituency seats. Two of Labour's seven seats, plus all those won by the Liberal Democrats (five), Greens (two) and UKIP (two), were top up seats.

European Parliament

From 1979 to 1994, elections to the European Parliament held in Great Britain were conducted by FPTP using large single-member constituencies. By the mid-1990s, the UK was the only EU member state not to use some form of proportional representation for European Parliament elections. In the 1994 election, Labour won 62 of the UK's 87 seats on 44% of the vote. This result had an important bearing on the party balance in the European Parliament, as it helped to make the Socialists the largest group.

The Blair government decided to replace FPTP with a proportional representation system. But its choice of a closed list system of PR was a controversial one. The closed

Table 3.5 Elections to the European Parliament (GB only), 2004

	Conservative		Labour		Liberal Democrat		UKIP		Green		SNP/ Plaid Cymru	
	Vote (%)	Seats (%)	Vote (%)	Seats (%)	Vote (%)	Seats (%)	Vote (%)	Seats (%)	Vote (%)	Seats (%)	Vote (%)	Seats (%)
East Midlands	26.4	33.3	21.0	16.6	12.9	16.6	26.1	33.3	5.4	0	0	0
Eastern	30.8	42.9	16.2	14.3	14.0	14.3	19.6	28.6	5.6	0	0	0
London	26.8	33.3	24.7	33.3	15.3	11.1	12.3	11.1	8.4	11.1	0	0
North East	18.6	33.3	34.1	33.3	17.8	33.3	12.2	0	4.8	0	0	0
North West	24.1	33.3	27.3	33.3	15.8	22.2	12.2	11.1	5.6	0	0	0
South East	35.2	40.0	13.7	10.0	15.3	20.0	19.5	20.0	7.9	10.0	0	0
South West	31.6	42.9	14.5	14.3	18.3	14.3	22.6	28.6	7.2	0	0	0
West Midlands	27.3	42.9	23.4	28.6	13.7	14.3	17.5	14.3	5.1	0	0	0
Yorks and Humberside	24.6	33.3	26.3	33.3	15.5	16.6	14.5	16.6	5.7	0	0	0
Scotland	17.8	28.6	26.4	28.6	13.1	14.3	6.7	0	6.8	0	19.7	28.6
Wales	19.4	25.0	26.4	50.0	10.5	0	10.5	0	3.6	0	17.4	25.0
Great Britain	26.7	36.0	22.6	25.3	14.9	16.0	16.2	16.0	5.8	2.7	2.4	4.0

Turnout (GB): 38.9%

Source: the Electoral Commission, www.electoralcommission.gov.uk

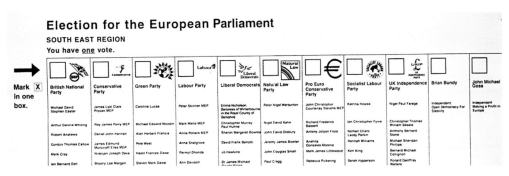

A specimen ballot paper for the European elections, 1999

list gave significant power to party officials, who were responsible for deciding the order in which candidates would be placed on the list. By placing candidates who were loyal to the party line at the top of the constituency list and those who were 'off-message' outside the top few places, party managers could influence the character of the UK representation decisively. Electors therefore cast their vote for a party list or an independent rather than for specific party candidates. Regional constituencies elect between four and 11 MEPs.

The Conservatives and Labour won most of the seats in the two European Parliament elections conducted under PR (1999 and 2004). The Greens and the United Kingdom Independence Party (UKIP) won their first seats in the European Parliament in 1999. In 2004, UKIP polled 16% of the vote and won 12 seats. But the allocation of seats by the voting system treated large parties more favourably than small parties (see Table 3.5). Northern Ireland's three MEPs are elected by the single transferable vote system to ensure cross-community representation.

Closed list systems are also used to determine additional members in the AMS elections to the Scottish Parliament, the National Assembly for Wales and the Greater London Assembly.

Northern Ireland Assembly

The 1998 Good Friday Agreement paved the way for the creation of a Northern Ireland Assembly. The single transferable vote system is used to elect the 108-member assembly. The existing 17 Westminster constituencies each send six members to the assembly. Under the Droop quota, a candidate needs to achieve 14.3% of the vote to be elected.

In the first elections to the assembly (1998) the Ulster Unionist Party (UUP) emerged as the largest party, with 28 seats. Importantly for the functioning of the new institutions, the transfer of votes to 'pro-agreement' candidates turned an 'anti-agreement' majority of first preference votes within the unionist bloc into a 'pro-agreement' majority among unionists. The second elections were held in 2003, even though the assembly had been suspended. The anti-agreement Democratic Unionist Party (DUP) overtook the UUP in the unionist bloc, and Sinn Fein overtook the moderate Social Democratic and Labour Party (SDLP) in the nationalist bloc (see Table 3.6 overleaf).

Table 3.6 Election to the Northern Ireland Assembly, 2003

	First preference vote (%)	Seats
Unionists		
Ulster Unionist Party	22.7 (+1.4)	27 (-1)
Democratic Unionist Party	25.7 (+7.6)	30 (+10)
Progressive Unionist Party	1.2 (-1.4)	1 (-1)
United Kingdom Unionist Party	0.8 (-3.7)	1 (-4)
Other unionists	0.5 (-2.4)	0 (-3)
Nationalists		
Social Democratic and Labour Party	17.0 (-5.0)	18 (-6)
Sinn Fein	23.5 (+5.8)	24 (+6)
Others		
Alliance Party	3.7 (-2.8)	6 (+0)
Women's Coalition	0.8 (-0.8)	0 (-2)
Independent (K. Deeny, West Tyrone)	0.9 (+0.9)	1 (+1)

Note: Figures in brackets refer to change since 1998. Turnout: 64.0%.
Source: the Electoral Commission, **www.electoralcommission.gov.uk**

Directly elected mayors

A number of UK cities now have a directly elected executive mayor. The supplementary vote system is used in each case. The most powerful of these elected mayors is the Mayor of London. Ken Livingstone won the London mayoral elections in 2000 (as an independent) and 2004 (as the Labour Party candidate). On both occasions he defeated Conservative Steve Norris after second preferences had been added (see Table 3.7).

A victorious Ken Livingstone salutes the cameras, 2000

Eleven local authorities (excluding London) had adopted the model of a directly elected mayor by 2005. Independent candidates won five of the 11 contests, Labour four and the Conservatives and Liberal Democrats one each. Among the independent victors were former police detective superintendent Ray Mallon in Middlesbrough and, in Hartlepool, Stuart Drummond, who was best known as Hartlepool United's mascot H'Angus the monkey. Non-aligned candidates benefited from protest votes, low turnouts, and their association with local issues. Independents fared less well when the mayoral posts came up for re-election.

Impact of the new electoral systems

The new electoral systems have already had an impact on UK politics, though it will take further rounds of voting before the picture becomes clear. The most significant effects of the move to multiple electoral systems are as follows.

Table 3.7 Election of Mayor of London, 2004

Candidate	Party	First preference vote (%)	Second preference vote (%)	Final (%)
Ken Livingstone	Labour	35.7	13.0	55.4
Steve Norris	Conservative	28.2	11.6	44.6
Simon Hughes	Liberal Democrat	14.8	24.3	
Lindsey German	Respect	6.2	3.3	
Frank Maloney	UKIP	6.0	10.0	
Julian Leppert	BNP	3.0	3.7	
Darren Johnson	Green	2.9	10.9	
Others	(3)	3.1	6.1	

Turnout: 36.9%

Source: www.londonelections.org.uk

More complex voting patterns

The move to proportional representation has helped to produce a more complex pattern of voting behaviour. Minor parties and independent candidates have performed better in elections using the new systems than in general elections using FPTP. Table 3.3 shows that minor parties have fared better in the list votes than in the constituency votes in elections to the Scottish Parliament. Electors recognise that a vote for a minor party is less likely to be wasted under AMS. One in five voters engaged in 'split-ticket' voting in the 1999 Scottish Parliament elections (more did so in 2003), supporting a major party in the constituency vote but giving their list vote to another (often minor) party.

Multiparty systems

The results of elections using PR and mixed electoral systems have made it more apparent that the UK has a number of party systems rather than a standard, nationwide two-party system. Both Scotland and Wales have multi-party systems. The number of parties securing meaningful representation (say 5% of seats) in the devolved assemblies is far greater than at Westminster. Nationalist parties are the second-placed parties in the Scottish Parliament and Welsh Assembly. Minor parties and independents won a total of 17 seats in the Scottish Parliament in 2003. The use of STV in Northern Ireland has seen fringe parties win seats in the assembly. Some 35% of votes cast in the 2004 European Parliament election were for minor parties and independents. UKIP performed far better in this election than it did in the general election a year later. This was a result of both PR and the high profile of European issues in the 2004 campaign.

Minority and coalition administrations

None of the elections to the new institutions in Scotland, Wales, Northern Ireland and Greater London has produced a decisive winner. No party has scored a majority of the popular vote or won a majority of seats. Whereas the Labour Party was used to winning most of the Westminster seats available in Scotland and Wales, it failed to achieve a decisive result in the 1999 elections conducted under AMS. In Scotland, Labour entered a coalition government with the Liberal Democrats, which continued after the 2003 contest. Labour initially formed a minority administration in Wales, but then constructed a coalition with the Liberal Democrats after Rhodri Morgan became Welsh Labour leader in 2000. The coalition ended in Wales when Labour won 30 of the 60 assembly seats and decided to govern alone. When Labour assembly member Peter Law left the party to sit as an independent in 2005, Labour became a minority administration. Labour and the Liberal Democrats agreed another coalition in Scotland after the 2003 election. Ken Livingstone has won the backing of Labour, Liberal Democrat and Green members of the Greater London Assembly. The Good Friday Agreement effectively requires that the Northern Ireland Executive must include members drawn from the major unionist and nationalist parties.

The use of more proportional electoral systems and the greater willingness of electors to vote for minor parties mean that coalition or minority governments are likely to become the norm in Scotland and Wales. This changes the nature of party competition, parliamentary politics and the conduct of election campaigns. The Liberal Democrats have been partners in coalition governments in Scotland (since 1999) and Wales (2000–03), but they continue to oppose Labour at Westminster. Coalition partners may find themselves supporting policies in one parliament that they oppose in another.

Public familiarity

Voters are becoming familiar with the new electoral systems. Surveys of attitudes to the new systems in Scotland and Wales suggest that most voters approve of them. But public opinion on electoral reform for Westminster has not changed dramatically. Few voters have strong feelings on the issue.

A sizeable minority of voters have found the new systems complex. Voters in London took part in five contests in June 2004, each using a different electoral system. In the mayoral election, 17% of second preference votes were ruled invalid as voters had completed the ballot paper incorrectly. The new electoral systems have not, though, produced an increase in turnout.

Electoral reform for Westminster

The operation of the new electoral systems appears to have confirmed Tony Blair's doubts about the suitability of PR for Westminster elections. The experience of coalition government in Scotland and Wales has not been a particularly happy one for the Labour Party. In Scotland, Labour retreated from its manifesto position on tuition fees in response to demands from its Liberal Democrat coalition partner. Labour's relatively poor showing in the elections in Scotland, Wales and a number of English local authorities has further persuaded many Labour MPs that the party would not achieve a decisive election victory if PR were used in general elections. These elections allowed voters to express their disapproval of New Labour and of Blair's attempts to impose his favoured candidates on reluctant local parties. Ken Livingstone triumphed as an independent candidate in

2000, while Alun Michael, Blair's favoured candidate for leadership of the Welsh Labour Party, enjoyed little popular support during his brief spell in power. The decision to use a closed list rather than an open list electoral system for the European Parliament elections also provoked a political backlash against the government.

Summary

The UK's multiple electoral systems

- ➤ Westminster Parliament: first-past-the-post
- ➤ Scottish Parliament: additional member system
- ➤ National Assembly for Wales: additional member system
- ➤ Greater London Assembly: additional member system
- ➤ European Parliament: regional list system (closed list)
- ➤ Northern Ireland Assembly: single transferable vote
- ➤ directly elected mayors: supplementary vote

Key terms

- ➤ **Devolution.** Political power moves away from a central authority (the Westminster Parliament) to local, regional or national governments (e.g. the Scottish Parliament).
- ➤ **Minority administration.** A government formed by a political party without an overall majority in the parliament or assembly.

Electoral reform in the UK

The campaign for electoral reform in the UK has a long history. English lawyer Thomas Hare devised the STV system in 1859. The Proportional Representation Society — a forerunner of the modern Electoral Reform Society — was formed in the 1880s. In 1918, a Speaker's Conference recommended that a hybrid electoral system (with a proportional representation element) should replace FPTP for general elections. A bill introducing the alternative vote was passed by the House of Commons, but was rejected by the House of Lords in 1931.

Labour and electoral reform

Labour's interest in electoral reform revived as it came to terms with the Conservatives' four consecutive general election victories between 1979 and 1992. Neil Kinnock set up a committee, chaired by Professor Raymond Plant (later Lord Plant), to examine the case for reform. In a series of reports, Plant backed AMS for elections for a Scottish Parliament and a regional list system for elections to the European Parliament. The Labour leadership accepted both. However, Plant's recommendation that the supplementary vote should be used for Westminster elections was more contentious. John Smith, Kinnock's successor as Labour leader, did not accept this recommendation, but he did promise that a Labour government would hold a referendum on electoral reform for Westminster.

Tony Blair maintained Smith's pledge and it was included in Labour's 1997 election manifesto. Labour and the Liberal Democrats were by this time working together on a range of constitutional issues including devolution, with both parties backing AMS for Scotland and Wales. As we have seen, the Labour government has put in place a number of new electoral systems that voters are starting to get accustomed to.

The Jenkins Report

Replacing the FPTP system used for general elections remains the main goal of proponents of electoral reform. In 1997 the Blair government established an Independent Commission on the Voting System to examine the case for moving away from FPTP for general elections. It was chaired by Lord (Roy) Jenkins, a Liberal Democrat peer and former Labour cabinet minister. In reaching its recommendations, the commission was instructed by the home secretary to find a system that observed four requirements:

> broad proportionality
> the need for stable government
> an extension of voter choice
> the maintenance of a link between MPs and geographical constituencies

Jenkins was also concerned about the regional divisions produced by FPTP, under which Labour and the Conservatives did not have parliamentary representation in some parts of Great Britain.

The commission considered the merits of a number of electoral systems (see Table 3.8). The Jenkins Report of 1998 then recommended a unique system called *AV plus* (AV+). Under this system, electors would cast two votes: one vote for a constituency MP and one for a top-up MP chosen from an open list of candidates. A clear majority of MPs (80–85%) would be elected in single-member constituencies (numbering between 530 and 560) under the alternative vote system. To win, a candidate would have to get an overall majority of the votes cast. The second preferences of the lowest-placed candidates would be transferred until one candidate achieved over 50%.

Table 3.8 How electoral systems score: the Jenkins Report verdict

	FPTP	AV	AMS	STV
Proportionality	1	2	5	4
Stable government	4	3	2	2
Voter choice	1	3	3	5
Constituency link	5	5	3	3

Note: Electoral systems were awarded a score between 1 (lowest) and 5 (highest) on the four criteria.
Source: D. Agnew, 'Electoral reform in the United Kingdom', *Politics Review*, vol. 8, no.1, 1999, p. 15.

The remaining 15–20% of MPs would be additional members drawn from 80 top-up areas of the UK. The boundaries of these areas would largely follow existing county and metropolitan council boundaries. Each area would have at least one top-up MP; the most populous areas would have two. Electors would cast one vote for either a party or an individual candidate. The additional members would then be allocated to parties on a correctional basis to produce a more proportional outcome. Under AV+, the 1997 election would have given Labour a majority of 77 (instead of 179), while the 1992 election would have produced a hung parliament. If the AV or SV systems had been used in 1997, the result would have been even more disproportional than that which occurred under FPTP (see Table 3.9). Labour would have increased its parliamentary majority still further, at the expense of the Conservatives. The Liberal Democrats would have performed best under STV.

Lord Jenkins

Table 3.9 Seats won in Great Britain using different electoral systems, 1997

	FPTP	AV and SV	List	STV	AMS (50:50 version)	AV+
Con	165	110	202	144	203	175
Lab	419	436	285	342	303	359
Lib Dem	46	84	110	131	115	91
Others	11	11	34	24	20	16

Adapted from: Source D, *Politics Review*, April 2002, p.21; Report of the Independent Commission on Electoral Reform 1998.

Impetus lost

The Liberal Democrats supported the Jenkins Report even though it rejected their favoured system, STV. But Labour's failure to hold a referendum on electoral reform strained Labour/Liberal Democrat cooperation on constitutional issues. The Conservatives remained implacably opposed to electoral reform. Proportional representation would have brought them greater rewards in 1997, 2001 and 2005. But Tory strategists recognised that the most likely outcome of elections conducted under PR or AMS would be a Labour/Liberal Democrat coalition.

Though he welcomed the Jenkins Report, Blair's doubts about PR appear to have hardened. In June 2001 he said that PR was unfair, as it delivered undue influence to small parties that held the balance of power. His concern had been reinforced by Labour's unhappy experiences with AMS in Scotland and Wales. Labour won a majority of seats in both Scotland and Wales in Westminster elections. But the decision to use AMS in elections to the Scottish Parliament and the Welsh Assembly denied Labour the chance of governing in its own right. In coalition with the Liberal Democrats, the Scottish Labour Party was forced to make unwelcome policy concessions (e.g. on STV for local elections).

Many Labour MPs at Westminster are unwilling to get rid of an FPTP system that has handed them parliamentary majorities on a minority of the popular vote. Calculations of political self-interest had prompted greater support for electoral reform in the Labour Party when it was in the political wilderness in the early 1990s. Similar calculations made it less appealing when Labour enjoyed political dominance, although some Labour MPs expressed support for reform after the 2005 election. The alternative vote, an element of the AV+ system suggested by Jenkins, has attracted some support. But it is less proportional than FPTP and would have delivered even bigger majorities for Labour.

The impetus for further electoral reform has been lost. Labour's pledge to hold a referendum on Lord Jenkins's recommendations was effectively dropped. In its 2001 and 2005 election manifestos, the party promised only a review of the experience of the new electoral systems. Two potential key players in this review — the secretary of state for constitutional affairs, Lord Falconer, and John Prescott, chair of a cabinet subcommittee on electoral issues — oppose PR. The odds appear stacked against a change to the FPTP electoral system.

Changes to the electoral systems used in Scotland and Wales are more likely. STV will be used in Scottish local elections from 2007. Four different systems will then be in use in Scotland: FPTP for Westminster, AMS for the Scottish Parliament, STV for local authorities and the closed-list PR system for the European Parliament. The UK government set up the independent Arbuthnott Commission to examine this, as well as the use of different constituency boundaries for elections to Westminster and the Scottish Parliament. Labour proposes changes to AMS, citing tensions between constituency and list MSPs. It also wants candidates defeated in constituency contests to be prevented from being elected via the list system.

In Wales, the Richard Commission (2004) also recorded scepticism about the constituency functions of list members. It proposed that STV be used for elections to an enlarged assembly. This has been rejected by the UK government, but reform of AMS is expected.

Suggested reading

Baimbridge, M. and Darcy, D., 'Putting the "proportional" into PR?', *Politics Review*, vol. 9, no. 4, April 2000.

Curtice, J., 'The electoral system: biased to Blair?', in P. Norris (ed.), *Britain Votes 2001* (Oxford University Press, 2001), pp. 239–50.

Denver, D., 'Whatever happened to electoral reform?', *Politics Review*, vol. 13, no. 1, 2003.

Independent Commission on PR, *Changed Voting, Changed Politics. Lessons of Britain's Experience of PR since 1997* (Constitution Unit, 2004).

Johnston, R., Pattie, C. and Rossiter, D., 'Equalising voter power', *Politics Review*, vol. 10, no. 3, February 2001.

McNaughton, N., 'Evaluating electoral systems', *Politics Review*, vol. 10, no. 1, September 2000.

Margetts, H., 'Electoral reform', in J. Fisher, D. Denver and J. Benyon (eds), *Central Debates in British Politics* (Longman, 2002), pp. 64–82.

Websites

Elections and electoral systems (gateway to UK and international sites):

www.psr.keele.ac.uk/election.htm

Electoral Reform Society (pro-reform pressure group): www.electoral-reform.org.uk

Independent Commission on PR (Report by the Constitution Unit):

www.ucl.ac.uk/constitution-unit/icpr

The Jenkins Report (full text): www.archive.official-documents.co.uk/document/cm40/4090/4090.htm

Labour Campaign for Electoral Reform (includes list of pro-PR Labour MPs):

www.electoralreform.connectfree.co.uk

Make My Vote Count (pro-reform campaign): www.makemyvotecount.org.uk

Exam focus

Using this chapter and other resources available to you, answer the following source-based questions.

From Table 3.1 and your own knowledge:

1 Present the main arguments in favour of reforming the Westminster electoral system.

2 Advance a case for keeping the present Westminster electoral system.

3 Why might some political parties be opposed to reforming the electoral system for the Westminster Parliament?

4 Why is it difficult for some smaller parties, such as the Liberal Democrats, to make an electoral impact in elections to the Westminster Parliament?

From Tables 3.1–3.6 and your own knowledge:

5 How far do you agree with the view that electoral systems based on proportional representation inevitably produce weak governments?

6 To what extent do you agree with the view that proportional representation systems produce results that reflect patterns of voting more accurately than does the FPTP system?

7 Explain why the electoral system used for the Scottish Parliament produces different outcomes from the system used in general elections for the Westminster Parliament.

Chapter 4

The UK party system

Anyone who wants to understand the political process in any country or region must pay close attention to the prevailing party system. Different party systems shape and reflect political institutions, and they offer valuable insights into different *political cultures*. This chapter concentrates on the party systems in the UK, exploring the various ways in which they can be interpreted. It also compares the Westminster party system with those at other levels of government.

Key questions answered in this chapter
➤ Does the UK have a two-party system?
➤ What are the alternative analyses of the UK party system?
➤ What party systems are there in Scotland, Wales and Northern Ireland?
➤ What are the implications of these systems for the types of government formed?

The UK as a two-party system

Classifying party systems is not just a matter of counting the number of parties that compete for office through elections. The decisive factor is the number of parties that compete with *a realistic chance of forming part of a government*. So a reliable definition of a two-party system is one in which *only two parties compete for office with a realistic chance of forming part of a government*.

The UK is usually identified as having a two-party system. The assumption that this is the case is built into many of its political institutions. The idea of an 'official opposition', with a leader who is paid a special salary, implies a system of *adversarial politics*.

Even the seating arrangements in the House of Commons, with government ministers facing their opposition 'shadows', reinforces this impression.

A brief historical survey points to the same conclusion. For almost all of modern British political history only two parties have had a chance of holding office at any one time, starting with the Whigs and the Tories from the seventeenth to the nineteenth centuries. The extension of the right to vote to the working class and women, between 1867 and 1928, made very little difference to the system as such, although there was a brief period of adjustment during the 1920s when the Liberals, Labour and the Conservatives all had a chance of winning. The Liberals (now the Liberal Democrats) have not been elected to form a government on their own since before the First World War. No third party has had any share of power since 1945. The dominance of the Conservatives and Labour became so marked after the Second World War that the political scientist and television pundit Robert McKenzie devoted only three pages out of nearly 700 to the poor Liberals in his classic study of *British Political Parties* (1955). At the time, the combined vote of the two electoral Goliaths accounted for more than 95% of the total, and there were only six Liberal MPs (see Tables 4.1 and 4.2).

Table 4.1 Combined share of the UK popular vote for Labour and the Conservatives, 1945–70

1945	1950	1951	1955	1959	1964	1966	1970
88%	90%	97%	96%	93%	87.5%	89%	89.5%

Table 4.2 The plight of the Liberals in UK general elections, 1945–70

	Liberals		Conservatives	Labour
	Share of the vote (%)	Seats	Seats	Seats
1945	9.0	12	213	393
1950	9.1	9	298	315
1951	2.5	6	321	295
1955	2.7	6	344	277
1959	5.9	6	365	258
1964	11.2	9	304	317
1966	8.5	12	253	363
1970	7.5	6	330	287

Advantages of a two-party system

Many commentators who think that the UK has a two-party system go on to claim that the country is much the better for it. They argue the same for the USA, where in normal circumstances only membership of either the Republican or Democratic Party offers a realistic chance of winning high office. The main advantages of a two-party system are as follows:

> The elections tend to result in a clear majority for one of the parties, leading to strong government.
> Even so, the government will be *accountable* because there should be a strong alternative government trying to take advantage of its mistakes.
> It is reasonable to expect that the parties will take regular turns in office, so that no single party begins to feel that it has a monopoly of power.
> The parties tend to be moderate because of the need to attract maximum support from different social groups in different areas of the country.
> If minor parties come up with popular ideas, one or the other of the main parties will usually adopt them. Thus there is still a good chance that 'minority' views will be reflected in government policy at some stage, and most voters should feel that they have an adequate choice at election time.

Disadvantages of a two-party system

All this sounds very reasonable. The important thing to note, however, is that all of the advantages have to be qualified. So in a two-party system voters *ought* to have a clear choice between opposing party programmes, the parties *tend* to be moderate, etc. But this tendency does not amount to an invariable law of politics. In other words, the advantages of the two-party system depend on *circumstances*.

When Robert McKenzie wrote *British Political Parties*, the advantages of a two-party system seemed obvious. Labour and the Conservatives agreed broadly on the best policies for the country, and the UK economy had recovered reasonably well from the Second World War. At the same time, though, there were differences of emphasis in the parties' respective positions, and at any time the official opposition was regarded as a viable alternative 'government in waiting'. So it could be argued at that time that the UK electorate had all the choice that it needed, and governments were held to account for their decisions.

The breakdown of 'consensus'

In the 1970s, however, the two-party model came under greater scrutiny, for two different reasons. First, society was changing rapidly. In the 1950s, most members of the working class voted Labour, while the Conservatives were the 'natural' party of the middle and upper classes. Twenty years later these categories were blurring, so that instead of being a reflection of social reality the two-party division looked like a relic from the past.

Second, the UK economy was struggling again. Even so, critics noted that at election time Labour and the Conservatives continued to bid against each other for public support, as if they were taking part in an auction. When they had to go back on their promises, people found it increasingly difficult to trust politicians in general.

The circumstances of the 1980s added new complaints to the list. The experience of 'Thatcherism', and the growing influence of Labour's socialists (see Chapter 7), suggested the following:

> When two parties are dominant, they can move to opposite extremes of the political spectrum.
> Elections held under the first-past-the-post system can produce inflexible, dogmatic governments even on a minority of the vote.
> Accountability can become meaningless because the debate between the two main parties is conducted on grounds of ideology, rather than in the interests of the country as a whole.

The Liberals and the 'middle ground'

In the 1980s the criticisms of the UK's two-party system came most frequently from the Liberal Party and its allies. With the two main parties polarised, there should have been room for a moderate alternative party to 'come through the middle' and win a majority of the votes. For a time in the early 1980s it looked as if this might happen. After the formation of an alliance between his party and the newly formed Social Democratic Party (SDP), in September 1981 the Liberal leader David Steel told his supporters to 'go back to your constituencies and prepare for government'. At one time, opinion polls suggested that over half of the electorate supported the Alliance.

Yet at the 1983 general election these hopes were dashed. The SDP/Liberal Alliance won more than a quarter of the popular vote, but the Conservatives won the election comfortably and the Alliance was left in third place, more than 2% behind Labour in the popular vote (see Table 4.3). The Alliance leaders had spoken confidently of 'breaking the mould' of the two-party system. Their despair after coming third rather suggests that instead of wanting to change the system, they had really wanted to take Labour's place within it.

The pain of coming third in the vote was made far worse by the outcome in terms of seats. Although the result was one of the worst in Labour Party history, it still had 209 MPs. The SDP/Liberal Alliance only had 23! Alliance supporters who advocated electoral reform could claim that under the present system the votes of their supporters

Table 4.3 The rise of the Liberals and their allies, 1974–2005

	Share of the vote (%)	Seats
Feb 1974	19.3	14
Oct 1974	18.3	13
1979	13.8	11
1983 (SDP/Liberal Alliance)	25.4	23
1987 (SDP/Liberal Alliance)	22.5	22
1992 (Lib Dem)	17.8	20
1997 (Lib Dem)	16.8	46
2001 (Lib Dem)	18.8	52
2005 (Lib Dem)	22.0	62

A confident David Steel, 1981

were worth little more than a tenth of a Labour vote. The two-party 'mould' had apparently triumphed after all.

Key terms

> **Adversarial politics.** A situation typical of two-party systems, where the governing party is faced by an opposition that provides a contrasting policy programme and tries to gain political advantage from government difficulties.

> **Consensus politics.** A situation in which the main parties are in broad agreement on principles and, instead of offering sharply contrasting programmes, seek support by claiming greater competence than their rivals. This also seems to be linked with a two-party system, leading to a fight between the 'ins' and the 'outs'. There is scarcely room for other parties, which will be forced to offer highly distinctive programmes that run the risk of alienating moderate voters.

Impact of the voting system

For Alliance supporters, the result in 1983 produced yet more evidence that the two-party system was failing the country. Their experience showed that the 'winner-takes-all' electoral process tended to reinforce the dominance of the two main parties, even if they were no longer an accurate reflection of social realities or public opinion. The voting system meant that:

> Voters do not take third parties seriously as potential governments.
> Since voters tend to choose the party that they would prefer as the next government, they have little reason to vote for minor parties even if they agree with their views.
> A party that enjoys a reasonable level of support across the whole country can end up with no seats at all, whereas a party with strong appeal in one constituency, but lacking any relevance to the problems of the country as a whole, can win representation in parliament.
> The 'first-past-the-post' system can hand a clear majority to a party that is the first preference of a very small minority of voters. Indeed, a party can end up governing the country even when a clear majority of voters dislike it intensely.

Alliance supporters thought that the disadvantages of the two-party system now clearly outweighed its benefits. The answer, they argued, was to introduce a system of proportional representation (see Chapter 3).

Summary

The UK as a two-party system

> Party systems are classified according to the number of parties that have a realistic chance of forming part of a government.
> In two-party systems, two parties have a realistic chance and they regularly alternate in power.

> It is commonly argued that the UK has been a two-party system since the Second World War (if not earlier). There is plenty of evidence to support this view, but we need to examine alternative explanations before reaching a verdict.

Multiparty systems

The Alliance was certainly justified in thinking that a change in the voting system was the most promising way of breaking the two-party mould. According to our definition of a party system, the key factor is the number of parties that can hope to participate in government. Countries that have adopted proportional representation are almost always multiparty systems with *coalition governments* because even parties with relatively low levels of support will win some seats, and their support might become necessary to a party trying to construct a government.

Advantages of multiparty systems

Supporters of multiparty systems point to several advantages:
> Voters have a wide choice, and are more likely to vote for a party that reflects their views closely.
> Under PR, the election outcome will be a closer reflection of the true preferences of the voters.
> If one party really enjoys overwhelming support, it can still form a strong government.
> If a coalition is necessary, the ruling parties will compromise with each other. Even if the outcome is a policy programme that few individuals would have chosen as their first preference, most people will find something to agree with.

Disadvantages of multiparty systems

Supporters of multiparty systems, and of PR electoral systems, tend to be moderates who believe that compromise is a good thing. Unsurprisingly, opponents tend to be people with very fixed views, or with intense party loyalties. They are quite prepared to take their chances under first-past-the-post because they would rather be in opposition than make deals with their opponents. However, they can criticise multiparty systems from a more objective viewpoint too:
> Sometimes tiny parties that hold extreme views can join a coalition and influence policies, even though hardly anyone has voted for them.
> The negotiations often take a long time, leaving the country without an effective government and giving extreme parties the opportunity of looking more dynamic.
> The withdrawal of small parties from a coalition can cause it to collapse, thus creating almost endless instability.
> Alternatively, a party that does not enjoy majority support can govern almost indefinitely, if it can make up the required numbers by forming a coalition with a few small groups.

➤ A small, moderate party can form part of coalition governments almost indefinitely because it will tend to be courted by parties of both left and right, which cannot form a majority government on their own.

The opponents of multiparty systems can illustrate their arguments with numerous European examples. In the old Federal Republic of West Germany, for example, the moderate Free Democrat Party was almost always included in coalitions, despite its low level of support. In Italy the Christian Democrats (CD) were almost constantly in office between 1945 and 1990, although they rarely received more than a third of the popular vote. Confident of retaining power whatever their performance, some politicians in the CD were always likely to become corrupted over time. Since 1990 some have received gaol sentences. During the period of CD rule, Italy did not even have the advantage of political stability: the coalition governments lasted only 10 months on average.

Multiparty UK?

Against the experience of some European states, advocates of multiparty systems can point to other examples where stable and popular governments have existed, while voters feel that they have a wide range of choices. The deciding factor, they argue, is the political culture of the country in question. In response, opponents of electoral reform in the UK argue that a switch from first-past-the-post would in itself change the political culture, increasing the opportunities for corruption.

Blair and Ashdown agree on constitutional reforms, 1998

The debate is set to continue, but in the meantime it could be argued that the British situation has been changing without any reform of the voting system, or even formal electoral pacts. The Liberal Democrats have still to take a share in government offices, but before the 1997 general election they looked likely to do so. The party won 46 seats in that contest — a result that could have made it a coalition partner after each of the 1974 general elections, which instead produced weak Labour governments. In the expectation of a close result in the 1997 election, the Liberal Democrat leader, Paddy Ashdown, held talks about some kind of governing pact with Labour. In the end, Labour's landslide victory meant that significant cooperation was unnecessary. But in 2001 the Liberal Democrats performed even better, climbing to 52 seats with just over 18% of the vote, and in 2005 it won 62 seats with 22% support.

It seemed as if the first-past-the-post system was becoming kinder to the Liberal Democrats, mainly due to the growth of *tactical voting*. This involved supporters of one of the other two parties switching to the Liberal Democrats in order to defeat a candidate representing their main rival. Even if a large slice of its support came from people who still refused to see it as a potential government, the growing strength of the party at Westminster was likely to change that perception.

Between them, the two major parties won less than 74% of the total UK vote in 1997. Four years later, the tally dipped to 72.4%, and in 2005 it plummeted to 67.5% (see Table 4.4). But it is too early to start describing the UK as a multiparty system. Significantly, the Liberal Democrats still seem intent on overtaking the second-placed party (at present the Conservatives), as if they regard the old 'mould' as a natural state of affairs. Only if the party continues its present rate of progress at the expense of both Labour and the Conservatives could one begin to say that three parties had realistic chances of forming part of a government. Almost certainly the UK would then have entered an age of coalitions. The price of Liberal Democratic entry into a coalition would be the introduction of a PR system that would probably make multiparty coalitions the rule rather than the exception in future.

Table 4.4 Combined share of the UK popular vote for Labour and the Conservatives, 1974–2005

Feb 1974	Oct 1974	1979	1983	1987	1992	1997	2001	2005
75.0%	75.0%	80.8%	70.0%	73.1%	76.3%	73.9%	72.4%	67.5%

Key terms

➤ **Coalition government.** A formal agreement between two or more parties to hold power together. Coalitions usually arise when no single party can form a majority government, which is frequently the case in countries with a PR system. But sometimes, during a national emergency, a majority party will invite others to join it in order to create a feeling of national unity. Thus from 1940 to 1945 Winston Churchill led a coalition that also included members of the Labour and Liberal parties, even though when he became leader of the Conservatives he could have governed without any allies. Coalitions normally involve policy compromises between the various members, and a division of ministerial jobs to reflect the electoral support for each party.

➤ **Electoral pact.** A formal agreement between rival parties not to compete against each other in particular seats. Electoral pacts tend to arise in countries with a first-past-the-post electoral system. Thus between 1981 and 1988 the SDP/Liberal Alliance was an electoral pact, under which representatives of each party decided who would stand in each seat. In 1988 the two parties decided to *merge*, resulting in the formation of what is now the Liberal Democratic Party.

➤ **Majority government.** A majority government can be formed under any electoral system, but is most common under first-past-the-post. It arises when a single party has more seats than all the other parties combined, and can thus form a government on its own.

➤ **Minority government.** A minority government may arise when no single party wins more seats than the combined total won by its opponents. In the UK, where peacetime coalitions are rare, the party with the most seats can try to form a government, in the hope that the other parties will not unite to vote against it on key issues. Such

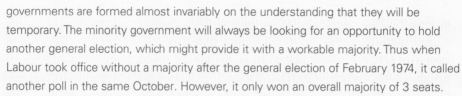

governments are formed almost invariably on the understanding that they will be temporary. The minority government will always be looking for an opportunity to hold another general election, which might provide it with a workable majority. Thus when Labour took office without a majority after the general election of February 1974, it called another poll in the same October. However, it only won an overall majority of 3 seats.

➤ **Pact.** A formal agreement between two or more parties to cooperate on specific policies, but where the 'junior' parties do not join the government. Thus between 1977 and 1978 the Liberal Party formally agreed to vote with the minority Labour government on key issues. Although Labour made some policy compromises, no Liberals joined the cabinet.

Summary

Multiparty systems

➤ In multiparty systems, more than two parties have a chance of forming part of a government, and coalitions are the rule rather than the exception.

➤ Proportional representation is associated with multiparty systems, while two-party and dominant-party systems flourish best under first-past-the-post.

➤ Alternatively, the rise of the Liberal Democrats in recent years suggests that the UK is becoming a multiparty system even without electoral reform.

Dominant-party systems

Thus, as we have seen, the UK cannot be described as a multiparty system. However, before agreeing with the majority of commentators who place it among two-party states, we need to look at other possible interpretations. Some analysts also speak of *dominant-party systems*. These must be distinguished carefully from *single-party* states, where no organised opposition is allowed (see Box 4.1). In contrast, in a state where one party is dominant, a number of parties may be in competition for power, but one of them consistently overshadows the rest, to the extent that opposition groups are seen as virtually irrelevant. So, for example, between the Second World War and 1993 Japan was clearly a dominant-party system. Although it was not without challengers, the Japanese Liberal Democratic Party held power continuously.

Is the UK a dominant-party system?

During the period of Conservative Party rule between 1979 and 1997, the UK showed some of the characteristics of a dominant-party system. One of the main features of this type of system is that the governing party begins to assume that it will be in office indefinitely. With no powerful enemies to keep it united, it begins to split into factions. Sometimes these are based on ideological differences, but there is also a tendency for people to divide over personalities. This is because the future leadership of the party

Box 4.1 | Single-party systems

During the Cold War (between the late 1940s and the end of the 1980s), it was usual for Western commentators to describe the Soviet Union and its satellites as 'one-party states'. In these countries, opposition parties were outlawed and dissidents even within the ruling Communist Party ran the risk of imprisonment or worse. The ruling parties tended to reinforce their dominance by taking over the whole machinery of the state and monopolising the key positions in social and economic institutions. Thus, for example, membership of the party might become as important to someone who wanted to run a factory as to a civil servant or the head of the secret police.

Single-party systems still exist, for example in the People's Republic of China, and in states where the ruling parties are vehicles for the ambitions of a charismatic leader. The latter variety seem particularly unstable, since one would expect the party to dissolve when the leader dies. But sometimes a nominated successor (often a favourite child) can hold on to power (a recent example is North Korea).

The very absence of choice tends to make people more likely to take to the streets at times of social or economic crisis. Moreover, the security forces cannot always be trusted to repress movements that they might secretly support. The most promising route for a monopolistic party is to relinquish its hold on society and allow the maximum possible freedom outside the political arena. If this makes the state more prosperous (as seems to be the case in China), so much the better. But it remains doubtful that people will be satisfied with economic and social freedom, while being denied the right to choose their leaders. The Soviet leader, Mikhail Gorbachev, attempted a similar experiment in the 1980s, leading to the break-up of the Soviet Union.

seems to carry with it the automatic succession to the highest political office. As a result, candidates start jostling each other long before the incumbent leader is ready to retire. Ironically, this kind of internal squabbling often helps to bring about the end of the period of dominance.

This seems to fit with the experience of the Conservatives, particularly after their third consecutive general election victory in 1987. Margaret Thatcher was replaced as prime minister in 1990 — just after the Conservative Party conference, where her admirers had chanted that she should stay in power for 10 more years! The leadership question continued to dominate discussion in the party up to its defeat in 1997, and beyond. The main policy issue which divided the party was the European Union (EU). Although feelings on this subject had always been strong, there is good reason to think that Conservatives would not have indulged in such bitter feuding if they had felt more respect for the Labour opposition. It can even be argued that the Conservative Party's failure to recover in the years after the 1997 defeat was due largely to the habit of mind it had adopted in office. Still thinking of themselves as the dominant party, Conservatives kept on arguing as if the New Labour victory had never really happened.

It might seem that any attempt to portray the UK as having a dominant-party system is mistaken, for the simple reason that since 1979 two different parties have held power.

In addition, the Major government was very weak between 1992 and 1997, and to the electorate the Conservatives hardly *looked* like a dominant party during those years. However, this evidence could actually be taken as supporting the idea that the UK has become a dominant-party system. This view sees the Thatcher years as teaching the electorate to expect very strong government. For a variety of reasons, the Conservatives could no longer provide this kind of rule after 1992. Internal party discipline collapsed, and they were turned out of office at the first opportunity.

In fact, the Conservative Party had only become dominant because its opponents were divided. A more typical dominant party sets out deliberately to win overwhelming support, by courting as many sections of the electorate as possible. This is far more characteristic of New Labour than it ever was of the Conservatives. The strategy clearly worked in 1997 and 2001, despite the significant fall in voter turnout. With huge overall majorities of 179 (in 1997) and 177 (in 2001), Labour had a parliamentary advantage that would provoke envy from many other 'dominant' parties across the globe. Even after the general election of 2005, when Labour's majority was reduced to 67, the party was well placed to implement its programme, provided that it avoided internal divisions.

Problems of a dominant-party system

Another reason to take seriously the idea that the UK has had a dominant-party system since 1979 is that the Conservative governments of 1979–97, and the Labour administrations since 1997, have been subjected to the kinds of criticism that are highly characteristic of these systems.

➤ **Politicisation and patronage.** In a dominant-party system, dominant parties begin to take over the bureaucracy, just as they do in single-party states. From early in Thatcher's period in office it was being claimed that the civil service had become 'politicised'. It was argued that certain officials were promoted because they seemed to share the thinking of one party, rather than being impartial as their traditional ethos demanded. Committed Conservative supporters were also appointed to semi-official bodies, known as *quangos*, which took over many areas of responsibility from the civil service. Similarly, New Labour was criticised because it brought in an army of 'special advisers', who took over certain civil service roles. Many of the civil service's information officers were replaced by spin doctors, who were more interested in showing Labour's record in a positive light than in providing the public with impartial facts concerning the government's activities.

➤ **Corruption.** Dominant-party systems are also associated with corruption. For example, this happened in Japan during the period of Liberal Democratic dominance in that country. The spate of scandals in the last few years of Conservative rule — 'sleaze', as it was popularly known — is significant in this context. New Labour was soon

Peter Mandelson facing mounting pressure over his financial affairs, 1998

damaged by stories about party funding, and in the case of Peter Mandelson, who accepted a loan of more than £300,000 from a fellow Labour MP, personal finances were involved too.

➤ **Faction fighting**. As has been noted above, when a governing party lacks a serious challenge from the official opposition it can become divided into factions pressing the claims of possible future leaders. This problem began to affect the Conservatives after Mrs Thatcher's third election victory in 1987. Many observers claim that New Labour suffered from faction fighting even before the party won power in 1997. Regular stories of tension between Tony Blair and his chancellor, Gordon Brown, illustrate the tendency of parties in a dominant position to divide over personalities rather than policy issues.

Summary

Dominant-party systems

➤ In one-party systems, opposition parties are banned outright.
➤ By contrast, in dominant-party systems, opposition parties are permitted. Even so, only one party stands a realistic chance of forming a government.
➤ In recent years, the UK has exhibited some of the most familiar features of a dominant-party system.

The UK: two-party, multiparty or dominant-party?

So we have to sort through some conflicting evidence before taking our own view on the nature of the UK party system. The rise of the Liberal Democrats, which continued at the 2005 general election, suggests that we might be entering a period of genuinely multiparty politics. At the same time, for most of the last quarter of a century governments have behaved as if they enjoyed 'dominant' status. Yet the idea that the UK is a two-party state is so familiar that most people continue to think that this is still the case.

In the 1950s it would have been quite safe to say that the UK had a two-party system. Now we need to be more cautious, and various answers to the question are possible. The important thing is to explain the reasons behind our conclusion, and to show that we are aware of the other points of view.

It is undeniable that UK governments since 1979 have usually behaved as if their parties were 'dominant' and the opposition irrelevant. We might be tempted to argue that this is just a temporary phenomenon, which has come about because parliamentary majorities have tended to be large. But something has certainly changed since 1959, when the Conservatives won a third consecutive election victory with a majority of exactly 100. Despite Labour's failure to launch a serious challenge at that election, the subsequent behaviour of the Conservative government did not give rise to the kind of criticisms that have become common since 1979. The opposition could not expect to win any parliamentary votes, but at least it was generally respected.

Reasons for the rise of a dominant-party system

A number of reasons have been given for the rise of a dominant-party system in recent decades:

- **The media.** One crucial development since 1959 is the far greater role of the media. Handled skilfully, this can make the prime minister seem a dominant figure — and emphasise the impotence of opposition leaders. At the same time, when a government hits trouble the media can exaggerate its weakness (as it did during the Major years). This makes it much more likely that, when power changes hands, the incoming government will be given a landslide majority and dominate the political scene.

- **Increasing professionalisation of UK politics.** In the past, the loss of office or even of a parliamentary seat might have been something of a relief for people who could return to their original professions. By contrast, today's politicians, many of whom have devoted most of their lives to the battle for power, have a vested interest in trying to carve out and maintain a dominant position. Senior ministers still have an excellent chance of well-paid employment after an election defeat. But even they will struggle to come to terms with a life outside politics. Ordinary backbenchers usually have even less to look forward to if the opposition takes over. Because of the *adversarial* nature of UK politics, the loss of power will disillusion party supporters in the constituencies even if the change of ruling party does not result in a radical change of policies. So at all levels, a defeated party will tend to be more demoralised than it would have been in the period of undoubted two-party dominance, from 1945 to 1970. This makes it more likely that the existing government will easily win the following election too, and begin to behave as if the opposition parties are irrelevant.

- **Changes under Thatcher.** While the above factors are largely outside political control, the deliberate changes of the Thatcher years must also be considered. After 1979, the Conservative governments fought against a succession of institutions — trade unions, local councils, the churches and even the Confederation of British Industry (CBI). These campaigns were largely successful, and bodies that at one time might have been important sources of resistance to any government are generally less 'party political' than they used to be. UK governments, in short, now dominate public life as they never have before, even if their power on the world stage has been eroded over the last century.

- **Patronage.** Finally, governments now have far more patronage than they had in 1959. Public bodies, especially quangos, are generally headed by strong government supporters, appointed by ministers. Rightly or wrongly, even lowly employees who disagree with government policy are often reluctant to voice their opinions. As we have seen, this is highly characteristic of states with a dominant-party system, and carries a clear threat of corruption.

Ironically, when they were in opposition Labour's leaders often alleged that the Conservatives were turning the UK into a 'one-party state'. Some of their policies may be different, but the style of government has barely changed since 1997. If we accept that their former complaints were sincere, this suggests strongly that experience in office has led ministers to accept a radical change in the system from the days of two-party politics.

The Westminster party system and the 2005 general election

Taken together, these factors strongly suggest that in 2005 the UK is best understood as a dominant party system. The fact that since 1979 there has been a change of dominant party does not matter in this context. The reduction of Labour's majority to 67 at the 2005 general election is not in itself a sign that the party's dominance is coming to an end. The gap between Labour and the Conservatives has narrowed, but the official opposition still does not look like a government-in-waiting. In short, there is little sign of a return to two-party politics.

However, there are good reasons for expecting some significant change in the near future. Labour's 67-seat majority was based on a lower level of public support than any other postwar government. Amazingly, its vote share was less than it had been in 1979, when it was decisively defeated by Thatcher's Conservatives. Only the quirks of the electoral system meant that in 2005 this smaller percentage gave it 86 more seats compared to 1979.

The relatively small vote share of the two main parties in 2005 greatly strengthens the argument for proportional representation. The Liberal Democrats still have little chance of winning an election, but in addition to their 62 seats they came second in more than 160 contests. In itself, the perceived unfairness of the present electoral system could easily affect the result next time, producing a parliament with no overall majority and leading to the subsequent introduction of PR. As we have seen, this system would almost certainly lead to genuine multiparty competition and coalition governments.

Other party systems in the UK

Local government

The situation in UK local government is affected strongly by the electoral timetable. Councillors serve 4-year terms, but elections in a proportion of seats are held every year, and there are frequent by-elections. This means that the results are affected by short-term changes in public opinion, and overall control of the closest-fought councils can change hands frequently. Furthermore, although local issues are very important, there is also a strong temptation for voters (particularly in England) to treat elections rather like opinion polls on the national record of the main parties. For example, the general election of 1997 was held on the same day as the local government elections of that year, 1 May. An important reason for Conservative disarray after those elections was that local councillors who lost their seats blamed the bad publicity attracted by their colleagues at Westminster for their own defeats.

Turnout for local government elections tends to be desperately low, especially in some inner-city areas. Thus in May 2002, a year after Labour was re-elected with a landslide majority, the turnout was only 32.8%. But at least this was an improvement on the 29% of the electorate who took the trouble to vote in 1998, the last occasion on which these particular seats were contested.

While councillors in England, Scotland and Wales are elected on the FPTP system, there is no reason to expect that the pattern of party conflict will be the same as at Westminster. Council constituencies are very much smaller than their Westminster counterparts, making it possible for parties to win seats with a tiny percentage of the overall national electorate. Popular local figures can win seats if they stand as 'Independents' or 'Local Residents', although in the past these labels have usually been a disguise for Conservative supporters.

On the face of it, the 2004 local election results make this level of UK politics look like a genuine multiparty system (see Table 4.5). Certainly Labour's dominant position in parliament was not reflected in the distribution of local council seats. After the 2004 local elections, the Conservatives were the largest party of local government in England and Wales, holding 7,912 seats compared to 6,155 for Labour, 4,550 for the Liberal Democrats and 2,150 for Independents and others.

However, these figures conceal wide variations in different parts of the country. Indeed, instead of one overall party system in local government, it would be more accurate to describe UK local government as having a number of different systems. In the metropolitan districts — the large cities outside London — Labour is sometimes so strong that its councils can act like rulers of a one-party state. But the Liberal Democrats have done well in recent years in places like Liverpool, Newcastle and Norwich. By contrast, while the Conservatives have been struggling for many years in the metropolitan areas, they are dominant in many of the more rural district councils. The 2005 local elections, held on the same day as the general election, mainly took place in counties which were already dominated by the Conservatives. They made further gains, as did the Liberal Democrats.

Outside England, the pattern is inevitably more complicated because of the presence of nationalist parties that do not contest English elections. Local elections in Northern Ireland are conducted under the STV system of proportional representation. The results in 2005 produced a multiparty system, with the four major parties strongly represented (see p103). In Scotland and Wales the local government party system is broadly similar to the

Table 4.5 Local government election results, 2004

	Approximate share of the vote (%)
Conservatives	29.6
Labour	38.1
Liberal Democrats	21.9
Independents/ others	10.4

contest for Westminster seats. Labour is the strongest party, but the Liberal Democrats and the nationalist parties (the SNP in Scotland and Plaid Cymru in Wales) enjoy a significant presence, while the Conservatives can still present a serious challenge in some areas.

Local elections often produce *hung councils*, where no single party is able to outvote the others. Decisions in hung councils are taken by coalitions that vary according to the relative local strengths of the parties, and (in some cases) the relationships between local councillors. But these are not very reliable 'trial runs' for coalition government at the national level. Local government reform since the 1980s has left councillors with far less opportunity to make distinctive policy decisions that reflect their ideological preferences. This makes cooperation much easier even between Labour and Conservative groups. In contrast, the adversarial tradition at Westminster makes such an alliance quite unthinkable.

Devolution in Scotland and Wales

In the years when the Conservative Party was dominant at Westminster, many people living outside England felt that they were being deprived of a voice. The Conservatives seemed mainly interested in England, and particularly after their fourth consecutive election victory in 1992 the only option for the Scots and Welsh people who consistently voted for other parties seemed to be some form of devolution, if not complete independence.

Ironically, of course, Westminster's control over subnational institutions meant that devolution had to wait until the national victory of a more sympathetic party. When the first elections were held to the assemblies of Wales and Scotland in May 1999, the additional member system (AMS) of proportional representation was used. As we have seen, PR is closely associated with multiparty systems, and in Wales and Scotland this was always the likely outcome, given that in addition to the main Westminster parties both countries have relatively strong nationalist bodies which do not contest elections in other parts of the UK.

The results, shown in Table 4.6, were a vivid demonstration of the effect of a voting system on the pattern of party representation. In the 1997 general election the Conservatives had failed to win a single seat in either Scotland or Wales, despite winning 17.5% of the vote in Scotland and 19.6% in Wales. Although the 1999 outcome under AMS was less than a resounding success for the party (which had opposed devolution), in certain circumstances it might have secured it a place in a coalition government in either country. Ironically, the result meant that after years of being dominant in both Scotland and Wales but impotent at Westminster, Labour now found itself having to share power in the devolved governments while the party enjoyed an overall majority of 179 in the UK parliament.

After the 1999 elections Labour established coalition governments with the Liberal Democrats in both Scotland and Wales. These arrangements proved reasonably stable,

Table 4.6 Results of elections to Welsh Assembly and Scottish Parliament, 2003 (1999 results in brackets)

Wales		Scotland	
Party	**Seats**	**Party**	**Seats**
Labour	30 (28)	Labour	50 (56)
Plaid Cymru	12 (17)	SNP	27 (35)
Conservative	11 (9)	Conservative	18 (18)
Liberal Democrat	6 (6)	Liberal Democrat	17 (17)
Other	1 (0)	Greens	7 (1)
		Scottish Socialists	6 (1)
		Independents	4 (1)

and the two parties agreed joint policy programmes. Although the Liberal Democrats came fourth in the elections in both countries, their combination with Labour provided a solid governing majority. This alliance was not a total surprise, since Labour and the Liberal Democrats had cooperated in pressing the case for devolution before 1997. But it was clearly premature to suggest that the Liberal Democrats, who are proud of their independent tradition, would join Labour permanently as a junior partner in either Scotland or Wales. This point was driven home when the Welsh Labour Party decided to form an administration on its own, rather than seek to form a coalition, after the elections of 2003. Although the results of that year were a serious setback to the nationalists in Scotland and Wales, they still have reason to hope that in future they might do well enough to force their way into a coalition of one kind or another. For their own part the Conservatives retain a strong presence in both countries. Thus Wales and Scotland should be regarded as multiparty systems at present.

Implications for Westminster

Some commentators believe that the experience of coalition governments in these countries will have a knock-on effect on Westminster, making cooperation between parties seem more natural at the UK level. In this respect, it is particularly interesting that coalitions have been formed between Labour and the Liberal Democrats. For many years some senior Liberals and their allies have lamented the split between themselves and Labour, regarding the members of each party as 'progressives' who should unite against the Conservatives. From this perspective, the 'Lab–Lib' coalitions in Scotland and Wales could be the first step towards unity, or at least regular cooperation, at general elections.

However, at Westminster there is little sign of peace breaking out between the parties. The devolved institutions still tend to be regarded as little more than glorified local councils. In addition, even if parties find themselves advocating very similar positions, ordinary members often have something like a tribal attachment to their own organisation, and regard those who endorse the principle of coalition government as traitors. The new evidence that PR systems almost invariably lead to coalitions might actually make a revision of the first-past-the-post system for Westminster *less* likely. Labour and the Conservatives would rather risk years of political impotence than accept the alternative of endless power sharing with another group in the most powerful elected institution of the UK. As long ago as 1852, the Conservative Party leader (and later prime minister) Benjamin Disraeli declared that 'England does not love coalitions'. It certainly remains true that most British politicians would prefer to avoid them if at all possible.

Northern Ireland

If the party contests in Scotland and Wales seem unlikely to have a significant impact on politics at Westminster, Northern Ireland has always been regarded as a case apart. It used to be thought of as an excellent example of a dominant-party state, with all the associated problems of corrupt government and faction fighting among the ruling Unionist Party.

Much has changed since the Westminster government took direct responsibility for governing Northern Ireland in 1972. In June 1998 elections were held to a new 108-seat devolved assembly, under the single transferable vote (STV) system. The results are given in Table 4.7. Elections were also held in 2003, though the devolved institutions were suspended at the time.

The choice of STV was particularly significant. This 'purer' form of proportional representation (see Chapter 3) was ideally suited to producing an outcome in which all the various viewpoints in Ulster could feel represented. The arrangement illustrates the extent to which Ulster is a genuinely multiparty system. Even under the first-past-the-post system still used for Westminster elections, the old Ulster Unionist Party (UUP) dominance among Protestant voters has crumbled since the 1980s. The party held 10 seats in 1997, but after the 2005 general election it was reduced to a single seat. Support has increased for the Democratic Unionist Party (DUP), whose supporters are less willing to make concessions over Ulster's position within the UK and are opposed to the Good Friday Agreement, which established the new devolved institutions. At the same time, the moderate Social Democratic and Labour Party (SDLP) has been overtaken in the battle for the nationalist (mainly Catholic) vote by Sinn Fein, the political wing of the Irish

Table 4.7 Results of elections to the Northern Ireland Assembly, 2003 (bracketed figures show 1998 results)

	Seats	Share of first preference votes (%)
Ulster Unionist Party	27 (28)	22.7 (21.3)
Social Democratic and Labour Party	18 (24)	17.6 (22.0)
Democratic Unionist Party	30 (20)	25.6 (18.1)
Sinn Fein	24 (18)	23.5 (17.6)
Others	3 (16)	14.5 (21.0)

Republican Army (IRA). Although levels of support for the four main parties has fluctuated, in the subsequent five Ulster-wide contests after the assembly elections (the 1999 European election, the general elections of 2001 and 2005, and the two council elections held in the same years) none of them received less than 15% of the vote, and none more than 30%. But the new political situation in Northern Ireland was reflected in the distribution of seats after the 2005 general election: DUP 9, Sinn Fein 5, SDLP 3, UUP 1. A coalition was formed after the first assembly elections, but it was rather an unusual one in which all the main parties were represented (four members from the UUP and from the SDLP, two each from Sinn Fein and the DUP). The intention was to overcome traditional enmities by making representatives of the various traditions work together, without the kind of initial negotiation and compromise that normally follow elections in multiparty states. So an election that produced a 'natural' reflection of public opinion in Ulster resulted in an 'unnatural' coalition. The internal tensions between the various parties led to the collapse of the assembly and the restoration of direct rule from Westminster in October 2002. If the institutions are restored, it remains to be seen whether the arrangement proves any more stable than the European coalitions that have given multiparty states a bad name.

European elections

Like local government elections, the battles in the UK to win representation in the European Parliament also create a picture of multiparty politics. However, the results of the last two elections, held in 1999 and 2004, have to be treated with some caution because Conservative voters were far more likely than their Labour counterparts to turn out, while the United Kingdom Independence Party (UKIP) polled strongly on what was its main campaigning issue. As with local government elections, the European contests always suffer from a lack of interest. In 1999 turnout plummeted to just 23%. In 2004 it climbed to 38.5%, assisted by all-postal voting in some regions. However, for a nationwide poll this was still a disappointing level of participation.

European issues certainly play a part in deciding the outcome; the performance of UKIP in 2004 underlined this point. Politics at the national level intrude on these contests at least as much as they do in local elections. So, for example, the Conservatives beat Labour by 60 to 17 seats in 1979, just after Mrs Thatcher's first general election victory. By contrast, in 1994, when John Major's government was deeply unpopular, Labour won by 62 to 18. That election, though, saw the first use of proportional representation, based on 11 separate regions.

The outcome of the 2004 election (see Table 4.8) makes the UK look like a multiparty

Table 4.8 Results of the European elections, 2004 (bracketed figures show 1999 results)

	Share of the vote (%)	Seats
Conservative	26.7 (34.8)	27 (36)
Labour	22.6 (27.0)	19 (29)
Liberal Democrat	14.9 (12.1)	12 (10)
UKIP	16.1 (7)	12 (3)
Green Party	6.3 (6.3)	2 (2)

Note: The number of UK seats was reduced from 84 in 1999 to 75 in 2004.

system. Although the relatively low turnout provides an inadequate basis for confident conclusions, this suggests that the likely effect of a PR system for Westminster elections would be similar. The very limited impact of the party system for European elections on the shape of party conflict at Westminster is well illustrated by the fate of the Green Party. It won nearly 15% of the vote in 1989, knocking the recently merged SDP/Liberal Alliance into fourth place. But the party never approached this level of performance in subsequent general elections, although under PR it did finally secure two Members of the European Parliament (MEPs) in 1999. It remains to be seen whether UKIP will ever make the kind of impact at Westminster that it had in the 2004 European elections (after which it lost its best-known member, Robert Kilroy-Silk).

Thus the European parliamentary elections reinforce the main conclusion of this chapter — namely that electoral systems are by far the most important factor affecting the nature of party competition.

Summary

Other party systems in the UK

➤ On the surface, the electoral battle for local government in the UK looks like a multiparty system. However, there are wide variations throughout the country.

➤ The new devolved institutions in Scotland, Wales and Northern Ireland have multiparty systems, based on different models of PR.

➤ If these institutions become more powerful, and the turnout rises, the party systems in each country might have a significant impact on the Westminster system. As yet there has been little sign of change.

➤ UK elections to the European Parliament are now conducted under PR and have produced a multiparty system.

Suggested reading

Bradbury, J., 'Labour power under pressure in Wales: UK general election', *Politics Review*, vol. 15, no. 2, November 2005.

Denver, D., 'Four-party competition in Scotland: UK general election', *Politics Review*, vol. 15, no. 2, November 2005.

Fisher, J., 'All change? Party systems in Britain', *Politics Review*, vol. 13, no. 1, September 2003.

Ingle, S., 'The Glorious Revolution and the party system', *Politics Review*, vol. 1, no. 3, February 1992.

Ingle, S., *The British Party System*, 3rd edn (Pinter, 2000).

Lynch, P., 'Scottish devolution and coalition government', *Politics Review*, vol. 11, no. 2, November 2001.

McKenzie, R., *British Political Parties* (Macmillan, 1955).

Robins, L., Blackmore, H. and Pyper, R., *Britain's Changing Party System* (Leicester University Press, 1994).

Sartori, G., *Parties and Party Systems: A Framework for Analysis* (Cambridge University Press, 1976).

Tonge, J., 'DUP and Sinn Fein truimph in Northern Ireland: UK general election' *Politics Review*, vol. 15, no. 2, November 2005.

Exam focus

Using this chapter and other resources available to you, answer the following questions.

1 Present the case for the UK having a two-party system.

2 What are the advantages and disadvantages of a two-party system?

3 How might the two-party mould be broken?

4 Outline the advantages and disadvantages of multiparty systems.

5 Is the UK a dominant-party system? Give reasons for your answer.

6 What is the nature of the party system in local government?

7 Outline the nature of the party system for European elections.

8 What impact has devolution had on the party systems in (a) Scotland; (b) Wales?

9 Explain the party system in the Northern Ireland Assembly.

10 'There are now party systems rather than a party system in the UK.' To what extent do you agree with this view?

Chapter 5

Voting behaviour

The outcomes of general elections in the UK are decided by a number of factors. Some voters know which party they are going to support well in advance of the election date. They may have a long-term attachment to the party that best represents the interests of their social class. Other voters may decide how to vote based on considerations of the performance of the government or the economy, or make judgements about party leaders and issues.

Key questions answered in this chapter
➤ How important is social class in determining voting behaviour?
➤ What role do factors such as gender, age, ethnicity and geography play?
➤ How important are issues, party leaders, personal economic prospects and the perceived competence of parties?
➤ Which theories of voting behaviour provide the most convincing accounts of the outcomes of recent general elections?

Class voting

Studies of voting behaviour in the period 1945–70 focused on the social characteristics of voters. They claimed to demonstrate a strong correlation between social class and voting. Social class was defined in terms of occupation and lifestyle. Manual workers made up the working class; non-manual workers the middle class. A majority of the working class voted for the Labour Party while most of the middle class backed the Conservatives. People voted for their 'natural' class party: that is, the party that best represented the interests of their social group.

Partisanship

Partisanship was also an important feature of UK politics. Most voters had stable, long-term feelings of positive attachment to one of the main parties. In other words, they identified themselves as a Labour supporter or a Conservative supporter. The two main parties had a large *core vote* of loyal supporters who voted for them habitually. This party identification developed through socialisation or social learning in the home (most people voted for the same party as their parents), school, workplace, neighbourhood and so on. These influences reinforced the individual's class identity and strengthened the link between class and voting.

Exceptions

Yet even in this period of class voting, there were important 'deviant' groups that did not vote according to their social class. 'Working-class Conservatives', who comprised some 25–30% of the working class, helped the Tories win three general elections in the 1950s at a time when the working class outnumbered the middle class (see Table 5.1). Various explanations were offered for this:

Table 5.1 UK general election results, 1945–2005

	Conservative		Labour		Liberal Democrat		Others		
	Vote (%)	Seats	Vote (%)	Seats	Vote (%)	Seats	Vote (%)	Seats	Turnout (%)
1945	39.6	210	48.0	393	9.0	12	3.4	25	72.8
1950	43.4	298	46.1	315	9.1	9	1.4	3	83.9
1951	48.0	321	48.8	295	2.6	6	0.6	3	82.6
1955	49.7	345	46.4	277	2.7	6	1.2	2	76.8
1959	49.4	365	43.8	258	5.9	6	0.9	1	78.7
1964	43.4	304	44.1	317	11.2	9	1.3	0	77.1
1966	41.9	253	48.0	364	8.6	12	1.5	1	75.8
1970	46.4	330	43.1	288	7.5	6	3.0	6	72.0
1974 (Feb)	37.9	297	37.2	301	19.3	14	5.6	23	78.8
1974 (Oct)	35.8	277	39.2	319	18.3	13	6.7	26	72.8
1979	43.9	339	36.9	269	13.8	11	5.4	16	76.0
1983	42.4	397	27.6	209	25.4	23	4.6	21	72.7
1987	42.3	376	30.8	229	22.5	22	4.4	23	75.3
1992	41.8	336	34.2	271	17.9	20	6.1	24	77.7
1997	30.7	165	43.4	419	16.8	46	9.3	29	71.5
2001	31.7	166	40.7	413	18.3	52	9.3	28	59.4
2005	32.3	197	35.2	355	22.1	62	10.4	31	61.3
Mean 1945–70	45.1		46.5		7.0		1.5		78.2
Mean 1974–2005	37.6		36.1		19.4		6.9		71.7

Note: Liberal Democrat includes Liberals (1945–79) and SDP/Liberal Alliance (1983–87). Northern Ireland MPs are included as 'Others' from 1974.

> deference (i.e. respect for the Conservative Party and its leaders)
> the authoritarian values of some working-class voters
> rising living standards
> working-class voters wrongly perceiving themselves as lower middle class

'Middle-class socialists', meanwhile, voted for Labour. They often worked in the public sector or had a liberal education.

Summary

Class voting

The success of the class voting model in explaining and predicting voting behaviour from 1945 to 1970 was a result of:

> British society having a relatively stable class structure
> class alignment — people saw politics in terms of class and voted for 'their' class party
> partisan alignment — most voters had a strong and enduring allegiance to their class party
> a stable two-party system — together the two main parties won 92% of the vote in this period

Class and partisan dealignment

Since 1970 both class voting and partisanship have declined. This has produced greater electoral volatility — more people switch their votes from one election to the next. Two linked trends have been apparent: class dealignment and partisan dealignment. *Partisan dealignment* refers to the decline in voter identification with Labour and the Conservatives. Fewer voters have a strong attachment to one of the two main parties. The parties' core vote has shrunk and party membership has declined. *Class dealignment* refers to claims that the relationship between social class and voting has weakened, with fewer people voting for their class party.

In addition, the party system was destabilised as the share of the vote won by the two main parties declined (to an average of about 70% since 1974). The nationalist parties in Scotland and Wales gained support and the fortunes of the Liberal Party and its successors revived.

Explaining class dealignment

There is no single accepted explanation for why (or indeed *if*) class voting has declined. A number of social changes have been suggested as contributory factors:

> The distinctions between social classes have been eroded. The spread of affluence, improved standards of living, greater social mobility and greater access to further and higher education have blurred the boundaries between the middle class and working class.
> Structural changes have altered the character of the working class. In the 1980s, Ivor Crewe argued that the 'old working class' had declined. This group consisted of

manual workers who belonged to trade unions, were employed in heavy industry (e.g. coal, steel and shipbuilding) and lived in Scotland, Wales and northern England. A 'new working class' had emerged, working in the private sector in southern England, having better qualifications and owning their own homes. Significant numbers of the new working class voted for Thatcher's Conservative Party in the 1980s.

➤ Sectoral cleavages emerged, first between people working in the public sector and those in the private sector, and second between those relying on public services (for housing and transport, etc.) and those using private provision.

➤ Finally, changes in the labour market, such as the increased number of women workers, part-time workers and the self-employed, raised questions about the usefulness of definitions of class that are based on occupation.

Explaining partisan dealignment

A number of explanations for partisan dealignment have been put forward too:

➤ Some academics claim that Labour and Conservative voters became disillusioned with the performance of their parties in government during the political and economic crises of the 1970s.

➤ The ideological links between party leaders and party members (particularly activists) were weakened. Left-wing Labour supporters were alienated by the policies pursued by the governments of Harold Wilson (1974–76) and James Callaghan (1976–79), while one-nation Tories were uneasy with the New Right policies adopted by Thatcher after she became Conservative leader in 1975.

➤ Other accounts emphasise social change, such as better education and the decline of class loyalties.

Defining social class

The perceived decline in class voting since the 1970s raised questions about how social class should be measured. The traditional method, used by the British Market Research Society, used the following categories:

➤ AB — professional and managerial
➤ C1 — white collar (non-manual)
➤ C2 — blue collar (skilled manual)
➤ DE — semi-skilled, unskilled and reliant on state benefits

However, the academics Anthony Heath, Roger Jowell and John Curtice argued that these categories failed to take account of the structural changes mentioned above. They devised their own categories:

I   Salariat — managers, administrators, professionals, semi-professionals.
II   Routine non-manual — clerks, secretaries, sales workers.
III Petty bourgeoisie — small proprietors, self-employed manual workers, farmers.
IV   Foremen and technicians — blue-collar workers with supervisory functions.
V   Working class — rank-and-file manual workers in industry and agriculture.

They also disputed claims that there had been a decline in *absolute* class voting, arguing instead that there had only been a fall in *relative* class voting. A decline in working-class support for Labour would produce a fall in the level of absolute class voting. But for there to be a fall in relative class voting, this would have to be accompanied by an increase in the number of working-class voters supporting parties other than Labour. Most electoral analysts believe that class voting has declined in both absolute and relative terms over the last 30 years.

Key terms

- ➤ **Class.** A social group defined by social and economic status, the key groups being the working class (manual workers) and middle class (non-manual).
- ➤ **Class dealignment.** A decline in the correlation between social class and voting behaviour.
- ➤ **Class voting.** A strong correlation between occupational social class and voting behaviour, with a majority of the middle class supporting the Conservatives and a majority of the working class voting Labour.
- ➤ **Electoral volatility.** Significant changes in voting patterns from one election to another.
- ➤ **Partisan dealignment.** A decline in the strong attachments felt by voters to the Conservative and Labour parties.
- ➤ **Partisanship.** The strong party identification of voters and their feelings of attachment to the Conservative and Labour parties.
- ➤ **Socialisation.** The process by which individuals learn and acquire their values and beliefs. Key agents include the family, school, work and neighbourhood.

Class and voting since 1970

Class and partisan dealignment raised important strategic questions for the main parties, but particularly for the Labour Party. In the period 1945–70, Labour relied heavily on the support of the 'old working class'. By the late 1970s, the working class had shrunk and the Conservatives were gaining support from the 'new working class' (sometimes dubbed 'Essex man'). Ivor Crewe warned that Labour faced long-term problems as social change was producing a 'glacial shift to the right'. Labour lost four successive general elections from 1979 to 1992, averaging just 32% of the vote.

The main parties both reacted to and contributed to class dealignment by consciously altering their appeal. The Conservatives in the 1980s, then Labour in the 1990s, targeted voters who fell outside their core support. Mrs Thatcher's popular capitalism promised the sale of council houses and nationalised industries. New Labour strategists recognised that to win power, the party had to regain votes from the skilled workers (the C2 group) and make gains in middle-class constituencies in the south (often referred to as 'middle England').

Recent general elections

The general elections of 1997, 2001 and 2005 provided further confirmation of class dealignment (see pp. 123 and 124). Class-based voting was less important in 1997 than in previous elections, then fell still further in 2001. Labour made gains among blue-collar (C2) and manual workers (DE), but made similar gains across all social groups, making significant inroads into the middle-class vote (AB and C1). New Labour had become a 'catch-all' party, occupying the electoral centre ground and achieving a cross-class appeal. Labour was no longer reliant on the working class; many middle-class former Conservative voters switched directly to Labour. In 2001, Labour made further gains among middle-class voters, though its working-class support fell slightly. Four years later, the Conservatives made gains in the C1, C2 and DE social groups, but again lost support from AB voters. The biggest falls in support for Labour were in the C2 and DE groups.

Social class is a less important predictor of voting behaviour than it was in the early postwar period. Nevertheless, Labour remains the most popular party among working-class voters and the Conservatives still perform best among middle-class voters. People with manual occupations are more likely to vote Labour than are non-manual workers or those with professional and managerial jobs. Today, however, the class voting model is less effective as an explanation of electoral outcomes and as a predictor of how people will vote.

Other structural factors

Before considering alternative theories of voting behaviour, it is worth mentioning other social or structural factors that might have an impact on voting. These include gender, age, ethnicity and region.

Gender

For much of the postwar period, women were more likely than men to vote Conservative. This *gender gap* perhaps reflected social attitudes of the time and the fact that relatively few women went out to work. This gender gap first disappeared in the 1990s and was then reversed. Labour made significant gains among women voters in 1997 and has enjoyed healthy leads in this social group in the last three general elections.

Age

The narrowing of the gender gap reflects changes in the voting behaviour of young female voters. Younger women are likely to be in work, are more left wing than older women and in many cases have embraced elements of feminist politics. Labour was the most popular party among voters aged under 35 in 1997, 2001 and 2005, even though it suffered a sizeable fall in support from those aged 25–34 in 2005. Conservative support is ageing: the party performs best among older voters. In 2001 and 2005, the Tories led Labour only among voters aged over 55. All parties courted those aged over 55 in 2005 because this group constituted 35% of the electorate and, as they are more likely to vote than young people, 42% of voters.

Ethnicity

Ethnic minorities in the UK make up 7.8% of the population. Operation Black Vote identified 70 constituencies in 2005 in which the size of the ethnic minority population exceeded that of the winning party's margin of victory. Turnout among black voters has, though, been consistently lower than among the white population. An overwhelming number of ethnic minority electors (over 80% in the 1980s and 1990s) have voted Labour. However, in 2005 support for Labour fell significantly in constituencies with large Muslim populations.

Political parties have stepped up their efforts to attract ethnic minority voters in recent years. A record number of ethnic minority candidates (113) stood for the three main parties at the 2005 election, but only 15 were elected. Shamit Saggar has cast doubts on the effectiveness of campaigns aimed at mobilising ethnic minorities. He argues that the UK's ethnic minority voters are not a homogeneous group. Asians are more likely, for example, to vote Conservative than are African-Caribbeans — though Labour enjoys comfortable leads in both groups. Nor do ethnic minority electors vote primarily on the basis of 'race' issues. Instead they tend to vote along class lines.

Regional voting patterns

There are important regional variations in voting behaviour in Great Britain (see Table 5.2). These were particularly pronounced in the 1980s, when a 'north–south divide' appeared. Conservative support became concentrated in the south of England,

Table 5.2 Regional variations in voting (% votes cast), 1997–2005

	2005			2001			1997		
	Con	Lab	Lib Dem	Con	Lab	Lib Dem	Con	Lab	Lib Dem
North East	20	53	23	21	60	17	22	61	13
Yorks and Humberside	29	44	21	30	49	17	28	52	16
North West	29	45	21	29	51	17	27	54	14
West Midlands	35	39	19	35	45	15	34	48	14
East Midlands	37	39	19	37	45	15	35	48	14
Eastern	43	30	22	42	37	17	39	38	18
London	32	39	22	31	47	18	31	50	15
South East	45	24	25	43	29	24	41	32	21
South West	39	23	33	39	26	31	37	26	31
Scotland	16	39	23	16	43	16	18	46	13
Wales	21	43	18	21	49	14	20	55	12

Source: MORI, www.mori.com

the suburbs and rural areas. Labour's electoral strongholds were found in the north of England, Scotland and Wales, in large urban areas and on council estates. At the 1997 general election, support for the Conservatives fell in all regions of Great Britain, but the greatest decline was in London (–14%) and the south east (–13%). Conservative support was concentrated in southern England; the party won no seats in Scotland or Wales in 1997. Labour gained ground in the south and the suburbs, but its strongest support was still found in northern Britain and cities. The Labour vote fell slightly in these strongholds in 2001, but its support held up in the south. Labour's share of the vote fell across Great Britain in 2005. Only in southern England did the Conservatives improve their position; they won just five seats in the six English metropolitan areas outside London. Despite winning more votes than Labour in England, the Conservatives had 93 fewer seats (see Chapter 3).

Regional patterns of support are explained partly by the distribution of social classes (with manual workers concentrated in urban areas, for example), but also by local political factors (e.g. effective Liberal Democrat campaigns in southwest England) and tactical voting. It is important to recognise that there are significant variations within regions as well as between them. In 2005, for example, the Conservatives overturned a 5,500 Labour majority in Enfield Southgate (where Michael Portillo was defeated in 1997), but not a 2,300 Labour majority in neighbouring Enfield North.

Summary

Structural factors

- social class
- age
- socialisation
- ethnicity
- gender
- region

Rational choice theories

The class voting model focuses on the social characteristics (notably social class) and partisan loyalties of voters. The importance of the individual voter is downplayed. Voters develop strong and stable loyalties to a party relatively early in their life and these are highly significant in determining how they vote. The model claims that short-term factors, such as election campaigns, are of limited importance as most voters already identify with a political party and will vote for it habitually.

Alternative explanations of voting behaviour focus on the choices made by individual voters. These put the individual at the centre of their analysis. The individual voter is a rational actor who decides how to vote by weighing up the relative merits and demerits of the main parties. There are four main variants of the 'rational choice' model:

- issue voting
- party leaders
- economic voting
- governing competence

Rational choice theory has been criticised for exaggerating the extent to which voters think rationally and make informed political choices. Levels of political knowledge and interest are not as high as these accounts might lead us to believe. Few voters will be aware of, or interested in, the detailed programmes put forward by parties in their election manifestos. Nonetheless, in an era of electoral volatility, voters are likely to choose between political parties on the basis of particular issues, their personal economic prospects or their perceptions of the main parties.

Issue voting

Proponents of the issue voting model claim that people decide how to vote by comparing the policies put forward by political parties on the major issues of the day. This assumes that voters perceive differences between the parties and vote for the one closest to their own position. To have a significant impact on the election result, issue voting must be *disproportional*. In other words, a majority of electors must feel an issue is important, must identify the same party as having the best policy and must then vote accordingly.

Doubts about issue voting

The importance of individual issues for election outcomes is, however, open to doubt. The Conservatives won the 1987 and 1992 general elections even though opinion polls revealed that most voters preferred Labour's policies on the key issues of the day (notably health, education and unemployment). Indeed, Thatcherite values were never widely accepted by the electorate even though the Conservatives won four successive general elections from 1979 to 1992. A majority of people preferred higher public spending to tax cuts, but this was not reflected at the ballot box.

Figure 5.1 Important political topics, 1988–2005

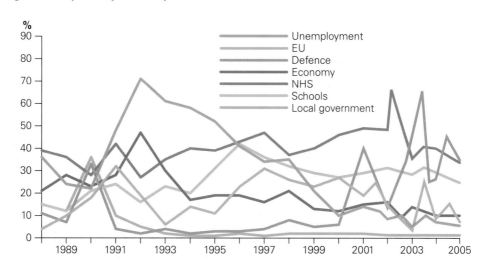

Source: MORI, www.mori.com

Note: The figure shows responses to MORI opinion poll questions on the 'most important issue' and 'other important issues' facing Britain.

Expectations of favourable personal economic prospects under the Conservatives trumped Labour's opinion poll leads on the public services.

Labour enjoyed healthy opinion poll leads over the Conservatives on most of the issues rated by voters as important in determining how they would vote in 1997, 2001 and 2005. Figure 5.1 shows the fluctuating importance of various issues between 1997 and 2005. As well as maintaining healthy leads on their traditional strengths (e.g. health, education and unemployment), Labour also established leads in areas such as law and order where the Conservatives had previously scored well. Significantly, Labour was the party considered best able to manage the economy at each of the 1997, 2001 and 2005 elections. Both main parties have put forward similar policies on health, education and the economy in recent elections. It was not, then, ideological differences that mattered to voters, but which party would deliver goals that were universally accepted.

Dramatic events can have a significant impact on party support. The 1982 Falklands War contributed to an upturn in the fortunes of the Conservative Party. Some commentators claimed that the 'Falklands Factor' was a key element in the Conservatives' 1983 general election victory, although others maintain that an upturn in the economy was more significant. Sterling's ejection from the Exchange Rate Mechanism (ERM) on 'Black Wednesday' in September 1992 brought about a sharp and lasting fall in the standing of the Conservative Party. It also shattered the Conservatives' claims to be the most effective managers of the economy.

New issue cleavages

As the socioeconomic policies of the two main parties moved closer together in the 1990s, new issues emerged to divide them. The politics of identity provides the two most prominent: Europe and race.

Europe was a potential vote winner for the Conservatives in 1997 and 2001, as the Tory position on membership of the European single currency was more popular than Labour's. But the Conservatives did not reap significant electoral rewards. In 1997, voters lost interest in the Tories because of their divisions over Europe. A 'Save the Pound' message featured prominently in the 2001 Tory election campaign but did not rank highly among voter concerns. It brought the Conservatives limited gains among elderly and working class voters, but for some young and middle class voters it reinforced the caricature of the Conservatives as extreme and 'out of touch'. Europe hardly featured in the 2005 campaign, in part because Labour had promised a referendum on the EU constitution.

Asylum is an increasingly important election issue

Table 5.3 Party strengths on key election issues, 2005

Issue	% saying issue was important in helping them decide which party to vote for	% Labour lead on issue
Health	67	+14
Education	61	+15
Law and order	56	−12
Pensions	49	+2
Taxation	42	−6
Asylum	37	−41
Economy	35	+30
Environment	28	−11
Housing	27	+20
Public Transport	26	+16
Unemployment	25	+31
Defence	19	−14
Europe	19	−11
Iraq	18	−29

Source: MORI, www.mori.com

Voters rated asylum and immigration as the ninth most important issue in 2001. It increased in saliency during Labour's second term to become the second most important issue facing the country in 2005. The Conservatives made immigration a central plank of their campaign because it was the issue on which they enjoyed their biggest lead over Labour.

Party leaders

The impact that party leaders have on the electoral performance of their parties is disputed. More electors vote for their favoured party or policies than for their favoured leader. A popular leader will not bring victory for their party if the message and policies that party espouses are unpopular. Public perceptions of party leaders may, however, be significant if a sizeable gap exists in popular views of the leaders of the two main parties. Voters in 1992 preferred John Major to Neil Kinnock and, in a close contest, this may have influenced the outcome.

Party leaders have become more important in shaping electoral outcomes in recent years because of two trends. First, perceptions of their relative strengths and weaknesses are more likely to sway voters who do not have strong partisan loyalties. Second, television and press coverage of politics is skewed heavily towards party leaders. Saturation coverage of the party leaders focuses more attention on their personalities. Leaders are the public face of their party and carry much of the responsibility for 'selling' party policy.

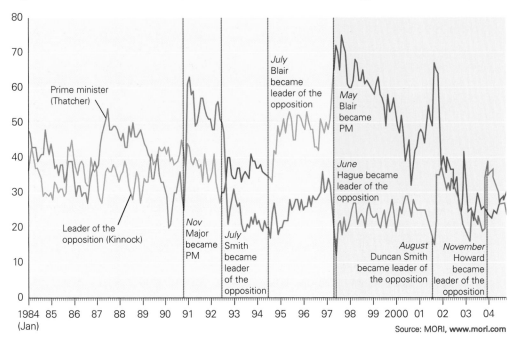

Figure 5.2 Public satisfaction with prime ministers and leaders of the opposition, 1984–2005 (%)

Source: MORI, www.mori.com

Blair's popularity

Tony Blair's approval ratings were higher than those for John Major in 1997, William Hague in 2001 and Michael Howard in 2005 (see Figure 5.2). In his first term as prime minister, an average of 56% of those surveyed by MORI said they were 'satisfied' with Blair's performance. Only 23% were satisfied with Hague. The Conservatives did not lose the 2001 election simply because Hague was unpopular, but he did become an obstacle to Tory recovery rather than a catalyst for it.

Blair's popularity declined during his second term, in part because the war in Iraq raised questions about trust. Dissatisfaction with Blair was a factor in the desertion or abstention of some former Labour voters in 2005. Although many voters were unhappy with Blair, they preferred him to the alternatives. Blair outperformed Michael Howard and Charles Kennedy in polls asking who would make the most capable prime minister.

Economic model

An alternative account, again drawing on rational choice theory, focuses on the perform-ance of the economy. The economic voting model posits a correlation between the economic performance of the government and voting behaviour. Voters are more likely to support the governing party if it has delivered a healthy economy. The *Essex model*, developed by David Sanders, used data on the economy (notably inflation and interest rates) and voters' personal economic expectations (i.e. whether they would be better or worse off) to predict voting patterns. It predicted accurately the outcome of the 1992 general election. Despite a recession, the Conservatives convinced enough people at the 1992 election that they were the party most likely to provide future economic prosperity.

In 1997 the economy was in better shape, but the Conservatives were defeated heavily. Crucially, economic recovery was not accompanied by a widespread 'feel good factor'. Though inflation and interest rates were low, voters remained worried about their personal economic prospects given job insecurity and problems in the housing market. The Conservatives thus did not gain credit for the economic upturn: for them, it was a 'voteless recovery'. Some voters felt that recovery had occurred despite the government rather than because of it. They associated the Major government with tax rises, high interest rates and sterling's exit from the ERM. The economic voting model correctly predicted both a Labour victory and a slight upturn in Conservative fortunes in the months leading up to the election. Labour benefited from its record of low inflation and low interest rates in the 2001 and 2005 elections. Many voters also recalled the economic problems under the Conservatives in the 1990s.

Governing competence

This perspective suggests that voters make a judgement about the overall performance of the government when deciding how to vote. David Denver refers to this as 'judge-mental voting'. If the governing party is widely perceived to have performed well in office, it will be rewarded at election time. Attributes of governing competence might include policy success (particularly a sound economy), strong leadership, developing a clear agenda and maintaining party unity. Conversely, governments that are judged to have failed to demonstrate a modicum of governing competence can expect to be punished at the polls. Policy failures (especially in economic policy), weak leadership, a lack of direction and obvious disunity will undermine a governing party's chances of securing another term in office.

But a general election is not just a verdict on the record of the government, although this is an important factor. At a general election, voters are presented with a choice between possible alternative governments. As well as judging the record of the govern-ment, electors will also reach a judgement on whether the main opposition party would be likely to perform better if it were in power. Voters thus make an overall judgement about the relative merits of the parties, including their ideology, policy programme, leaders and 'trustworthiness' to run the country. In short, politics matters!

The judgemental voting perspective offers a convincing account of the outcome of the 1997, 2001 and 2005 general elections. In 1997 voters reached a negative verdict on the Conservatives' performance in government and believed New Labour would prove more effective. Voter satisfaction with New Labour then declined by 2001 and, in partic-ular, 2005. Opinion polls revealed discontent with government policies (e.g. the war in Iraq), disappointment with its record on public service reform and a lack of trust in Blair.

However, public perceptions of the Conservatives were even more negative. They were still associated with the failings of their last spell in power, trailed Labour on many of the key issues and had an unpopular leader.

Summary

Rational choice model
- issue voting
- party leaders
- the economy
- governing competence

Key terms
- **Dealigned electorate.** An electorate in which class identities and party loyalties are weak.
- **Economic model.** Voters support the political party most likely to improve their personal economic situation.
- **Issue voting.** Electors vote for the party presenting the policy programme that best fits their own interests.
- **Judgemental voting.** Voters exercise judgements (about party image, issues, leaders, personal economic prospects, etc.) when deciding how to vote.
- **Rational choice model.** An approach to the study of politics that focuses on the actions of rational individuals pursuing their own interests.

The 1997 general election

Many studies of the 1997 general election focused on voters' perceptions of the two main parties. The old adage that 'opposition parties don't win elections, governments lose them' seemed to be confirmed. The Conservatives were in many respects the authors of their own downfall. They faced a number of (often self-inflicted) disadvantages:

- The ERM exit and tax rises undermined their reputation for sound economic management.
- The party was badly divided over Europe.
- The party was tainted by 'sleaze'.
- Major was perceived as a weak leader.
- Much of the 'Tory press' had deserted the Conservatives.

Neil Hamilton, centre of the 'cash for questions' scandal, which added to the Conservatives' reputation for 'sleaze'

Large numbers of voters felt it was time for a change of government. Crucially, they also felt that the Labour Party was now electable. New Labour entered the 1997 election campaign with more in its favour than 5 years previously:
- It was seen as a moderate party.

- ➤ It was seen as a united party.
- ➤ It was viewed as trustworthy, notably on economic management.
- ➤ Blair was a popular leader.

A record-breaking election

The 1997 general election set a number of records, including:

- ➤ Labour's largest ever number of seats (419) and parliamentary majority (179)
- ➤ a record postwar swing (10.5%) from the Conservatives to Labour
- ➤ the Conservatives' lowest share of the vote (30.7%) since 1832 and lowest number of seats (165) since 1906
- ➤ the then best postwar performance by a third party in terms of seats (46 Liberal Democrat MPs)
- ➤ the then lowest postwar turnout

The Blair family enters 10 Downing Street after Labour's landslide victory, 1997

Labour thus won a stunning landslide victory. It increased its support across all classes and all regions (see Table 5.4). Labour's strongest support came from working-class

Table 5.4 The 1997 general election (% votes cast)

	Con	Lab	Lib Dem
Share of vote (GB)	31.5 (−11.3)	44.4 (+9.2)	17.2 (−1.2)
Social class			
AB	42 (−11)	31 (+9)	21 (+0)
C1	26 (−22)	47 (+19)	19 (−1)
C2	25 (−15)	54 (+15)	14 (−4)
DE	21 (−8)	61 (+9)	13 (0)
Home ownership			
Home owners	35 (−12)	41 (+11)	17 (−3)
Council tenants	13 (−6)	65 (+1)	15 (+5)
Union membership			
Union members	18 (−9)	57 (+7)	20 (+2)
Gender			
Men	31 (−8)	44 (+6)	17 (−1)
Women	32 (−11)	44 (+10)	17 (−1)
Age			
18–29	22 (−18)	57 (+19)	18 (−3)
30–44	26 (−11)	49 (+12)	17 (−3)
45–64	33 (−9)	43 (+9)	18 (−2)
65+	44 (−3)	34 (−2)	16 (+2)

Note: figures in brackets show change since 1992.

Sources: BBC/NOP exit poll; J.Curtice, 'Anatomy of a non-landslide,' *Politics Review*, vol.7, no.1, September 1997.

and blue-collar workers, with the party gaining a majority of votes from the crucial C2 category of electors. The party's most notable gains were made in middle-class areas, it becoming the most popular party with white-collar workers. This was reflected in the regional voting pattern: Labour strengthened its grip in its geographical heartlands and made spectacular gains in supposedly solid Conservative suburban areas.

The Conservative Party was pushed back into its heartlands in rural and southern England. No Conservative MPs were elected in Scotland, Wales or most large cities. The total Conservative vote fell from a record 14 million in 1992 to 9.6 million in 1997 as former voters switched to Labour, supported the Eurosceptic Referendum Party or abstained. The defeat was made worse by tactical voting.

Tactical voting

Labour's parliamentary landslide was achieved on 44% of the vote — less than the party had scored when defeated in 1951 (see Table 5.1). Anti-Conservative tactical voting boosted Labour's majority and cost the Tories some 48 seats. Tactical voting occurs when voters decide to transfer their support from their favoured party to the party best placed to defeat the political party they least like. In 1997 some Labour supporters in Conservative-held seats where Labour had been the third-placed party in 1992 transferred their support to the second-placed Liberal Democrats, as they had the best chance of defeating the incumbent Conservative.

The narrowing of the ideological gap between Labour and the Liberal Democrats meant that supporters of both were more willing to vote for their second-choice party. Voters also appeared more knowledgeable about which party was best placed to defeat the Conservatives, thanks to effective local campaigning and media publicity. Tactical voting in 2001 helped Labour and the Liberal Democrats hold on to many of the seats they had won 4 years earlier. But in 2005, the Liberal Democrats did not make great inroads in Conservative-held seats in southern England because Labour voters remained loyal rather than switching to the Liberal Democrats.

It is worth recalling that the electoral system is biased towards Labour (see Chapter 3). In 1992, the Conservatives won 41.8% of the vote but a parliamentary majority of only 21 seats. Five years later, Labour won 44.4% of the vote and a majority of 179 seats. In 2005, it won a 66-seat majority on 35.2% of the vote, the lowest share ever recorded by a winning party.

The 2001 general election

The 2001 general election saw a near repeat of the 1997 result, but without the drama. Only 21 seats in Great Britain changed hands. But the absence of significant change was itself extraordinary, as it confirmed that Labour's 1997 landslide, rather than being a one-off, had reshaped the electoral landscape.

The electoral coalition of traditional working-class Labour voters and middle-class voters who switched their support to New Labour in 1997 held together (see Table 5.5). But the number of people voting Labour fell as turnout plunged to 59.4% (the reasons for this are discussed in Chapter 2). Voters had been disappointed by the performance of the Blair government, especially its record on public services, but were prepared to give Labour another chance. The Conservatives were not seen as a credible alternative government. They made a net gain of just one seat and an extra percentage point of the popular vote. But Conservative support among middle-class (AB and C1) voters fell to a new low. In pursuing a right-wing agenda of tax cuts and Euroscepticism when voters were most concerned about failing public services, the Conservatives misread the public mood.

Table 5.5 The 2001 general election (% votes cast)

	Con	Lab	Lib Dem
Share of vote (GB)	32.7	42.0	18.8
Social class			
AB	39	30	25
C1	36	38	20
C2	29	49	15
DE	24	55	13
Home ownership			
Home owners	43	32	19
Council tenants	18	60	14
Union membership			
Trade unionists	21	50	19
Gender			
Men	32	42	18
Women	33	42	19
Age			
18–24	27	41	24
25–34	24	51	19
35–44	28	45	19
45–54	32	41	20
55–64	39	37	17
65+	40	39	17

Source: MORI, www.mori.com

The 2005 general election

Each of the three main parties had reasons to be cheerful at the outcome of the 2005 general election, but also causes for concern. Labour won a 66-seat majority but its share of the vote fell to just 35.2%, as it lost support in all social classes and regions.

Table 5.7 The 2005 general election (% votes cast)

	Con	Lab	Lib Dem
Share of vote (GB)	33	36	23
Social class			
AB	37	28	29
C1	37	32	23
C2	33	40	19
DE	25	48	18
Home ownership			
Home owners	44	29	20
Council tenants	16	55	19
Gender			
Men	34	34	22
Women	32	38	23
Age			
18–24	28	38	26
25–34	25	38	27
35–44	27	41	23
45–54	31	35	25
55–64	39	31	22
65+	41	35	18

Source: MORI final aggregate result, **www.mori.com**

Labour's 9.6 million votes was the party's lowest total since its 1983 nadir. The Conservatives made a net gain of 33 seats but failed to pass the 200 MP mark. They polled 32.3% of the vote, an increase of 0.6% — smaller than the increase made in 2001. The Liberal Democrats won 62 seats on 22.1% of the vote, their highest share since 1987. They took 12 seats from Labour, but suffered a net loss of two seats to the Conservatives.

Support for Labour fell in all regions and among all key social groups. Labour's share of the vote fell most in constituencies with a large Muslim population and in university constituencies containing large numbers of students and academics. The higher than average swings from Labour to the Liberal Democrats in these seats reflected the unpopularity of the Blair government's policies on Iraq and tuition fees. Women and upper-middle-class voters were more likely to stick with New Labour, even though these groups had been pro-Conservative in the 1980s.

The Conservative share of the vote increased in Greater London (by just 2%), but remained static in many regions and declined in the North East and Yorkshire (see Table 5.2). They were not the main beneficiaries of discontent with the government. The Conservatives lost support from middle-class and women voters for the third successive election, and performed poorly in middle-class suburban constituencies in the provinces. Support for the Liberal Democrats was highest in the AB social group, but they failed to gain ground in middle-class constituencies in southern England. Instead, they benefited from disenchantment with Labour among students and Muslim voters. Minor parties also gained from the fragmentation of the Labour vote. The Greens, Respect, the British National Party (BNP) and UK Independence Party (UKIP) all performed better than in 2001. But UKIP failed to make the breakthrough that its performance in the 2004 European elections had hinted at.

An electoral sea change?

The last three general elections have produced results of historic significance. Labour has won three successive victories, each with large majorities, for the first time in its history. The Conservatives suffered their worst defeat in a century in 1997, followed by their second worst and fourth worst performances in 2001 and 2005. The Liberal Democrats, meanwhile, have achieved their highest number of MPs for more than 70 years.

A typology of general elections used by electoral analysts such as Pippa Norris provides one way of assessing the significance of Labour's 1997 victory. It identifies three categories of election outcomes:

➤ *Maintaining elections*: traditional left–right issues dominate the campaign and existing patterns of support remain largely intact.
➤ *Deviating elections*: there is a temporary downturn in the normal share of the vote for the majority party, caused primarily by short-term issues or personalities.
➤ *Critical elections*: significant and durable realignments in the electorate which have major consequences for the party system occur. Realignment is evident in three areas: the social basis of party support, the partisan loyalty of voters, and the ideological basis of party competition.

Critical elections are rare events in UK politics. Labour's landslide victory in 1945 is the only unambiguous postwar example. The case for classifying the 1997 general election as a critical election is not clear cut, although it did bring about significant changes in the electoral landscape which have continued to resonate. These were:

➤ The social basis of party support changed as a significant swing from the Conservatives to Labour occurred among middle-class voters. Labour then suffered smaller than average losses in this group in 2001 and 2005. Middle-class support for the Conservatives fell in each of the three contests, but they made small gains among working-class voters in 2001 and 2005.
➤ More voters than usual switched directly from the Conservatives to Labour in 1997. The incidence of tactical voting also increased.
➤ The ideological gap between the two main parties narrowed in 1997 as New Labour occupied the electoral centre ground. The Liberal Democrats were now positioned to New Labour's left while the Conservatives were placed on the right of centre.

Issues such as Europe and asylum became more significant as differences on socio-economic policy waned.

However, it is far from certain that these changes represent the significant and durable realignment necessary for the 1997 contest to be labelled a 'critical election'. The trends outlined above can be seen as evidence of electoral *dealignment* rather than *realignment*. Class dealignment and partisan dealignment have been underway since the 1970s. Class voting has fallen to new lows in recent elections. The 1997 election marked the continuation of a trend, not its beginning or end. New Labour's success

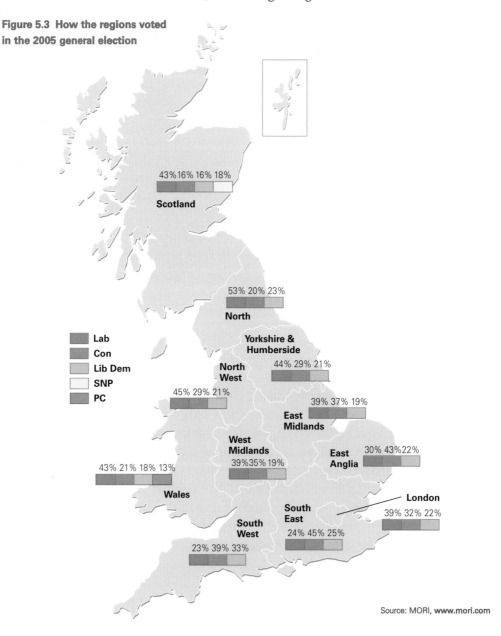

Figure 5.3 How the regions voted in the 2005 general election

Source: MORI, www.mori.com

in developing a cross-class appeal and the sizeable fall in support for the Conservatives mark a sharp disjuncture from the 1979 to 1992 period in which the Tories won four general elections in a row. But relatively few New Labour voters feel a strong sense of attachment to the party, as low turnout and the decline in working-class support for Labour confirm. The number of people voting for the two main parties has also fallen in each of the last three elections.

The ideological basis of party competition was transformed by the emergence of New Labour in the mid 1990s. New Labour is a 'catch-all' party with a broad appeal rather than a narrow, class-based one. It achieved this by positioning itself in the electoral centre ground — the position of the average voter — and persuading voters that it could be trusted to manage the economy. By accepting the market economy, abandoning its former 'tax and spend' outlook, and promising not to raise income tax, New Labour won over voters who were dissatisfied with the Conservatives' performance in office in the 1990s.

The ideological gap between the two main parties thus narrowed ahead of the 1997 election. In 2001 and 2005, most voters saw little difference between the policies proposed by the main parties. But it is still too early to know whether the ideological change that saw New Labour move to the centre ground will survive Tony Blair's eventual resignation.

Chancellor Gordon Brown and election coordinator Alan Milburn on the campaign trail in 2005. Labour aimed to persuade voters it could be trusted with the economy

Divisions between Labour and the Conservatives have been evident on issues such as Europe, asylum and devolution, but these have not persuaded large numbers of voters to change allegiance. The major issues in recent elections have been familiar ones, namely health, education and the economy. The perception that Labour, rather than the Conservatives, is the party best able to manage the economy has been a significant change. But New Labour has benefited from a combination of circumstances — a sound economy, a weak opposition and a biased electoral system — that cannot last indefinitely.

Key terms

- **Catch-all party.** A political party with limited ideological conviction and a broad rather than class-based electoral appeal.
- **Core vote.** A party's loyal or habitual supporters; the minimum support a party can expect at an election.
- **Critical election.** An election that brings significant, long-term changes in party support.
- **Electoral centre ground (or 'middle ground').** A political position thought to be occupied by a majority of voters. This need not be in the *ideological* centre, but falls roughly halfway between extremes of left and right.
- **Tactical voting.** Voting for the candidate of a political party that is not one's first preference in the hope of preventing a victory for the candidate of one's least favoured party.

Future prospects

There are clear limits to Labour's electoral hegemony. The electoral coalition of middle-class and working-class voters held together in 2001 and (to a lesser extent) in 2005. But this was a result of a combination of short-term factors — a healthy economy, Labour leads on key issues and the unpopularity of the Conservatives — rather than an enduring shift in allegiance. Only a minority of Labour voters identify themselves as strong supporters of the party. Labour has also performed relatively poorly in local and European Parliament elections.

War in Iraq and the marketisation of the welfare state contributed to a fraying of support on Labour's left flank in Blair's second term. Voter trust in the government and satisfaction with Blair's performance also declined significantly. These difficulties are not as severe as those that brought the period of Conservative predominance to an end in the 1990s, but serve as a reminder that New Labour's cross-class appeal and reputation for competence is not invulnerable. Economic downturn and tax increases could test the loyalty of those middle-class voters who turned to Labour in 1997. Under new leadership, however, Labour may attract back voters who deserted them in 2005.

The Conservatives' standing in the opinion polls has barely moved since 1997, hovering around the 30–33% mark for much of this time. The narrowing of the gap between the two main parties since 2001 resulted mainly from a fall in support for

Labour, rather than an increase in Tory support. To recover, the Conservatives must develop a coherent narrative, attractive headline policies and re-establish a reputation for economic competence. The 2001 and 2005 elections show that the party still has much work to do.

After the 2001 election, Liberal Democrat strategists believed that their best hope of advance lay in taking Conservative-held marginal seats. But with Labour ensconced in the electoral centre ground and the Liberal Democrats positioned to their left, winning votes from the centre-right was not easy. Though they perform better among middle-class than working-class voters, the Liberal Democrats failed to gain ground in many Conservative-held seats in southern England in 2005. Instead, they attracted more votes from Labour and emerged as their main challengers in 104 of the 355 seats held by Labour. The unpopularity of both main parties meant that the 2005 election offered unusually favourable circumstances. However, it is far from certain that they will be able to turn tactical or protest voters into committed supporters. Indeed, support for the Liberal Democrats tends to be 'softer' than that for Labour and the Conservatives.

Competing for votes

Voting behaviour in the UK is far less predictable than it was 40 years ago. Labour and the Conservatives used to have a large reservoir of core voters who were tied to them through class and party loyalties. Class and partisan dealignment have increased the numbers of voters who change allegiance from election to election. Such voters require greater persuasion to both turn out to vote and to support a particular party than used to be the case. Political parties thus invest more energy in marginal constituencies and particular social groups whose support might make the difference between winning and losing. Dealignment and the proximity of the ideological positions taken by the main parties also means that many voters make up their minds on the basis of likely governing competence. Judgements about which party would provide a sound economy and effective public services, and which has the most able team of leaders, have been critical factors in recent general elections.

Suggested reading

Butler, D. and Kavanagh, D., *The British General Election of 2005* (Palgrave, 2005).

Curtice, J., 'Anatomy of a non-landslide', *Politics Review*, vol. 7, no. 1, September 1997.

Curtice, J., 'General election 2001: repeat or revolution?', *Politics Review*, vol. 11, no. 1, September 2001.

Curtice, J., 'Historic truimph or rebuff? 2005 UK general election', *Politics Review*, vol. 15, no. 1, September 2005.

Denver, D., 'Making the choice: explaining how people vote', *Politics Review*, vol. 12, no. 1, September 2002.

Denver, D., *Elections and Voters in Britain* (Palgrave, 2002).

Norris, P., 'A critical election? Understanding the outcome of the 1997 general election', *Politics Review*, vol. 6, no. 4, April 1997.

Norris, P and Wlezien, C. (eds), *Britain Votes 2005* (Oxford University Press, 2005).

Saggar, S., 'The race card, again', in P. Norris (ed.), *Britain Votes 2001* (Oxford University Press, 2001), pp.195–210.

Websites

BBC 2001 election site (includes full results): www.news.bbc.co.uk/vote2001/

BBC 2005 general election site (includes full results):
http://news.bbc.co.uk/nol/ukfs_news/hi/uk_politics/vote_2005/default.stm

Department for Constitutional Affairs (includes reports on recent UK elections):
www.dca.gov.uk/elections/index.htm

MORI (highly recommended site containing a wealth of opinion poll data):
www.mori.com

Richard Kimber's 2005 general election site (gateway to hundreds of election-related sites): www.psr.keele.ac.uk/area/uk/ge05.htm

Exam focus

Using the chapter and other resources available to you, answer the following questions.

1 Explain the term 'class dealignment'.
2 Explain the term 'partisan dealignment'.
3 What is class-based voting?
4 Discuss the main factors that have influenced recent voting behaviour.
5 Explain the importance of issue voting compared to other factors determining voting behaviour.
6 Why might the 1997 general election be regarded as 'a record-breaking election'?
7 Why might the 2001 general election have appeared 'uninteresting'?
8 Explain why each of the three main parties had reasons to be cheerful but also causes for concern at the outcome of the 2005 general election.
9 Explain tactical voting.
10 How far do you agree that Labour is a 'catch-all' party?
11 Discuss the importance of regional factors in Labour's 2005 general election success.
12 Present the case that social class plays only a minor role in influencing voting behaviour.
13 Present the case that social class remains an important factor in determining voting behaviour.

Chapter 6

UK political parties

Political parties are an inevitable feature of representative democracies like the UK. Individuals can sometimes win parliamentary seats without the assistance of a formal party organisation. But a permanent body that can build up a reliable body of support over the years is a significant advantage in an age when individual candidates are normally strangers to the majority of their electors. As we shall see in this chapter, parties have many other potential advantages. Recently, however, some of their activities have made them unpopular, and it can no longer be taken for granted that their overall influence on democracy is a healthy one.

Key questions answered in this chapter
➤ What are the main roles of political parties?
➤ How open and democratic are their structures and procedures?
➤ How are they funded and how should they be funded?
➤ Do parties enhance or threaten democracy?

The role of political parties

Histories of UK political parties usually begin in the seventeenth century, when 'Tories' were opposed by 'Whigs'. But these were not political parties in the modern sense. They were loose alliances of parliamentarians, who lacked any kind of professional organisation beyond Westminster and had no need for campaigning machinery at a time when few people had the right to vote in elections. Modern UK parties, by contrast, have arisen from the need to mobilise consent within a mass electorate, and began to develop in the second half of the nineteenth century, as the number of voters increased.

Political parties vary widely, depending on their context. The functions of modern UK parties are influenced strongly by a political culture that the country shares with most Western states. This culture is characterised as a *liberal democracy* (see Chapter 1). In such states, parties can be defined as *voluntary organisations whose members share broadly similar views, whose purpose is to participate in government by securing the election of their candidates.*

In liberal democracies, the typical functions of political parties include:

- **Representation.** Parties in liberal democracies compete for public office through free elections. In order to be successful, they must represent the interests and opinions of a significant section of the electorate, which (with some small exceptions) consists of the whole adult population. Even if they cannot satisfy everyone, they try to build a *consensus* and accommodate popular demands as far as possible.
- **Recruitment of leaders.** Parties normally supply the leading politicians in liberal democracies. In the UK, political leaders are almost always people who have devoted much of their adult lives to their parties. As party members, politicians learn important skills, such as the ability to communicate and a sense of what is politically acceptable.
- **Government.** Organised parties help to ensure stable government. At national and local level, they exert discipline over their representatives, who usually vote for their party's policies even when they have serious doubts on specific issues. Voters can expect with some confidence that the programme of the democratically elected government will be implemented. At the same time, opposition parties give people who disagree with the government a sense that their views are being aired, and reassurance that an alternative group exists to replace any government that loses the public's confidence.
- **Policy formulation.** Parties offer voters a choice between competing policy programmes in published documents called *manifestos*. Although a party's policy is influenced by other factors, the programme must be broadly acceptable to party members, and there will normally have been some kind of internal consultation before a manifesto is published. Since the middle of the twentieth century, the proposals of UK parties have tended to become much more detailed. After an election, the successful party almost invariably claims to have secured a *mandate* from the people to put the policy ideas into operation.
- **Participation and mobilisation.** Under a system of representative government, voters usually do not participate directly in the law-making process. But the main political parties have local organisations in every UK constituency, providing citizens with the opportunity to join and make their views known on a regular basis. At

election time, the local parties try to encourage ordinary voters to turn out. They are important agents of political education in the UK.

Summary

The role of political parties

In a representative democracy, political parties perform five key functions:

➤ representation   ➤ recruitment of leaders
➤ stable government   ➤ policy formulation
➤ participation and mobilisation

Elitism or pluralism?

Before looking in detail at the organisation of the main parties, we should consider the two main approaches to analysing political parties.

The elitist model

The book *Political Parties*, published in 1911 by the German sociologist Robert Michels, is a classic expression of the *elitist* approach to political analysis. Michels argued that political leaders have a vested interest in imposing unity on their followers, and they usually have the necessary power, skills and knowledge to get their way. He believed that ordinary members want to be given direction by someone, and accept leadership gratefully.

Michels thought that *oligarchy* (the rule of a few) was an inescapable feature of all large organisations, however democratic they might claim to be. He concluded that the parties which did not conform to his model would fail, and were thus irrelevant. So he claimed that his findings amounted to something like the laws of natural science.

Elitists do not agree on every detail. But broadly speaking, in a party that conforms to the elitist model we should expect the following:

➤ Parliamentary candidates are chosen by the leadership.
➤ Most parliamentary candidates have similar backgrounds and characteristics.
➤ The party leader is chosen by a small, select group.
➤ The party leader is powerful.
➤ Party conference is little more than a rally to show support for the leadership.
➤ Policy is decided by the leadership.

The pluralist model

Unlike elitists, pluralists believe that key stated principles of liberal democracy are realistic. They consider Michels's view to be far too pessimistic. For them, parties provide opportunities for everyone with the necessary talent and drive to compete for office. They can point to recent prime ministers, such as the Conservatives Edward Heath and

John Major, who came from relatively humble backgrounds. Pluralists also argue that, far from pursuing their own interests, party leaders have to listen carefully to the views of their grass-roots members.

Like elitists, pluralists differ in their detailed views. But, broadly speaking, in a 'pluralistic' party we should find the following:

> Parliamentary candidates are chosen by the whole constituency membership.
> Parliamentary candidates reflect a wide range of backgrounds and characteristics.
> The party leader is chosen by the whole membership.
> The party leader has limited powers.
> The party conference is an open forum for debate.
> Policy is decided either by the whole membership or by a large representative group.

Compromise positions

While it is useful to compare the state of UK parties today with the contrasting checklists for both elitism and for pluralism, we should not confine ourselves to these rigid models. For example, we might agree with elitism in identifying an elite at the top of the main parties, but also accept that these leaders can come from almost any social background. Like the elitists, though, we might conclude that whatever their origins, successful leaders tend to behave in similar ways once they have reached the top. At the same time, we can follow the pluralists in recognising that if any leader loses touch with rank-and-file opinion, he or she runs the risk of being deposed.

Although our approach might adopt elements of the competing theories, it is unlikely that at any given time the parties will reflect a perfect compromise between the two. So, if we think that the parties are more 'elitist' than 'pluralist', our position could be described as one of *modified* (or *qualified*) *elitism*. If we think that on balance pluralism provides a better explanation, we could say that UK political parties reveal a tendency towards *modified* (or *qualified*) *pluralism*.

Party structure: Labour and the Conservatives

Historical background

For convenience, the main focus of our discussion will be a comparison between Labour and the Conservatives, which have dominated UK politics for most of the period since 1918. Although we are interested here in the present day and the recent past, it is important to note a few background factors relating to the long-term traditions of Labour and the Conservatives:

> The Conservative Party is the direct descendant of the 'Tories', who opposed democratic participation on principle, and the party developed when most people in Britain lacked the right to vote.

- Labour was founded in 1900, when the majority already had the vote.
- The Conservative Party was tied closely to the aristocracy and the affluent middle class.
- Labour was founded to represent the interests of the largest group in society — the working class.
- Membership of the Conservative Party has always been based on individual affiliation.
- A large proportion of Labour Party members have joined through their affiliation to other bodies, notably the trade unions.

With these points in mind, it is not surprising that the Conservative Party has traditionally been regarded as a *hierarchical* organisation, conforming quite closely to the elitist model. For its part, Labour has been viewed as more of a pluralist organisation. These tendencies reached their logical conclusion in the 1980s, when the Conservatives were regarded as benefiting from strong leadership, while Labour was seen as almost unmanageable.

Yet circumstances have a profound effect on the development of political parties. As far back as 1955, the political scientist Robert McKenzie argued that, on closer inspection, Labour and the Conservatives were actually difficult to distinguish in terms of their structures and practices. His argument lent strong support to Michels's elitist thesis, by stressing the power of the leadership within each organisation.

Since McKenzie put forward his arguments, both of the main parties have suffered badly from internal divisions — Labour after 1979 and the Conservatives since 1990. The impression of division is highly damaging, particularly when the media are so interested in stories about internal differences. So it is no surprise that both parties have tried to reassert control. At the same time, though, parties are voluntary bodies and many members join because they hope to have their opinions heard. If these expectations are disappointed, the result can be mass defections from the party. For us, the important question is: *how open and democratic are the structures and procedures of the two main parties today?*

Cultural factors

Before looking in more detail at the two main UK parties, we should also note three general developments in UK culture and society that have exerted a crucial influence on political life:

- **The media.** Political leaders are now under intense scrutiny, not only at election time but also when important political issues arise. The result has been a marked increase in the number and influence of spin doctors, who advise senior party figures and try to present their views in the most positive light. These figures exercise far more influence than ordinary backbenchers, let alone grass-roots party members. Fear of the media has made both major parties more wary than ever of internal dissent. New Labour's leaders are often accused of being 'control freaks', but the same tendency has affected the Conservatives. This development adds weight to the *elitist* model.

> **The decline of deference.** People nowadays are faced with an increasing range of choices in every aspect of their daily lives. Party leaders can still draw to a certain extent on stubborn loyalty among ordinary members — but it would be a grave mistake to take it for granted. It is more important than ever to make party members feel that their opinions matter. This development supports the *pluralist* view.

> **The decline of class voting.** In the early postwar period, Labour and the Conservatives could rely on a high degree of loyalty from the working class and the middle and upper classes respectively. Social divisions in the UK are less obvious nowadays. Instead of living in one place and holding the same job throughout their lives, people are more geographically mobile. They are less likely to develop stable attitudes to issues and parties because they come into contact with a wider range of groups in the course of their lives. This factor is also likely to work in the direction of greater *pluralism*.

The combined effect of these conflicting factors makes it less likely that we will be completely satisfied with either of the 'pure' models of elitism and pluralism.

Candidate selection

The first-past-the-post electoral system in the UK ensures a close relationship between candidates and constituencies. It is possible to win a seat even if a strong faction within the local party strongly disapproves of the selected candidate. But the task is made much harder if people with an intimate knowledge of the area refuse to help with the campaign. So it makes sense for national parties to give constituency organisations a significant role in the selection process.

On the other hand, a controversial local candidate can be an embarrassment to the central party, particularly in by-election campaigns conducted under an intense media spotlight. As a result, the central parties can be expected to demand an important role in the selection process.

Candidate selection in the Conservative Party

Conservative Party activists pride themselves on their independence. The usual practice is for the local party committee to draw up a shortlist, from which the successful candidate is chosen at a meeting open to all the members. A recent example of a constituency resisting pressures from outside came before the 1997 general election, when the Conservatives in the seat of Tatton refused to deselect their controversial candidate, Neil Hamilton, despite pressure from the central party.

However, the central party does play an important role. The first step for would-be Conservative MPs is to win a place on a list of approved candidates, which is supervised by a vice-chairman of the national party (appointed by the leader). Since the 1997 general election campaign, the central party can also rely on an Ethics

Committee with the power to block candidates in the last resort. Notoriously, this body failed to act when Lord Archer was chosen as the Conservative candidate in the London mayoral election of 2000, before being persuaded to stand down. But it may well prove more effective in the long run: before the 2005 general election it exercised a surprising assertion of power when a sitting MP, Howard Flight, was deselected as a candidate after making unwelcome comments about Conservative taxation policy.

Lord Archer campaigning to become Conservative candidate for the London mayoral election, 1999

Profile of Conservative candidates

After the party's landslide defeat in the 1997 general election, senior Conservatives accepted that something had to be done to change the profile of their parliamentary party, which was dominated by married white males from professional backgrounds. Traditionally, Conservative selection meetings had preferred this type of person, often subjecting women, and men without families, to more difficult questioning.

In 1998 the Conservative leader, William Hague, proposed that women should make up at least a quarter of the final shortlist in constituency candidate selection contests. His initiative failed, and there was no attempt to put the issue to a vote of the whole membership. At the 2001 general election, 93 Conservative candidates were women — an increase of 27 since 1997, but still 65 behind Labour. Only 1 out of 38 new Tory MPs elected in that year was a woman. As for the ethnic minorities, only one Asian candidate was chosen in a seat which the Conservatives could possibly have won. As it turned out, he was defeated.

After the second election defeat, a plan was drawn up to introduce quotas of female and ethnic minority candidates in winnable seats. This was seen as a step too far, given the traditional independence of constituency parties. Instead, the central party relied on *constituency profiling*, recommending the selection of female candidates in seats where they would have a better chance of winning than a man. However, senior figures in the party expressed a strong desire for change. The problem remained one of persuading local activists to break with their old prejudices. Considering the party's ethos the results were impressive. In the 2005 general election the Conservatives fielded 122 women candidates and 41 candidates from ethnic minorities. The contest produced the party's first black MP, Adam Afriye, who won the safe seat of Windsor, along with the Asian MP Shailesh Vara in northwest Cambridgeshire.

Despite this success, it will prove extremely difficult to bring the occupational background of Conservative MPs into line with the population as a whole. In 1997, only one of them (out of 165) had been a manual labourer; 109 had been to a public school and 84 had attended either Oxford or Cambridge universities. The underlying problem was that many of the party's grass-roots members rather liked the fact that they were not representative of society as a whole.

Candidate selection in the Labour Party

On paper, local Labour constituencies seem to enjoy even more independence than their Conservative counterparts. A list of approved people is kept by the central party organisation, but the successful applicant does not need to be on it. Affiliated societies, notably the trade unions, can nominate people provided that they are members of the party.

In practice, the situation is very different. For the New Labour leadership, the power to select (or deselect) candidates is particularly sensitive. Rule changes in the early 1980s made it easier for constituency activists to get rid of an uncongenial candidate, and although this power was not often exercised it was an integral part of Labour's 'unelectable' image at that time. Candidates can still be removed by a constituency party; for example, in March 2003 the MP for Reading East, Jane Griffiths, was deselected even though she was an outspoken supporter of Tony Blair.

In other respects the influence of the central party has been growing since the late 1980s. For example, party rules decree that there must be at least one woman on every shortlist. In 1994–95 the central party went so far as to impose all-women shortlists in 38 winnable seats. Now that the 2002 Sexual Discrimination (Election Candidates) Act has clarified the legal position on 'positive discrimination', the party's rules decree that at least half of a region's seats where a sitting Labour MP has announced an intention to retire must be filled by a woman. Moreover, if the selected candidate is regarded as unsuitable — usually because he or she is a critic of the leadership — the choice can be overruled on the pretext of 'procedural irregularities' (for example, this happened to Liz Davies at Leeds North East in 1995). However, misjudgements by the central party over candidate selection can still result in rejection by the electorate. At the 2005 general election Labour lost one of its safest seats, Blaenau Gwent in Wales, to a popular former party member who stood against an official candidate selected from an all-woman shortlist.

Shaun Woodward, who defected from the Conservatives to the Labour Party in 2000

In the last resort, the national leadership can disband the local party entirely, as it did in the case of Doncaster in 1997. But more often it gets its way without taking such drastic measures. It also has another useful method of ensuring the selection of a favoured candidate. Senior backbenchers can be persuaded to stand down close to an election, allowing the central party to impose a candidate on the grounds that it is too late for the local activists to hold the full selection process. Just before the 2001 general election, a vacancy arose in the Labour constituency of St Helens. The local party selected the former Conservative MP Shaun Woodward, who was strongly favoured by the leadership. But he had no obvious links with the area and, as the husband of a millionairess, he hardly fitted the traditional profile of a Labour MP. This case was so controversial that the central party decided that it had to allow a contest of sorts, but it was alleged that Woodward's main rivals had been excluded from the shortlist.

Profile of Labour candidates

An obvious result of Labour's recent reforms has been a dramatic increase in the number of women candidates in winnable seats. In 1987 there were only 21 Labour women MPs; 10 years later there were 102. In 1987, 69 women stood unsuccessfully on Labour's behalf; the figure in 1997 was only 54. This reduced failure rate shows that Labour is not just better than it used to be at running female candidates; it is clearly serious in its declared intention of securing their election to parliament, too. In 2005, 171 women candidates stood for Labour; a third of the candidates standing for the party for the first time were women, compared with less than a quarter for the Conservatives and the Liberal Democrats.

With this notable exception, however, the profile of New Labour in parliament has much in common with its main rival. Although Shaun Woodward looked out of place in St Helens, he was much more at home with his new colleagues at Westminster. The figures after the 1997 general election were distorted by the overwhelming Labour landslide. But the 'workers' party' now had more graduates from Oxbridge (61) and former public school pupils (67) than manual labourers. Of the new MPs, 188 came from the professions. Compared to the Conservative Party, Labour still had fewer business-people (37, compared to 65); but this was still a remarkable figure, given the common assumption that 'Old' Labour had been anti-business.

Leader selection

Leader selection in the Conservative Party

Until the election of Edward Heath in 1965, Conservative leaders had been chosen after informal discussions within the parliamentary party. The introduction of formal rules, giving all MPs a vote on the leadership, made the Conservatives look more 'modern' — but only at the cost of increasing instability, even when the party was in power. Margaret Thatcher was challenged unsuccessfully in 1989, and defeated in 1990. Her successor, John Major, grew so impatient with rumours of a challenge that he triggered a leadership election himself, in 1995. He defeated John Redwood, but his position was weakened further.

When the Conservatives returned to opposition in 1997, ordinary members demanded a say in the choice of leader. After submitting his own leadership to a 'referendum' of party members, William Hague introduced the following changes under the slogan 'Fresh Future':

➤ Instead of choosing the leader themselves, MPs would reduce the number of candidates to two in a preliminary round of ballots.

➤ The membership as a whole would then choose from the two remaining candidates.

➤ Instead of allowing a challenge to the leader at a set date in every year, a leadership election could be triggered at any time if the leader fails to win a vote of confidence from MPs. Such a vote would be held if demanded by 15% of the parliamentary party.

Although Hague presented his reforms as a move to 'democratise' his party, some commentators argue that they actually strengthen the leader's position. The level of dissent required to generate a leadership election is far higher than it was in 1990, when Margaret Thatcher's challenger, Michael Heseltine, needed only a proposer and a seconder. Moreover, if the leader narrowly survives the vote of MPs and proceeds to the second-round vote of ordinary members, he or she is much better placed to win this run-off than Mrs Thatcher would have been had she chosen to fight on in 1990. Rank-and-file members are traditionally more deferential to a leader than are MPs.

When the reformed system was first used in 2001 the grassroots members elected Iain Duncan Smith, rather than the first choice of MPs, Kenneth Clarke. Duncan Smith was not a success, and in November 2003 he lost a vote of confidence among his parliamentary colleagues. His successor, Michael Howard, won unopposed. It seemed that the drive to democratise the Conservative Party had merely underlined the importance of having a leader who enjoyed the support of MPs rather than ordinary members. After the 2005 general election Howard emphasised his hope that the system would be reformed, and his views were echoed by Hague himself. The party had already been working on possible alternatives for over a year. Despite the pressure for a return to a system which gave the final choice to MP's, activists were most reluctant to give up their decisive role.

Leader selection in the Labour Party

After its general election defeat of 1979, Labour changed its own rules for choosing a leader. Instead of confining the choice to MPs as before, there would now be a complicated procedure allowing 30% of the vote to MPs, the same proportion to constituency associations and 40% to the trade unions.

Critics claimed that the new system meant that Labour's leaders would depend upon the trade unions more than ever. In 1993 the proportions were changed, so that the three sections of the party each controlled a third of the vote. More importantly, while in the past union leaders had been able to cast votes on behalf of their members without consulting them, a new system of *one member, one vote* (OMOV) meant that the unions and the constituency parties had to ballot all of their members in advance. Tony Blair was the first leader to benefit from this system, in 1994.

The incumbent Labour leader can be challenged, but his or her position is more secure than that of a Conservative leader. In office, a leader can only be unseated by a two-thirds majority vote of the party conference. In opposition, 20% of Labour MPs have to call for an election.

The effect of this system was illustrated in 2003, when Tony Blair was strongly criticised for his policy on Iraq. If he had been a Conservative prime minister facing such a high level of dissent on any issue, there is every chance that he or she would have faced a formal leadership challenge. As it was, talk of a looming contest was dismissed, and actually encouraged wavering MPs to rally behind Blair. In 2004 Blair announced that if Labour won the next election he would continue to serve as prime minister, but would not seek a fourth term in office. Even though his reputation within the party continued to fall, he still implied that he would stay on as leader until a time of his own choosing.

Power of the leaders over personnel
Leadership power in the Conservative Party
It used to be thought that Conservative Party leaders enjoyed far more power than their Labour counterparts, based on the unthinking loyalty of MPs and constituency members. But since 1975, three Conservative leaders have been 'sacked' by their MPs, and John Major's premiership was weakened seriously by internal dissent. By comparison, Labour's recent leaders have been much more secure.

The exaggerated popular view of the power of the Conservative leader owes something to the party's traditional deference, but also reflects the fact that, in theory, the leader has a free choice over senior colleagues and party officials, whether or not the Conservatives are in office. In practice, however, the leader is heavily influenced by the power of factions within the party, whatever the party's circumstances. Thus John Major complained about disloyal members of his cabinet, who could not be sacked because they would cause more trouble on the back benches. William Hague had to include the charismatic Michael Portillo in his shadow cabinet, even though he was bound to prove a dangerous rival. By contrast, before the 2005 general election Michael Howard acted swiftly to ensure that a dissident MP, Howard Flight, was not only dismissed as party vice-chairman but also deselected as a candidate.

Leadership power in the Labour Party
When the party is in opposition, the Labour leader cannot nominate the members of his or her shadow cabinet, which is elected by the parliamentary party. When Labour wins power, government offices have to be shared out among this group of people.

However, the contrast with the Conservative leadership is not as sharp as it might seem. The shadow cabinet elections in the Labour Party are little more than a formal means of registering the power of various party factions, and calculations of this kind always exert a strong influence on the choices of the Conservative leader. In addition, once Labour is in office the prime minister can conduct *reshuffles*, which gives a powerful leader the chance to dispose of awkward colleagues, and, in Tony Blair's case, to promote close allies and friends whether or not they have ever been elected. Blair has even used his position as prime minister to transform the institutional structure of his party. Until 2001 the Labour Party chairman was elected by the conference, and was mainly concerned with organisational matters. By contrast, Blair hand-picked a person (originally Charles Clarke) who spent much of his time defending government policy on television. This brought Labour into line with traditional Conservative Party practice, but it could be argued that such an important change should have been subject to the approval of the conference.

Box 6.2 Robert McKenzie on party leadership

'Whatever the role granted in theory to the extra-parliamentary wings of the parties, in practice final authority rests in both parties with the parliamentary party and its leadership.'

R. T. McKenzie, *British Political Parties*, 1963.

Party conferences
Conservative Party conferences

In the past, the annual Conservative Party conference was regarded as nothing more than a public relations exercise, or a rally to lift the spirits of ordinary members. On some issues, notably law and order, spokespeople had to work hard to avoid criticism. But motions for debate were chosen carefully, and the conferences' decisions were regarded as purely 'advisory'. In practice, they were often ignored. The leader's speech closed the conference, and was invariably the signal for a prolonged standing ovation.

After the party's election defeat in 1997 it looked as though the Conservative conference would become more difficult to manage, as ordinary members demanded more influence. But the annual gathering still lacks any formal power. At most, it provides leaders with an opportunity to test the reaction of members to policy ideas — and registers the current popularity of senior figures, who compete for the warmest reception.

Labour Party conferences

Labour's 1918 constitution gave the party conference formal powers over policy making. As a result, meetings tended to be tense and the debates could be dramatic. Instead of rallying ordinary members with a rousing speech, leaders often found themselves apologising for unpopular decisions.

Since the 1980s, it has been a primary goal of Labour's 'modernisers' to reduce the importance of the party conference. This campaign reached its climax at the 1997 conference, which endorsed the document *Partnership in Power*. From now on, the conference would be little more than a 'rubber stamp' for policy decisions taken elsewhere (see p. 144). As with the Conservative conference, the leader's speech, which closes the meeting, dominates media coverage. Although Tony Blair seems to inspire respect rather than love, his carefully phrased speeches usually receive a prolonged ovation.

However, the conference does still have some influence. In 2000 a critical vote helped to persuade the chancellor, Gordon Brown, to increase pensions. On the other hand, the warm reception in that year for the Northern Ireland secretary, Mo Mowlam, may have contributed to her removal from office. Just like the Conservative gathering, the Labour conference is something of a 'beauty contest' for potential leadership candidates — and the present incumbent is unlikely to be pleased if rivals prove to be a little *too* attractive!

Policy making
Policy making in the Conservative Party

Formally, the Conservative leader has overall responsibility for policy making. During the 1992 general election campaign, this point was underlined by John Major when he confirmed that his party manifesto was 'all me' (if anyone doubted this, the front cover was dominated by his photograph). In office, the leader can interfere in the detailed decisions of even the most important ministers, as when Margaret Thatcher criticised the economic policy of her chancellor, Nigel Lawson, leading to the latter's resignation in 1989.

In opposition, Conservative leaders tend to have less influence. So, for example, in July 2000 William Hague was forced to agree when his shadow chancellor, Michael Portillo, dropped the party's pledge to reduce the overall burden of taxation during the forthcoming parliament.

However, Hague was also keen to give ordinary members more say in policy decisions. A referendum of party members was held to endorse his decision to rule out UK membership of the euro zone, and the draft of the 2001 election manifesto was also approved by a party-wide vote. Critics pointed out that members had been given a 'take it or leave it' choice, instead of being asked for their own suggestions, and that they were always likely to follow the preferences of the leader. But Hague's 'Fresh Future' reform package of 1998 also introduced a system of *policy forums*. Like the conference, the forums were purely advisory, but they gave ordinary members the chance to air their views on a regular basis. In 2000 the party's policy of restoring tax incentives for married couples was amended after consultations uncovered a surprising level of opposition among grass-roots members.

Policy making in the Labour Party

Traditionally, Labour's manifesto was compiled by the National Executive Committee (NEC), the body elected by the conference to oversee the day-to-day business of the party between its annual gatherings. Resolutions that had been passed by the conference with a two-thirds majority were expected to be included in the party's official programme. This system produced the 1983 election manifesto, dubbed 'the longest suicide note in history' because of its radical commitments. Labour's programme is usually blamed for its heavy defeat in that election.

While the 1945 Labour government implemented most of its ambitious manifesto commitments, this was more the exception than the rule. The two minority Labour governments of 1974–79, for example, were criticised savagely by left-wing party members for departing from election promises. The leadership could argue that circumstances had prevented them from sticking to the programme. However, a feeling remained that most ministers had been rather relieved to have an excuse not to do as their members wanted. As a result, left-wing members of the party launched a campaign to 'democratise' Labour's policy making. They only succeeded in making their party look more disunited than ever.

Reforms under the last two Labour leaders, John Smith (1992–94) and Tony Blair, do give ordinary members a chance to influence policy (see Box 6.3). Like the Conservatives, Labour holds a series of policy forums. These meetings are often informal, which encourages people to attend and to put forward their views. They provide a useful opportunity to uncover and respond to dissent among the party faithful before the issues spill over into debates at the party conference, where the extra publicity can still cause major political embarrassment. This was the case before 2005, when the leadership made tactical concessions to trade unionists at a National Policy Forum. Figure 6.1 outlines Labour's policy-making process.

However, under Tony Blair Labour's policy-making process has been heavily influenced by the findings of focus groups made up of people who are not party members. In November 2003 Blair launched the 'Big Conversation', which invited the general public to contribute ideas on policy. The initiative was dismissed by other parties as a gimmick, and was hardly ever mentioned again. But it illustrated Blair's tendency to heed the views of uncommitted voters rather than those of party members.

The Liberal Democrats

Although this chapter follows the usual approach of comparing Labour and the Conservatives, the recent rise of the Liberal Democrats has attracted increasing attention to the party. The Liberal Democrats also provide an interesting sidelight on the Michels thesis and the general arguments of this chapter.

The party has a federal structure, with separate bodies for England, Scotland and Wales overseen by a federal executive. There are also specified associated organisations, including groups representing women, ethnic minorities and other groups with a

Box 6.3 The abolition of Labour's Clause IV

An excellent illustration of changes within the Labour Party is the fate of Clause IV of its original constitution, which referred to the need for a Labour government to nationalise key industries. Feeling that this commitment was a liability for his party, Hugh Gaitskell (leader from 1955 to 1963) hoped to remove it, but was defeated at the 1959 party conference.

After becoming Labour leader in 1994, Tony Blair seized on the issue as the perfect way to make New Labour seem more 'electable', and to reinforce his own authority at the same time. Previous reforms of the party made his task much easier than it had been for Gaitskell. However, Blair enjoyed other key advantages, particularly much greater access to the media, and a 'honeymoon' with the voters that seemed certain to last until the next election because the Conservative government was so deeply unpopular.

Blair made the most of his advantages. The issue was debated within the party for 6 months in advance of a special conference. This 'consultation exercise' might be regarded as an excellent example of pluralism at work. But, in fact, only 6% of members participated in the exercise — a sign that many potential opponents regarded the result as a foregone conclusion. At the special conference, in April 1995, it was found that less than half of the members had bothered to vote. The result was a comfortable victory for Blair's new Clause IV, which dropped any reference to nationalisation. It was a useful lesson for all party leaders. In certain circumstances, and with skilful management, ordinary party members could be persuaded to give 'democratic' endorsement to a leader's radical reforms, greatly strengthening his or her chances of pushing through more changes in the future.

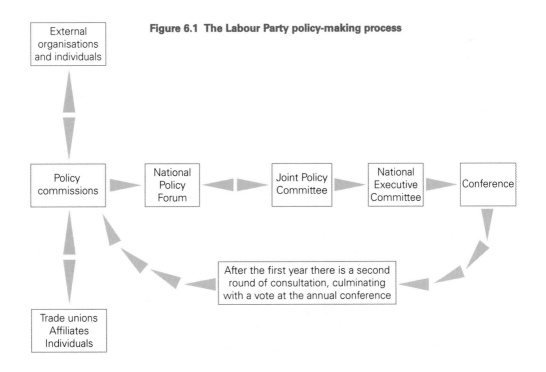

Figure 6.1 The Labour Party policy-making process

External organisations and individuals

Policy commissions

National Policy Forum

Joint Policy Committee

National Executive Committee

Conference

After the first year there is a second round of consultation, culminating with a vote at the annual conference

Trade unions
Affiliates
Individuals

less formal association, which campaign on specific issues like the environment and electoral reform.

The party constitution states that the leader is elected by the whole party membership. Liberalism is a highly individualistic ideology (see Chapter 7), and it could be argued that this provision merely reflects the beliefs of the party's members. Yet during all the years in which the Liberals were a party of government, the ordinary members had no say in the choice of leader. Indeed, the vote was restricted to MPs until 1976.

The leader, now elected by the whole membership, plays a central role in policy presentation. In the years before the 1997 general election, Paddy Ashdown (leader from 1988 to 1999) tried to persuade his party to move closer to Labour, with a view to a possible coalition government. If the election result had been less conclusive, it would have been interesting to see how his party would have reacted. As it was, Ashdown was included in a Cabinet Constitutional Reform Committee. Although the New Labour government did not deliver electoral reform as Ashdown had wanted, the impression that the Liberal Democrats were taking part in policy discussions at the highest level was bound to increase the prestige of the leader.

The Liberal conference has traditionally been difficult to control, and it is still far removed from the 'rally' style of Labour and Conservative gatherings. Yet with the Liberal Democrats now holding 62 seats, and looking well placed for further gains, the pressure for unity behind the leader has increased noticeably. After the 2005 general election, during which he played a dominant role, the leader Charles Kennedy announced that there would be a wide-ranging review of party policy. He indicated that the influence of the party conference over policy would be reduced, following trends established by Labour and the Conservatives.

Overall, it is safe to conclude that as the Liberal Democrats have increased in significance, they have become more like the two major parties. They are subject to the same background influences that have affected Labour and the Conservatives, and have tried to strike a similar compromise between upholding the authority of the leader and pleasing grass-roots activists. Not every Liberal Democrat was satisfied with Charles Kennedy's conduct of the 2005 election, but there was no formal challenge afterwards. His position might not have been so strong if the party had not emerged as a potential partner in a future government. Thus the history of the Liberal Democrats lends qualified support to the elitist critique of pluralism.

Power of leaders over MPs

In order to carry out his or her policy programme, a UK prime minister needs the consistent support of MPs, whether or not they are ministers. In the nineteenth century, governments often fell from office because of adverse parliamentary votes, and in 1940 the Conservative Neville Chamberlain resigned even though he won a parliamentary vote of confidence by 81 votes, because more than a hundred of his party's MPs had either voted against him or abstained. In 1979 the Labour prime minister James

Callaghan was forced to call a general election (which his party lost) after a parliamentary vote of confidence.

The crucial importance of mustering the maximum parliamentary support has led to the establishment in all parliamentary parties of a system known as *whipping*. The party whips are chosen for their powers of persuasion and their loyalty. Their task is to keep a close eye on opinion among specific groups of MPs, to report back any rumblings of discontent and to ensure that would-be rebels turn out to vote for the party. Before the most important votes, the party issues instructions underlined three times. MPs who defy these *three-line whips* can be subjected to a range of penalties, including the withdrawal of some privileges, the denial of promotion and, for the most serious offenders, expulsion from the parliamentary party (*loss of the whip*).

Sometimes the imposition of discipline through the whipping system can backfire on a leader. In November 1994, for example, seven Conservative MPs were deprived of the whip for voting against the European legislation of the Major government. Another MP resigned the whip in sympathy, and in April 1995 the government had to back down, restoring the whip to the seven rebels.

This incident of the 'whipless ones' merely illustrates that leaders who are already weak can make matters worse for themselves. But even a strong leader can stir up serious discontent, leading ultimately to serious rebellions. In March 2003, 121 Labour backbenchers defied Tony Blair by voting against a three-line whip in a vote on the threatened war with Iraq. The government's overwhelming majority, bolstered by support for the war on the Conservative benches, meant that its motion passed comfortably. By contrast, in January 2004, when the Conservatives and Liberal Democrats joined Labour rebels on the issue of university top-up fees, the government's majority fell to just 5.

In response to these examples, a pluralist might conclude that even the disciplinary power of the whips is insufficient to stifle damaging displays of dissent, and that a wise government should always keep backbench opinion in mind rather than trying to force MPs to vote against their real views. An elitist, by contrast, would argue that, without strong discipline, effective government would become impossible.

UK parties — elitist or pluralist?
Referring back to our checklists for elitism and pluralism, we can see that there is evidence to support both views.

Arguments for elitist parties
Those who argue that UK parties are elitist can make the following points:
➤ The central parties have a strong influence over candidate selection.
➤ Candidates for both parties resemble each other increasingly. Women and ethnic minorities are still under-represented, and the recent increase in their numbers owes more to the demands of the national parties than to local activists.

- Although the right to help choose a leader has been extended, ordinary members still have less say than MPs.
- Skilful leaders can dominate their parties.
- Party conferences are stage-managed to avoid embarrassment and to create the impression of unity behind the leader.
- Recent changes in both major parties give the impression of consultation with ordinary members, but the initiative on policy making still lies with senior party members and with the leaders in particular.
- Both of the main parties need a system of whips to enforce discipline.

Arguments for pluralist parties

The following points can be made by those who argue that UK parties are pluralist:

- Constituency parties still have an important say in candidate selection.
- Candidates come from a wide range of backgrounds. If there is a tendency for more 'professional' people to enter the House of Commons, this merely reflects the fact that politics demands specific skills nowadays.
- Ordinary members now enjoy far more say in the choice of leader.
- Leaders are more vulnerable than ever if they prove to be inadequate.
- Party conferences still offer the opportunity to voice dissent.
- Party members have ample opportunity to make their views known on policy matters. If they do not take the opportunities provided for them, they have only themselves to blame.
- Although whips are a regrettable necessity, their powers in both of the main parties are still limited and can never be absolute while MPs have opinions of their own.

It certainly appears that the two main UK parties are coming to resemble each other more and more. Beyond this, probably the safest conclusion is that both elitist and pluralist analyses of UK political parties are *partially* true. We may think that the *tendency* of recent developments is towards one model or the other. In other words, we may plump for 'qualified pluralism' or 'qualified elitism'. The important thing, as the major parties continue to respond to a rapidly changing context, is to evaluate the evidence as objectively as we can.

Summary

Structure of the main UK parties

- While not conforming exactly to Robert Michels's 'iron law of oligarchy', the main political parties in the UK are vulnerable to criticism from pluralists because ordinary members have relatively little say in their decisions.
- Recent changes in the structure of both the main UK parties make them look more democratic and open, in theory. But in practice, skilful leaders are as dominant as ever — if not more so.

Party funding in the UK

Parties in decline?

As we noted earlier, people seem to be growing more selective in their political activities. Leaders can no longer depend upon blind loyalty from their members. It would be fair to say that people who criticise UK parties tend to do so on pluralist grounds: that is, they claim that politicians are insufficiently representative of ordinary people, and that voters do not have an adequate range of choice.

The pluralist argument is challenged by a sharp recent decline in UK party membership — a trend that is affecting parties throughout western Europe. Before William Hague's reforms, the Conservative Party did not have national membership figures. But the total was estimated at around 400,000 in 1997. In 2002 it was put at 330,000 — despite the fact that Hague himself had hoped for 1 million members by the year 2000. By the 2005 general election, the party probably had around 300,000 members.

Labour has fared no better. After Blair became leader in 1994 there was a boost in membership, and in 1996 the party had just over 400,000 members. In 2004 the figure had fallen below 250,000. Meanwhile, the Liberal Democrats also suffered (around 100,000 in 1994, declining to 70,000 in 2004).

Paying for parties

The fall in party membership was a clear symptom of declining public interest. But it threatened to make the problem worse. One reason for disillusionment was the reliance of the major parties on rich donors. In the years before the 1997 general election, the association of the Conservative Party with 'sleaze' was reinforced by unsavoury stories about the sources of party funding. Similarly, for many years Labour had been attacked because the trade unions provided the vast majority of its funds (two-thirds of the party's income in 1992). But if parties can no longer rely on a mass membership to provide small donations, how else can they pay their bills?

While their costs are minuscule compared to their US counterparts, the major UK political parties are increasingly expensive to run. In the 1997 general election, the Conservatives spent £28 million, provoking genuine fears about possible bankruptcy. Labour's campaign cost £26 million. After the introduction of limits on spending under the Political Parties, Elections and Referendums Act (2000), the figures fell in 2001: the Conservatives spent £12.75 million, Labour £11 million and the Liberal Democrats £1.36 million.

This situation creates obvious risks. The sums required by the two main parties are still too large to be met by ordinary members. At the same time, though, they are well within the reach of many business concerns. Some of these might want to help a party out of principle. But people with deep pockets and a selfish interest in particular policies can easily be tempted to make a large donation. Even if the donor fails to secure the immediate goal — either pushing through helpful legislation or blocking proposals that endanger profits — a grateful government is likely to bear the donation in mind when drawing up future policies.

New Labour and party funding

The 'sleaze' scandals of the Major years led to the establishment of a Committee on Standards in Public Life (popularly known as the Nolan Committee after its first chairperson). Ironically, although New Labour had posed as a party that was 'whiter than white' on such questions, it was involved in a similar scandal almost as soon as it took office in 1997. By this time it was relying on the trade unions for only 40% of its funding; 55% now came from individual and corporate donors.

Bernie Ecclestone, whose donations to the Labour Party caused controversy

The Formula One motor racing supremo, Bernie Ecclestone, had previously given large sums to the Conservative Party. In late 1997 it emerged that he had switched his generosity to Labour, providing it with £1 million. The story broke after the new government had decided to exempt Formula One from its promised ban on tobacco advertising. Most voters concluded immediately that the policy change had much more to do with the donation than with the estimated tally of job losses arising from the ban. They were more likely to make this assumption because they had previously linked trade union influence over Labour policy with the funding that unions provided.

In its 1997 manifesto Labour had promised an investigation into party funding, and had proposed the following:

> All donations above a certain figure should be publicly disclosed.
> Donations from non-UK individuals and firms should be banned.
> The system of party funding should be subjected to a thorough review.

These ideas, which led to the passage of the Political Parties, Elections and Referendums Act in 2000, were clearly aimed at the Conservative Party. It had been a long-standing beneficiary of overseas donations, and generous gifts and loans from individuals who remained anonymous. Between 1992 and 1997, the party had received 17 donations in excess of £1 million. At the same time, the Conservatives had been able to attack Labour because of its financial dependency on the unions — even though an act of 1984 had forced unions to consult their members on a regular basis before contributing to Labour funds. In the light of the Ecclestone affair, and subsequent revelations that the offices of Tony Blair and Gordon Brown had been financed by a secretive 'blind trust', it seemed that New Labour had only escaped from one generous sectional interest by throwing itself into the hands of another.

State funding

As long ago as 1976, a parliamentary committee recommended the state funding of political parties, but nothing had been done. An independent report of 1981 had recommended a severe cap on individual donations, and argued that the state should match the total raised by each party from its voluntary supporters. When the Committee on Standards in Public Life reported in 1998, it put forward the following proposals, which were less radical, but far-reaching nonetheless:

➤ Donations over £5,000 (£1,000 if given to local parties) should be publicly disclosed.
➤ Anonymous donations over £50 should be banned.
➤ Foreign donations should be banned.
➤ 'Blind trusts' should be outlawed.
➤ Companies proposing to make political donations should ballot their shareholders in advance.
➤ Parties should submit details of their funds and spending to an Electoral Commission.
➤ Parties should spend no more than £20 million on general elections.
➤ Existing state funding for parties should be increased.

The day-to-day activities of the parties were already subsidised out of public funds, through the arrangement known as 'Short money' (after Edward Short, the Labour Leader of the Commons who negotiated the deal in 1975). An amount linked to the number of votes won at the preceding election was given to the parties, to pay for such facilities as secretarial support. Although the Short money itself could not be spent on campaigning, it freed other funds to be spent by the parties on their electoral activities. In addition, local candidates in general elections were subsidised, having the right to hire halls for meetings without charge and to post one election address to each voter.

Although most of the Committee's proposals were implemented in 2000, they did not apply to the 2001 general election. That contest underlined the reliance of the main parties on a few rich individuals. In the months before the election, just three donors gave more than £6 million to Labour, while three donors contributed £11 million out of the £12.4 million given to the Conservatives in this period. Recently there have been demands for even more far-reaching reforms. In 2004, the independent Electoral Commission proposed a cap of £15 million on national spending and a £10,000 limit on individual donations. However, it is possible that such measures could still be bypassed by wealthy individuals giving money in the form of loans.

Party funding aroused controversy after the 2005 general election, when Tony Blair appointed Lord Drayson to a junior ministerial position. Drayson had given £1 million to Labour during 2004, and his links to the government had already been criticised because his company PowderJect had previously won a lucrative contract to supply smallpox vaccine. Whether Drayson was really the best-qualified candidate for the job or not, his appointment did nothing to reassure critics of the existing funding system.

Arguments for state funding

- The major parties would no longer be placed under any kind of obligation to sectional interests.
- The secrecy that surrounds party funding, and brings democracy into discredit, would be removed.
- The parties would no longer be distracted from their central tasks by the need to raise funds.
- Reliable and adequate sources of funding would allow the parties to plan their future activities on a more rational basis. For example, they could give long-term job security to policy researchers.
- It would bring the UK into line with many other European democracies.

Arguments against state funding

- Once accepted as a principle, state funding could be abused by incumbent governments, which might fix the rules to their own advantage.
- Although this kind of reform requires cross-party support, it would be difficult to devise a formula that would satisfy everyone.
- Unless devised carefully, the terms of a reform could be avoided by the same methods that allow wealthy individuals to avoid income tax.
- If funding were linked to the level of support at the previous election, it would tend to reduce the chances of minor parties making a breakthrough.
- While guarding against corruption, reform could prevent idealistic, wealthy individuals from helping unorthodox ideas to win a hearing.
- The results of state funding in other countries have been mixed. In Italy, it was abolished amid claims that it had actually increased corruption.

UK parties and democracy

It can be argued that the major parties have brought most of their current problems on themselves. Having taken the loyalty of voters for granted for too long, they are now looking for the kind of solutions, such as funding by the taxpayer, that would only enjoy widespread support if the parties were still popular. As it is, voters are unlikely to respond favourably to the argument that parties should be bailed out in this way.

Some theorists believe that political parties are a bad thing in themselves, and that direct democracy is the only valid form of government. In a modern, complex society, this view seems unrealistic (see Chapter 1). While the UK remains a representative, liberal democracy, it is difficult to see how electoral politics, and the process of orderly government, could go on without political parties of one kind or another. In this sense, the question 'Do parties enhance or threaten democracy?' answers itself. A more relevant question is: 'Could our existing political parties do a better job of upholding democracy?'

At the beginning of this chapter we drew up a list of party functions. On the basis of our discussion, these functions can be used to decide whether or not parties are an asset or a threat to democracy:

Representation
- The main UK parties do try to build coalitions that represent the interests of significant elements in the population.
- But declining membership and electoral apathy suggests that the parties no longer generate much enthusiasm.

Recruitment of leaders
- The parties still provide national leaders who reach the top by demonstrating their political skills and their electoral appeal.
- But the leaders of the main parties are often accused of being 'out of touch'.

Government
- The parties usually provide stable government, despite periods of uncertainty like the Conservative Party's problems in John Major's second term (1992–97).
- But the appearance of stability is sometimes imposed at the cost of principle, when MPs are forced by party whips to vote against their consciences.

Policy formulation
- In theory ordinary members of the main parties enjoy an important role in designing and endorsing policies.
- But in practice policy-making is firmly under the control of party elites. Leaders often prefer to listen to focus groups made up of non-members.

Participation and mobilisation
- The main parties have tried hard to increase participation and improve the electoral turnout.
- But far from making people more inclined to participate, the parties' efforts seem to have made the public more apathetic.

These considerations suggest that parties are not a positive *asset* to democracy. But this is not to say that they represent an active *threat*. For this to be the case, their poor performance would have encouraged speculation about alternative systems of government (e.g. a dictatorship of some form). Things have yet to reach such a crisis.

However, it is worrying that the main failings of UK parties lie in the areas that are most important for a healthy democratic society — representation and participation. Interestingly, these are the areas that are least under the control of the parties themselves. Nowadays they are trying to attract support from an increasingly diverse and distracted society, and are constantly harassed by powerful media that enjoy many advantages denied to politicians (exercising 'power without responsibility', as Prime Minister Stanley Baldwin complained back in 1931).

Defenders of the existing UK political parties argue that, despite all their handicaps, they tend to produce (relatively) honest, hard-working politicians who genuinely hope to make life better for the majority of citizens. It can be argued that in recent years their critics have made matters worse by making impossible demands. Once politicians find that they are criticised for failings that would be excused in any other walk of life, their sense of distance from 'ordinary' people is bound to increase. In particular, they will find it more difficult to own up to genuine mistakes, and to distinguish the successful media presentation of their spin doctors from real achievements.

Clearly, UK parties could do better in all of their areas of activity. Before answering questions about their performance, though, we need to be sure that the demands we make are realistic, and that their shortcomings are their own fault, rather than merely reflections of wider developments in society.

Summary

UK parties, funding and democracy

➤ In common with parties across most of the Western world, UK political parties have encountered increasing criticism in recent years.

➤ These criticisms arise partly from general trends in society, partly from increasing demands from voters, and partly because of the parties' own conduct.

➤ Other critics have attacked the parties for their fundraising methods. In theory, state funding could help to overcome this difficulty, but the task of devising a fair and workable system is highly problematic.

Suggested reading

Beetham, D., Byrne, I., Ngan, P. and Weir, S., *Democracy under Blair: A Democratic Audit of the United Kingdom* (Politicos, 2002).

Cowley, P. and Fisher, J., 'The Conservative Party', *Politics Review*, vol. 10, no. 2, November 2000.

Cowley, P. and Fisher, J., 'The Liberal Democrats', *Politics Review*, vol. 10, no. 3, February 2001.

Fisher, J., 'The future of British political finance', *Politics Review*, vol. 8, no. 4, April 1999.

Fisher, J., 'Party finance: new rules, same old story?', *Politics Review*, vol. 12, no. 4, April 2003.

Fisher, J. and Cowley, P., 'The Labour Party', *Politics Review*, vol. 10, no. 1, September 2000.

Kelly, R., 'Power in the Conservative Party — towards a new assessment', *Politics Review*, vol. 1, no. 4, April 1992.

Kelly, R., 'Power in the Labour Party — the Blair effect', *Politics Review*, vol. 8, no. 2, November 1998.

Kelly, R., 'Farewell conference, hello forum!', *Politics Review*, vol. 11, no. 1, September 2001.

Kelly, R., 'Tough times for the Tories', *Politics Review*, vol. 13, no. 3, February 2004.

Kelly, R., 'The making of party policy', *Politics Review*, vol. 15, no. 2, November 2005.

Outnwaite, D., 'How should parties be funded?', *Politics Review*, vol. 14, no. 2, November 2004.

Websites

Conservative Party: www.conservatives.com

Electoral Commission: www.electoralcommission.org.uk

Labour Party: www.labour.org.uk

Liberal Democrats: www.libdems.org.uk

Exam focus

Using this chapter and other resources available to you, answer the following questions.

1 What are the functions of political parties?

2 How do the structures of the main parties differ?

3 How do the different parties select their candidates?

4 Compare the ways in which the main parties select their leaders.

5 What role do party conferences have in the main parties?

6 Are UK parties elitist or pluralist? Give reasons for your answer.

7 How are the main parties funded?

8 Why has the funding of political parties become a controversial issue?

9 Discuss the arguments for and against the state funding of political parties.

10 To what extent do political parties enhance or threaten democracy?

Chapter 7

Party ideologies

In the previous chapter we looked at the structures of UK political parties. This chapter argues that our understanding of party conflict is incomplete without an examination of ideas. Ideology is one of the most controversial aspects of political studies and it can be confusing. When approaching the subject two important points must be kept in mind. First, ideological differences go deeper than arguments about the details of policy; and second, when we write about political ideas our job is to understand their nature, even if we happen to disagree with them.

Key questions answered in this chapter
➤ What is ideology?
➤ What are the differences between 'Old' and 'New' Labour?
➤ What are the differences between traditional conservatism and Thatcherism/ New Right ideas?
➤ What are the main beliefs of the Liberal Democrats?
➤ What are the beliefs of the main nationalist parties in the UK?

What is ideology?

An ideology is best understood as *a guiding set of core political, economic and social beliefs or values* (see Box 7.1). These beliefs or values can arise from a variety of sources, such as family background and personal experience. Marxists, for example, argue that beliefs are closely related to a person's economic status (see Box 7.2). Whatever their origins, ideologies have a powerful effect on our reactions to political issues. Even those of us who like to think of ourselves as 'objective' are predisposed to be hostile or friendly towards particular policies and parties because of our existing beliefs.

Box 7.1 The history of 'ideology'

The word 'ideology' was first used at the time of the French Revolution. Originally it was used by people who thought that politics could be studied 'objectively'. In fact, this goal is impossible to achieve because people have core values that shape their view of the world (even if they insist that their ideas represent nothing more or less than plain 'common sense').

Since the nineteenth century, the word has changed its meaning completely. Marxists have always used it as an insult, to attack people who are biased against the interests of the working class. More commonly nowadays, commentators use the word 'ideologue' to describe people whose beliefs are so strong that they will follow them regardless of the consequences. Hence Hitler and Stalin are often depicted as typical ideologues.

Even today some people dislike the word 'ideology'. But values and beliefs are important in politics, whether they are strongly held or not — and ideology is as good a word as any to use when we study them.

Box 7.2 Marxism

More than most ideologies, Marxism has been debated fiercely by its devotees. Fortunately we don't have to look at these controversies in detail because the ideology has had only a marginal impact on political parties in the UK. But despite the popular association between Marxism and conflict, its core premise is a belief that human beings are naturally *cooperative*. Since it stimulates competition between individuals, and results in social and economic inequality, private property is regarded by Marxists as being evil in itself.

Marx himself believed that capitalist states could only ever be run in the interests of the dominant class, regardless of the party in office. He felt that the only hope of establishing a harmonious society lay with the workers, who (he thought) would have no interest in tyrannising others if they took power. So the workers must seize control of the state and use it to abolish property. This could only be achieved through violence because the owners of property would never give up their privileges unless they were forced to do so. But once property had been abolished, human beings could return to their 'natural' state of cooperation. Eventually the state would 'wither away' (as Marx's follower Lenin put it) because there would no longer be any need for laws designed to enforce the control of a dominant class.

In practice, Marxism proved far less benign than the theory suggested. Events in the Soviet Union and elsewhere forced some Marxists to rethink their beliefs, but others argued that Stalin and other leaders had failed to apply the theory properly. This is a typical ideological reaction — after all, people often prefer to blame the weaknesses of other people rather than reassess their own views! In contrast, supporters of the capitalist system have tended to blame the ideology, thus creating a misleading impression of Marxist thinking.

Some people have argued that contrasting beliefs offer the best explanation of political activity as a whole — that parties are groups of people who share common views, and organise to uphold those principles. People who share general principles can disagree about the details of policy, according to their judgement of a specific situation. But they can continue to co-operate because these differences are superficial. The classical expression of this view is the remark of the eighteenth-century conservative Edmund Burke, who wrote that: 'A party is a body of men united for promoting by their joint endeavours the national interest upon some particular principle in which they are all agreed.'

Although this is a fine ideal, it was never a very accurate description of UK political parties. People join parties for a variety of reasons. More importantly, politics, particularly at the highest levels, almost invariably demands compromises. Even ordinary party members have often been asked by their leaders to support policies that go against their fundamental convictions. In particular, Tony Blair's acceptance of Conservative policies on a range of issues has challenged the consciences of many Labour MPs, who joined the party in order to oppose them. In March 2003, 139 Labour MPs voted against the war on Iraq; only Blair's eloquence persuaded other party colleagues to join him in supporting the action.

Tony Blair using all his eloquence to drum up support from Labour MPs for a war against Iraq

At the other extreme, others argue that politics is not about principles at all. On this view, politicians are interested in power only for the status and financial benefits that it can bring. They might talk about their ideals, but only to disguise their real intention to serve the selfish interests of themselves and their closest allies. Needless to say, the people who take this view of politicians tend to be those who are most disillusioned with the profession. A less jaundiced view, often aired by political scientists, is that whatever their personal ideals when they entered the profession, politicians have to work within institutions like Westminster and Whitehall. The traditional values and practices of such institutions have a dramatic effect on the thinking of anyone who is exposed to them for any significant length of time.

A realistic assessment of the role of ideas in politics would place it somewhere between these two extremes. It might just about be possible for politicians to rise to senior positions in their parties without believing a word they are saying. But even they will find it necessary to pretend. No politician wants to be accused of being 'unprincipled', and they usually find it hard even to admit that they have changed their minds. Principles might be irrelevant to them, but they can be vital to party members, who do not face the pressures that force professional politicians to be flexible. Sincerity means a lot to uncommitted voters, too, even if they disagree with the stated views. Equally, people do find their views changing when they work in institutions. Yet people in Whitehall and Westminster do not think exactly alike. In fact, some politicians with very fixed views (such as Margaret Thatcher) seem to have affected government institutions more than those institutions affected them.

Although ideas are still important in UK politics, there is no doubt that the ideological differences between the main parties have narrowed in recent years. There are several reasons for this development, including:

➢ The need to attract the support of 'floating voters' in order to win elections.
➢ The increasing use of focus groups, which give all the main parties a broadly similar picture of the preferences of floating voters.
➢ The tendency of the media to concentrate its critical attention on any radical elements in a party programme, or on real and potential splits within a party, forcing parties which aspire to office to seek the 'middle ground'.
➢ The influence of a globalised economy, which greatly reduces the scope for radical initiatives in economic policy (e.g. rich individuals may leave a country with a high level of income tax, and companies can move production elsewhere if a government increases taxation on business).

These factors tend to mean that the main parties offer broadly similar policies, an important reason why people are becoming increasingly disillusioned with party politics. However, this does not mean that ideas are becoming irrelevant. If anything, the fact that the main parties have broadly similar ideas makes it more important than ever to understand the nature of those ideas.

Summary

What is ideology?

➤ Ideology is 'a guiding set of core political, economic and social beliefs or values'.

➤ Ideological differences do not explain all political disagreements, but they play an important role in most debates and in the formation of political parties.

Political ideologies in the UK

Although there are many competing academic approaches to ideology, our definition suggests that the best starting point is to look closely at the 'core' ideas of each tradition. Ultimately, we can trace different ideologies to contrasting views about human nature. In modern times, the most important UK ideologies have been conservatism, socialism, liberalism and social democracy.

Conservatism

The first important thing to notice is that, like liberalism, conservatism shares its name with that of a political party. There are sound historical reasons for this, but it still gives rise to confusion, which can only be avoided by using a small 'c' when writing about the ideology. When people write about 'Conservatism' with a capital 'C', they are usually implying that the ideology and the beliefs of the party are the same thing. As we shall see, this is not necessarily the case.

As its name suggests, conservative ideology is based on a preference for things as they are, and the view that all change is potentially dangerous. In turn, this usually arises from a particular view of human nature. Traditional conservatives believe that human beings are difficult to predict — it is certainly a mistake to think of them as 'rational', and many are capable of evil. If individual people are so unreliable, no one can know in advance how change will affect society as a whole. So in politics the tried and tested is always to be preferred to an experiment, and plans for radical, far-reaching change forced through in the name of ideas like 'equality' (or even 'freedom') are potentially disastrous.

Most traditional conservatives have a positive view of the state, as the guardian of a stable social order. In an ideal world, it would restrict itself to keeping the peace. But conservatives think that the world is far from ideal, and accept the need for at least some state intervention in the economy when times are hard. They pride themselves on their *pragmatism*, thinking that politicians should never be afraid to change their policies because life never turns out as planned (see Box 7.3).

Box 7.3 Macmillan on politics

'Events, dear boy, events.'

Conservative prime minister Harold Macmillan (1957–63), when asked what he feared most in politics.

Socialism and revisionism

Many people regard Marxism as a variety of socialism, and the ideologies do share a core belief in the cooperative nature of human beings (see Box 7.2). Socialists are also concerned primarily with economic power, believing that equality (or something close to it) is essential in any society that claims to be truly free and fair. They reject the idea of *equality of opportunity* as understood in a capitalist society, because it means that some people will become richer than others. In any case, they argue, it is a misleading idea, because differences in family circumstances will mean that some children have far better life chances than others (see Table 7.1).

The crucial difference is that socialists are much less hostile than Marx and his followers to the state. Indeed, far from thinking that the state should be abolished, social-ists see it as potentially the key instrument in creating social justice. A socialist state would control 'the means of production and exchange' (or at least the most important ones) in the interest of the workers, and would enforce economic equality. While some socialists follow Marx in assuming that such a state could not be established without a violent revolution, later *revisionist* thinkers (or *democratic socialists*) argued that mass democracy can ensure a peaceful road to socialism. Most leaders of the Labour Party have fallen into this 'revisionist' camp; although the party's opponents have freely associ-ated it with revolutionary ideas and intentions, very few Labour MPs have accepted Marx's ideas in full.

Liberalism

Although Marxists go too far when they argue that beliefs are always significantly shaped by economic interests, there is certainly a tendency for people's ideas to reflect their status in society. Traditional conservatism is associated with a rural society, ruled by landed aristocrats. It was given its most eloquent expression when this dominant group came under economic and political attack from the unsettling social forces released by the industrial revolution, beginning in the eighteenth century. Equally, socialism has an obvious appeal for low-paid workers who feel that they are exploited.

Liberalism is usually associated with the interests of the middle classes (the 'bourgeoisie', as Marxists would say). The core principle of *classical liberalism*, which dominated British politics during the Victorian period, is that individuals should be free to do as they wish, not just in economics but in all spheres of activity, unless they do harm to other people. In turn, this is based on the idea that people are *rational* by nature — if they are left alone, they will tend to make the best decisions for themselves. Classical liberals assume that rational individuals will put themselves and their families above all other considerations. Competition is natural and beneficial, particularly in economic matters where it ensures the maximum choice for consumers.

There are obvious connections here, not just with the individualistic spirit that drove the industrial revolution, but with the rise of literacy, and with Protestantism. As such, liberalism seems ideally suited to many countries in the West today, since the idea that everyone's vote should be of equal value is rightly identified with 'liberal democracy' (see Chapter 1) — but it is especially well suited to the UK and the USA. The characteristic liberal concept of *rights*, which human beings are supposed to possess by virtue of their rationality, is upheld in most Western states (see Chapter 12). Ironically, although the Liberal *Party* was out of office for most of the twentieth century, the period can be seen as one of *liberal* dominance in the ideological sphere, whichever party was in power in the UK (see pp. 176–77).

'Classical' and 'new' liberalism

However, during the same years people who regarded themselves as liberals began to disagree on one of the key political issues: the role of the state. *Classical liberals* still regarded the state as at best a necessary nuisance. Governments, they felt, should confine themselves to the establishment and enforcement of laws (mainly to protect private property, but also to safeguard 'rights' in general). In their opinion, high taxation punished the rich and successful, and unless someone was physically or mentally incapable of working, he or she should not be supported in idleness.

This classical version of liberalism was widely accepted in Britain during the Victorian period — at least among the 'political classes', since this was a pre-democratic age. Towards the end of the nineteenth century, however, its appeal began to fade. The emerging *new liberals* still believed in the importance of the free, rational individual, but they had a far more positive attitude towards the state. This arose because the experience of the industrial revolution had led them to doubt whether classical liberalism really guaranteed freedom in any meaningful sense. When people had to devote so much of their lives to work — often in unhealthy conditions — they were in no position to develop as rational individuals. Thus new liberals argued (among other things) for compulsory state education, better working conditions and some public provision to insure workers against ill health, unemployment and old age.

Social democracy and the postwar consensus

The history of liberalism illustrates clearly that ideologies cannot be understood in the abstract. While they help to shape events, they are themselves the products of circumstances. As people respond to developments, they can reach very different conclusions even when they start from similar viewpoints about human nature. In the case of classical and new liberalism, people who share a belief in the free, rational individual can reach conflicting conclusions on a range of vital issues, including the role of the state, economic inequality and the justice of taxation (see Table 7.1).

At the same time, circumstances can make people from different ideological 'families' take a broadly similar view on policy matters. Between 1945 and the mid-1970s something like this happened in the UK, so that the period is often described as one of political *consensus*. Although political disagreements continued during these years, most people were broadly happy with the general policy framework pursued by successive Labour and Conservative governments. Only full-blooded socialists, and classical liberals, were fiercely opposed, for very different reasons.

Clement Attlee's Labour governments of 1945–51 are usually regarded as marking the high point of socialism in the UK. But it makes more sense to characterise the party's policies as revisionist, democratic socialist or (in the more familiar term) social democrat. Like socialists, Labour's leaders regarded the state as a positive force for social justice. But the very fact that a government had been elected with an ambitious programme to help the underprivileged seemed to prove that radical change — including the development of the *welfare state* and the nationalisation of some inefficient industries like the railways — could be secured without violence or far-reaching reforms to the existing institutions of government.

Table 7.1 Attitudes of the major ideologies

Issue	'Classical' liberalism	Socialism	Conservatism	Social democracy/ new liberalism
Competition	Perfectly natural: neither good nor bad in itself	Unnatural	Natural for most but not all: can cause social tension	Natural within limits
Private enterprise	Morally good and economically efficient	Morally destructive and inefficient	Morally neither right nor wrong in itself, but on balance the most efficient economic system	Good within limits
Equality of opportunity	Morally good and guaranteed by free market	Meaningless under capitalism	Morally good in theory, but impossible in practice	Essential in a good society; requires state intervention
Inequality of income	Morally justified and efficient	Morally destructive	Unavoidable and morally justified within limits	Morally destructive unless kept to a minimum
State ownership	Evil and inefficient	Morally justified for all major industries and services	Acceptable for basic utilities	Necessary for basic utilities
Welfare state	Morally dangerous; only permissible to prevent starvation	Morally justified and necessary under capitalism	Morally justified; regrettable necessity	Morally justified and necessary
Private education	Morally acceptable	Morally abhorrent	Morally acceptable	Morally justified only if access open to all

New liberals continued to give priority to individuals rather than society, while Labour's social democrats thought in *collective* terms. This underlying difference in their core principles helps to explain why the declining Liberal Party remained independent from Labour, despite the striking similarity of the policy ideas that arose from their beliefs. Nevertheless, there was very little in the government's programme to unsettle a 'new' liberal. They saw nothing wrong in the state running essential public utilities such as the railways, water, electricity and gas, so long as more 'commercial' enterprises were left alone. In addition, the Attlee government's welfare reforms built on earlier measures introduced by the 'new liberal' governments of H. H. Asquith before the First World War. The creation of the National Health Service (1948) was particularly welcome to new liberals (see Box 7.4).

Box 7.4 **'New' liberalism and the 'postwar consensus'**

To illustrate the close agreement on policy matters between new liberals and social democrats after the Second World War, the two main architects of postwar policy were liberals, whose ideas were warmly embraced by a Labour government dominated by social democrats.

The brilliant economist *John Maynard Keynes* (1883–1946) was almost a stereotype of new liberal thinking. He regarded capitalism as the best system for creating wealth, but appreciated its tendency to lurch from 'booms' to 'busts'. He recommended policies that promised to iron out the peaks and the troughs, resulting in a more stable upward curve of prosperity. Fiercely opposed by the Treasury at first, his policies gradually won acceptance as the best way of saving capitalism from itself.

The social scientist *William Beveridge* (1879–1963) was a dynamic civil servant who was asked to head an official inquiry into social services during the Second World War. His report, published in 1942, caused an immediate sensation. It promised to protect British citizens from 'Five Giants': poverty, ignorance, want, squalor and idleness. Together with Keynes, Beveridge strongly influenced government proposals aiming at full employment, and his report pointed the way towards the creation of a postwar welfare state.

For their part, traditional conservatives could not be impressed by claims that the Labour reforms would create a 'new Jerusalem'. As we have seen, conservatives are deeply sceptical about any plan to make the world radically better. But after two world wars and many years of unprecedented social upheavals, most traditional conservatives were willing to accept any ideas that promised to bring some stability, and they had no principled objection to the increase in state activity. Over time, members of the Conservative Party who thought like this became known as *one-nation Conservatives*.

From Table 7.1 we can understand why social democrats, new liberals and even traditional conservatives could accept the outlines of the postwar consensus, and why socialists and classical liberals disliked it so much. This provides a crucial background for understanding more recent developments.

The breakdown of consensus

One reason why members of different ideological families could support the policies of the postwar consensus was that they suited the circumstances of the UK at that time. More exactly, they promised to prevent a gradual decline in economic strength from developing into an overwhelming crisis for the UK. Thus, the welfare system protected people from economic hardship, and consumer demand could be increased by the Treasury through changes in the tax system, to prevent prolonged recessions. To the majority of observers, these policies seemed only sensible because the effects of the Second World War had underlined the weakness of the UK's economy in relation to its competitors.

However, as memories of the war began to fade, living standards improved for most citizens. As a result, it seemed that the liberal/social democratic consensus had achieved its main objective and was set to become a permanent fixture. Future general elections would not be about ideological differences at all, but instead would revolve around the relative abilities of the two main parties to implement the policies upon which most people were broadly agreed.

All this changed after the worldwide economic crisis that began in 1973, when oil prices soared as a result of conflict in the Middle East. Arguably, the impact of the resulting inflation was most serious of all in the UK, since the country had been falling behind its competitors for so long (Britain's own oil reserves in the North Sea had yet to be exploited). The Conservative Party lost power in 1974, and Labour could do nothing to stop inflation. The ideas of the consensus suddenly seemed impotent. After all, they had been designed to stop a bad situation getting worse, yet the UK had been plunged into a full-scale crisis without warning, and neither of the main parties seemed to have an answer. The time was ripe for alternative views to win renewed attention.

Key terms

➢ **Classical liberalism.** The belief that all human beings are competitive, and that the rational pursuit of self-interest is natural.

➢ **Conservatism.** The belief that human beings require strong leadership and a stable framework of laws because the vast majority are incapable of independent rational behaviour.

➢ **Rights.** Fundamental freedoms possessed or claimed by a country's citizens. In particular, they are associated with liberal democracies such as the UK, where many rights (e.g. the right to free speech) are protected by law.

➢ **Social democracy/new liberalism.** The belief that human beings have a natural sense of justice, and that the best form of society is one that fosters a genuine equality of opportunity for all.

➢ **Socialism.** The belief that human beings are naturally cooperative. Private enterprise causes conflict and should be abolished; production should be organised by the state in order to satisfy need.

Summary

British political ideologies

➤ The fortunes of ideologies are tied closely to circumstances.

➤ Specific policy ideas arising from ideologies can change, but the basic core principles remain the same.

➤ It is a mistake to assume that parties always stick to their ideological traditions.

➤ In the modern UK, the most important ideological groups in all parties have been classical and new liberals and social democrats. Traditional conservatives and socialists have played only a marginal role.

Thatcherism and the modern Conservative Party

The emergence of Thatcherism

When Margaret Thatcher became leader of the Conservative Party in 1975 she was opposed by many of her senior colleagues. She had served in the cabinet of Edward Heath (1970–74) apparently without objecting to consensus policies. But privately her opposition to one-nation Conservatives like Heath amounted to something like contempt.

There was nothing original about 'Thatcherism'. Even the certainty with which Mrs Thatcher held her convictions would have been no surprise to the Victorians. Some have argued that Mrs Thatcher's beliefs were an odd mixture — that she combined unflinching support for individualism with a belief in a strong state (see Box 7.5). Yet this, too, would have been a familiar position to Victorian liberals. Like them, Mrs Thatcher thought that the state should concentrate on the maintenance of law and order. At times of economic distress, rather than intervene in the economy, nineteenth-century governments inspired by classical liberalism had not hesitated to repress social discontent.

We have argued already that no senior politician can ever act in complete accordance with his or her core principles: compromise is inevitable from time to time. If we take this into account and run down the checklist of classical liberal principles in Table 7.1, Mrs Thatcher gains a strong 'pass' mark in every category. She believed that people were naturally competitive; that private enterprise was morally justified because it rewarded effort and produced greater prosperity than any conceivable alternative; that attempts to reduce inequality were deplorable because redistribution of wealth through taxation meant the confiscation of the just rewards for effort; that no one should be denied opportunities, but that the gifted would find their way to the top without any direct assistance from the state; that the welfare state was morally corrupting and actively deterred people from looking after themselves; and that private education was perfectly justified because consumers should be free to spend their money as they like.

Some commentators have argued that Thatcherism was just another variety of conservatism. To do so, however, flies in the face of clear evidence. If we look again at the core values of conservatism and classical liberalism, we can see that they are very strongly opposed (see Box 7.6). Ultimately, the disagreement between the two traditions arises from views of human nature that could hardly be more different. It would be an exaggeration to say that traditional conservatism was destroyed by Mrs Thatcher. Given its origins in an aristocratic, rural society, its appeal had been declining for many years. People who thought of themselves as traditional conservatives did tend to stay loyal to the party after 1975, but only because they had no other political refuge. Whether they are aware of the fact or not, it makes sense to place those who agreed with the Conservative Party's principles after 1975 firmly in the classical liberal camp.

Box 7.5 Margaret Thatcher's classical liberalism

Perhaps the best evidence of Mrs Thatcher's classical liberalism is her much-quoted remark that there is 'no such thing as society'. Taken at face value, this shows an extreme commitment to the individual, but the real meaning of the words has been disputed. Fortunately, there are many other quotations that illustrate her views.

➤ 'Without the strong, who would provide for the weak? When you hold back the successful you penalise those who need help.' (1978)

➤ 'Some socialists seem to believe that people should be numbers in a state computer. We believe they should be individuals.' (1975)

➤ '[Victorian values] were values when our country became great.' (1982)

The last quotation is particularly interesting as an indication of how ideological commitment can shape our view of history. It would be far more accurate to say that 'Victorian values' were a *product* of Britain's economic power, rather than the cause of it as Mrs Thatcher obviously thought.

Box 7.6 Differences between traditional conservatism and Thatcherism

Traditional conservatism	Thatcherism
➤ hostility towards radical change	➤ strong support for radical change
➤ suspicion of individualism	➤ fixation on the individual
➤ fear of excessive liberty	➤ love of liberty, particularly in economics
➤ acceptance of welfare state	➤ hostility towards welfare state
➤ desire for cooperation with unions and other pressure groups	➤ hostility towards unions and other pressure groups
➤ affection for local government	➤ hostility towards local government

Despite her remarkable success as Conservative leader, Mrs Thatcher remains a highly controversial figure. Her downfall in November 1990 can be traced directly to her views. She disliked the system of rates to pay for local government services because it allowed the poor to vote for increased services without bearing more than a small fraction of the cost. But the community charge, or poll tax, that she introduced was widely opposed because it meant that rich and poor under the same local authority would pay the same for council services.

Although the unpopularity of the poll tax was the main reason for Mrs Thatcher's departure from office, the leadership election was actually triggered by her opposition to deeper European integration. None of the major continental governments was socialist at the time, but Mrs Thatcher was convinced that closer cooperation with them would endanger her record of 'rolling back the state' in the UK. In short, economic liberalism was both her inspiration and her nemesis.

The Conservative Party after Thatcher

Since 1990 the Conservative Party has remained true to Mrs Thatcher's legacy. Between 1990 and 1997 the state was 'rolled back' still further, through the sale of nationalised industries like the railways. Conservative ministers continued to attack 'scroungers', who allegedly preferred life on state benefits to holding down a job. The poll tax was replaced, but there was no return to the rating system. There were none of the spectacular reductions of income tax that had marked the Thatcher years, but the Conservatives continued to present themselves as the party of low taxation and they did make modest cuts when resources allowed.

Since 1997 the Conservatives have struggled to get their message across. To a considerable extent, they are victims of the history of their ideology. The classical liberals of the nineteenth century were able to sound a confident note because they lived at a time when most people agreed on the 'correct' standards of moral conduct. So when the classical liberals argued on behalf of freedom in both economic and social terms, they could safely ignore the possibility that more than a small minority might take this as a signal to embark on 'experimental' lifestyles.

Today's social context is very different. Logically, as classical liberals the Conservatives should advocate the maximum freedom for individuals in all spheres of life. Some of them do. But others are unwilling to take a step which would decriminalise many activities that they find distasteful, such as drug-taking. Equally, the theory of classical liberalism gives no reason to oppose mass immigration. Within obvious limits required by national security, people ought to be free to move just as they like. However, Mrs Thatcher spoke out against the supposed threat of being 'swamped' by people from other cultures, and most of her supporters agreed with her view that immigration should be greatly reduced, if not ended entirely.

Many critics claim that such views betray a lingering streak of traditional conservatism within the party bearing that name. However, we have seen that traditional conservatives have misgivings about all sources of social instability, whereas Thatcherites oppose specific developments while accepting others (notably rising economic inequality) with enthusiasm. The fact that some Conservative Party members continue to oppose certain social freedoms while accepting the free market is something of a puzzle, because there is clearly a link between the two. What is clear is that this tension underlying the policies of the Conservative Party has contributed to its unpopularity in recent years. This was recognised in 2002 by the then party chair Theresa May, who admitted that its stance on issues like homosexuality made people think of the Conservatives as 'the nasty party'. It is also more appropriate to argue that many Conservatives today oppose mass immigration because of *nationalism*, rather than distinctive conservative ideology. As is argued below (pp. 177–79), members of many ideological families can exhibit nationalistic tendencies.

The Conservatives and the 2005 general election

Mrs Thatcher herself did not feature in the 2005 general election campaign. But this did not mean that the party had changed its ideological stance. After all, its leader, Michael Howard, had been an enthusiastic supporter of Mrs Thatcher when she held office.

If the party's platform had a single unifying theme, it was the idea of increasing choice for the individual. This was illustrated by the familiar Conservative Party promise to cut taxes when circumstances allowed, giving 'hard-working families' extra options. Although the party pledged to match Labour's promised spending on health and education, it argued that these essential public services would need to be reformed to widen choice and maximise efficiency. In true Thatcherite style, the Conservatives also emphasised the scope for savings through significant cuts in state bureaucracy.

One eye-catching element of the 2005 Conservative programme was its pledge to link the value of the state pension to average earnings rather than the rate of inflation. This policy, which was likely to make pensioners better off in future, was clearly dictated by the fact that existing pensioners were more likely to vote than other age-groups, and to support the Conservatives. The proposed change was purely tactical, and would actually have reversed a decision taken under Mrs Thatcher for the ideological purpose of reducing public spending.

Summary

Thatcherism and the modern Conservative Party

➤ Within the Conservative Party, Thatcherism is best understood as a revival of classical liberalism.

➤ It has dominated the party since the perceived failure of the new liberal/social democratic consensus that previous Conservative leaders had accepted.

From 'Old' to New Labour

In 1997 the Conservatives were swept from office by Tony Blair and New Labour. The reasons for the landslide defeat were complex, but the most notable were the Major government's loss of a reputation for economic competence, and repeated allegations of financial and sexual misconduct by ministers. Yet one should not discount ideological factors. In particular, many voters now feared that, because of their classical liberal principles, the Conservatives could not be trusted to preserve the National Health Service and other popular public services.

Before winning the 1979 general election, Mrs Thatcher had played down her radical intentions in case many voters took fright. To some, it seemed that Tony Blair carried off the same trick in 1997, and that the new government would show its true 'socialist' colours as soon as it was in power. But it soon became clear that Blair was perfectly sincere when he promised that his government would govern as New Labour. The Conservatives found it difficult to present convincing arguments against a man who broadly accepted most of the key assumptions of their own classical liberalism.

The origins of New Labour

The Labour Party had certainly travelled a long way since it lost power in 1979. Until the late 1980s it was torn by ideological strife, between activists who wanted to make it into the fully socialist organisation that it had never been, and moderates who called themselves social democrats but who were difficult to distinguish from new liberals.

Social democrats within the Labour Party had always felt confident that they could water down any socialist ideas proposed by more radical members. This was particularly true after the 1950s when they began to argue that capitalism did not need to be abolished because its worst aspects had already been reformed. This new, sophisticated *revisionism* suggested that socialism was irrelevant because economic power had already passed peacefully from the owners of capital to professional managers. The old antagonism between classes was therefore fading away and Britons could look forward to a harmonious, just society without a revolutionary upheaval.

This position cut no ice with Labour's socialists. Even before the 1979 defeat, they were arguing (like the supporters of Thatcherism) that the new liberal/social democratic consensus had failed, so it was time for a radical new direction. Michael Foot, leader between 1980 and 1983, tried to sustain a compromise position between Labour's socialists and social democrats. But for many in the party there could be no halfway house. Four senior revisionist figures left to establish the Social Democratic Party (SDP) in 1981; they were soon joined by 25 Labour MPs (and one Conservative).

The hopes of the SDP came to an end in 1982, when the Falklands War transformed Mrs Thatcher's public standing. In the 1983 general election the new party (in alliance with the Liberals) nearly matched Labour in its share of the national vote, but it was a long way behind in terms of seats. The threat to Labour's position as a major national party was not over, but the episode had taught some valuable lessons. If Labour wanted to form a future government, it seemed that its leaders would have to make a decisive break with socialism, instead of talking like socialists and acting like social democrats, as they had in the past.

The road to New Labour

After the 1983 election Labour chose the dynamic (but increasingly moderate) Neil Kinnock as leader. Kinnock confronted his socialist critics within the party and eventually destroyed their power. Unfortunately for him, his public image never recovered from bitter attacks launched against him by Mrs Thatcher's allies in the press. Thus, although Kinnock did much to modernise his party, it was left to his successors to reap the rewards (see Box 7.7).

In 1992, a fourth consecutive general election defeat inspired forecasts of everlasting opposition for Labour. Kinnock resigned immediately. His successor, John Smith, took steps to remove one of the main grievances of the SDP defectors, abolishing the *block vote* used by the trade unions at party conferences (see Chapter 6). Although Smith died after only 2 years as leader, his contribution to Labour's revival should not be underestimated. He spoke with conviction about social justice, and this moral commitment helped him both to retain the loyalty of members who might otherwise have abandoned the party, and to persuade union leaders to back his reforms.

Neil Kinnock, Labour Party leader, making a speech in 1987

Box 7.7 Landmarks on the road to New Labour

1976: James Callaghan tells the party conference that high public expenditure to counter the impact of recession is 'no longer an option'. Widely seen as a decisive break from the economic ideas of the 'consensus' years.

1981: SDP defections threaten Labour's future as potential party of government. Denis Healey, backed by party moderates, beats the socialist Tony Benn for post of deputy leader.

1983: Neil Kinnock becomes leader, with social democrat Roy Hattersley as his deputy.

Mid-1980s: Kinnock purges party of 'militant' socialists.

Late 1980s: policy review. Kinnock drops commitment to unilateral nuclear disarmament.

1993: changes in procedure for leadership ballots. Trade unions and constituency parties to hold ballots of individual members (one member, one vote) before backing candidates for office or voting on key policy decisions at the party conference.

1995: party agrees to abandon commitment to nationalisation (Clause IV).

Smith's successor, Tony Blair, was well placed to complete Labour's transition into 'SDP Mark II'. The original SDP had now disbanded, and many of its former members were welcomed back into the Labour fold. Labour's remaining socialists had been crushed long before Blair's 1997 election victory, which made his reforms unassailable. He had even managed to cajole his party into giving up its historic commitment to state ownership — the policy known as *Clause IV*, which had deterred many new liberals from joining Labour (see Box 6.3 on p. 145).

Yet Labour's social democrats, who continued to look back to the Attlee government for inspiration, had new reasons to feel uneasy. Blair won his battle over nationalisation largely because his personal popularity with uncommitted voters promised to end Labour's long years of opposition since 1979. At the time, social democrats rejoiced because they shared Blair's view that Labour would never regain power until it was able to deny any charge that it was still a socialist party.

But in his anxiety to turn his back on the past, Blair made commitments that went beyond social democracy and new liberalism. He pledged that his party would not increase income tax rates for the better off — despite the fact that this meant retaining Mrs Thatcher's tax cuts, which had previously been denounced by Labour as immoral. There would be no reversal of privatisation, public schools were in no danger at all (Blair himself was a product of one), and Conservative union reforms would be modified but not repealed. Blair went out of his way to befriend staunch classical liberals like the newspaper proprietor Rupert Murdoch, and he even praised Margaret Thatcher. New Labour had not been in office for many months before veteran social democrats who had stayed loyal to Labour throughout the difficult 1980s, such as the former deputy leader Roy Hattersley, began to launch ideological attacks on the prime minister. In turn, these critics were dismissed as relics of what became known as 'Old' Labour (see Box 7.8).

Box 7.8 Differences between 'Old' and New Labour

'Old' Labour believes...	New Labour believes...
in state ownership	in a public/private mix; preference for the latter
in a significant reduction of economic inequality	in equality of opportunity regardless of outcome
that unemployment is a greater evil than inflation	that, on balance, inflation is a greater evil than unemployment
in an intimate link with unions	that unions should be kept at arm's length
that business interests should be kept at arm's length	that business interests should be courted
that constitutional change is relatively unimportant	that constitutional change should be a high priority
that it is better to lose elections than abandon fundamental principles	that politics, ultimately, is about winning elections

Just as Mrs Thatcher's allies had derided traditional conservatives as 'wets', Blair's supporters used 'Old' Labour as a term of abuse to identify any member of the party who disagreed with the leadership. It encompassed people like Hattersley and the socialist figurehead Tony Benn, who had fought each other bitterly since 1979. After 1997 they found themselves in uncomfortable agreement, in their criticisms of Blair if not in their suggested policy alternatives.

A new consensus?

So is Blair a classical liberal? Are the 'Thatcherites' still in power, trading under a different name long after the public thought they had been consigned to history? Is there, in fact, a new consensus in the UK, embracing both of the parties with a realistic chance of forming a government and thus depriving voters who disagree with classical liberalism of a meaningful choice?

At the time of writing, these questions still cannot be answered with complete confidence. As we have seen, the subject of ideology is riddled with problems of definition. We have put forward the view that differing interpretations of human nature lie at the heart of these questions. On this score, Tony Blair would provide a better fit with new liberalism than with the classical variant (see Box 7.9). While Mrs Thatcher and her allies regretted that the welfare state had ever been invented, Blair clearly believes that the better-off in society have a duty to help the disadvantaged, and he does not think that this can be achieved through private charity only, as Thatcherites tend to do. His government has also

Box 7.9 The Third Way

Tony Blair has made various attempts to produce an eye-catching label to encapsulate his beliefs and distinguish them from Thatcherism, socialism and social democracy. The 'Third Way' is the best-known label, because academics and thinkers friendly to Blair have tried hard to define it, while his critics have found it easy to scoff at. It is, indeed, a most elusive concept.

Probably the most important thing about the Third Way for students of ideology in the UK is the fact that Blair thought it necessary in the first place to find a new name for his beliefs. We have seen that new liberalism has much in common with social democracy, and that both of these positions could be seen as a 'third way' because they represent a compromise that would 'humanise' the capitalist system. One can understand why Blair does not want to call himself a new liberal. But his uneasiness with the social democratic label is highly significant because it would have connected him to an honourable tradition within his own party. In fact, Blair's Third Way is really a fourth one — a compromise between revisionist social democracy and classical liberalism. Some moderate members of the Conservative Party, influenced by European Christian democracy, provided a suitable name for this approach some time ago — the 'social market'. But despite his deep religious convictions Blair has not accepted this label either, making him even more difficult to pin down. His evident desire to escape identification with any established tradition of political ideology probably reflects an unwillingness to alienate any potential supporters.

Box 7.10 **Ideology and the 2001 and 2005 general elections**

Some observers argued that the mass voter abstentions in the 2001 general election were the product of a lack of ideological choice. Labour and the Conservatives had presented broadly similar policies on key subjects like taxation, education, health, pensions and law and order.

The big difference between the two main parties concerned their attitudes to Europe, and in particular the single currency. Yet opinions on this issue cut across ideological lines, and many socialists were as hostile to the EU as the classical liberals in the Conservative Party. Meanwhile, although the Liberal Democrats argued for an increase in income tax in 2001, few voters regarded them as serious candidates for office. In any case, the Liberal Democrats were not recommending that the rate of tax should rise to anything like the level it had been in the mid 1980s.

If anything, the 2005 contest revealed even less ideological division. All three main parties broadly agreed on the issues that divided them in the 1980s:

➤ They concurred that the free market economy was by far the most efficient generator of wealth.

➤ None of the parties argued for substantial increases in taxation to redistribute wealth (the Liberal Democrat proposal for a new 50% higher rate was far below the level for top earners in the mid 1980s).

➤ All the parties agreed that there should be more funding for key public services, such as health and education.

➤ They all echoed public concern about antisocial behaviour.

➤ Although the Conservatives' proposals on immigration and asylum were attacked by their opponents, all the parties wanted to see firmer action against people who entered the country illegally.

➤ The Liberal Democrats showed the greatest concern for the environment, but none of the parties was prepared to take radical measures against the threat of global warming.

The most striking evidence of basic ideological agreement was the extent to which the two largest parties concentrated their campaigning on personal attacks against the respective leaders, the Tories branding Blair a 'liar' and Labour accusing Michael Howard of harbouring a secret, extremist policy agenda.

enforced a minimum wage, which demonstrates the prime minister's belief that the demands of the free market should give way when the alternative is blatant exploitation of low-paid workers. He has also committed his government to abolishing child poverty, though this goal is more closely associated with his chancellor, Gordon Brown.

Yet there is still room for doubt. Differing opinions about human nature give rise to various ideas of the kind of society we would like to live in. Blair would obviously prefer a society governed in accordance with social justice. However, before the election, Blair denied that there is anything wrong with economic inequality. Indeed, he would be happy to see the gap between rich and poor grow wider. This belief cannot easily be squared with new liberalism, let alone with social democracy. It is the sort of development that makes even traditional conservatives uneasy. Before he became prime minister, Blair had himself attacked those who tolerated rising inequality.

Labour and the 2005 general election

After the 2001 general election the Blair government increased spending on public services, notably in the key areas of health and education. This was compatible with a social democratic approach. But much of the money was raised through an increase in national insurance, which affected the low-paid as well as the rich. The government also distributed wealth to the poorest in society, but this was not enough to stop, let alone reverse, the trend towards greater economic inequality.

Much of the discussion during the run-up to the 2005 election concerned the relationship between Tony Blair and his chancellor, Gordon Brown. It was widely understood that Brown was more sympathetic than his leader towards the social democratic tradition. However, the party's manifesto once again ruled out income tax increases for the better off, even though many commentators believed that some taxes would have to rise after the election. Brown also accepted an increased role for the private sector in the provision of public services.

In 2004 Blair announced that he would retire at some point after the election, and despite their uneasy personal relationship it was assumed that Brown would succeed him. But to judge from the party's manifesto, supported by both Brown and Blair, there was unlikely to be any radical change of policy. Labour's proposals in areas like immigration, asylum and crime were broadly similar to the tougher measures promised by the Conservatives, and were clearly a response to the perceived demands of the electorate. After the election Blair argued for a restoration of respect in most spheres of life, almost in the manner of John Major's 1993 promise to bring Britain 'Back to Basics'. The party's concern to stamp out antisocial behaviour and to introduce identity cards echoed the kind of authoritarian policies that had earned the Conservatives the reputation of being 'the nasty party'.

Summary

From 'Old' to New Labour

➢ Within the Labour Party, the ideas of the new liberal/social democratic consensus are still popular, but the present leadership is strongly attracted by many of the core values of classical liberalism.

➢ The eclipse of the traditional debate within the Labour Party is signified by the tendency of commentators to lump social democrats (and the few remaining socialists in the Labour Party) into the category of 'Old' Labour, even though these people have different ideas about human nature.

Liberal Democrats

Until recently, commentators paid little attention to the ideas of the Liberal Democrats because, despite their respectable support among the electorate, they won few parliamentary seats. It was too often assumed that the party had no ideological identity of its own, and merely tried to 'split the difference' between Labour and the Conservatives.

However, it can be argued that since the merger of the Liberals and the Social Democratic Party (SDP) in 1988 the Liberal Democrats have been more consistent in their ideological outlook than the other two main parties. Indeed, this consistency can be traced much further back, to before the Second World War, when the old Liberal Party embraced new liberalism, rejecting the classical variant. We have seen that new liberalism is broadly similar to social democratic ideas, so the merger between the two parties was a natural development accepted by the overwhelming majority of their members. The main disagreements arose over questions which were practical rather than ideological, such as the effectiveness of nuclear weapons as a deterrent against attack.

The SDP was founded in 1981, mainly as a result of fears that the Labour Party was coming under the control of hard-line socialists. At the same time, the Conservative Party was embracing classical liberalism under Mrs Thatcher. This polarisation between the two main parties left the Liberals and the SDP as a moderate alternative — a natural home for disillusioned voters. But this position had not been adopted for tactical reasons: the Liberal–SDP alliance monopolised the middle ground of UK politics because the other parties had moved away from a position which they had all shared until the breakdown of the consensus. Opinion surveys repeatedly showed that its ideas were shared by a majority of British people, but the effects of the party system (see Chapter 4) condemned it to political impotence.

Under the leadership of Paddy Ashdown (1988–99) it looked as if the Liberal Democrats would serve in a coalition with New Labour if it failed to secure an overall parliamentary majority. This idea came to nothing because Blair won so easily in 1997, and had no need of a coalition partner. Although Blair often spoke of forging a permanent 'progressive alliance' with the Liberal Democrats, after 1997 there was increasing friction between the parties, which in part reflected ideological differences. As we have seen, New Labour has adopted many of the classical liberal ideas of the Conservative Party. As a result, the Liberal Democrats have attracted several high-profile defectors from Labour, including the former MP Brian Sedgemore who joined the party during the 2005 general election campaign.

The Liberal Democrats and the 2005 general election

In 2001 the Liberal Democrats argued for a small increase in the basic rate of income tax to pay for improved public services. The Conservatives and New Labour attacked the proposal, although in recent years both parties have increased the tax burden in other ways, even for average earners. In 2005, the Liberal Democrats advocated a new higher rate of 50% on earnings of over £100,000 per year. This was a modest proposal, which would have been accepted by most Thatcherites until 1988, when the rate was cut to 40%. Once again, though, the idea was attacked by Labour and the Conservatives on the grounds that it would reduce the incentive to work hard — an argument characteristic of classical liberals.

In 2005 the Liberal Democrats argued that the extra money raised by taxation would pay for care for the elderly, and proposed scrapping Labour's policy of charging university students for their tuition fees. The party also promised to oppose Labour's plans to introduce a system of identity cards. This was a reminder of the traditional Liberal/Liberal Democrat concern for the freedom of the individual. Although the party wanted to increase overall government expenditure, there was also an echo of hostility towards an over-intrusive state in the proposal to abolish the Department of Trade and Industry.

However, during the election campaign these domestic issues were overshadowed by the party's stand against the Iraq war. Some commentators claimed that this was a tactical decision on the part of Charles Kennedy, the Liberal Democrat leader. However, his party had a longstanding commitment to international law and the United Nations. As in other respects, the electoral dividends gained by the Liberal Democrats because of the Iraq war can be attributed to principle rather than opportunism. This even applies to its support for changing to a proportional electoral system, since Liberal Democrats argue that the votes of all individuals should have equal weight. The remaining question is whether the party will continue to base its policies on traditional liberal priciples if it ever achieves a decisive breakthrough and begins to be considered as a serious contender for office. Whatever its lofty stance at the national level, it has often been accused of adopting dubious tactics when it has a chance of winning by-elections.

Nationalism in the UK

No account of ideology in UK politics could be complete without a reference to nationalism. Nationalism is best defined as *a belief in one's country's national independence and self-determination*. Parties like the Scottish National Party (SNP), Plaid Cymru in Wales, and Northern Ireland's Sinn Fein pursue distinctively nationalistic agendas. In addition, the most passionate arguments within the Conservative Party are those of nationalistic 'Eurosceptics', such as Lady Thatcher herself.

We have already suggested that the easy equation of ideology with 'extremist' or noisy politics is highly misleading. It is an echo of the old tendency to call anyone an 'ideologue' if we do not like the person's views. It may well be accurate to call some of the loudest nationalists 'extreme', but are they ideologues, in the sense we have described here?

We have argued that ideology is best understood as a set of basic principles, arising from particular views of human nature. Typically these ideas inspire some kind of vision of the best form of political association, addressing questions such as: how much freedom should the citizens enjoy, and how should they contribute to the costs of government (or, as an anarchist would ask, should there be a government at all)?

If we tried to locate some common themes among nationalists, we would get little further than noticing their belief that specific communities should govern themselves. Only rarely do nationalists in different communities agree on anything beyond this, and indeed they often disagree about what constitutes a 'nation'; this can be based on geographical boundaries, language, culture or other factors. As Box 7.11 shows, the UK contains nationalist parties with sharply contrasting views on key subjects such as the role of the state, social justice and tolerance. It is even possible for sincere-sounding nationalists in one country to deny self-determination to similar movements abroad. For example, in the 1950s French nationalists were strong supporters of war against the Algerian independence movement. More recently, the Serbian nationalist Slobodan Milosevic used violence in an attempt to repress separatist movements elsewhere in the former Yugoslavia.

Even nationalists within the same community can disagree violently on the best kind of institutional arrangements once independence has been won (or a threat to established 'national sovereignty' beaten off). For example, nationalist feelings in Scotland were encouraged during the 1980s by resentment at the fact that Conservative policies, imposed from Westminster, seemed to hit hardest north of the border. One might expect that Scottish nationalists would have turned violently

---

| Box 7.11 | Prominent UK nationalist parties and their key 2005 general election proposals |

British National Party (BNP): An end to all immigration and multiculturalism; withdrawal from the European Union; the restoration of capital punishment.

Plaid Cymru, the Party of Wales: A full parliament for Wales, rather than the present assembly; greater environmental protection and better living standards for all Welsh people; a 50% tax rate on incomes over £50,000 per year.

Scottish National Party (SNP): A stronger Scottish parliament, leading to full independence; Scottish control over North Sea oil revenues; opposition to Labour's plans for the abolition of Scottish army regiments; greater social justice in Scotland.

Sinn Fein: A united Ireland and the withdrawal of British troops from Northern Ireland; an end to discrimination on any grounds; greater social justice.

UK Independence Party (UKIP): Withdrawal from the European Union; new restrictions on asylum and an end to economic immigration except in 'very exceptional circumstances'; crackdown on crime; big reductions in state bureaucracy.

against classical liberal economic ideas, and in 2005 the SNP advocated many policies which would have been endorsed by 'Old' Labour. But for many years they drew support from people known as 'Tartan Tories', who agreed wholeheartedly with the economic policies of the Conservative Party.

It seems, on due reflection, that nationalism is a little like feminism (see Box 7.12) and environmentalism (see Box 7.13 overleaf). That is, it is not *in itself* a distinctive ideology, but rather a belief that can be held in tandem with a range of views about the best kind of human association. Some forms of nationalism, like fascism, have become attached to distinctive ideas about the best way to run a state. Membership of the German Nazi Party implied agreement with these views, which arose from a (perverted) interpretation of human nature. Thus fascism seems to qualify as an ideology, on our terms, although thankfully it has had a minimal effect on internal UK politics. But with most other nationalist movements, we are dealing with members of more than one ideological 'family'. Their underlying disagreements on fundamental political questions would emerge as soon as they achieved self-determination.

Box 7.12 Feminism

The achievements of the feminist movement in the UK have been considerable. However, it is doubtful whether many of the remarkable advances in the economic and legal status of women can be attributed to followers of a distinct feminist ideology. Most people who support the feminist movement do so as part of a broader ideological allegiance. In other words, for example, there are liberals who think that no society is fair unless women enjoy equal opportunities; and there are socialists who believe that capitalism invariably exploits women. But consistent liberals believe that *everyone* can and should enjoy equality of opportunity, regardless of their sex or ethnic origin. Similarly, consistent socialists believe that under capitalism *everyone* is exploited. So to call these people 'liberal feminists' or 'socialist feminists' seems unnecessarily cumbersome. They simply carry their liberalism and socialism to its logical conclusion. In fact, most of Labour's female MPs are obviously liberals, who press for reform within the existing capitalist system.

According to our view of ideology, only *radical feminists* qualify as members of a truly distinctive tradition. Their views, which focus on the aggressive nature of men, point towards the segregation of the sexes. They continue to argue for radical social and political reform, whereas other self-styled moderate feminists seem broadly satisfied with recent changes. Indeed, some commentators now talk of an era of postfeminism, in which many women even seem tolerant of hardcore pornography.

The end of ideology?

For more than a century, and despite the existence of various party labels, liberalism has dominated political debate in most Western states. The UK is a key example of this.

In 1992 the American writer Francis Fukuyama published a book that heralded an end of ideology. Taking the view that major historical events had arisen from clashes of principle, he argued that the ever-increasing popularity of Western liberalism across the world promised an era of relative peace and prosperity for all. This closure of ideological conflict would thus bring an 'end to history', as defined by Fukuyama.

Since 1992 the world has not exactly been peaceful, and this seems enough to dispense with Fukuyama's claims. But our discussion has revealed an even more telling objection. As a citizen of the United States, which was founded on liberal values, Fukuyama apparently thought that liberalism was not an ideology at all; it was just a common-sense approach to life. By contrast, we can see that it is simply one among many ways of interpreting the world. The evidence of this chapter suggests that the operation of democracy in the UK has tended to reinforce the attraction of liberalism for the main parties; after all, the idea of 'one person, one vote' is highly individualistic, and parties tend to assume that the best way of winning support from 'rational' individuals is to present them with policies which will benefit themselves and their families rather than the community as a whole. However, since the fortunes of ideologies are closely tied to circumstances, there is no way of telling whether the twenty-first century will 'belong' to liberalism, or whether some other ideology will rise to take its place.

Box 7.13 Environmentalism

In some respects, environmentalism resembles feminism. It is perfectly possible for members of the traditional ideological 'families' to have a serious concern for the environment, although this does fit rather better with some ideologies (notably conservatism) than with others. Liberals and socialists, for example, have tended to concentrate on the way in which wealth is distributed, and have claimed that their own way of running an economy would ensure the greatest prosperity for the greatest number. Thus Tony Blair has regularly claimed that environmental damage is the greatest threat to human wellbeing, but he has also admitted that no serious politician would dare to take radical action against it. By contrast, environmentalists put the long-term health of the planet above all other considerations. Their values imply that people in the economically developed world should reduce their living standards, rather than dreaming of ever-increasing material prosperity.

While most UK politicians have to claim that they are sensitive to the needs of the environment, it seems sensible to confine the word 'environmentalist' to those who argue for radical change in our lifestyles. Although these ideas lie behind much recent pressure group activity (see Chapter 8), and are wholly endorsed by the Green Party in the UK, they have made little impact on the policies of the main political parties. Most elections are won by the party that seems best equipped to increase prosperity, and on present trends it would be very difficult for anyone to win power with the argument that we all need to give up our affluence. However, this might all change in the light of growing evidence of environmental damage.

Suggested reading

Beachill, B., Spoor, C. and Wetherly, P., 'Return to Old Labour politics?', *Politics Review*, vol. 12, no. 2, November 2002.

Bradbury, J., 'The third way: where next for New Labour?', *Politics Review*, vol. 12, no. 1, September 2002.

Cowley, P. and Fisher, J., 'The Liberal Democrats', *Politics Review*, vol. 10, no. 3, February 2001.

Garnett, M., *Principles and Politics in Contemporary Britain* (Longman, 1996).

Garnett, M., 'The Blair essentials', *Politics Review*, vol. 10, no. 4, April 2001.

Gilmour, I., *Inside Right: Conservatism, Policies and the People* (Quartet, 1978).

Grant, M., 'Is the Labour Party still a socialist party?', *Politics Review*, vol. 15, no. 2, November 2005.

Jones, B., 'Is Tony a Tory?', *Politics Review*, vol. 14, no. 1, September 2004.

Leach, R., *Political Ideology in Britain* (Palgrave Macmillan, 2002)

Websites
British National Party (BNP): www.bnp.org.uk
UK Independence Party (UKIP): www.independenceuk.org.uk
Plaid Cymru: www.plaidcymru.org
Sinn Fein: www.sinnfein.ie
Scottish National Party (SNP): www.snp.org

Exam focus

Using this chapter and other resources available to you, answer the following questions.

1 What is the role of ideas in politics?
2 Outline the core ideas of: (a) conservatism; (b) socialism; (c) liberalism; (d) social democracy.
3 What were the key ingredients of the postwar consensus?
4 Why did the 'consensus' break down?
5 Distinguish between classical and new liberals.
6 Outline the key features of Thatcherism.
7 Distinguish between traditional conservatism and Thatcherism.
8 What are the key features of New Labour?
9 Outline the differences between 'Old' and 'New' Labour.
10 To what extent do you agree with the view that a new consensus is emerging in the UK?
11 Outline the beliefs on the main nationalist parties in the UK and explain how and why they differ.
12 Is there an 'end of ideology'? Give reasons for your answer.

Chapter 8

Pressure groups

The UK, like all representative, liberal democracies, is vulnerable to the charge that ordinary citizens have insufficient opportunities for meaningful participation. For the system's defenders, the existence of numerous *pressure groups* is sufficient to refute the charge. Even if citizens are only called upon to cast a vote every few years, between elections they are free to organise in an attempt to influence the policy decisions of government and businesses. Pressure group activity is therefore a crucial element in any liberal democracy. But like any important political phenomenon, it has generated a great deal of controversy.

Key questions answered in this chapter
➤ How do pressure groups differ from political parties?
➤ What is the role of pressure groups in a pluralist democracy?
➤ Why do some pressure groups succeed and others fail?
➤ In what ways have pressure groups changed in recent years?
➤ Do pressure groups enhance or threaten democracy?

What are pressure groups?

The first thing to notice about pressure groups is that the term sounds somewhat negative. The idea of 'pressure' makes us think of *force*. It implies that these groups set out to make elected governments take decisions against their will. For this reason, some people prefer to use the more neutral term *interest group* to describe such bodies. But the term 'pressure group' ties in with our discussion of politics in Chapter 1. No matter how apolitical a group might appear to be, there will almost always be occasions when its members seek to influence some aspect of government policy.

Whatever we choose to call them, the focus of this chapter is on *organisations whose members share common interests and which seek to influence government*. This is a good definition, so far as it goes, but political parties are organisations that seek to influence government, too. So what distinguishes pressure groups from political parties?

➤ Parties put up candidates for election; most pressure groups do not.
➤ While parties want to form a government of their own, pressure groups want to *influence* governments, whichever party is in power.
➤ Parties produce manifestos, covering all the key policy areas. Although pressure groups frequently issue literature to illustrate their arguments, these tend to focus on a single issue or policy area.

While these are the main distinctions, they are sometimes difficult to draw. For example, a pressure group can win useful publicity by running candidates in elections. In the UK general election of 2001, the independent candidate Dr Richard Taylor won the seat of Wyre Forest after a campaign that focused almost entirely on the fate of the local hospital. Dr Taylor retained the seat at the 2005 general election. In total, there were more than 150 independent candidates in 2005, some standing for frivolous reasons but others supporting a wide range of causes. The key point is that, unlike parties, electioneering is not the main activity of these groups.

Additionally, some pressure groups produce policy ideas on a wide range of issues. This is particularly the case with environmental groups such as Greenpeace (founded in 1971), since concern for the environment extends to matters like trade and foreign policy.

Types of pressure group

The term 'pressure group' covers a wide variety of organisations, but for convenience political scientists assess them under different categories, depending on their motivation, geographical scope, durability, status and methods of campaigning (see Box 8.1). The main types are as follows:

➤ **Sectional groups.** Broadly speaking, sectional groups are involved in defending their own economic interests (e.g. trade unions and employer's organisations).
➤ **Cause or promotional groups.** These are organisations that campaign on behalf of causes with no direct link to economic self-interest. For example, few campaigners on behalf of animal rights think that their actions will make them any richer.
➤ **Local groups.** A local group may spring up, for example, to oppose the closure of a particular hospital or the building of a new road.
➤ **National groups.** Instead of forming their own separate group, local campaigners on behalf of a hospital or against a new road may join forces with existing national bodies concerned with health or the environment.
➤ **Transnational groups.** Some pressure groups (e.g. the environmental organisation Greenpeace) are active across national boundaries. So the local people opposing the

Protesters at the Newbury bypass site, 1996

new road might try to win support from Greenpeace, which has a much larger membership and far more campaigning experience. Equally, transnational bodies can set up their own local bodies. The organisation Friends of the Earth (FOE), for example, has around 200 local groups in the UK.

> **Peak or 'umbrella' groups.** These are organisations that speak for a variety of similar, smaller groups. UK examples include sectional groups like the Confederation of British Industry (CBI) and the Trades Union Congress (TUC).

> **Temporary groups.** A body that saves a local hospital, or stops the building of a new road, can disband once its objectives have been secured. On a national level, a good example is the National Campaign for the Abolition of Capital Punishment (1955–69), which was wound up when the suspension of the death penalty was made permanent.

> **Permanent groups.** As a general rule, sectional groups are more likely to be permanent than cause groups. But having saved its hospital, a local group may decide to stay together as a permanent fundraising body, and to oppose any future threats. A more familiar example is a group like Oxfam (founded in 1942), which will probably have to continue its fight against global poverty indefinitely. Sadly, world poverty is a permanent problem. But even in the hypothetical case of a world entirely free from poverty, the group would almost certainly stay in existence because it would be logical to expect famine to make a quick return somewhere in the world.

Box 8.1 Pressure group strategies

Direct

➤ lobbying key policy-makers (whether in the EU, in London or at local levels)

➤ writing to MPs or local councillors

➤ funding political parties

➤ boycotting firms

➤ breaking controversial laws (e.g. the mass refusal to pay the community charge, or poll tax, in 1990)

Indirect

➤ distributing leaflets

➤ using the media and new technology

➤ demonstrating (e.g. the anti-poll tax demonstration of March 1990)

Note that demonstrations, and other very public forms of pressure group campaigning, are frequently described as forms of 'direct' action. But most demonstrations in a liberal democracy are clearly 'indirect' — they aim to mobilise public opinion, which may, in turn, bring pressure to bear on governments or firms.

Problems of classification

All pressure groups fall into more than one of these categories. For example, it would be uncontroversial (if rather long-winded!) to describe Greenpeace as a 'permanent transnational cause group'. But people join groups for different reasons and sometimes the classification on the basis of motivation is more difficult. For example, some local shopkeepers might join an organisation opposing a new bypass for their village, not because they object to the building of new roads for environmental reasons, but because they fear that they will lose customers. For them the organisation is a sectional group. But neighbours with a more general, principled objection to road-building will see it as a cause group. In classifying pressure groups, then, we usually have to make a judgement about the motives of a *majority* of members.

This task is made a little trickier by the tendency of groups to try to act as if they are cause groups, thinking that they will win more support if they avoid the impression that they are motivated by self-interest. So, for example, the British Medical Association (BMA) campaigns for improved pay and conditions for its members, who are employed in health organisations. If it can justify its claim by referring to the general cause of good

The Countryside Alliance has held various demonstrations, like this one in Whitehall

healthcare for patients, so much the better. Again, we have to make a judgement on the *real* purpose of the organisation in question.

One rather spectacular and controversial example to reinforce the point is the recent debate over hunting. The pro-hunting Countryside Alliance (founded in 1998) has tried to emphasise its credentials as a cause group. So, for example, it has appealed for support from anyone who wants to preserve the countryside, regardless of where they live; and it also claims that freedom in general will be under attack if hunting is banned.

In response, the anti-hunting lobby has exploited the association between hunting and the upper classes, in an attempt to portray the Alliance as a narrowly-based sectional group. The latter argument is barely relevant because the rich will not be any less wealthy if they are deprived of their hunting. However, the opponents of hunting find the class argument useful, not least because it deflects attention from practices such as angling, which also infringes the 'rights' of living creatures (see Chapter 12), but has broader social appeal.

Two final points arising from this example are that pressure groups often spring up to oppose each other, and that their tactics are heavily influenced by their circumstances. When the anti-hunting lobby was associated with militant hunt saboteurs rather than respected animal welfare groups, such as the Royal Society for the Prevention of Cruelty to Animals (RSPCA, founded in 1840), its influence at Westminster was weak and there seemed little reason for its opponents to organise.

After the election of New Labour in 1997, public perceptions of the debate on hunting were transformed. The continuing activities of anti-hunt protestors were rarely publicised. By contrast, the Countryside Alliance was forced to organise and to adopt more 'militant' tactics. These included mass demonstrations in London in 1999 and 2002, and repeated pledges that its members (around 100,000 in 2003) would ignore the ban on hunting which was introduced in 2005. The tables have been turned — now it is the hunting lobby that knows that the parliamentary arithmetic is against it, so it concentrates on legal challenges and mobilising public opinion in the hope that the ban will be lifted.

Insider and outsider groups

From the point of view of political scientists, the most important way of classifying pressure groups arises from their status as insider or outsider groups (see Box 8.2). *Insider* groups are those that enjoy direct access to ministers and policy-makers as a matter of daily routine. An excellent example is the National Farmers' Union (NFU), which has traditionally enjoyed a close relationship with ministries concerned with agriculture — currently the Department for Environment, Food and Rural Affairs (Defra) — regardless of the party in government. Indeed, the Agriculture Act (1947) made it a legal requirement for ministers to consult the NFU before taking decisions that might affect farming.

While the NFU is obviously a sectional group, it is also quite possible for cause groups with specialist knowledge to win insider status. For example, the Howard League

Box 8.2 Insider and outsider groups

Insiders

British Medical Association (health)

National Farmers' Union (agriculture)

National Trust (environment)

Confederation of British Industry (economics)

Law Society

Royal Society for the Prevention of Cruelty to Animals

Royal Automobile Association (motoring)

Outsiders

Countryside Alliance (environment)

National Anti-Vivisection Society (animal welfare)

OutRage (homosexual rights)

Campaign for Nuclear Disarmament

Life (anti-abortion)

Keep Sunday Special

Fathers 4 Justice (parental rights)

(founded in 1886), which campaigns for prison reform, usually wins respectful attention from the Home Office despite a membership that in 2002 numbered only 2,768.

In fact, such groups can be worth cultivating by ministries even if they are sometimes moderately critical of government policy. By studying the practical results of policy decisions, they can bring the attention of ministers and civil servants to real problems, which could cause wider political damage unless they are addressed quickly. The reward for providing such valuable information can be admission to a *policy network* (see p. 190).

Outsider groups are those which are not usually consulted. This usually puts them at a serious disadvantage compared to the insiders, but they can sometimes bring about dramatic policy changes. For example, since its objections had been ignored by the government, the Anti-Poll Tax Federation established to oppose Margaret Thatcher's poll tax encouraged non-payment. It also organised a mass gathering in London in March 1990 (which ended in a riot). As well as helping to secure a change in the law, the Anti-Poll Tax Federation can claim to have played a significant part in the removal of Mrs Thatcher from office in November 1990.

A less spectacular route to influence for outsider groups is to brief sympathetic individual backbench MPs or members of the House of Lords before debates on legislation that affects their cause. Even if they lose the vote in the first instance, a campaign of well-informed critical speeches can embarrass governments sufficiently to persuade them to withdraw specific clauses.

'In', 'out' or 'in-between'?

It would seem obvious that the goal of all pressure groups should be to win insider status. But some cause groups are quite happy to stay as outsiders, feeling that they would lose some of their credibility if they were in regular contact with policy-makers. This kind of group is more common nowadays, at a time when conventional political activity is increasingly unpopular.

More traditional pressure groups can be 'in' or 'out', depending on circumstances. Even since 1997 it would be misleading to call the anti-hunting lobby an insider group, but it certainly has more chance of an invitation to Downing Street than it had before the election of New Labour. Labour has always been close to the trade unions, which helped to found the party in the early twentieth century. Under Tony Blair, though, the unions have found their influence greatly diminished. In fact, some complain that the situation has barely improved since the days of Margaret Thatcher. Equally, the employers' organisation, the Confederation of British Industry (CBI), used to expect warm relations with Conservative ministers, but during the economic recession of the early 1980s the CBI chairman warned that if policy did not change he would take on the government in 'a bare-knuckle fight'.

While the distinction between 'ins' and 'outs' is useful, it is not clear-cut. For some groups, the ideal situation is to be neither fully 'in' nor fully 'out'. Campaigning bodies such as the housing pressure group Shelter (1966) and the Child Poverty Action Group (1965) seem able to embarrass governments at one moment and then collaborate with them the next, such is their reputation for detailed research in their areas of social policy. Almost the only certainty is that groups which resort to terrorism will be 'out' — at least until they show a readiness to negotiate (see Box 8.3).

Box 8.3 **Terrorism**

In Chapter 1 we saw that some people define politics in a way that specifically excludes terrorism, along with other forms of violence. On this showing, terrorism is very like war — it is what happens when politics fails comprehensively. Logically, people who take this view reject the idea that terrorist organisations should be seen even as very extreme pressure groups. They argue that respect for the rule of law is an essential element of liberal democratic systems. At most, pressure groups should confine their tactics to illegal protests that do not involve violence. Such tactics are known as campaigns of *civil disobedience*, like the refusal to pay the poll tax in 1990.

Yet things are not quite so simple. The definition of a 'terrorist' includes the idea that such people are using terror to bring pressure to bear on governments. Many groups take up arms in support of claims that are clearly political in character. Moreover, as in the case of the Irish Republican Army (IRA), they can at times support peaceful attempts at conflict resolution while pursuing a campaign of violence directed towards the same goal.

Terrorism arouses very strong emotions, and students of politics can hardly be immune from these feelings. In the end, a decision to include or exclude terrorist organisations from discussions of pressure groups will depend on our attitude towards the causes they claim to uphold and our assessment of the system they operate in.

At the same time, some insider groups are never accepted fully. They might force themselves through the door, but governments are obviously looking for the first chance to boot them out. In the early postwar period, even Conservative governments were anxious not to alienate the trade unions, which were often invited for talks at Downing Street. Under the Labour government of 1964–70, journalists began to talk of 'beer and sandwiches at Number 10' whenever the unions visited the prime minister, as if they were so powerful that they could even dictate the variety of refreshments on offer. Labour's current leaders are far less friendly towards the unions and are more likely to consume claret and caviar with the representatives of big business.

New pressure-points

Pressure groups have to respond to institutional developments and target their campaigns at the relevant level of policy making. So while it makes sense for local cause groups to lobby their council, those who want to change a national policy will focus their attention on Westminster or Whitehall. But the growing importance of the EU, and the new interest in global issues, has encouraged some groups to look elsewhere. European institutions are particularly attractive, since the activities of many pressure groups in Brussels or Strasbourg benefit from official subsidies.

It is possible to be 'in' at one level of government and comprehensively 'out' at another. For example, in the early 1980s gay rights campaigners won a sympathetic hearing from some Labour-run councils. Even relatively small grants to such bodies were greeted with sensational headlines in some sections of the press. The extent to which gay rights were 'out' for the then Conservative government was signalled by the insertion of a clause in the Local Government Act (1988), banning councils from 'promoting' homosexuality. In the late 1980s British trade unions, faced with an unremittingly hostile government at Westminster, began to look towards the European Community for new allies.

The introduction of devolved governments in Scotland, Wales and Northern Ireland provides obvious opportunities for groups who feel that their arguments are being ignored in London. There is also a marked new trend for pressure groups either to lobby European politicians and officials directly, or to employ Brussels-based lobbyists to do this work for them. This recognises Europe's growing importance as a source of subsidies, and of regulations that are binding on the UK. The sight of the president of the European Commission, Jacques Delors, being warmly applauded by the 1988 conference of the Trades Union Congress (TUC) probably helped to inspire Mrs Thatcher's deepening dislike of the EC.

Recently some groups (particularly those concerned with poverty or the environment) have turned their attention to transnational institutions. In November 1999, for example, there were large demonstrations during the meeting of the World Trade Organisation in Seattle, USA. Environmental bodies such as Greenpeace have been active at global events like the Earth Summit at Rio de Janeiro in June 1992, the similar meeting at Johannesburg 10 years later, and the G8 meeting at Gleneagles in July 2005.

The new prominence of global movements has led to another interesting trend. Increasingly these bodies are tempted to bypass governments, focusing instead on the companies whose activities they find objectionable. A fascinating example was the Brent Spar incident of 1995 (see Box 8.4). Alternatively, activists who want to change government policy can take action against multinational firms, hoping that in turn these powerful organisations will pressurise objectionable governments. In the 1980s many students boycotted Barclays Bank, which had important investments in racist South Africa. Such action probably played some part in bringing the apartheid system to an end.

Greenpeace's demonstration at Brent Spar, 1995

Box 8.4 The Brent Spar incident

In 1995, the giant oil company Shell proposed to sink its disused oil platform Brent Spar in the sea rather than towing it away and dismantling it on land. The pressure group Greenpeace protested angrily, claiming that the company's preferred option would cause far more pollution. The UK government gave Shell its full support. But after a Europe-wide boycott of the company's products, Shell backed down.

Key term

> **Policy network.** An informal community consisting of government ministries and insider bodies that are consulted regularly during the policy-making process.

Summary

What are pressure groups?

> Pressure groups are organisations whose members share common interests and seek to influence governments.

> They can be classified in several different ways. The most important distinction is between insider and outsider groups.

Pressure groups and democracy

Corporatism

In the early 1960s, amid increasing concern about the UK's relative economic decline, many commentators began to feel that conflict between powerful economic interest groups was holding the country back. The notion that the government favoured one group over another — for example, the trade unions over employers' groups — was an obvious source of friction. In response, the Conservative government led by Harold Macmillan set up new institutions in which unions and employers could meet on a regular basis. Not only would the groups feel that the government was giving everyone an equal hearing, but (it was hoped) both sides of industry would begin to understand each other's positions. Cooperation between the key economic groups would replace the previous divisions, in a new 'corporate' institutional setting.

But *corporatism* has always been something of a dirty word in the UK. It was associated with fascism — indeed, in his early days the Italian dictator Benito Mussolini had won British admirers precisely because his corporate approach seemed to promise industrial harmony, and thus greater efficiency. By the mid-1970s, critics of the arrangement were able to argue that corporatism had done nothing to reverse the UK's decline, and after 1979 Margaret Thatcher abandoned it. It has not been revived by New Labour.

Whether corporatism or other factors were to blame for economic decline is still a bone of contention. One can argue, for instance, that successive governments failed to take it seriously enough, and it certainly never approached the situation in Mussolini's Italy. But for many critics, corporatism was simply wrong in principle. It was anti-democratic because, although the various parties talked openly among themselves, the electorate as a whole was excluded from their deliberations.

Elitism and Marxism

In Chapter 1 we introduced the concept of *elitism*. It is easy to see that the idea of corporatism should appeal to elitists. Under any political system, they think, the key decisions will be taken by a relatively small number of powerful people. For a government to consult with the leading representatives of the most powerful pressure groups may be anti-democratic, but it is quite unavoidable. So according to this view, governing through corporate institutions is the only honest way of proceeding. It is also more efficient because political leaders will not have to waste their time pretending to consult outsider groups.

Some take the elitist approach further, and look at the social backgrounds of those who take part in the key decisions, many of whom have attended public schools and Oxbridge colleges. The idea that everyone from these backgrounds inevitably shares a common interest may be taken too far. Even so, at the very least there will be a tendency for people who have attended the major public schools to speak the same sort of language, which will be unfamiliar to those from less privileged backgrounds. And no one can pretend that Old Etonians are under-represented among the most powerful people in the UK.

The *Marxist* critique of capitalist societies can usefully be seen as a variant of elitism. Although the ideology has spawned many different interpretations, Marxists tend to regard all pressure groups of any importance in a capitalist country as sectional. Stripped of their superficial characteristics, they all represent the interests either of property-owners or of the propertyless workers.

From the Marxist viewpoint, the idea of corporatism as practised in the UK in the 1960s and 1970s was meaningless. Since the governments of all parties were seen as defenders of the capitalist system, any consultation with the workers could be nothing more than window-dressing. Instead of allowing the two sides of industry to understand each other's positions, corporate institutions were seen merely as ways of coaxing union leaders into seeing things from the bosses' point of view. Thus a small elite group of employers and their allies would always get their way.

Pluralism

By contrast with elitists, *pluralists* believe that competition between pressure groups is the hallmark of a healthy democracy (see Chapter 1). It can be argued, in fact, that without pressure groups like the Suffragettes, the UK would not be a democracy at all. Pluralist theory portrays governments as acting like a neutral umpire, judging arguments by their quality rather than by the status of the people who put them forward. Provided that its arguments are good enough, even the poorest organisation can reasonably hope to influence government policy.

Pressure groups represent a key element of *civil society* — the part of any society that is independent of the state. They are voluntary organisations and, provided that they restrict themselves to lawful activity, they are free to campaign however they choose. They compete against each other for public attention and, as we have already noticed, the success of one group tends to inspire another one to oppose it with more vigour. Each side will try to put forward the best possible arguments supporting its point of view, and back them with detailed research. Thus the free competition between pressure groups will help governments to reach informed and fair decisions.

The most eloquent expressions of this pluralist view were written in the USA during the 1950s. This timing is no accident. It was the period in which commentators were adjusting to a divided world, as the Soviet Union consolidated its control of eastern Europe and supported communist movements elsewhere. Whether consciously or not, those who depicted the capitalist West as a world of pluralism were comparing it with its ideological opponents and arguing that it should be defended as a beacon of freedom. Voluntary associations were virtually unknown behind the Iron Curtain; where they continued to exist they were warmly supported by Westerners. But for such observers, the principle was more important than the people who upheld it. They believed that civilised life was impossible without the right to organised dissent, and this is the essence of the pluralist theory.

We have already produced significant evidence to underline the value of pluralism as a means of explaining UK politics. For example, those who demonstrated against the poll tax tended to be poor, but they still managed to win the (partial) revision of the government's plans. More recently, in the late summer of 2000 a determined group of protestors forced the government to backtrack slightly from its policy of high fuel taxes. It might be argued that these examples are noteworthy only because they are so unusual. But we have already seen that, under liberal democracy, outsider and insider groups can swap places, depending on changing circumstances.

Thatcherism and the New Right

Although the pluralist theory was very popular with opponents of the Soviet Union, Margaret Thatcher seemed to dislike most organised groups as a matter of principle. In this respect she was true to the general principles of the New Right (see Chapter 7), which followed the seventeenth-century political philosopher Thomas Hobbes in thinking of organised groups as 'worms within the entrails of a natural man'. Translated to a democratic age, this argument rests on the idea that governments are elected to take decisions, not to spend all their time trying to satisfy the various pressure groups. If the public does not like the decisions, they can always vote the government out.

Box 8.5 Pluralism and the media

The electronic and printed media present a particularly thorny problem for pluralists. On the one hand, they can argue that a free press is an essential element of a pluralist society, guaranteeing a market for information in which well-educated citizens can make up their own minds on the key issues of the day. On the other hand, pluralists have to accept that the owners of newspapers and television channels are likely to have their own sectional interests and, on balance, very few of them are likely to support causes such as the worldwide movement against global capitalism (see p. 189).

Pluralists argue that unless a single media outlet secures a complete monopoly, all causes can hope to win publicity. A media organisation that presses the case of one pressure group is likely to inspire competition from another. Yet it is clear, for example, that a newspaper that gives glowing coverage to the anti-globalisation movement would be unlikely to receive much advertising revenue from transnational corporations. Biased reporting, exaggerating the extent of any violence associated with a demonstration (or underestimating the number of protestors), is only one aspect of the problem. The most powerful weapon for media owners is their refusal to report certain campaigning activities at all. For example, protests against the 2003 war on Iraq were hardly reported at all on certain television channels in the United States.

Once media tycoons allow their editors to give a decent hearing to a cause that they do not like, it is a sure sign that the campaigners have won already. So protestors are faced with a 'Catch-22' situation: in order to win the argument they have to reach a wide audience, but they cannot depend upon a wide audience unless and until they look like winning the argument.

By the end of her term of office, Thatcher had upset almost every important interest group, including bodies normally associated with the Conservatives such as the Law Society, the Police Federation and the CBI. But even she had to relent on occasion. For example, she suddenly took notice of environmental arguments towards the end of her premiership, after the Green Party performed surprisingly well in the 1989 elections to the European Parliament. But her downfall in 1990 can be traced directly to her opposition to pressure groups. The poll tax was introduced after limited consultation, so the government was taken by surprise by the strength of the reaction. Whatever they felt about the specific issue, pluralists everywhere could believe that Thatcher's downfall vindicated their position.

Pluralism and democracy

If pluralism were an accurate description of life in liberal democracies, all the claims about its importance to a free society would be verified. The humblest citizen would have as much chance of a serious hearing as the richest property owner or the most powerful official. Far from being the only chance for ordinary citizens to have a meaningful say, elections would be contests to decide which group of neutral 'umpires' would get the next turn to preside over the continuing contest between freely organised bodies. As an added bonus, since each group would enjoy equal access to the media (see Box 8.5), the public would be better informed, as the well-researched and objective findings of each group increased the stock of public knowledge.

Unfortunately, though, the pluralist theory was always at best an idealistic over-simplification. Even its best-known advocates have admitted that groups do not compete on an 'equal playing field'. Their new position, known as *neopluralism*, is actually a significant shift. Instead of assuming that governments act as impartial umpires, the neopluralists argue that they should side with the disadvantaged to ensure that the battle is fair. This is rather like recommending that football referees should allow Nationwide League teams to field more than 11 players when they face Manchester United! In reality, as we have seen in the example of hunting, the political 'referees' have their personal favourites among the teams. Provided that they enjoy a reasonable majority in parliament, there is little to prevent governing parties from rewarding their friends.

Pluralism and 'sleaze'

While the Iron Curtain existed, the pluralist theory could win advocates in the West even if they found it something less than a perfect description of political realities in countries like the UK and the USA. Significantly, criticism of pressure group activity has grown since the end of the Cold War denied commentators the luxury of comparing Western freedom with Soviet totalitarianism.

While Mrs Thatcher's governments were relatively untainted by allegations of 'sleaze', her successor John Major was seriously damaged by a stream of negative media stories. In particular, the 'cash for questions' scandal (see Box 8.6) gave rise to fears that MPs

Box 8.6 Lobbying firms

Under the Major government, the public grew accustomed to news stories about the activities of professional lobbying organisations. Such firms are contacted by organisations or individuals, and in return for a fee they will present arguments to policy makers in the hope of influencing their decisions. The most famous (or notorious) of these bodies was the firm Ian Greer Associates, which was involved in the 'cash for questions' scandal, when MPs accepted payment in return for raising issues in parliament.

To some pluralist theorists, lobbying is an essential feature of a healthy democracy. Busy people, such as those running businesses, may lack the time and the communication skills to present their arguments. Without lobbyists they might lose the battle for influence, not because their arguments are poor in themselves, but because their opponents are more eloquent. On the pluralist assumption that governments are neutral, it is still vital that the cases for and against a proposal are presented with equal clarity.

However, some people regard lobbying as a form of political corruption. Those firms that enjoy the closest relationship with policy makers can command the highest fees, whether or not they happen to be very good at presenting an argument. Thus the group or individual with the deepest purse will secure their objectives; and at the same time, the best-placed lobbyists will thrive at the expense of more able rivals who lack their insider status.

were willing to grant special access to individuals who were willing to pay, after a *Sunday Times* investigation revealed that some MPs were open to bribery. Despite the lengthy 'honeymoon' of the Blair government, similar allegations have, if anything, become more serious since 1997. In the first few months of the New Labour government, it emerged that the motor racing tycoon Bernie Ecclestone had donated considerable sums to both of the main parties. Even the most naive pluralist would have found it difficult to argue that Mr Ecclestone had acted out of a concern for the health of the democratic process. But his persuasive powers were such that Blair modified his manifesto pledge to outlaw tobacco advertising, despite the powerful arguments of the anti-smoking lobby. In the following year, lobbyists with close links to New Labour were exposed for offering access to ministers in return for cash.

Returning again to the question of whether pressure groups are good for democracy (see Box 8.7 overleaf), these examples suggest a pessimistic response. An elitist could argue that, however good it might be in theory, *in practice* pluralism is actually damaging to democracy. Politicians might try to convince the electorate that they are both open-minded and incorruptible, but as this is far from the truth, it just makes voters increasingly cynical about democracy. They begin to see all politicians as liars, and withhold their votes at election time. Recent evidence of declining turnout seems to suggest that this has indeed been happening, not just in the UK but throughout the Western world. For an elitist, the only way out of the downward spiral of apathy is for politicians to admit that genuine pluralism operates only in those rare and trivial cases where money is not an issue.

> **Box 8.7 Pressure groups: for and against**

For

➤ They allow participation between elections.

➤ They give a voice to minority groups.

➤ They can provide objective information to government and voters.

➤ They reinforce the credibility of liberal democracy, by showing that policy outcomes do not always depend on the economic resources of different groups in society.

➤ Their use of headline-grabbing stunts to win publicity is healthy, because it widens the terms of political debate.

Against

➤ Single-issue groups channel enthusiasm away from elections.

➤ They can allow well-organised and even corrupt minorities to drown out the voice of the general public.

➤ They often provide biased and conflicting evidence to government and voters.

➤ They merely expose the unequal opportunities for influencing policy in a state governed by elites.

➤ Their use of headline-grabbing stunts is at best irresponsible, and sometimes dangerous.

It is open to question whether pressure groups are any more democratic than political parties. The larger ones, in particular, are vulnerable to Robert Michels's 'iron law of oligarchy' (see Chapter 6).

Summary

Pressure groups and democracy

➤ In theory, pressure groups are an asset in a democratic society. They allow ordinary people to participate in politics, and even small groups with little money have the chance to influence government policy in the right circumstances.

➤ This positive view of pressure groups is called pluralism.

➤ On balance, however, the evidence tends to support the contrasting 'elitist' position that, although everyone is free to organise on behalf of a favourite cause, certain individuals and groups have an overwhelming advantage in winning government attention.

➤ Recent scandals in the UK show that, contrary to the pluralist position, a dubious argument backed by wealthy people can overcome well-informed opposition from groups with fewer resources.

➤ Even so, a large number of factors affect the fortunes of pressure groups and the result of their activities is rarely a foregone conclusion.

The new politics of pressure

In the light of this discussion, it is not really surprising that pressure group activity seems to be growing while electoral participation and party membership are in sharp decline. Turning away from a world in which elected leaders cut shady deals, people are seeking outlets for their idealism elsewhere. Naturally they tend to choose cause groups for their energies, rather than bodies that are formed to pursue the economic interests of their members. One spectacular example is the membership of the Royal Society for the Protection of Birds (RSPB), founded in 1889. By the 1960s it had 10,000 members, but this figure had risen to 100,000 by 1972 and membership topped 1,000,000 in 1997.

Another important reason for this development is the general rise in living standards in the period since the Second World War. This means that more people have the spare time — and the relative freedom from financial worries — to participate in campaigning. The RSPB has benefited from the increase in the number of pensioners with enough financial security to engage in birdwatching. Of course, sectional groups like the trade unions have played an important part in the general improvement in living standards. So, ironically, one could say that *cause* groups are inheriting the earth fertilised on their behalf by *sectional* organisations.

Another irony is that many of these groups are protesting against the results of the very affluence that gives them the freedom to protest. Environmental bodies reflect a growing concern for the damage that has been done to our planet in the search for higher living standards. At the same time, while Marxism is generally held to be in decline, an increasing number of activists are protesting against the perceived injustice of global capitalism. Again there is an irony here, because technological change allows protestors to communicate with ease across national boundaries. The major companies that provide this technology are themselves giant transnational concerns, so the activists are likely to be using the products (and thus increasing the profits) of their enemies! The protestors might reply that, if there were no global capitalism, there would be no reason for people to use the technology to organise demonstrations. Even if they have to buy the companies' products, they might argue, this is a case in which the ends justify the means.

Anti-globalisation protestors are obviously outsider groups, and their tactics are designed accordingly. In the UK, perhaps the first of this new breed of cause groups was the Campaign for Nuclear Disarmament (CND, founded in 1958), whose members have always attracted close interest from the security services. But in 1960, and again in 1981, Labour Party conferences voted in favour of unilateral nuclear disarmament. The policy was finally abandoned before the 1992 general election. When New Labour came to office there was predictable curiosity from the press, to see how many current or former members of this outsider group had suddenly vaulted into the centre of political power.

More recent examples of outsider group activity are anti-road protestors, who sometimes use dramatic tactics to obstruct new developments. Some animal rights activists have even resorted to planned acts of violence, evidently in the belief that human beings who conduct experiments on defenceless creatures have thereby forfeited their own rights (see Box 8.8 overleaf).

There is some reason to suppose that, while most 'traditional' pressure groups have sought to become insiders, winning and consolidating a place within a policy network, the new groups will be content with outsider status. To some people, membership of a pressure group that is wholly opposed to the dominant trends in modern society can bring its own satisfactions. There is a tendency for new groups to attract middle-class professionals, who can provide skills that are directly relevant to the running of publicity campaigns, and who may well relish a battle of wits against the state and transnational companies. In September 1998, environmentalist campaigners from Sweden, Poland, France and Germany attended a training camp in Staffordshire to learn obstructive tactics, such as the art of tunnelling and how to build tree-houses! More and more inventive tactics can be expected in the future, thanks to developments in information technology and the growing influence of the media.

Pressure groups and the 2005 general election

Apart from the increasing tendency for pressure groups to put up candidates in general elections, such bodies can also attract publicity by staging stunts which will be reported by a media hungry for news. During the 2005 general election campaign there were more protests against high fuel taxes and several incidents involving supporters of the group Fathers 4 Justice, which claims that mothers enjoy favourable treatment by the courts when parents split up. The most spectacular stunt was carried out by Greenpeace activists, who installed solar panels on the roof of the house of Deputy Prime Minister John Prescott. But the most significant intervention may have come from the Countryside Alliance, which claimed that its efforts led to the defeat of 27 anti-hunting MPs.

Fathers 4 Justice protesters, dressed as Captain America, Robin and Batman, scale the Foreign Office, 2005

These incidents followed a year of high-profile protests, mostly involving Fathers 4 Justice and the Countryside Alliance. In May 2004 two supporters of Fathers 4 Justice managed to throw flour bombs at the prime minister from the gallery of the House of Commons. In September, hunt supporters infiltrated the Commons chamber itself, despite the tightened security resulting from terrorist threats. The success of such tactics, at least in terms of winning publicity, suggests that they will be used more frequently in future.

Pressure groups: success and failure

We have seen that the world of pressure groups is very complicated, and becoming more so. In presenting a list of factors that affect their fortunes, we have to be aware that there are always exceptions. Nevertheless, the following factors can be suggested:

> **Political context.** A group has an obvious advantage if a sympathetic political party controls the government at the relevant level.

> **Climate of opinion.** Even a powerful and generally popular government cannot hope to be supported by the public on every issue. In 2000 New Labour enjoyed high opinion poll ratings, but its policy on fuel taxes was so unpopular that it had to reduce them under pressure from mass protests backed by the media.

> **Resources.** Running an effective campaign can be very expensive, so wealthy supporters provide an obvious advantage.

> **Membership.** Even if the organisation is relatively poor, a large membership is a great help. Most members will also be voters, as will their families and friends, and political parties will hesitate before dismissing the claims of large organisations. A mass membership can help to communicate with strangers, by delivering campaign literature or holding big demonstrations to win media attention.

> **Motivation of members.** A small but enthusiastic and knowledgeable membership is more promising than a large body of passive supporters. The Howard League, with fewer than 3,000 members, has certainly made a significant impact on the treatment of prisoners.

> **Organisational factors.** Sectional groups seem to have an advantage in organising themselves. For example, all workers in a particular trade are potential members of the relevant union, so the organisation will be able to target them. By contrast,

---

Box 8.8 **The campaign to close Huntingdon Life Sciences**

The company Huntingdon Life Sciences (HLS) was the subject of a Channel 4 documentary in 1997, which exposed cruel animal testing. The company had already been targeted by animal rights activists, but the pressure increased after the documentary. The tactics of protestors included attacks on staff and property, and boycotts of firms which invested in the company. Their aim was to drive HLS out of business.

The episode has now become a trial of strength between the UK government and the animal rights movement. Special legislation has been introduced to increase prison sentences for activists to 5 years and to prevent known protestors from causing 'economic damage' through intimidation. The government has also taken steps to protect the company and its investors from the financial effects of boycotts. It accepts that the animal tests carried out at HLS provide important benefits for the UK and that its practices are now more humane. For their part, the protestors argue that animal testing of any kind is cruel and unjustified.

a body like the Consumers' Association (founded in 1946) might be relevant to every single citizen of the UK, but organising all of them for specific campaigns would be very difficult.

➤ **Quality of leadership.** A charismatic leader is an important asset for any pressure group in a media age.

➤ **Celebrity supporters.** In the battle for media attention, any group that can enlist well-known personalities has a significant advantage.

➤ **Strength of opponents.** Even a relatively large pressure group, such as CND in the 1980s, could make little headway against well-organised opponents with committed supporters in the media.

On this showing, a well-funded pressure group with a large, highly motivated membership and charismatic leaders should have little trouble in convincing a sympathetic government to act on its behalf. If only things were so simple!

Summary

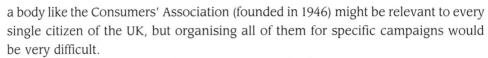

The new politics of pressure

➤ Pressure group activity in the UK is increasing.

➤ This is happening partly because of disillusionment with political parties, partly because of rising living standards, but also because institutional changes offer new opportunities for campaigning bodies.

Suggested reading

Batchelor, A., 'UK and US interest groups: similarities and differences', *Politics Review*, vol. 12, no. 1, September 2002.

Garnett, M., 'Groups and democracy', *Politics Review*, vol. 15, no. 2, November 2005.

Grant, W., 'Insider and outsider pressure groups', *Politics Review*, vol. 9, no. 1, September 1999.

Grant, W., 'Outside in! Insider groups under challenge', *Politics Review*, vol. 11, no. 2, November 2001.

Jackson, N., 'Pressure group politics', *Politics Review*, vol. 14, no. 1, September 2004.

Outhwaite, D., 'How pressure groups influence political parties', *Politics Review*, vol. 10, no. 2, February 2000.

Websites

Countryside Alliance: www.countryside-alliance.org

Friends of the Earth: www.foe.co.uk

Greenpeace: www.greenpeace.org.uk

Howard League: www.howardleague.org.uk

Liberty: www.liberty-human-rights.org.uk

Exam focus

Using this chapter and other resources available to you, answer the following questions.

1 What are pressure groups?
2 Distinguish between sectional and cause or promotional groups.
3 List three examples each of sectional and cause or promotional groups.
4 Distinguish between insider and outsider groups.
5 Outline the problems of classifying pressure groups.
6 Discuss the tactics used by different types of pressure group.
7 How are pressure groups funded?
8 Why are the media more important to some pressure groups than to others?
9 Why do some groups lobby the new devolved governments rather than or in addition to Westminster?
10 Why do some groups lobby at the EU rather than or in addition to Westminster?
11 Discuss the role of pressure groups in maintaining a pluralist society.
12 'Pressure groups exert power and influence over the executive.' To what extent do you agree with this view?
13 How far do you agree that pressure groups represent vested interests and are therefore a threat to democracy?
14 Is there a new politics of pressure? Give reasons for your answer.

Chapter 9

The constitution and constitutional reform

A constitution is an authoritative set of laws, rules and practices specifying how a state is to be governed and the relationship between the state and the individual (see Box 9.1). It provides the framework for the political system, establishing the main institutions of government and outlining their powers and the relationship between them. It also determines where sovereignty — that is, ultimate decision-making power — resides within the state. The relationship between the state and its citizens should be spelled out, with the basic rights of citizens guaranteed. A constitutional document also outlines a special procedure for its amendment.

Key questions answered in this chapter
> What are the key features of the UK constitution?
> What are the main strengths and weaknesses of the traditional constitution?
> What have been the most significant constitutional reforms introduced by the Labour government since 1997?
> To what extent have Labour's reforms produced a new constitutional settlement?

Constitutions and politics

Constitutions do not inhabit a lofty world above normal political activity. Instead, they have an important impact on day-to-day politics and are inherently political. A constitution is not static: the rules and practices it provides for have to be interpreted and sometimes adapted to meet changing circumstances. Nor are constitutions neutral: the framework they provide (e.g. the electoral system) may favour some actors, while others may seek to change it.

The UK's 'unwritten' constitution

A distinction is frequently made between written and unwritten constitutions. In the case of a *written* constitution, the main principles and rules governing the state are enshrined in constitutional law. Where these rules are found in convention and tradition, a constitution may be described as *unwritten*. In practice, however, all constitutions contain a mixture of written and unwritten rules.

The British constitution is often described as 'unwritten', as no single constitutional document exists for the UK. In this respect, the UK is one of only three liberal democratic states (Israel and New Zealand being the others) that does not have a single constitutional document. By contrast, the USA has the world's first written constitution, dating back to 1787. It consists of just seven articles and 27 amendments, the first ten of which make up the Bill of Rights. Many of the constitutions found in western Europe were rewritten after the political upheaval of the Second World War.

Box 9.1 The constitution defined

The House of Lords Select Committee on the Constitution (2001) defined a constitution as: 'the set of laws, rules and practices that create the basic institutions of the state and its component and related parts, and stipulate the powers of those institutions and the relationship between the different institutions and between those institutions and the individual'.

An uncodified constitution

Classifying the UK constitution as 'unwritten' is misleading. Instead, the UK is best described as having an *uncodified* constitution. In the case of a *codified* constitution, the key principles and rules of the state are collected together in a single authoritative document. This document is often, as in the USA, referred to as 'the Constitution', although in reality the constitution includes judicial decisions and conventions. As the UK lacks a document of this kind, it is classified as having an uncodified constitution. Some of the most important rules governing the political system in the UK are written down, but not in a single codified document. Instead, they can be gleaned from a variety of sources, many of which date back to the nineteenth century. Some rules are written down as Acts of Parliament or judicial rulings, but others take the form of unwritten conventions.

The absence of a codified constitutional document raises problems of clarity and interpretation in UK politics (see Boxes 9.2 overleaf and 9.3 on p. 214). However, it is worth remembering that students of American government would not gain a full understanding of that system simply by examining the US constitution. Although it outlines the framework of the US political system, the constitution does not explicitly provide for a strong president, nor does it mention important actors such as the bureaucracy and political parties. Furthermore, the US constitution has had to be constantly reinterpreted by the Supreme Court so that eighteenth-century principles make sense in the modern world. A written constitution is not a detailed instruction manual but a reference point for an evolving political system.

Box 9.2 Codified versus uncodified constitutions

Strengths of a codified constitution

- The major rules, principles and institutions of the political system are entrenched in a single authoritative document.
- The powers of the executive and legislature are clearly constrained and the location of sovereign authority is identified.
- The independence of the judiciary is protected.
- The basic rights of citizens are identified and safeguarded.
- Special procedures for amending the constitution are set out.
- The constitutional document has educative value, as it outlines the values and structures of the political system.
- Constitutional crises are less likely to arise because of confusion about what amounts to 'unconstitutional' behaviour.

Strengths of an uncodified constitution

- The constitution is sufficiently flexible to adapt to changing circumstances.
- It is easier to amend constitutional law and update the rights of citizens to reflect social change.
- The major rules, principles and institutions have evolved and proved their worth over time, rather than being created artificially.
- Decisions on constitutional issues are largely in the hands of elected politicians rather than unelected judges.

Key terms

- **Codified constitution.** The laws, rules and principles specifying how a state is to be governed are laid out in a single constitutional document.
- **Constitution.** The set of laws, rules and practices that specify how a state is to be governed, and which define the relationship between the state and the individual.
- **Constitutional.** Political behaviour that is in accordance with accepted rules and norms.
- **Constitutional government.** Government that operates within an agreed set of legal and political constraints.
- **Uncodified constitution.** The laws, rules and principles specifying how a state is to be governed are not set out in a single document, but are found in a variety of sources.
- **Unconstitutional.** Behaviour that falls outside the accepted rules and norms of the political system.

Sources of the constitution

In the absence of a codified document, we have to look for the key rules and practices of the political system in different places. There are five principal sources of the UK constitution:

> statute law
> common law
> conventions
> authoritative works
> European Union law

Statute law

Statute law is law created by parliament. In the legislative process, Acts of Parliament have to be approved by the House of Commons, the House of Lords and the monarch before they are placed on the statute book (i.e. gain the force of law). They are then implemented by the executive and enforced by the courts.

Some Acts of Parliament have a greater constitutional significance than others. Important historical examples are the Great Reform Act (1832), which extended the franchise; the Parliament Act (1911), which established the House of Commons as the dominant chamber of parliament; and the European Communities Act (1972), by which the UK joined the European Economic Community. More recent examples of statute law that were of major constitutional significance include: the Scotland Act (1998), creating a Scottish Parliament; the Human Rights Act (1998), enshrining key rights in UK law; and the House of Lords Act (1999), removing most hereditary peers from the upper chamber.

Statute law is the most important source of the principles and rules making up the UK constitution. This is because, under the doctrine of parliamentary sovereignty (discussed later in this chapter), parliament is the supreme law-making body in the UK. However, this doctrine also means that parliament may amend or repeal any existing act — so the post-1997 Labour government has been able to push through a programme of constitutional reform.

Common law

The common law includes legal principles that have been developed and applied by UK courts. The courts interpret and clarify the law where there is no clear statute law. Judicial decisions have thus clarified the rights of citizens *vis-à-vis* the state. Such rulings become part of the body of the common law, taking precedence over earlier decisions and serving as a guide to future lawmakers. However, ministers may seek to clarify or amend common law through Acts of Parliament.

The common law also includes customs and precedents that have become accepted practice. They relate to the role of the monarchy, parliament and the executive. Particularly important here is the *royal prerogative* — the powers exercised in the name of the Crown. Although the UK is a constitutional monarchy, the Crown retains a number of formal powers that date back to the period before Britain became a constitutional monarchy in the late seventeenth century. The royal prerogative includes the power of the Crown to:

➤ declare war and negotiate treaties
➤ dissolve parliament
➤ appoint government ministers
➤ appoint judges

These powers no longer rest with the monarch. It is government ministers who exercise prerogative powers in the name of the Crown. It is the prime minister who declares war, decides the date of a general election and appoints government ministers and judges. The prime minister will inform the monarch of his or her decision, but the monarch has no real power to veto prime ministers' actions or dissuade them from their chosen course. Even in the award of the Queen's Birthday Honours, it is government ministers who draw up the list of recipients.

Conventions

Conventions are rules or norms that are considered to be binding. Long usage gives conventions their authority — they are neither codified nor enforced by courts of law. The UK constitution is regarded as flexible because some of its key components, such as those dealing with the monarchy, are based on convention.

By convention, the monarch must assent to Acts of Parliament. If the queen were to refuse to assent to an act, a constitutional crisis would ensue. The monarch also accepts the advice of ministers on making treaties and on declarations of war.

It is the monarch who appoints the prime minister. Convention dictates that the leader of the largest party in the House of Commons will be invited to Buckingham Palace after a general election and invited to form a government. The last member of the House of Lords to become prime minister was Alec Douglas-Home in 1963. It had become a convention that the prime minister should be a member of the House

The monarch traditionally has responsibility for the state opening of Parliament

of Commons, so he resigned from the Lords and successfully fought a by-election to take a seat in the Commons.

The first-past-the-post electoral system usually produces a clear outcome, rendering the decision on which party will form the next government a formality. However, should a general election produce a *hung parliament* — one in which no single party has an overall majority — the monarch may face a tricky and hugely important decision. After the February 1974 general election produced no clear winner, the defeated prime minister Edward Heath explored the possibilities of forming a coalition government with the Liberals. Only when he admitted defeat was Harold Wilson, the leader of the largest party in the Commons, invited to form a minority Labour government.

Ministerial responsibility

The circumstances under which government ministers might be expected to resign are governed by convention, too. The convention of *collective ministerial responsibility* suggests that ministers who cannot accept a policy position agreed by the cabinet should resign. In 2003, Robin Cook and Clare Short resigned from the cabinet in protest at the prime minister's policy towards Iraq. The convention of *individual ministerial responsibility* holds that ministers should resign if they, or their department, are guilty of serious political mistakes.

In reality, neither convention holds fast. There are abundant examples of ministers who disagree with cabinet decisions remaining in government and briefing the media about their dissatisfaction. A clear-cut example of the convention of individual ministerial responsibility in action is the resignation of three ministers, including the foreign secretary Lord Carrington, after criticism of their political judgement before the Argentine invasion of the Falkland Islands in 1982. But, as Chapter 11 explains, many ministerial resignations in the last 30 years came about because of personal misconduct rather than political or policy mistakes.

Authoritative works

A number of established legal and political texts have become accepted as works of authority on the UK constitution. These texts have no formal legal authority but prove helpful in interpreting the more obscure areas of constitutional practice. They act as a guide to the workings of institutions and the political system in general.

There are only a handful of examples of authoritative works. Erskine May's *Treatise on the Law, Privileges, Proceedings and Usage of Parliament* (1844) is regarded as the 'Bible' of parliamentary practice, as it provides a detailed guide to rules and precedents. A. V. Dicey's *An Introduction to the Study of the Law of the Constitution* (1884) examined the relationship between the law and the nineteenth-century constitution. It described a system of responsible cabinet government in a parliamentary democracy with a constitutional monarchy, where parliament was legally sovereign and the people politically sovereign.

European Union law

On 1 January 1973, the UK became a member of the European Economic Community (EEC). The EEC was subsequently renamed the European Community (EC) and, since the Maastricht Treaty came into force in 1993, the European Union (EU). The treaties establishing the European Union, legislation emanating from the EU and judgements of the European Court of Justice have all become a part of the UK constitution.

Summary

Sources of the UK constitution

- statute law (i.e. Acts of Parliament)
- common law (i.e. court decisions and customs)
- conventions
- authoritative works
- European Union law

Key terms

- **Common law.** Law derived from decisions in court cases and from general customs.
- **Convention.** An established norm of political behaviour rooted in past experience rather than the law.
- **Precedent.** A judicial ruling that becomes an authority when deciding later cases.
- **Royal prerogative.** Discretionary powers of the Crown that are exercised in the monarch's name by government ministers.
- **Statute law.** Law derived from Acts of Parliament and subordinate legislation.

Key principles of the UK constitution

Four core principles formed the building blocks of the traditional UK constitution:
- parliamentary sovereignty
- the rule of law
- the unitary state
- parliamentary government

Membership of the European Union has added a fifth main characteristic.

Parliamentary sovereignty

The doctrine of parliamentary sovereignty is the cornerstone of the UK constitution. It basically states that the Westminster Parliament is the supreme law-making body in the United Kingdom. *Sovereignty* means legal supremacy: parliament has ultimate law-making authority. This legislative supremacy is constructed around three propositions:
- Legislation cannot be overturned by any higher authority.
- The Westminster Parliament can legislate on any subject of its choosing.
- No parliament can bind its successors.

The Houses of Parliament at Westminster

These propositions theoretically give parliament great power within the UK polity. In practice, the government of the day exercises significant control over the legislative process — for example, through the whip system of party discipline and control over the legislative timetable. So it is the executive branch that has dominant status. Parliamentary sovereignty has contributed to the centralisation of power in the UK state: power is concentrated in the hands of the executive, while other institutions are not constitutionally protected. As no parliament can bind its successors, a future UK government is free to legislate to abolish the Scottish Parliament, return hereditary peers to the House of Lords or withdraw from the European Union.

Bills that have important constitutional implications are normally considered in a Committee of the Whole House rather than in a standing committee. However, in many other states, the amendment of constitutional law must follow additional stages in the legislative process, such as achieving a weighted majority in parliament or approval in a referendum. This is not the case in the UK.

Constraints on parliamentary sovereignty

The doctrine of parliamentary sovereignty means that, in theory, parliament can make or unmake any law of its choosing. In practice, however, a series of constraints limit the range of issues on which parliament can hope to legislate successfully. Some areas of life lie outside the reach of parliamentary power. No Parliament can, for example, change the laws of physics or ensure that England will win the next World Cup.

Of greater political relevance, membership of the European Union and the provisions of the Human Rights Act (1998) are constraints on parliamentary sovereignty, as these set limits on permissible legislation. The European Communities

Act (1972) stated that European Community (now European Union) law overrides UK law when the two are in contradiction. EU law, not the statute or constitutional law of an EU member state, has supremacy. In the case of the Human Rights Act, all UK legislation passed since the act came into force has to comply with the provisions of the European Convention on Human Rights. Despite these limitations, however, parliamentary sovereignty remains valid. Parliament retains ultimate legislative authority as it can repeal either act.

Conventions and traditional modes of behaviour may also shape opinion on what is practicable and desirable. It is expected, for example, that proposals for significant constitutional reform will have been highlighted in the election manifesto of the governing party, giving the government a *mandate* to act. Governments have also sought to bolster the legitimacy of constitutional reform measures (e.g. devolution) by holding *referendums*. The outcome of a referendum is not strictly binding on parliament, but the increased use of referendums nonetheless challenges the notion of the supremacy of parliament.

There is no overriding constitutional bar to a future government legislating to abolish the Scottish Parliament. But significant political and practical obstacles would present themselves. An attempt at abolition might provoke a constitutional crisis, particularly if most people in Scotland continued to support the Scottish Parliament and if the UK government relied on the votes of English MPs to push legislation through the Westminster Parliament.

The rule of law

The rule of law is concerned with the relationship between the state and its citizens, ensuring that state action is both limited and responsible. In the UK it means that all UK citizens are under the law, including members of the royal family, the executive, legislature and judiciary. All citizens must obey the law and are equal under it. Equality before the law means that the courts can hold government ministers, police officers and public officials accountable for their actions, if they have acted outside the law or have been negligent in their duties.

The rule of law also holds that laws passed by parliament must be interpreted and applied by an independent judiciary, free from political interference. The rights of citizens are thus protected from arbitrary executive action. Aggrieved citizens can take the government or a local authority to court if they feel they have been treated improperly. Individuals charged under the law are entitled to a fair trial and should not be imprisoned without due regard for the legal process.

The rule of law is an essential feature of a liberal democracy. The doctrine of parliamentary sovereignty theoretically enables parliament to abolish these rights. However, a sustained effort to overturn the key elements of the rule of law would be widely regarded as illegitimate and anti-democratic, making it untenable. Yet governments of both main parties have legislated to restrict the rights of citizens (and of third-country nationals, such as asylum seekers) to have full recourse to the legal process.

A unitary state

The United Kingdom is made up of four component nations: England, Scotland, Wales and Northern Ireland. The UK has traditionally been viewed as a *unitary state*. A unitary state is a centralised state in which political power is located at the centre in national institutions. Subnational institutions do not have autonomous powers that are constitutionally safeguarded — they are either politically weak or non-existent. In the case of the UK, parliamentary sovereignty has ensured centralisation and weak local and subnational government. By contrast, power is shared between national (i.e. federal) and regional (i.e. state) governments in federal systems such as the USA and Germany. Their constitutions grant each tier of government autonomy and specific powers.

Unitary or union state?

Some political scientists (e.g. James Mitchell) have argued that the description 'unitary state' does not reflect accurately the character of the multinational UK. Mitchell prefers to think of the UK as a 'union state'. A classic *unitary state* exhibits a high degree of both centralisation and standardisation: all parts of the state are governed in the same way and share a common political culture. In a *union state*, by contrast, important political and cultural differences remain. These asymmetries reflect the different ways in which parts of the state were united.

The component nations of the UK came together in different ways: Wales was invaded by England, Scotland joined the union by means of an international treaty, while Northern Ireland remained part of the UK after the establishment of the Irish Free State. Political and cultural differences survived: Scotland retained its own legal system, Wales its own language and Northern Ireland separate institutions and political parties.

Nonetheless, political power was concentrated at the centre in Westminster and Whitehall. By the second half of the twentieth century, the interests of each nation were represented in London by a government department headed by a cabinet minister. But the Scottish Office, Welsh Office and Northern Ireland Office were also agents of central government, implementing policy in these nations. Important policy decisions were made at the centre and imposed on the rest of the UK even when the local population signalled its discontent.

Key terms

➤ **Devolution.** The transfer of political power from central government to subnational government.

➤ **Federalism.** The sharing of power, enshrined in a constitution, between national (federal) and regional (state) authorities.

➤ **Union state.** A state in which there are cultural differences and where, despite a strong centre, different parts of the state are governed in slightly different ways.

➤ **Unitary state.** A homogeneous state in which power is concentrated at the political centre and all parts of the state are governed in the same way.

Parliamentary government in a constitutional monarchy

Under the UK constitution, government takes place through parliament under a constitutional monarchy. Government ministers are politically accountable to parliament, are legally accountable to the Crown and must face the verdict of the electorate at least once every 5 years. Between general elections, a government relies upon its majority in the House of Commons to survive and enact its legislative programme.

The balance of power between different institutions of the UK state has, of course, altered over time. The 'Glorious Revolution' of 1689 established the supremacy of parliament over the monarchy. The key conventions of the constitutional monarchy gradually fell into place. The monarch retained formal powers (e.g. to assent to legislation), but their usage was constrained. The extension of the franchise enhanced the position of the House of Commons; it had overtaken the House of Lords as the predominant legislative chamber by the early twentieth century. Political parties emerged as key actors in the conduct of government. The first-past-the-post electoral system and two-party system tended to produce single-party government. The majority party thus controlled the cabinet and exercised considerable discipline over its members in the House of Commons.

By the mid-nineteenth century, the UK political system was one of cabinet government. Cabinet was then the key policy-making body, but a century later considerable power was vested in the office of prime minister. This led some commentators to argue that prime ministerial government had replaced cabinet government (see Chapter 11).

Key terms

➤ **Cabinet government.** A system of government in which executive power is vested in a cabinet, whose members exercise collective responsibility, rather than a single office.

➤ **Constitutional monarchy.** A political system in which the monarch is the formal head of state, but the monarch's legal powers are exercised by government ministers.

➤ **Parliamentary government.** A political system in which government takes place through parliament, blurring the boundaries between the executive and legislative branches.

➤ **Prime ministerial government.** The view that the prime minister has become the dominant actor in UK government and is able to bypass the cabinet.

Membership of the European Union

Membership of the European Union has had important implications for the UK constitution. The basis for UK membership of the then EEC was provided for by the European Communities Act (1972). Its provisions on the basis of Community law (now European Union law) in the UK have important constitutional implications:

➤ The act gave legal force to existing and all future EC law. EC regulations do not need to receive the explicit assent of parliament before they become binding.

➤ EU law has precedence over domestic UK law. In the event of a conflict between the two, EU law takes precedence and must be applied. This may mean that UK law has to be amended. The Merchant Shipping Act (1988) had to be repealed when the House of Lords found, in the 1991 *Factortame* case, that parts of it infringed EC law on the registration of fishing boats.

➤ The UK courts apply EU law directly. Where questions of interpretation of EC law arise, they are referred to the European Court of Justice for a ruling.

Membership of the EU thus challenges parliamentary sovereignty. The courts can set Acts of Parliament aside, as the *Factortame* case illustrated. However, parliament remains formally sovereign as it retains the right to repeal the European Communities Act (1972). This would signal the UK's intention to leave the EU, but difficult negotiations would then be required to determine issues such as the UK's relationship with the EU single market. The UK courts would be faced with a thorny question should parliament deliberately pass legislation that infringed EU law.

The UK government does not enjoy sole policy-making power in many important areas of public policy. The range of policy areas in which the EU has policy competence has increased significantly since the single market programme was launched in the mid-1980s. Most UK government departments work with the EU in developing and implementing policy. The EU has exclusive competence in trade, agriculture and fisheries policy. Policy responsibility for issues such as regional policy, working conditions and environmental policy is shared between the EU and its member states. The Council of Ministers, which acts as the EU's co-legislature with the European Parliament, increasingly takes decisions by qualified majority voting. This means that a member state opposing a policy decision cannot veto it. But unanimity remains the norm for particularly sensitive issues such as taxation and treaty change.

Summary

Key principles of the UK constitution

➤ The Westminster Parliament is sovereign.
➤ The rule of law governs the relationship between individuals and the state.
➤ The UK is a unitary state in which power is concentrated at the centre.
➤ Government takes place through parliament in a constitutional monarchy.
➤ The UK is a member of the European Union.

Strengths and weaknesses of the traditional constitution

Strengths

Supporters of the traditional constitutional settlement argue that it has a number of enduring strengths (see Box 9.3). While they recognise that improvements are required, adherents to this *Westminster model* argue that reform should be limited and pragmatic. Changes should work with the grain of the existing constitution rather than seek to overhaul its key components.

One perceived strength of the traditional constitution is its proven worth. The constitution has proved its value by operating effectively over many years. Pragmatic reforms, introduced where there is a clear case for change, have enabled the constitution to adapt to changed circumstances. This flexibility is another positive feature, as the mechanics of the constitution can be adapted smoothly and speedily.

Conservatives view the constitution as an organic body of rules rather than an artificial creation. It has evolved over time and reflects the history and enduring values of the British people. The rules and practices that make up the constitution form a coherent and intelligible whole.

The Westminster model provides for strong and effective government. The doctrine of parliamentary sovereignty establishes supreme authority within the political system. But it is the government, particularly the core executive, rather than parliament that

---

Box 9.3 **Strengths and weaknesses of the traditional constitution**

Strengths
- ➤ It provides a coherent system of government.
- ➤ It has evolved over time, reflecting the values of the British people.
- ➤ Parliamentary sovereignty ensures a clear centre of authority.
- ➤ The rule of law protects the rights of citizens.
- ➤ Government is responsible — it is accountable to parliament and the electorate.
- ➤ Government is effective — governments can implement their policy programmes.
- ➤ The constitution is flexible and can be easily adapted.

Weaknesses
- ➤ Parliamentary sovereignty and a strong executive produce centralised government.
- ➤ Local and subnational governments are not constitutionally protected.
- ➤ The rights of citizens are weak and not safeguarded effectively.
- ➤ Pre-democratic elements (e.g. the monarchy and House of Lords) survive.
- ➤ Constitutional rules and conventions are unclear and can be overridden.
- ➤ Changes to the constitution do not require special procedures (e.g. a referendum).

is at the heart of the policy-making process. In the UK, the process of government is conducted by political parties: the cabinet is party-based and the governing party exercises significant control over the legislative process in the House of Commons. Power is thus concentrated at the centre, enabling the government of the day to implement most of its political objectives successfully. Ministers, not judges or bureaucrats, make crucial political decisions.

Strong government is also responsible government under the UK constitution. The government is accountable to parliament, which scrutinises its activities, and responsive to the electorate. In a general election in a two-party system, voters effectively choose between alternative governments. The first-part-the-post electoral system usually gives the winning party a parliamentary majority, allowing it to fulfil its mandate. An unpopular government will pay the price at the polls. Government is also responsible, as the rule of law protects citizens against arbitrary power.

Weaknesses

Critics of the traditional constitution argue that it had a number of serious weaknesses that could only be rectified by a significant reform programme (see Box 9.3). The uncodified nature of the constitution creates problems of clarity and interpretation. It is not always clear when a government has acted unconstitutionally: conventions on ministerial responsibility, for example, are unclear. Parliament, which is controlled by the government of the day, is the final arbiter of the constitution. This is potentially dangerous because there is no constitutional court to check the power of the state and defend civil liberties.

Power is concentrated dangerously at the centre. There are few safeguards against the arbitrary exercise of state power. Parliamentary sovereignty means that even the key tenets of the rule of law are not fully enshrined in constitutional law. A government with a strong majority can force through legislation undermining civil liberties and weakening other institutions. There are insufficient checks and balances within the constitution and no formal separation of powers. The executive exercises considerable control over the legislative process. Neither local nor subnational government has constitutionally protected status. In June 2003, the Labour government announced plans to end the situation under which the Lord Chancellor is a senior member of the executive (as head of a government department with a seat in cabinet), the legislature (as Speaker of the House of Lords) and the judiciary (with the power to appoint judges).

Critics of the traditional constitution depict it as outdated, inefficient and un-democratic. Conventions are unclear and key elements of the common law, notably the royal prerogative, date back to a pre-modern era. The House of Lords is also a throwback to a pre-democratic era: the hereditary principle cannot be justified in a liberal democratic state.

Summary

Strengths and weaknesses of the traditional constitution

Strengths:
➤ coherent and tested
➤ clear source of political authority
➤ rule of law
➤ flexible

Weaknesses:
➤ undemocratic and outdated
➤ excessive centralisation of power
➤ weak civil liberties
➤ prone to manipulation

The constitution under pressure

For much of the twentieth century, there was broad political consensus in support of the constitution and the key institutions of the UK state. The constitution continued to evolve, but in a largely peaceful and pragmatic fashion. Governments of all political persuasions were happy to work within the existing constitutional framework. Political elites and the electorate regarded the constitution as legitimate and effective.

However, the constitution was not always a uniting factor in twentieth-century political life. At times it was the focus of serious political dispute. These moments of dispute coincided with periods of political dislocation, with the main parties opposing each other's positions on the major constitutional issues of the day. The 'Irish Question' dominated UK politics in the late nineteenth and early twentieth century. It came close to provoking civil war before a solution of sorts was reached in 1921–22 with the creation of the Irish Free State (which later became the Republic of Ireland) and a six-county Northern Ireland that remained part of the UK. A constitutional crisis also arose when the House of Lords refused to support the 'People's Budget' introduced by the Liberal government in 1909. It was not resolved fully until the Parliament Act (1911), reducing the powers of the Lords, was passed. Both crises went to the heart of the UK constitution and altered its fundamental principles decisively: the unitary state and parliamentary sovereignty respectively.

The 1970s

Further challenges to the established constitutional settlement arose in the 1970s, and the political system appeared ill equipped to deal with them. They included economic decline, ineffectual government, direct rule in Northern Ireland and membership of the EEC. Support for the two main parties declined and consensus politics broke down as Labour moved to the left and the Conservatives embraced New Right thinking.

Commentators questioned the efficacy of the constitution. In 1976, Conservative politician Lord Hailsham warned that executive dominance of the legislature was producing an elective dictatorship in which governments could ride roughshod over the rights of individuals. He and others (e.g. Lord Denning) argued that a Bill of Rights was needed to entrench the rights of citizens. Political scientist S. E. Finer believed that the first-past-the-post electoral system had produced *adversarial politics* and he advocated proportional representation (see Chapter 3).

The political turmoil of the 1970s did not produce a new constitutional settlement, but important changes were introduced. The most significant change was membership of the EEC, which qualified the sovereignty of parliament. Support for devolution grew in Scotland and Wales, but did not prove sufficient for the two referendums held in 1978 to achieve the requisite majorities for new assemblies to be created. The devolution referendums and the 1975 referendum on UK membership of the EEC also challenged the traditional view of parliamentary sovereignty.

Conservative governments, 1979–97

Conservative governments were elected in the four general elections held between 1979 and 1992. On each occasion, the Tories achieved a parliamentary majority under the first-past-the-post electoral system without winning a majority of the popular vote. Some of the policies introduced by the Conservatives, such as the weakening of local government, had important constitutional consequences. In other areas where the Conservatives maintained the status quo, their inaction was criticised. The constitution was once again a thorny political issue as the long period of Conservative rule strained both the legitimacy and the efficacy of the traditional constitution.

The governments of Margaret Thatcher (1979–90) and John Major (1990–97) were both traditionalist and radical in their approach to the constitution. They were traditionalist in upholding many of the key features of the constitution. Demands for devolution were rejected because the Conservatives viewed the UK as a unitary state. They also exploited the doctrine of parliamentary sovereignty to centralise power further. Constitutional radicalism came from the Conservative Party's adherence to the New Right's message of free market economics. Nationalised industries were privatised and the functions of local authorities dispersed to *quasi-autonomous non-governmental organisations* (quangos), whose members were appointed by government ministers.

Centralisation

Power became even more concentrated at the centre during the Thatcher and Major period. In much of the rest of Europe, subnational governments gained greater autonomy. But in the UK, the trend was towards centralisation as the centre gained additional power at the expense of local government. Local government autonomy was eroded as the government restricted the spending powers and policy-making role of elected local authorities. The Greater London Council and six metropolitan counties were abolished.

The concentration of power in Whitehall was felt most acutely in Scotland, where demands for devolution intensified. Conservative governments were returned in four UK general elections despite their growing unpopularity outside England. Thatcher paid little heed to Scottish distinctiveness, imposing her monetarist policies on a

UK-wide basis. John Major's administration sought to strengthen the Union by granting limited new powers to the Scottish Office, but this was not enough to turn the pro-devolution tide. A Scottish Constitutional Convention, attended by Labour and Liberal Democrat representatives, agreed a blueprint for a Scottish Parliament. Tory warnings that devolution would spell the break-up of the United Kingdom fell on deaf ears.

New forms of governance

Under the Conservatives, traditional methods of government gave way to new forms of governance. In the past, formal institutions such as central government departments and local authorities had been responsible for deciding on policy, allocating public funds and implementing policy decisions. By the 1990s, many of the traditional policy-delivery functions of the civil service and local authorities had been transferred to unelected agencies, which controlled significant amounts of public money. Government had been replaced by new forms of governance in which social activities were directed by a wide range of actors and involved a complex array of procedures. Nationalised industries such as electricity and the railways were privatised; new regulatory bodies oversaw their activities. Tasks formerly carried out by Whitehall were now undertaken by executive agencies (e.g. the Passports Agency), which operated at arm's length from their parent government department, while local authorities lost some of their functions to quangos.

Loss of faith in parliament

Parliament appeared ill equipped to challenge a government that was determined to press ahead with radical socioeconomic policies. Backbench Conservative MPs made life more difficult for the Major government in the 1990s as the issue of Europe divided the Tory Party. But the behaviour of some Conservative MPs damaged the image of parliament. High-profile cases of 'sleaze' exposed both a worrying decline in ethics in public life and the failure of parliament to keep its own house in order. In response, the Major government established a Committee on Standards in Public Life. Its recommendations on codes of practice for ministers, civil servants and MPs were introduced, but the damage had been done.

The conduct of government ministers was also questioned. The judicial review of the actions of the government became more prominent. In a number of cases, the courts ruled against ministers who had overstepped their powers. The 1996 Scott Report into the sale of arms to Iraq found that ministers had misled parliament, but no minister resigned. Finally, the transfer of functions from Whitehall to executive agencies made it more difficult for parliament to hold ministers accountable for policy problems.

Erosion of civil liberties

The New Right proclaimed the virtues of individual liberty in the marketplace. The Conservative governments presented their policies on trade union reform, privatisation and reform of the welfare state as giving the individual greater freedom of choice.

The Citizen's Charter improved the information available to citizens about the performance of the public sector and gave them greater redress of grievances.

However, the Conservative government restricted civil liberties too. Examples included restrictions on freedom of movement during the 1984–85 miners' strike, increases in the powers of the police and the prosecution of civil servants for leaking information classified under the Official Secrets Act. The government lost a number of high-profile cases in the European Court of Human Rights.

Royal scandals

Not even the monarchy escaped the loss of faith in the traditional constitutional settlement. Public support for the monarchy declined as the behaviour of some junior members of the royal family brought negative publicity. The role and future of the UK's constitutional monarchy became a matter for serious political debate, particularly after the death of Diana, Princess of Wales in 1997. Suggested reforms included amendments to the Act of Succession to end *primogeniture* — the practice whereby male heirs take precedence over female heirs. Ultimately, changes to the role of the monarchy were largely symbolic: the queen, for example, agreed to pay income tax.

Summary

The constitution under pressure

- centralisation of power
- new forms of governance
- decline of parliament
- erosion of civil liberties
- questioning of the monarchy

Key terms

- **Civil liberties.** Fundamental individual rights that provide protection from interference by the state.
- **Governance.** The range of institutions, networks and relationships involved in making social decisions.
- **Judicial review.** The power of the judiciary to review the actions of government and declare them unlawful.
- **Quango.** A quasi-autonomous, non-governmental organisation: that is, a public body that operates at arm's length from the government.
- **'Sleaze'.** In politics, behaviour characterised by low standards of honesty or morality.

The movement for reform

In the late 1980s and the 1990s, a coalition of political parties, pressure groups and commentators developed a coherent and influential case for reform. They argued that the actions, and the inaction, of the Conservatives had undermined the legitimacy of the traditional constitutional settlement. Radical proposals for reform emerged and were taken up by Labour and the Liberal Democrats. By 1997, only the Conservatives opposed a radical reform.

The Liberal Democrats, who have long placed constitutional reform at the heart of their programme, advocated radical change. But it was the pressure group Charter 88 that proved a catalyst for the emerging reform movement. As a non-partisan body, it won support from across the left and centre of UK politics with its demands for a written constitution, a Bill of Rights, electoral reform, devolution and an elected upper House. The left-wing Institute for Public Policy Research (IPPR) and right-wing Institute of Economic Affairs (IEA) both produced draft written constitutions. *The Economist*, the *Guardian* and the *Independent* voiced support for reform, too. Opinion polls conducted in the mid-1990s suggested that the public was becoming disillusioned with the traditional constitution.

Labour and the constitution

For much of its history, the Labour Party viewed constitutional reform as an unwelcome distraction from its main goal, namely to improve socioeconomic conditions for the working class. In government, Labour's few attempts to reform the constitution (e.g. the 1968 proposals for reform of the House of Lords) had failed, often because of opposition from backbench Labour MPs. In the early 1980s, the left were influential within the Labour Party. In its 1983 election manifesto, Labour adopted a socialist approach to the constitution, proposing large-scale nationalisation, the abolition of the House of Lords and withdrawal from the EC. Heavy election defeat forced a painful rethink.

Labour remained wary of constitutional reform in the late 1980s, but beneath the surface important changes were under way. Influential figures in the party began to embrace a liberal approach to constitutional reform. The liberal perspective focused on values such as decentralisation, civil liberties, open government, modernisation and electoral reform. It was voiced by a range of actors on the left of UK politics. In the English regions, Labour councillors and MEPs were attracted by the style of regionalism prevalent in other EU member states, and the political rewards it offered. The Scottish Constitutional Convention brought together Labour and Liberal Democrat politicians plus representatives from Scottish civil society to draw up an agreed blueprint for devolution.

By the mid-1990s, the Labour Party was advocating much of the liberal con-stitutional reform agenda, including devolution, a strengthening of civil liberties, reform of the House of Lords and greater freedom of information. Crucially, however, it did not support a written constitution, preferring a step-by-step approach to reform. Electoral reform proved the most contentious issue within the party. Under John Smith, Labour agreed to introduce forms of proportional representation for elections to a

Scottish Parliament and the European Parliament. But Smith and then Blair pledged only to hold a referendum on electoral reform for Westminster.

Cooperation between Labour and the Liberal Democrats on constitutional reform continued under Blair. Ahead of the 1997 general election, the two parties issued a joint report pledging support for a wide-ranging programme of reform. This included the end of hereditary peers in the House of Lords, a Scottish Parliament and Welsh Assembly to be elected by proportional representation, legislation on human rights and freedom of information, plus the creation of a commission to explore alternatives to the first-past-the-post system for general elections. After Labour's landslide victory, senior Liberal Democrats sat on a cabinet subcommittee examining constitutional reform.

Labour's reform proposals

In its 1997 general election manifesto, Labour included pledges on human rights, freedom of information, devolution, electoral reform and parliamentary reform (see Box 9.4).

Labour's case for constitutional reform was built around four main themes:

➤ **Modernisation.** Institutions such as parliament, the executive and the civil service were using outdated and inefficient procedures that were in need of reform.

➤ **Democratisation.** Participation in the political process would be encouraged through electoral reform and greater use of referendums.

Box 9.4 Labour's 1997 manifesto pledges on constitutional reform

The Labour Party promised to:

➤ hold referendums on devolution in Scotland and Wales

➤ establish a Scottish Parliament with legislative and tax-varying powers

➤ establish a Welsh Assembly with secondary legislative powers

➤ continue negotiations on power-sharing devolution for Northern Ireland

➤ following a referendum, establish a directly elected mayor and strategic authority for London

➤ establish Regional Development Agencies in the English regions

➤ create directly elected regional government in England where it is supported in a referendum

➤ reform local government and pilot the idea of elected mayors with executive powers

➤ incorporate the European Convention on Human Rights into UK law

➤ introduce legislation on freedom of information

➤ begin the reform of the House of Lords by removing hereditary peers

➤ modernise the House of Commons

➤ ban foreign donations to political parties

➤ introduce proportional representation for elections to the devolved assemblies, European Parliament and the office of Mayor of London

➤ establish an independent commission to examine the case for electoral reform for Westminster elections. If there is a positive case, hold a referendum on electoral reform

➤ hold a referendum on membership of the euro, should the government decide to seek entry

---

> **Decentralisation.** Decision-making powers would be devolved to new institutions in Scotland and Wales, and the role of local government would be enhanced.
> **Rights.** The rights of citizens would be strengthened and safeguarded.

Constitutional reform since 1997

The constitutional reforms introduced by the Labour government since 1997 are discussed in detail in the relevant chapters of this book. However, the main reforms are outlined below (and in Box 9.5) and their significance assessed.

Human rights

The Human Rights Act (1998) enshrined most of the provisions of the European Convention on Human Rights (ECHR) in UK law. The rights protected by the convention include:

> the right to life
> the right to liberty and security of person
> the right to fair administration of justice
> respect for private and family life, home and correspondence
> freedom of thought and expression
> freedom of peaceful assembly and association
> the right to marry and found a family
> freedom from torture and degrading treatment
> freedom from discrimination in the enjoyment of these rights

The ECHR was agreed in 1950 and falls within the remit of the Council of Europe. This intergovernmental organisation is separate from, and should not be confused with, the European Union. Alleged abuses of human rights are investigated by a European Commission on Human Rights and, if necessary, referred to the European Court of Human Rights (based in Strasbourg) for a ruling.

The UK was one of the original signatories but did not directly incorporate the provisions of the ECHR into domestic law. From 1965, UK citizens seeking redress of grievance under the convention could pursue their case through the court in Strasbourg, but could not do so through the UK courts. The process was complex, costly and time-consuming.

The UK has one of the worst records for violations of the convention. Examples of rulings against the UK government include cases on corporal punishment, telephone tapping, the rights of transsexuals and the rights of prisoners. The government was not legally obliged to alter legislation accordingly in such cases, but tended to do so for political reasons.

Incorporation into UK law

Under the Human Rights Act, UK courts and tribunals now hear and decide upon cases brought under the convention. Judges can declare legislation incompatible with the ECHR

Box 9.5 Labour and constitutional reform, 1997–2001

Devolution and decentralisation

Scotland Act (1998): established a Scottish Parliament with legislative and tax-varying powers.

Wales Act (1998): established a National Assembly for Wales with executive powers.

Northern Ireland Act (1998): established a Northern Ireland Assembly and power-sharing executive.

Regional Development Agencies Act (1998): established nine Regional Development Agencies in England.

Greater London Authority Act (1999): created an elected mayor and strategic authority in London.

Rights

Human Rights Act (1998): incorporated European Convention on Human Rights into UK law.

Freedom of Information Act (2000): provided greater access to information held by public authorities.

Elections, parties and referendums

Referendums (Scotland and Wales) Act (1997): provided for devolution referendums in Scotland and Wales.

Registration of Political Parties Act (1998): required political parties to register as legal bodies.

Greater London Authority Referendum Act (1998): provided for a referendum in London on an elected mayor and assembly.

European Parliamentary Elections Act (1999): established a 'closed list' system of proportional representation for elections to the European Parliament.

Political Parties, Elections and Referendum Act (2000): regulated the conduct of elections and referendums.

and overturn executive decisions. However, the courts cannot automatically overturn legislation that is declared incompatible: it is up to parliament to amend the legislation speedily. Should parliament fail to do so, a citizen would have to take the case to the European Court of Human Rights in Strasbourg, as the 1998 act did not incorporate Article 13 of the ECHR, which provides for a remedy against breaches. But the act does require the UK government to ensure that legislation is compatible with the convention. Since it came into effect on 2 October 2000, all bills introduced at Westminster must have received a declaration of compatibility with the ECHR from government lawyers. Legislation introduced in the devolved assemblies must also be declared compatible.

The act has the potential to bring about significant constitutional change by reshaping and clarifying the relationship between the individual and the state. The UK courts have already heard a number of cases brought against public authorities under the new legislation. In 2000, a Scottish court found that a provision in the Road Traffic Act (1988) that the owner of a car caught speeding must reveal the identity of the driver infringed the right to silence. In 2003, Radio One DJ Sara Cox was awarded £50,000 damages after a court ruled that the *Sunday People* had infringed her right to privacy by publishing nude photographs of her. More significant verdicts are likely in the coming years as the courts build up a body of case law on human rights and reach decisions that have important political ramifications.

The European Court of Human Rights, Strasbourg

Radicals argued that the Blair government should have drawn up a specific UK Bill of Rights, placing constitutional limits on the executive and increasing the statutory protection of individual rights from state encroachment. A Bill of Rights would have formed part of a new written constitution. Other critics, though, felt that the Human Rights Act had strengthened the hand of judges *vis-à-vis* Members of Parliament. Concerns were expressed about the socially unrepresentative nature of senior judges and the lack of accountability for judicial decisions.

Other measures introduced by the Blair government have restricted civil liberties. The 9/11 terrorist attacks in the USA led to new security legislation in the UK. The Anti-Terrorism, Crime and Security Act (2001) brought about a derogation (i.e. an exemption) from Article 5 of the ECHR (the right to liberty and security). This allowed the indefinite detention without trial of those foreign nationals suspected of terrorist activity who could not be deported to a safe country. In 2004, the House of Lords ruled that the detention of 12 people in this manner was unlawful as it discriminated against foreign nationals. The government responded by introducing the Prevention of Terrorism Act (2005), which applies to both UK citizens and foreign nationals, replacing indefinite detention with house arrest and surveillance. This ended the UK's temporary derogation from Article 5. Further restrictions were proposed following the July 2005 terrorist attacks in London.

Domestic legislation introduced by the Blair government allows complex fraud cases and cases where 'jury-nobbling' is suspected to be heard by judges alone, thereby restricting the right to trial by jury. The double jeopardy rule — that individuals acquitted of a serious crime should not be tried again for the same offence — was overturned by the Criminal Justice Act (2003). This act also enabled judges to allow juries to hear details of previous offences. Controversial proposals for the introduction of identity cards were reintroduced at the start of Labour's third term.

Freedom of information

In its 1997 election manifesto, Labour pledged to introduce legislation to provide individuals with greater access to information held by public bodies. The Freedom of Information Act (2000) disappointed liberal reformers, particularly as the government had retreated from some of the proposals contained in the 1997 White Paper, *Your*

Right to Know. The act gives individuals a general right of access to personal information held on them by some 100,000 public bodies. It also requires public authorities to publish a range of information, although there are a number of crucial exemptions. Information can, for example, be withheld on the grounds of national security or public safety, while citizens do not have an automatic right to see the policy advice provided to ministers. Since the act came into force fully in 2005, politicians, journalists and citizens have requested access to information on matters such as government policy, school inspections and the performance records of surgeons.

Devolution and decentralisation

Devolution is the transfer of powers from central government to subnational institutions. In the case of legislative devolution, the subnational bodies have legislative, executive and perhaps tax-raising functions. Legislative devolution existed for Northern Ireland between 1922 and 1972. Scottish and Welsh affairs were handled at the centre by territorial ministries — the Scottish Office and, from 1964, the Welsh Office.

Since 1997, power has been devolved to new institutions in Scotland, Wales and Northern Ireland. The government's proposals were approved in a referendum in each nation. Devolution has been asymmetric. Rather than following a standard blueprint, each of the devolved institutions has different powers and distinctive features. These variations reflect the different circumstances of the three nations in question. Pressure for devolution had been stronger in Scotland than in Wales. The new arrangements for Northern Ireland emerged from the talks held between the UK and Irish governments and Northern Ireland political parties that produced the 1998 Good Friday Agreement.

The Scottish Parliament has legislative and tax-varying powers. It and the Scottish Executive have sole responsibility for policy on issues such as education, health and local government. The parliament can also vary the rate of income tax by 3% (i.e. three pence in the pound). The National Assembly for Wales is a weaker body. Unlike its Scottish counterpart, the assembly does not have primary legislative authority. It has only secondary legislative and executive powers, which means that it can only fill in the details of, and implement, legislation passed by Westminster in policy areas such as education and health. The Northern Ireland Assembly has legislative powers over a similar range of policy areas to the Scottish Parliament. Special procedures exist in the assembly to ensure cross-community support. Following the first elections to the assembly, four political parties were entitled to ministerial posts in the power-sharing Northern Ireland Executive.

Constitutional implications of devolution

Devolution has already had a significant impact on the traditional constitutional settlement. The UK no longer fits the classic definition of a unitary state — although, as we saw above, even the pre-devolution UK was more like a union state. Nor does the

UK fit the standard definition of a federal state — that is, a state in which power is shared between different tiers of government, with autonomous subnational institutions enjoying significant authority.

The new constitutional settlement does have quasi-federal features: there is a formal division of powers and a new structure of intergovernmental relations, for example. The legislation creating the devolved institutions, however, sought to safeguard parliamentary sovereignty and place limits on the powers of the new bodies. The Westminster Parliament remains sovereign and retains the right to overrule or abolish the devolved institutions. The legislation also identified *reserved powers* that remain exclusive to Westminster. These include crucial areas such as economic policy, foreign and defence policy, and constitutional affairs.

Devolution has had further important implications for the UK constitution. These are discussed in more depth in Chapter 13 but are summarised here.

- **Differential policy.** The devolved institutions have introduced or proposed policies that differ from those in place in the rest of the UK. Northern Ireland and Wales abolished school league tables, while the Scottish Executive has abolished tuition fees for students and provides free personal care for the elderly.

- **Intergovernmental relations.** New mechanisms governing relations between central government and the devolved executives have been put in place. These include Concordats between government departments and the devolved bodies and a Joint Ministerial Committee where ministers discuss matters of common concern. In 2001, the Judicial Committee of the Privy Council made its first ruling on where competences lie in the post-devolution UK.

- **Electoral systems.** The devolved assemblies are elected by proportional representation. This has made it more apparent that the UK has multiparty systems rather than a two-party system. The executives in Scotland, Northern Ireland and (from 2000–03) Wales have all been controlled by coalition governments, which were previously rare in UK politics.

- **Changes at Westminster.** Procedures in the Westminster Parliament (e.g. questions to ministers and committee activity) have had to be amended. The number of Scottish constituencies was reduced from 72 to 59 at the 2005 general election.

- **Territorial ministries.** The posts of secretary of state for Scotland and secretary of state for Wales lost their status as single cabinet positions in their own right in 2003, when they were combined with other posts. The Scotland Office and Wales Office were subsumed in a new Department for Constitutional Affairs.

This list is likely to grow longer as the rules concerning government funding for the component nations of the UK (currently governed by the *Barnett formula*) are re-examined and the role of the Department for Constitutional Affairs is clarified.

The 'West Lothian Question' asks why Scottish MPs at Westminster should be able to vote on purely English matters when English MPs can no longer vote on matters devolved to the Scottish Parliament. In 2003–04, legislation on foundation hospitals and tuition fees for England was passed only with the support of Scottish MPs. Critics want Scottish MPs to be prevented from voting on English matters.

Devolution is a process, not an event. The devolved institutions in Scotland and Wales have bedded-in with few problems. But there have already been demands for changes to the electoral system in Wales and Scotland and an increase in the powers of the Welsh Assembly. In Northern Ireland, the new institutions have been suspended since October 2002; the situation has been made more problematic by a fall in support for parties in favour of the Good Friday Agreement, and remains fluid.

England

The English dimension of devolution is still to be addressed fully. In its first term in office, the Labour government established Regional Development Agencies to administer policy in the English regions. In its second term, Labour moved ahead with its proposals for elected regional assemblies (albeit with limited powers) in those English regions where public support is confirmed in a referendum. However, the 2004 'no' vote in a referendum on an elected assembly for the north east forced the government to shelve its plans.

Local government in England has been reformed. London was the first city to have a directly elected mayor and an assembly with executive power in areas such as transport and the environment. The first elected mayor, Ken Livingstone, introduced a congestion charge for motorists entering central London from 2003. Local councils were obliged to reform their political management, with the government favouring the elected mayor model. By late 2002, 30 local authorities had held referendums on introducing an elected mayor, but the change was supported in only 12 authorities.

Electoral reform

The Labour government's record on electoral reform is a mixed one. Proportional representation has been introduced for elections to the Scottish Parliament, Welsh Assembly, Northern Ireland Assembly and European Parliament, and for directly elected mayors in a number of towns and cities. These electoral systems are not uniform. However, no action has been taken to change the first-past-the-post system used in UK general elections.

A version of the additional member system (AMS) is used in elections for the Scottish Parliament and Welsh Assembly. A majority of representatives are elected by first-past-the-post in single-member constituencies, with the remainder elected as *additional members* under the closed list system of proportional representation in multi-member constituencies. These 'top-up' seats are allocated to political parties on a corrective basis. For elections to the European Parliament, the government opted for a closed list system of proportional representation. This system was criticised as it gives party chiefs the key say in candidate selection and denies voters an effective choice between candidates of the same party. Directly elected mayors in cities such as London are elected by the supplementary vote system. The single transferable vote system (STV) is used in elections to the Northern Ireland Assembly.

The Scottish and Welsh Labour parties have expressed dissatisfaction with AMS, claiming that it creates two classes of representative. From 2007, STV will be used for Scottish local elections. This means that four voting systems will be in use in Scotland — first-past-the-post for Westminster, AMS for the Scottish Parliament, the PR list system for the European Parliament, and STV for local elections.

The Jenkins Report

The Blair government established an Independent Commission on the Voting System (the 'Jenkins Commission') to examine the case for using proportional representation in general elections. The Jenkins Report (1998) recommended a unique mixed system called *AV plus*. In this system, electors would cast two votes: one for a constituency MP and one for an additional member (or 'top-up' MP); 80–85% of MPs would be elected by the alternative vote system in single-member constituencies. To win, a candidate would have to get an overall majority of the votes cast. The second preferences of the lowest-placed candidates would be transferred until one candidate received over 50%. The remaining 15–20% of MPs would be additional members drawn from 80 'top-up' areas of the UK. They would be allocated to parties on a correctional basis to produce a more proportional outcome.

Labour had promised a referendum on electoral reform for Westminster in its 1997 manifesto. However, Blair's already limited enthusiasm for PR waned still further after Labour's experiences in coalition in Scotland and Wales. The 2001 and 2005 Labour manifestos spoke only of a review of the experience of the new electoral systems. It now seems unlikely that the full Jenkins Report proposals will be put before the electorate.

Parliamentary reform

Reform of the House of Lords

The major development here has been the reform of the House of Lords. The Labour government initially intended to abolish the right of all hereditary peers to sit and vote in the Lords. However, it reached a compromise for the House of Lords Act (1999), allowing 92 hereditary peers to remain. Stage One of the government's reform programme thus produced a *transitional house*, which comprised mainly life peers and had greater balance in the representation of the two main political parties.

The government has made little progress with Stage Two of the process, when the final composition and powers of the reformed House would be settled. The Royal Commission on Reform of the House of Lords (the Wakeham Commission) recommended in 2000 that the reformed upper chamber should be partially elected with the majority of members chosen by an independent Appointments Commission.

The government's proposals were set out in the 2001 White Paper, *The House of Lords: Completing the Reform*. Its main proposals were as follows:

- The last hereditary peers would be removed.
- The new House would have 600 members — known as Members of the Lords (MLs) — serving 5- to 15-year terms.
- 120 members (20% of the total) of the House would be elected by proportional representation in regional constituencies.
- A further 20% of MLs would be non-aligned, selected by an independent Appointments Commission.
- Political parties would nominate MLs: the Appointments Commission would not have the final say on these nominations.
- The numbers of party representatives would reflect the party balance at the last general election.
- The powers of the House would remain largely unchanged, but it would lose its right to veto secondary legislation.

The proposals met strong opposition from across the political spectrum. The main points of contention were the low number of elected members (just 20% of the total) and the control that political parties would have over nominations for appointed members. Ministers were concerned that a mainly elected upper chamber would prove a serious rival for the House of Commons, creating legislative deadlock. They wanted the Commons to maintain its predominant position. The Conservatives, the Liberal Democrats, many Labour backbenchers and the House of Commons Public Accounts Committee all supported a mainly elected House of Lords.

In an effort to break the deadlock, the government set up a Joint Committee of both Houses to explore options and make recommendations. It presented seven options in late 2002, but the House of Commons rejected all seven in February 2003. The proposal for an 80% elected and 20% appointed House was defeated by just three votes. The House

Members of the Wakeham Commission, which reported in 2000

of Lords voted for an all-appointed House but this was the least popular option in the Commons, where it was defeated by 323 to 245. Blair and 12 other cabinet ministers voted for an all-appointed House, despite Labour's manifesto commitment to democratise the upper chamber.

The reform process has reached an impasse. The government issued a consultation paper but withdrew plans for legislation before the general election. The 2005 manifesto stated that the remaining hereditary peers would be removed but the future composition of the Lords would again be decided on a free vote. It is difficult to see how a consensus on reform might be forged. The government has also promised a review of conventions in the Lords and to impose a limit of 60 sitting days for the consideration of most bills in the upper House.

Reform of the House of Commons

Labour's initiatives to reform the House of Commons have been less spectacular. Changes to Prime Minister's Question Time and the working hours of the House, plus additional sittings in Westminster Hall, have modernised proceedings. The House of Commons Modernisation Committee has produced a number of proposals for change, including scrutiny of draft legislation and changes to the workings of departmental select committees. Devolution has affected procedures in the House too. The government has not backed electoral reform for Westminster.

Central government

Central government has not been a target of Labour's constitutional reform programme to the same extent as other institutions. However, many of the reforms introduced since 1997 have brought about structural and procedural change in Whitehall. The Human Rights Act (1998) requires government departments to comply with the European Convention on Human Rights. New relationships between central government and the devolved institutions have emerged and new procedures (e.g. Concordats) created to regulate them. The territorial ministries were initially reduced in size and renamed the Scotland Office and Wales Office. Then in June 2003 they became part of a newly created Department for Constitutional Affairs which would have overall responsibility for the devolution settlement. The offices of secretary of state for Scotland and secretary of state for Wales were also combined with other cabinet posts.

Labour has modernised the civil service further but the increased influence of special advisers has caused concern. The government produced a draft Civil Service Bill in 2004. It proposed only limited moves to protect the integrity of the civil service and is unlikely to reach the statute book in the near future. Little has been done little to reduce the number of quangos found at the fringes of government. Perhaps the most significant change in central government has been the gradual accretion of power at 10 Downing Street. The Prime Minister's Office and the Cabinet Office have been restructured, further strengthening the position of the prime minister. Three powerful units whose reach extends across Whitehall now exist at Number 10: a Policy Directorate, a Communications and Strategy Directorate and a Government Relations Directorate. The government argues that this centralisation of power is necessary for the delivery of effective, 'joined-up' government. However, critics believe that the prime minister's desire to exercise control over large areas of public policy has undermined the government's efforts to decentralise power.

The judiciary

Proposals for radical reforms to the judiciary were announced in 2003, first during an ill-thought-out cabinet reshuffle and then in White Papers. They included the abolition of the post of Lord Chancellor, the creation of an independent Judicial Appointments Commission, and a Supreme Court to replace the Law Lords. Of these, only the plan for an independent body to appoint judges received broad support from the legal profession.

The proposal to abolish the office of Lord Chancellor was meant to bring about the separation of the legislative, executive and judicial functions of the office. The Lord Chancellor was a member of the cabinet (with responsibility for the law and rights) and the legislature (as speaker of the House of Lords), and is head of the judiciary. But it proved difficult to disentangle these roles. The Constitutional Reform Act (2005) thus retained the office but transferred some judicial responsibilities.

The creation of a Supreme Court, scheduled for 2008, will see the 12 Law Lords taken out of the upper House to form a new court. This will also enhance the separation of powers, but the court will not have the authority to strike down legislation.

Elections, referendums and parties

The Labour government has sought to modernise and regulate the conduct of elections and referendums. The key piece of legislation was the Political Parties, Elections and Referendum Act (2000) which:

> established an independent Electoral Commission to administer, and make recom-mendations on, the conduct of elections and referendums
> set an upper limit on national campaign expenditure by political parties
> required parties to produce accounts containing details of donors and donations
> banned foreign donations to political parties

Concerned by falling turnout, the Blair government has also eased restrictions on voting (e.g. for those without a permanent residence) and encouraged alternative methods of voting (e.g. e-voting and all-postal ballots). But the increased use of postal voting has led to concerns about electoral fraud. Measures to tighten up procedures were put forward after the 2005 election.

Democratisation has been evident too in the greater use of referendums. Devolution referendums were held in Scotland, Wales and Northern Ireland, while a number of English towns and cities held local referendums on creating a directly elected mayor. In its 1997 manifesto, Labour pledged to hold a referendum on introducing proportional representation for Westminster elections, but this did not materialise. The government proposed two referendums on the UK's relationship with the EU. However, plans for a referendum on the EU constitution were shelved after 'no' votes in France and the Netherlands. A referendum on the European single currency will only take place if the cabinet recommends entry.

Summary

Constitutional reforms since 1997

> legislation on human rights

> extended freedom of information

> devolution of power to new institutions in Scotland, Wales and Northern Ireland

> decentralisation of power in London

> multiple electoral systems

> (partial) reform of the House of Lords

> proposals for a Supreme Court

> reorganisation of Whitehall

> greater regulation of the conduct of elections

> increased use of referendums

A new constitutional settlement

The changes introduced by the Blair government arguably amount to the most important package of constitutional reform ever introduced in the modern UK. Commentators have rightly talked of a new constitutional settlement replacing the traditional constitution. Many of the rules, procedures and principles of the traditional UK constitution have been affected by Labour's reforms: few key institutions remain untouched.

However, the reforms are not revolutionary. Change was introduced in a piecemeal rather than 'big bang' fashion. The government did not produce a written constitution or a tailor-made UK Bill of Rights.

Significantly, the underlying principles of the UK constitution have been adapted rather than overturned. The Blair government was careful to avoid too many direct challenges to the core principles of the constitution. The impact of the reforms on four principal features of the constitution is as follows:

> **The uncodified constitution.** Labour's reforms have not provided the UK with a codified constitution, but they have established key principles and procedures (e.g. human rights and devolution) in statute law.

> **Parliamentary sovereignty.** The Scotland Act (1998) states that the Westminster Parliament remains sovereign and retains the power to make laws for Scotland. It can also repeal the act itself. In practice, however, the Westminster Parliament will not legislate on matters devolved to the Scottish Parliament, so parliamentary sovereignty

> ### Box 9.6 Labour and constitutional reform, 2001–05
>
> **Devolution and decentralisation**
>
> ➤ Reduction of the number of Scottish MPs at Westminster from 72 to 59 (took effect in 2005).
>
> ➤ Publication of the 2002 White Paper, *Your Region, Your Choice: Revitalising the English Regions*, envisaging the creation of regional assemblies where there is sufficient popular demand and a unitary system of local government.
>
> ➤ 'No' vote in 2004 referendum in the northeast led the government to shelve plans for elected regional assemblies.
>
> **Parliament**
>
> ➤ Publication of the 2001 White Paper, *The House of Lords: Completing the Reform*, envisaging a partially elected second chamber. Proposals shelved after hostile response.
>
> ➤ Parliament fails to approve any of seven reform options — plans for further legislation on Lords reform shelved.
>
> **Central government**
>
> ➤ Department for Constitutional Affairs created in 2003, taking over the functions of the Lord Chancellor's Department, the Scotland Office and the Wales Office.
>
> **Judiciary**
>
> ➤ Constitutional Reform Act (2005) paves the way for changes to the office of Lord Chancellor, the creation of an independent Judicial Appointments Commission and the establishment of a Supreme Court.
>
> **Elections and referendums**
>
> ➤ All-postal ballots held in four regions in the 2004 European Parliament elections — increased electoral fraud reported.
>
> ➤ Sex Discrimination (Election Candidates) Act (2002) permits political parties to adopt positive action in candidate selection.

no longer means a real power to make law across the UK. The Human Rights Act (1998) also seeks to preserve the sovereignty of parliament. If the courts find legislation incompatible with the European Convention on Human Rights, that legislation is not automatically struck down: it is up to parliament to decide on amendments. The Constitutional Reform Act (2005) paves the way for a new Supreme Court, but this will not be able to overturn legislation.

➤ **The unitary state.** Labour's asymmetric devolution programme means that the component parts of the United Kingdom have different political institutions and political cultures. Policy differences are also emerging — those on issues such as care for the elderly and tuition fees mean that the welfare state is no longer uniform across the UK.

➤ **Rights.** The rights of citizens have been strengthened by the Human Rights Act (1998) and the Freedom of Information Act (2000). But government legislation has also restricted civil liberties (e.g. the right to trial by jury).

Reforms frustrated

Most of the reforms outlined above were introduced in the first term of the Blair government (1997–2001). The second term (2001–05) proved less effective (see Box 9.6). There was some tidying up of loose ends, for example the reduction in the number of Scottish MPs at Westminster. But efforts to bring about radical reforms ran into trouble and momentum was lost. Many of the issues tackled in this period will have to be revisited in Labour's third term (see Box 9.7).

Stage Two of the reform of the House of Lords failed to get off the ground. The government retreated from its commitment to democratise the House and withdrew the reform blueprint set out in its 2001 White Paper. Having finally spelled out its proposals for elected regional assemblies in England, the government was also forced to abandon its plans after the 'no' vote in the 2004 referendum in the northeast. The creation of the Department for Constitutional Affairs was a missed opportunity: it does not have full responsibility for the devolution settlement, for example. Radicalism was evident in the proposals for reforming the judiciary, but the government's plans were badly thought out and had to be amended.

Criticisms of New Labour reforms

The post-1997 reforms have been subject to criticism from two broad perspectives: a conservative perspective which holds that Labour has damaged the traditional UK constitution, and a liberal perspective which argues that Labour's reforms have not gone far enough. Both accuse the government of incoherence: changes have been introduced without sufficient thought to their impact, while some reforms remain incomplete. Reforms have also been implemented without the development of an overarching philosophy. Although constitutional reform will be a major part of his legacy, Blair has taken little interest in either the details or the overall vision.

The conservative critique

The conservative perspective was supportive of the pre-1997 constitutional settlement, arguing that it needed limited, pragmatic reform rather than the substantial overhaul that has occurred. Its critique argues that Labour's reforms have damaged the fabric of the constitution so that its component parts no longer form a coherent and effective whole. Indeed, the reforms have brought new problems in their wake. Devolution has raised questions about funding and the status of England; the Human Rights Act has increased the political role of the judiciary and opened up a can of worms on the nature of rights such as privacy.

Before Labour's 1997 general election victory, the conservative critique was most associated with the Conservative Party. The Conservatives opposed Labour's proposals for reform of the House of Lords, electoral reform and the incorporation of the European Convention on Human Rights into domestic law. They argued strongly that legislative devolution would bring about the break-up of the Union. The only constitutional reform measures signalled in the Conservatives' 1997 manifesto concerned changes to House of Commons procedures. Following their heavy election defeat, the Conservatives began to change their stance on constitutional reform. They accepted the 'yes' results in the Scottish and Welsh devolution referendums and pledged to work constructively with the new institutions. However, the Conservatives were unhappy with what they felt was the unfair treatment of England in the new settlement.

The Conservatives were critical of Labour's plans for reform of the House of Lords, fearing that the removal of hereditary peers would create an emaciated chamber packed with Labour appointments. They proposed a stronger elected element than that favoured by Blair. Electoral reform is one area where the Conservatives have not (yet) toned down their opposition to change. The Tories opposed using AMS for elections to the devolved assemblies, but became its main beneficiaries.

The liberal critique

New Labour's reforms grew out of a liberal agenda for constitutional change developed by senior figures in the Labour Party, as well as by Liberal Democrats, pressure groups and political commentators. By the end of Tony Blair's first term in government, many of those who had initially supported Labour's agenda were expressing their dissatisfaction with a perceived lack of progress and ambition.

Proponents of the liberal model of constitutional reform were critical of both the details and vision of Labour's reforms. They questioned the coherence and comprehensiveness of the party's constitutional settlement, arguing that it had developed neither a sufficiently coherent reform package nor a sufficiently radical one. Though much has

---

Box 9.7 Constitutional reform in Labour's third term

Proposals in Labour's 2005 manifesto

➤ Enhanced powers, plus a reformed structure and electoral system, for the Welsh Assembly.

➤ Devolve further responsibility for planning, housing, economic development and transport to existing regional bodies in England.

➤ Provide new opportunities for people to express their views on having a directly elected mayor.

➤ Remove the remaining hereditary peers from the House of Lords and allow a free vote on its composition; codify the conventions of the upper House and set time limits on the consideration of bills in the Lords.

➤ Review the experience of new electoral systems in the UK.

Other developments

➤ Referendum on the EU constitution.

➤ Identity Cards Bill to introduce identity cards.

➤ Electoral Offences Bill to improve security of postal voting.

---

changed, radical reformers argued that constitutional reform had followed a 'minimalist' rather than a 'maximalist' route. They argued that Labour had been too timid on reform of the House of Lords and freedom of information. Liberals were also concerned by perceived infringements of civil liberties, particularly when security was increased after the 11 September 2001 terrorist attacks on New York and Washington.

An alternative maximalist reform package might include:

➤ a written constitution
➤ a UK Bill of Rights
➤ a federal state with regional assemblies in the English regions and a federal parliament at Westminster
➤ an elected upper chamber of parliament
➤ proportional representation for general elections
➤ state funding of political parties
➤ a transfer of power from quangos to elected local authorities
➤ reform of the monarchy (or its abolition)

This liberal perspective is associated with the Liberal Democrats, who support many of the demands listed above. Under Charles Kennedy, the party retreated from its co-operative relationship with Labour on constitutional reform.

The UK constitution has changed significantly since 1997, and although the pace of change has slowed, further reforms are likely. Constitutions evolve over time. In areas such as devolution, Labour's reforms have raised new issues that need to be addressed. Other areas, notably reform of the House of Lords and English regionalism, have yet to be completed. Debates about the impact, coherence and comprehensiveness of Labour's reforms are set to continue.

Suggested reading

Bennett, A., 'The British and American constitutions compared', *Politics Review*, vol. 11, no. 1, September 2001.

Bogdanor, V., 'Constitutional reform', in A. Seldon (ed.), *The Blair Effect* (Little, Brown, 2001), pp. 139–58.

Forman, N., 'The state and the people: Britain's changing constitution', *Politics Review*, vol. 13, no.3, February 2004.

Hazell, R., 'Labour's constitutional revolution', *Politics Review*, vol. 9, no. 2, November 1999.

Magee, E. and Lynch, P., 'The changing British constitution', *Politics Review*, vol. 13, no. 2, November 2003.

Masterman, R. and Hazell, R., 'The constitution: Labour's continuing revolution', *Politics Review*, vol. 12, no. 2, November 2002.

Mitchell, J., 'Reviving the union state: the devolution debate in Scotland', *Politics Review*, vol. 5, no. 3, February 1996.

Zander, M., 'UK rights come home', *Politics Review*, vol. 7, no. 4, April 1998.

Websites

Charter 88 (constitutional reform pressure group): www.charter88.org.uk

The Constitution Unit (research centre whose *Monitor* newsletter provides regular updates on constitutional developments: www.ucl.ac.uk/constitution-unit

Department for Constitutional Affairs (government department responsible for rights, the legal system, reform of the House of Lords and electoral administration): www.dca.gov.uk

Electoral Reform Society (electoral reform pressure group): www.electoral-reform.org.uk

Liberty (civil liberties pressure group): www.liberty-human-rights.org.uk

Exam focus

Using this chapter and other resources available to you, answer the following questions.

1 What is a constitution?
2 Outline the difference between a codified and an uncodified constitution.
3 Summarise the main sources of the UK constitution.
4 Explain why the UK constitution has been criticised.
5 What is sovereignty?
6 What is parliamentary sovereignty?
7 Outline the main constraints on parliamentary sovereignty.
8 Where does sovereignty reside in the UK?
9 Is the UK a unitary or a union state? Give reasons for your answer.
10 Discuss the impact of EU membership on the UK constitution.
11 Outline the strengths and weaknesses of the traditional constitution.
12 Why were there demands for constitutional reform in the 1970s, 1980s and 1990s?
13 Discuss the significance of the main constitutional reforms since 1997.
14 Outline the main criticisms of New Labour's constitutional reforms since 1997.
15 'The biggest programme of change to democracy ever proposed.' Discuss this view of Labour's constitutional reform programme.

Chapter 10

Parliament and parliamentary reform

The UK's House of Commons is probably the best-known democratic institution in the world. But in recent years the politicians at Westminster have become deeply unpopular. A radical process of reform has begun in the upper chamber, the unelected House of Lords. Increasing public criticism suggests that the time has come to conduct the same kind of operation on the House of Commons itself. This chapter examines the workings of parliament, and asks whether there really are serious problems with the institution, or whether our expectations have become unrealistic.

Key questions answered in this chapter
➤ What is the role and significance of parliament?
➤ How effectively does parliament carry out its role?
➤ What is the case for parliamentary reform?
➤ What are the views of the main parties on parliamentary reform?

The functions and importance of parliament

The role of the Commons
People could be forgiven for thinking that parliament has never changed, and indeed the justification for some of its rituals and routine does lie in events and customs of the distant past. For example, it is thought that the opposing front benches in the House of

Commons were originally placed two sword-lengths apart in order to prevent bloodshed! The annual Queen's Speech, which reveals the government's legislative programme, is still printed on goat's skin although the monarch reads a copy printed on humble paper. But over the history of parliament, change has been as important as continuity. In particular, the UK's gradual transformation into a democratic nation has caused a shift in the role that its representative institutions are expected to play.

In recent times, the key roles expected of parliament have been as follows:

- **Passing legislation.** Parliament is the UK legislature, the supreme law-making body. Apart from passing new laws, it can (and frequently does) revise its previous decisions, under the convention that no parliament can bind its own successors. There is an expectation that legislation should be discussed fully before it is put to a vote.

- **Scrutiny of the executive.** Under the principle of *accountability*, ministers are responsible to parliament for their decisions (see Box 10.1). Governments can be dismissed if they lose the confidence of a majority of MPs.

- **Representation.** As an elected body, the House of Commons is expected to reflect public opinion to a considerable extent, and to respond to widely held grievances. Even if the government is supported by a clear majority of MPs, it is expected that minority viewpoints should at least be allowed a hearing.

- **Recruitment of ministers.** By convention, all ministers must be members either of the Commons or of the Lords. In other words, unlike in countries with a constitutional *separation of powers* (like the USA), members of the UK executive must also be part of the legislature.

- **Debate.** Apart from discussing legislation, parliament is regarded as the proper place to debate issues of national concern even if they cannot be affected by a change in the law. Thus in September 2002 parliament was recalled to discuss the possibility of war with Iraq. Earlier in the same year MPs returned from their holidays to pay tributes to the late queen mother.

All these functions of the House of Commons are important. But in recent years, critical attention has concentrated on the second one — holding the executive to account. Healthy democracies depend crucially upon the principle of accountability. Since the UK has a system of *representative government*, rather than a direct democracy

Box 10.1 Ministerial and collective responsibility

By convention, ministers take responsibility not just for their own actions, but for anything that goes on within their department. By the same token, the cabinet is held to be responsible collectively for decisions taken by individual members. In theory, if parliamentary criticism exposes serious departmental errors, a minister ought at least to offer his or her resignation to the prime minister, whether it is accepted or not. If a major policy decision agreed by the cabinet as a whole is seen to have failed, the whole government should resign.

These doctrines of ministerial and collective responsibility have rarely been followed. Cabinets and individual ministers normally soldier on even after disastrous mistakes. So, for example, when the UK was forced to leave the European exchange rate mechanism in 1992 no one resigned, although the incident was widely seen as a national humiliation and the prime minister himself had tied his credibility to the policy.

Nowadays, collective responsibility would seem to apply only when the nation's survival is at stake and a viable alternative government is available. (Even a discredited government is better than no government at all!) As the experience of the 1990s shows (see p. 246), individual resignations are caused by the exposure of 'misjudgements' in personal matters, far more than by professional errors. Ministerial responsibility tends to be enforced when:

➤ the minister can be shown personally to have taken a disastrous decision, with no excuses

➤ the minister has made a series of mistakes, possibly trivial in themselves but building up a general impression of incompetence

➤ the minister has become an embarrassment to the government as a whole

➤ the prime minister needs a scapegoat

In October 2002 many observers were surprised when the education secretary, Estelle Morris, resigned, admitting that the job had proved too difficult for her. Her case fell into the second category on the list above. However, the previous high-profile cabinet resignation, that of the transport secretary Stephen Byers 5 months earlier, was an instance of someone fulfilling *all* of the above criteria! As a result, Morris was hailed as a rare example of honesty in politics, and later returned to the government in a junior capacity.

Perhaps the most damaging ministerial resignations are those which occur when a prominent cabinet member disagrees with a key policy. Michael Heseltine (1986), Nigel Lawson (1989) and Geoffrey Howe (1990) all left Conservative governments over policy disagreements. In 2003, Robin Cook and Clare Short both resigned over policy towards Iraq. These examples can be seen as a product of the 'collective responsibility' doctrine, in that the ministers concerned were no longer prepared to say in public that they agreed with the government's line. More exactly, resignations of this kind take place when the minister's working relationship with the prime minister has broken down beyond repair. Thus the most notable resignations of recent years are a useful illustration of prime ministerial dominance within the executive (see Chapter 11).

(see Chapter 1), its citizens rely on their elected representatives to check any attempt by the executive to govern without paying due heed to people's general interests.

The problem is that, unlike in some countries where the legislature is separate from the executive and the judiciary, traditionally in the UK these branches of government are *fused*. That is, members of the executive (and the head of the judiciary) had to be members of the legislature. Officially, the head of the executive is the serving monarch. But real executive power lies with the prime minister, who commands a majority of votes in the House of Commons. How, then, can the executive be held accountable in any meaningful sense? This is the question that dominates discussion of the UK system of government.

The role of the opposition

Even though the government of the day commands a majority in the House of Commons, not all MPs are members of the executive. After the general election of May 2005, Labour had 356 MPs. This left 289 seats shared among the opposition parties. The Conservatives, with 197 MPs, formed the official opposition. They might be heavily outnumbered, but they have an obvious interest in holding the executive to account. Even if they cannot muster enough votes to defeat the government's bills, they can make damaging contributions in debates. The opposition leader can also use Prime Minister's Question Time to make public criticisms of the government's record. Other senior opposition spokespeople, known as *shadow ministers*, have similar opportunities to hold members of the executive to account.

It can be argued that every government needs a strong official opposition. The importance of the role has been acknowledged since 1935, when the opposition leader was first awarded a special salary. The sense of unchallenged power can lead to serious mistakes but, perhaps more importantly, the existence of a dangerous political enemy helps to keep the governing party united. Even a party in a dominant position, as Labour has been since 1997, has to keep reminding its backbenchers that rebellions will only play into the hands of an effective and ruthless opposition, ready to take advantage of any dissenting votes.

The role of backbench MPs

Box 10.2 Trollope on MPs

'It is the highest and most legitimate pride of an Englishman to have the letters of MP written after his name.'

Anthony Trollope on MPs in *Can You Forgive Her?*, 1865.

Backbenchers are MPs of all parties who are not members of the executive, or the teams of opposition spokespeople ('shadow ministers'). If they take their roles seriously, they can be equally busy as ministers. The key responsibilities are:

> **Representing their constituents.** MPs are expected to raise issues of particular concern for the people who live in their constituencies, whether they voted for the MP's party or not. For example, if a local factory closes, the MP is expected to raise the matter with a relevant minister, even if nothing can be done about it.

> **Serving constituents.** Apart from their work at Westminster, MPs make regular visits to their constituencies, where they can be approached by the residents for advice and, where possible, practical help. (In this context, see the work of the *ombudsman*, discussed in Chapter 12.)

> **Voting on legislation.** Every MP is entitled to cast a vote on a bill.

> **Debates.** Backbench MPs can speak in the most important debate on any bill — the second reading (see Box 10.3). But they do not have an equal right to speak. The

speaker, who presides over debates, normally gives preference to ex-ministers, especially on important issues. But in most cases an MP will enjoy the right to be heard if he or she wishes to say anything. MPs enjoy *parliamentary privilege*: that is, they cannot be sued for anything mentioned during a speech within the confines of Westminster. They can also initiate *adjournment debates*, which give them a chance to win publicity for their views on subjects important to them. They can put down *early day motions* for the same purpose, giving their views in writing in the hope that enough MPs will offer supporting signatures to win publicity for the cause. Early day motions are never debated, but they can serve to make a point provided that sufficient signatures can be obtained.

➤ **Committee work.** MPs with an enthusiasm for a particular subject can be chosen to serve on a *standing committee*, which deals with legislation in a specific area, or a *select committee*, which keeps an eye on the work of a department or several departments. The prestigious Public Accounts Committee, which was founded as long ago as 1862, oversees spending across Whitehall.

➤ **Private members' bills.** Although backbench MPs cannot hope to pass their own ideas into legislation without government support, if they are successful in a ballot they can introduce a bill. Again, the goal here is usually to win publicity for a favourite cause (or to impress constituents) because in most circumstances the bill fails through lack of time. But sometimes a private member's bill will be given either open or tacit support by the government and eventually reach the statute book. Some important social legislation of the 1960s, including the Abortion Act, originated in this way. It is a convenient method for governments to allow the passage of controversial legislation without being blamed by its opponents for having introduced the bill in the first place.

➤ **Executive scrutiny.** Conscientious backbenchers of all parties can dredge useful (and sometimes embarrassing) information out of the government. Apart from the regular Question Times, MPs can submit questions in writing and the relevant minister's answer is published in *Hansard* — the official record of parliamentary debates.

Box 10.3 **The legislative process in the UK**

1 **Queen's speech.** Once it has been agreed among cabinet members, the government's legislative programme is announced at the beginning of each parliamentary session. (The queen delivers the speech, but government officials write it for her.) This is often a difficult process, and an ambitious reforming government may be frustrated by the relative lack of time. Until Labour's recent reforms, governments sometimes had to resort to *guillotine motions*, which could be introduced to bring debate to a close in order to make sure that other parts of its legislative programme had time to go through the necessary stages. Nowadays the timetable for bills is usually agreed in advance, through *programme motions*. However, if an issue is particularly controversial, the government might actually be *pleased* to see it fail for lack of time.

2 **First reading.** This consists of a formal announcement that a bill will be printed, and introduced for debate at a certain time. In the Commons, there is no vote at this stage.

3 **Second reading.** This is the key stage, when MPs debate the principle of the bill. Ministers in the department most affected by the proposals begin and end the debate, which is followed by a vote.

4 **Committee stage.** Provided that the bill passes its second reading, it is allotted to the relevant *standing committee.* Each line of the bill is scrutinised, but significant changes are rare because the committee will have a built-in government majority.

5 **Report stage.** If the committee does suggest major changes, the House of Commons as a whole has to approve them in the form of amendments.

6 **Third reading.** Bills can no longer be amended at this stage (except in the Lords). They have to be accepted or rejected as a whole. This means that there are fewer debates and votes.

7 **House of Lords.** The bill has to negotiate a similar obstacle course in the Lords before it can be presented for the queen's signature. As discussed below, the Lords have lost the power to reject a bill, unless it has failed to pass it at the time that parliament is dissolved for a general election. But bills are quite often returned to the Commons with amendments. The Commons (in practice, the government) then decides whether or not to accept these changes. If they cannot accept them and vote accordingly, the Lords usually give way without further protest. However, the Lords put up protracted resistance over the Hunting Act (2004) and the Prevention of Terrorism Act (2005). In the first case, the government only pushed through the legislation by means of the Parliament Act of 1949 (see below).

8 **Royal assent.** This is necessary for the bill to become law, but it is a formality nowadays since no monarch has refused to sign legislation since Queen Anne in 1707.

The role of the House of Lords

Background

Originally the House of Lords was regarded as (at least) the equal of the Commons. But once the Commons was elected by something close to universal franchise, the Lords began to seem outdated, with an automatic Conservative majority built on the votes of *hereditary peers* — that is, members of the House of Lords who owed their right to attend and to vote to a title bestowed on one of their ancestors, not to their own merits. Its very existence was likely to come into question should it ever conflict with the Commons, particularly if the elected government was pushing for radical reforms against the resistance of heriditary peers.

Sure enough, in 1911, after a protracted struggle over the right of the Lords to challenge the government's budget, the Liberal government passed a Parliament Act, restricting the power of the upper chamber. The Lords could no longer reject legislation outright, but merely delay it. An act of 1949 reduced this delaying power further. If the Commons continued to insist on any piece of legislation, it would automatically become law after a year, whatever the Lords might think. If the Lords opposed a bill introduced within the year before a general election, the government would have to hope that it was re-elected to start the whole process again in the new parliament. But almost invariably these would be bills considered to be of minor importance by the government. Even this temporary power to kill off legislation could actually be more useful to the government than the Lords. It allowed the ruling party to blame the Lords for obstructing bills that the government never wanted to pass in the first place!

In 1958 the Life Peerages Act vastly increased the prime minister's powers to change the composition of the Lords. Instead of being dominated by hereditary part-time politicians with illustrious titles, the upper House became something like a retirement home for members of the Commons who had once held ministerial rank. New hereditary titles were virtually unknown — the last was awarded in 1983, to a politician who had no male heir. The Peerage Act (1963) allowed any heir to a hereditary peerage who was really serious about a political career to renounce the title and thus remain qualified for membership of the Commons. Further reforms were proposed later in the 1960s, but they failed to pass the Commons because of combined opposition from right-wing Conservatives, who hated to see the Lords tampered with, and left-wing Labour MPs, who wanted it abolished. It was left to the New Labour government of Tony Blair to return to the subject (see pp. 260–62).

Functions

Despite its outdated image, the House of Lords still performs some valuable functions — even in its current, semi-reformed state. These are:

> **Executive scrutiny.** Although most cabinet ministers are members of the Commons, some junior ministers are picked from the Lords. They are subjected to regular question-and-answer sessions, which actually tend to be more informative than the knockabout performances in the Commons.

> **Debates.** Although the crucial votes take place in the Commons, legislation is still debated in the Lords. Indeed, some bills are introduced there first, to relieve pressure on the government's timetable in the Commons. Although partisan point scoring is frowned upon in the genteel upper chamber, it is still possible for experienced ex-ministers to make telling speeches. The Lords also provides scope for independent-minded peers to raise issues for debate, thus winning publicity for causes that might otherwise be ignored.

> **Revision of legislation.** Party discipline in the Lords is relatively weak, so peers can be swayed by the quality of a debate. Although the power of the Lords has been restricted, it is well placed to make ministers 'think again', if only over the subsidiary clauses of major bills, or legislation that is not a high political priority. Since the House can be reformed at the whim of the Commons, peers try not to cause provocation by voting down legislation on a regular basis. As a result, the Lords can actually benefit from their weak constitutional position. Ministers can be fairly sure that peers must

feel very strongly if they take their opposition to the risky lengths of opposing the will of the Commons.

➤ **Recruitment of ministers.** The last peer to serve as prime minister was the Conservative Marquess of Salisbury, who left office in 1902. In 1940 Winston Churchill became premier rather than Lord Halifax mainly because his rival was unaccountable to the Commons. But as discussed, each government department has a junior spokesperson in the Lords; in addition, the Lord Chancellor has always been a member of the House (see Chapter 12). Since the Life Peerages Act, the Lords represents a remarkable pool of talent — of retired ministers who can draw on their experience, relatively young MPs whose career has been cut short by electoral defeat, or people from other professions who have been elevated to the Lords because of their specialist knowledge.

How does parliament perform?

Parliament is still central to UK political life, at least on paper. But is it really effective in performing its roles? If not, why not? And can anything be done about it?

One possibility that we need to consider at the outset is whether the current displeasure with parliament might be a reaction to unusual circumstances. After the 1997 general election, parliament seemed impotent because the New Labour government enjoyed an overwhelming majority. Backbenchers like Tony Benn, who disagreed with government policy, could be ignored safely. Conservative MPs seemed wholly irrelevant. Almost the only thing they could decide was the identity of their leader, and after William Hague's reforms of the selection process (see Chapter 6) they lost their previous dominance even on this question. Because there was no danger that the government would be defeated, parliament rarely appeared on the television news, apart from the weekly Punch and Judy show, Prime Minister's Question Time.

Unfortunately, although complaints about parliament have been increasing recently, they are far from new. Back in 1931, the former prime minister David Lloyd George told a parliamentary committee that 'the House of Commons has no real effective and continuous control over the actions of the executive'. In the 1960s, the apparent failings of parliament as a whole formed part of a general view that the UK's institutions needed a radical overhaul (see Box 10.4).

In 1969 one MP, Ian Gilmour, commented that complaining about the House of Commons had 'long been a minor industry'. Yet instead of improving since then, the

---

Box 10.4 **Richard Crossman on the workings of parliament**

'The whole of parliament is geared not to help backbenchers criticise ministers, but to help ministers overcome backbenchers.'

Richard Crossman, MP, 1966

(just after becoming leader of the House of Commons in Harold Wilson's Labour government)

situation seems to have deteriorated further. The Conservative government led by John Major (1990–97) was seriously divided over the question of European integration, and the very public wrangling over this issue did further damage to parliament's reputation. More seriously, there was a stream of scandals, either sexual or financial, involving ministers and backbenchers.

'Sleaze' and the Nolan Committee

'Sleaze' was a blanket term that became all too familiar in the 1990s. Many MPs — almost invariably Conservative ministers and backbenchers — were exposed for having committed a series of misdemeanours. Ministerial resignations over private affairs, such as David Mellor (1992: sex scandal, followed by stories about links with a Palestinian activist), Michael Mates (1993: links to a foreign businessman who left the country to avoid prosecution) and Tim Yeo (1994: sex scandal), have little or no direct relevance to parliament as an institution. But other incidents, notably the resignations of Tim Smith and Neil Hamilton over the 'cash for questions' affair, raised more serious issues.

The allegations (vigorously contested in Hamilton's case) created the impression that MPs were quite willing to abuse their positions, and to act as well-placed lobbyists for outside interests rather than focusing on the needs of their constituents (see Chapter 8). *The Sunday Times* exposed two more Conservative MPs who accepted money in return for raising questions in the Commons. In fact, the guilty pair were the only ones out of 20 MPs to fall into the newspaper's trap, which underlined the relatively low level of corruption among British politicians. However, that was not the impression gained by most voters.

The cash for questions affair persuaded John Major to appoint a Committee on Standards in Public Life, under Lord Nolan. When the committee reported in May 1995, it recommended that MPs should make a complete disclosure of their interests, including the full extent of any financial benefits. It established an ethical framework for public office-holders, who should demonstrate an unusual combination of 'selflessness, integrity, objectivity, accountability, openness, honesty and leadership'. It also recommended that an independent parliamentary commissioner should be appointed to keep a check on MPs' outside interests, reporting to a new parliamentary Select Committee on Standards and Privileges.

Lord Nolan, head of the Committee on Standards in Public Life

The proposals were strongly opposed by many MPs. It was felt by some that the new machinery implied that all parliamentarians were open to corruption. Thus, it would further reduce the public image of politicians. It might also deter successful people from other areas of public life from entering the Commons. Ironically, in the nineteenth century it was felt that outside interests were *essential* for all politicians, as a way of keeping in touch with developments in, say, the business world.

Despite their misgivings the Commons approved Nolan's report, in November 1995. Since then many people have remained sceptical that things have really improved. In particular, concerns are often raised about the number of retired ministers who, after a decent interval, take up well-paid jobs in firms that they formerly supervised. Can action be taken to prevent a minister from doing special favours for an individual or company, when the reward comes after the minister has left parliament?

One difficulty was that even if the Commissioner for Parliamentary Standards acted with full independence, the Select Committee for Standards and Privileges was too dependent on prime ministerial favour. Elizabeth Filkin, who was appointed to succeed the first Commissioner, Sir Gordon Downey, found that the committee rarely acted upon her recommendations. Even worse, Filkin was frequently obstructed in her work. For example, in 2000 the junior foreign office minister Keith Vaz refused to answer her questions, preventing her from investigating eight of the 18 charges against him, which included allegations that he had failed to declare payments from businessmen and made improper use of his ministerial position. It seemed that Vaz's attitude had wholehearted support from other members of the government. Eventually, Mrs Filkin left her post early, faced with a concerted attempt to reduce the status of her job.

Who is to blame?

At best, the problems encountered by Mrs Filkin revealed the insensitivity of MPs. The new system had been instituted to meet the complaints of members of the public who no longer trusted parliament to regulate itself, but almost immediately ministers and backbenchers worked together to undermine any signs of independent initiative in the Commissioner.

Yet it still seems unreasonable to blame parliament as an *institution* for all this. In every instance, the problems have related to the kind of people elected in recent years. This points to reforms of the electoral system, rather than parliament itself. Let us take two examples.

Scrutiny of the prime minister

Take, for example, Prime Minister's Question Time (PMQs). At the start of his premiership, Tony Blair changed the format for this ritual. Previously there had been two quarter-hour sessions, on Tuesdays and Thursdays. Now there would be only one session, lasting for half an hour on Wednesday afternoons while parliament is sitting. In theory, this should allow for a more sustained inquisition, subjecting the prime minister to greater pressure. At a time of crisis, opposition MPs and their leaders could return again and again to a specific problem, trying to goad the prime minister into damaging admissions. Parliament has been broadcast continuously on radio since 1975; television cameras were installed in the Lords in 1985, and they arrived in the Commons in November 1989. So under the spotlight of media coverage, the prime minister would have nowhere to hide.

But in practice, the image of PMQs has continued to decline. The nation now seems to expect petty point scoring, even when issues of real substance are under discussion. From recent experience it can also expect the government's supporters to line up with 'questions' that are often just flattering statements about the prime minister's supposedly magnificent record.

The committee system

Similarly, the system of select committees was reformed in 1979. This was a well-intentioned attempt to increase the power of backbenchers, to help them fulfil the key role of holding the executive to account. Reformers hoped that the resulting committees would be something like their counterparts in the US Congress, which are well resourced and have sweeping powers to cross-question ministers, officials and even private individuals.

In practice, though, the leaders of the political parties have undermined the UK committees. If members of a committee show signs of becoming too independent, steps are taken to remove them — sometimes on the most flimsy pretexts. For example, the outspoken Conservative backbencher Nicholas Winterton was removed from the Health Committee in 1992. Ministers have also ignored a summons to attend — sometimes, it seems, simply to snub the committees rather than to hide anything — and civil servants can only give evidence if their ministers agree. Keith Vaz is far from being the only minister who has attended a committee and refused to answer questions. The government is under no obligation to respond even verbally to the findings of a committee.

After the 2001 general election the government tried to eject two independent-minded committee chairpeople, Gwyneth Dunwoody and Donald Anderson (both Labour MPs). The move was defeated by a parliamentary vote, but MPs failed to draw the obvious lesson and make these posts subject to election by the whole House of Commons, rather than being under the control of the party business managers — the *whips*.

Under these constraints, the committee system has worked quite well, issuing a stream of often critical and well-publicised reports. But the feeling remains that the more effective it becomes, the more likely it is to be tampered with by the executive. If they want to keep their positions, committee members have to strike an unsatisfactory compromise: they have a free licence to probe, but not too far. Ironically, this means that a set of institutions set up to check the executive can end up actively helping the government of the day to neutralise criticism. The public is encouraged to *think* that the committees' conclusions are based on a fearless and thorough examination of the facts, whereas in reality they will usually be toned down to avoid a major quarrel.

The difficulties facing a committee which hopes to hold the executive to account were illustrated by a tragedy in 2003. The Foreign Affairs Committee summoned a government weapons inspector, Dr David Kelly, after media claims that the case for war against Saddam Hussein had been exaggerated. Kelly, who had been the main source for a critical BBC report, was subjected to blunt questioning by the committee. A few days later he committed suicide, and some committee members were criticised for their aggressive approach.

Dr David Kelly

Key terms

➤ **Bill.** A proposed piece of legislation, up to the moment when it passes all the necessary parliamentary stages and is signed by the monarch (the *royal assent*). Once it has passed all of these stages, the bill becomes an *Act of Parliament*.

➤ **Green Paper.** A document published by the government, typically setting out alternative proposals for future legislation. Green Papers are rather like invitations for interested parties (such as pressure groups) to express their views.

➤ **White Paper.** Usually more detailed than a Green Paper, this sets out more concrete proposals that will form the basis of a bill to be introduced in the near future. The appearance of a White Paper suggests that the government's mind is made up, but there is still time for consultation if interested parties have well-founded objections (or ideas to improve the proposals).

➤ **Whips.** Party officials (members of either House) entrusted with the task of ensuring the maximum turnout for votes. If an MP receives an instruction to vote underlined three times, this is known as a *three-line whip*, and failure to obey is considered a serious breach of discipline. If MPs lose the party whip, this means that they are no longer pestered to vote. But this is rather a mixed blessing because in a system so dominated by the main parties the loss of the whip amounts to expulsion, and usually (though not always) means the effective end of a political career.

Summary

The functions and importance of parliament

➤ The Westminster Parliament is still the centrepiece of UK democracy, despite devolution and the increasing importance of EU legislation.

➤ Its main functions are to represent constituency interests, to debate and pass legislation, to nurture and recruit government ministers and, most importantly, to hold the government to account.

Is parliament out of date?

So far, it looks as if parliament as an institution has fallen into disrepute mainly because of the shortcomings of those who attend it. Yet even if we think that standards have declined recently, British MPs have rarely been angelic. Perhaps circumstances have changed, so that institutional weaknesses in the parliamentary system that were once obscured have now come to the surface.

There are several good reasons for adopting this view. Until the nineteenth century, parliament tended to be *reactive* rather than *proactive*. It responded to the monarch's appeals for money, for example, or debated the conduct of wars. But the Victorians were enthusiastic reformers. They had a new confidence that social problems could be solved by the application of 'rational thinking' and new 'scientific' methods. As a result, government began to interfere in new areas, such as public hygiene and education.

At the same time, the gradual extension of the franchise meant that more and more people had at least *some* involvement in politics. A more literate population could also read about activities at Westminster in the newspapers. So voters tended to be more demanding and politicians were more willing to take action. The result was a massive expansion of government activity. Such twentieth-century innovations as the welfare state were logical extensions of this phenomenon, and not a radical break with the past.

The acceptance of vast new responsibilities suggested that parliament should equip itself for the challenge. To some extent, this has happened. For example, the old 'gentleman amateurs' who dominated parliament even in the nineteenth century have now disappeared almost entirely. Since 1911 — significantly, during a period when government was taking on new social responsibilities — MPs have been paid by the state, enabling them to regard politics as a separate career (if not as a source of great wealth). Since 1969 the taxpayer has covered at least a proportion of office costs, and since the mid-1980s this amount has actually exceeded MPs' salaries. So if parliamentarians are now dealing with a greatly expanded range of subjects — often at a high level of detail — at least they are now better equipped for the task.

The long decline of parliamentary government

Yet the greater scope of political action has brought other developments. In the mid-nineteenth century it was still possible to talk of the UK being governed by parliament. Indeed, every government between 1835 and 1874 fell as a result of votes in the House of Commons, rather than defeat at a general election. Even so, the economic and constitutional theorist Walter Bagehot (1826–77) claimed in *The English Constitution* (1867) that parliament had now joined the monarchy as no more than a 'dignified' element of the constitution. The cabinet — the truly 'efficient' element of the constitution — did the real work of government.

This argument had far-reaching constitutional implications. If Bagehot was right, the centre of power in Britain had shifted from the *legislature* to the *executive*. In the twentieth century his argument was taken further. The cabinet as a collective body seemed to be losing its power to the prime minister. Thus, according to this view, in the course of little over a century the UK had moved from parliamentary government to something approaching a 'presidential' system. In 1976 the Conservative politician Lord Hailsham went so far as to describe the system as an 'elective dictatorship'.

As we have seen, the political system in the UK is usually characterised by the idea of a *fusion* of powers, in contrast to countries like the USA where the legislature, executive and judiciary are separated. In the UK, the executive branch is currently supposed to be responsible to the legislature (parliament), and the head of the judiciary (the Lord Chancellor) is a member of both the legislature and the executive, as a cabinet member. This system, which caused many constitutional theorists to despair, evolved over time and not in accordance with any set plan.

The rise of the executive

The system is discussed in more detail in the next chapter. The main point to notice here is that, although power in the UK is indeed 'fused' on paper, the executive has clearly

---

Box 10.5 The media

One reason for parliament's current ill repute is the contempt in which politicians are held by certain influential sections of the media. In this context, there are arguments for and against the role of the media. In their favour, the following can be argued:

➤ The media merely reflect public attitudes towards politicians. If people disliked the nature of the coverage they would either refuse to buy newspapers or turn off their televisions.

➤ In recent years opposition parties have been unable to hold ministers to account. The media have filled the role.

➤ Politicians have become very good at avoiding questions on matters of substance. Therefore media interviewers have to be more aggressive and persistent to unearth the truth on behalf of the public.

Against these points it can be argued:

➤ To some extent, at least, the media shapes its audience. People have come to expect negative and intrusive reporting, often about the personal lives of politicians. This does not mean that they approve of the media's approach. Journalists are increasingly unpopular and newspaper sales have been declining.

➤ If the media investigated issues of real substance they would provide a welcome reinforcement to the elected opposition. However, they tend to overlook important matters and concentrate on gossip.

➤ Politicians have become less open and honest because the media are always trying to catch them out.

A final point in defence of politicians is that journalists do not face the pressures of decision-making. As a result, it is no surprise that many talented people now prefer the option of a media career, rather than going into politics.

tended to gain power at the expense of the legislature to which it is supposed to be accountable. Undoubtedly this development has reflected the increasing scope of government activity. Members of the executive still have to be part of the legislature, and they still have to be careful not to lose the confidence of MPs. But more and more of their work is conducted away from the House of Commons. Even when they attend the Commons or the Lords, there is a greater gulf between them and backbench MPs than there ever was in the past.

In the nineteenth century, when governments did far less and communications were fairly basic, ministers in most departments knew very little more about the situation in the country than their backbench colleagues. Except perhaps for ministers concerned with foreign policy, this equality of information was of little importance. But now ministers have a vital interest in being informed, to keep at least one step ahead even of friendly MPs, and particularly of the media (see Box 10.5). The process begins from the moment when an MP or a peer first receives the call from Downing Street. New ministers are briefed intensively by civil servants and, symbolically, are whisked around London in government cars. They are now privy to secrets, and may even be open to prosecution if they 'leak' sensitive information. Unless they have some tactical purpose, they will not be tempted to do so. After all, the possession of privileged information is a great source of power and security!

In short, appointment to office turns the 'poachers' of Westminster into 'gamekeepers' overnight. The legislature, executive and judiciary may technically be 'fused' in the UK. Yet although they are locked into the same institutions, they have very different outlooks and priorities — just like poachers and gamekeepers. From this perspective, we can appreciate that public dissatisfaction with the performance of parliament was almost inevitable, as soon as the *knowledge gap* between ministers and everyone else became a matter of profound importance. After the huge expansion of government activity, the work of the executive would be all but impossible if the legislature really performed its key role of holding ministers to account.

Avoiding accountability

As early as 1949, in the light of the postwar Labour government's nationalisation of key industries, which increased greatly the scope of state activity, the Conservative MP Christopher Hollis wrote a book entitled *Can Parliament Survive?* Since 1979, the complexity and ever-increasing scope of government action has prompted a further development, which threatens to destroy any illusion that ministers can be held to account. This is the development of *agencies*.

It was always rather difficult to claim that individual ministers could be held 'responsible' for decisions taken by obscure officials within their departments, whom they might never even have met. But to avoid any chance of being blamed for administrative mistakes within their huge department, ministers began to split them up into separate agencies. Thus, for example, the Prison Service Agency (formed in 1993) was still officially part of the Home Office, but it was given a chief executive who could be blamed if, for instance, some prisoners escaped (see Box 10.6).

Box 10.6 **Recent 'non-resignations'**

It is unrealistic to expect ministers to give up their offices whenever problems occur in their areas of 'responsibility', and such honourable decisions have always been the exception rather than the rule. The theory of parliamentary accountability must depend ultimately on a confidence that either by a direct vote, or (more usually) through damaging questions in the House, ordinary MPs should have the power to make a minister's position untenable. But in recent years the tendency has been for ministers to 'tough it out' with support from Downing Street, even when they have been caught red-handed.

➢ The chancellor of the exchequer, Norman Lamont, did not resign after the UK's enforced departure from the European exchange rate mechanism. If Lamont had gone, the prime minister, John Major, would have been under pressure to follow him out of office.

➢ Michael Howard, the home secretary, sacked the chief executive of the Prison Service Agency after three prisoners escaped from a high-security jail. Before the advent of the agency, his own position would have been far more vulnerable.

➢ There were no ministerial resignations in 1996 after the Scott inquiry found that parliament had been misled over the policy of selling arms to Iraq.

➢ In the same year, there were no resignations over the BSE disease in cattle.

The tendency has continued under New Labour. For example, the secretary of state for transport, Stephen Byers, only stood down in May 2002 after a long series of ministerial mishaps. Particularly controversial was his refusal to sack an aide who had described the terrorist atrocity of 11 September 2001 as a convenient opportunity to 'bury' bad news without attracting media attention.

Ministers tried to justify the 2003 war on Iraq on the grounds that Saddam Hussein was said to control weapons of mass destruction. However, these weapons were never located. No government minister resigned for having backed a war which was based on false intelligence. The Chairman of the Joint Intelligence Committee was actually promoted soon afterwards. By contrast, the Director-General of the BBC was obliged to resign because one of his reporters had made allegations against the government with insufficient evidence.

This was an important development. Ministers began to argue that they were still responsible for *policy* decisions, but that problems in day-to-day *operations* were in the hands of the agencies. In practice, this distinction was almost impossible to sustain. For example, if a government chose not to take the *policy* decision of increasing prison capacity despite severe overcrowding, and there were several riots as a result, who was to blame? The Home Office minister could argue that the Prison Service has to maintain order, but the staff of the service would merely reply that government policy was making their *operational* work impossible.

The power of parties

The other major problem facing would-be reformers of the Commons is the strength of party discipline. Ironically, this can be seen, at least in part, as a product of the 'professionalisation' of politics. The independent country gentlemen of the past could take politics or leave it. Very few of them were ambitious for the top offices, and they only attended parliament at all out of a sense of public duty. When government whips asked them to vote against their principles — or even to attend a debate in the first place when private business was pressing — they were likely to receive an impolite answer.

By contrast, nowadays only the bravest (or most foolhardy) backbench MPs refuse to toe the party line. Since the Second World War, whenever a government has been in danger of losing a division, even critically ill MPs have been brought into the precincts of Westminster to record a vote. (As a small concession, the gravely ill can be 'nodded through' by the whips — they do not have to be pushed through the lobbies in person.) Ambitious young MPs will overlook their misgivings, knowing that the whips have long memories and that any public show of dissent (even an abstention) will earn them serious disfavour and probably mar their chances of promotion. If they offend too often, their constituency parties might ultimately *deselect* them. Even elderly MPs on the verge of retirement will hesitate before defying the whips — the knighthood that even obscure backbenchers tend to expect as a reward for their silent services may well be denied if they do not watch their step.

Power, patronage and the 'presidential' prime minister

In short, the existing strength of the executive is further enhanced by extensive *powers of patronage* wielded by the executive. Whatever changes might be made to parliament itself, the key fact for all MPs to remember is that the prime minister of the day can make or break careers.

So is parliament now only a 'dignified' part of the constitution — an obedient (and expensive) rubber-stamp to the all-powerful executive? Does the UK now have a presidential system? On a literal view of the term, talk of a UK presidency is obviously exaggerated. In the USA, the president only visits the legislature once a year — to deliver the 'State of the Union' address to both Houses of Congress. If the House of Representatives and the Senate are both dominated by members of the opposite party, a president does not have to resign. Indeed, the instinctive independence of the legislature can be so strong that the president sometimes finds it easier to cooperate with political opponents than with supposed friends.

The president can be removed from office by a successful impeachment, although this process requires two-thirds majorities in both Houses of Congress. By contrast, the UK prime minister only needs to lose the confidence of the Commons — and in 1940 the government of Neville Chamberlain resigned, even though it had actually won a vote of confidence.

We return to the question of 'presidential' government in the next chapter. For now, we need only note that although the *formal* institutional arrangements mean that the UK cannot be a presidential system, under Tony Blair it has come as close to the US model as it ever has. Is there anything that parliament can do to shore up the system?

Summary

Is parliament out of date?

➢ In recent years, people have grown more disillusioned with the whole political process in the UK, and with parliament in particular.

➢ The main reasons for discontent are the power of the executive, the strength of political parties and the lack of independent initiative among MPs.

Proposals for reform

The House of Commons

During the 18 years of Conservative government after 1979, the opposition parties experienced the full force of executive power in the UK and there were repeated demands for change (see Box 10.7). In May 1996, the then Shadow Leader of the House of Commons, Ann Taylor, promised that a future Labour government would do much more than 'tinker' with the parliamentary system. The government's aim would be to make parliament more efficient as a law-making body, and to 'make MPs more effective in holding the executive to account'. Labour's 1997 manifesto echoed this pledge, and a new Modernisation Committee was established after the election.

Box 10.7 **Party attitudes to reform**

It is difficult to draw up hard-and-fast rules about party attitudes to parliamentary reform, as they depend crucially on circumstances, but some general tendencies are clear.

➢ In office with clear majorities, both Labour and Conservatives have been hesitant (at best) about change. Even when they complain in opposition about executive dominance, they find the institutional arrangements very convenient when they step into their opponents' shoes. But although a degree of cynicism is justified, there have been occasions when reforming governments have had the excuse of being blown off-course by 'events'. Thus when the Heath government won the 1970 general election, it had ambitious plans to 'modernise' parliament, but soon found itself preoccupied with industrial and economic problems.

➢ The Liberal Democrats (and their predecessors) have always been interested in the reform of parliament — an attitude that is consistent with their critical approach to the constitution in general. Again, a cynic might think that this merely reflects their failure to hold power independently since 1914.

This all seemed very encouraging to the supporters of reform. But we have seen that there were plenty of reasons to be sceptical. Opposition parties are always likely to argue for reforms. When they return to power, they tend to discover that the system was perfectly sound after all. So it was no great surprise that the Modernisation Committee soon turned its attention to 'tinkering'. An example of this was the changes to MPs' working hours (see Box 10.8). In a series of votes MPs decided to start sitting on Tuesdays and Wednesdays at 11.30 a.m. rather than 2.30 p.m., finishing at 7 p.m. rather than 11. On Thursday, the sittings would run from 10.30 a.m. to 6 p.m., reflecting the fact that many MPs have to travel back to their constituencies for the weekend. However, before long many MPs were complaining that these more orthodox hours actually made their lives more stressful; for example, there was no provision for a lunch break. In January 2005 the Commons voted to restore the old hours on Tuesdays. Even under the revised rules there was nothing to prevent all-night sittings in certain circumstances. In March 2005, when the Lords and the Commons were deadlocked over the Prevention of Terrorism Bill, they sat continuously for more than 40 hours.

Box 10.8 MPs under stress

The ambition to become an MP might seem eccentric at a time when politicians are unpopular, and it is even more difficult to explain in view of the demands of the job. In 1996, the occupational psychologist Ashley Weinberg carried out a survey of nearly 100 MPs. Half of them said that they worked between 55 and 70 hours per week. At the time, the average full-time working week in the UK was less than 40 hours, and even that was 5 hours more than the average in Germany and France. More than a third said that they had insufficient sleep, and a fifth complained of symptoms typical of people suffering from stress. No wonder MPs have been keen to reform their working hours!

The leader of the House at the time, Robin Cook, had expressed a wish to make the Commons 'more topical, more effective and more accessible'. There were some interesting changes; for example, MPs can now organise debates on topical issues in Westminster Hall. But his package of reforms still concentrated on timetable changes. Conservative critics had every reason to argue that these would make life more comfortable for the government, potentially making parliament even more unpopular. For example, PMQs have been brought forward to midday, so that the proceedings will catch the lunchtime news. MPs had incurred some criticism because of

Robin Cook, leader of the House of Commons, 2001–03

their prolonged summer break, but this has not been reduced. Instead, the holiday will begin and end 2 weeks earlier, so that parliament will sit briefly before the annual party conferences.

In the same vote of October 2002, it was agreed that an experiment of using Westminster Hall for wide-ranging debates should be made permanent. The Modernisation Committee has also considered ideas to make it easier to pass Private Members' Bills. But the most promising and controversial proposals focus on the select committees. It was agreed in principle that these bodies should be able to scrutinise legislation before it is introduced, supplementing the role of standing committees at a later stage of the process. Yet reformers are aware that this depends on the goodwill of ministers, who would have to ensure that the committees were given enough time to consider the bills.

The power of committees to summon witnesses could also be increased, and their members be given more assistance in their research efforts. But the reform movement suffered a serious setback in March 2002, when a plan to reduce the power of the party whips over the choice of select committee members was rejected in the Commons. Significantly, Robin Cook was the only cabinet minister to support the proposal, and it was rumoured that the prime minister warmly opposed his scheme. Cook resigned from his post in March 2003 during the Iraq crisis. It was expected that he would leave the government soon in any case, largely because of repeated disagreements with the prime minister over his plans for reform.

Perhaps the best hope is for the election in the near future of a minority government, which will have to take more account of backbench demands. Ironically, under a weak government there would probably be less demand for reform. Many voters would want such a government to be strengthened rather than fenced in by more effective checks. But if the curbs could be introduced, their value would be recognised the next time a government came to power with an overwhelming majority. For those who fear an

---

Box 10.9 Commons reform and the 2005 general election

Parliamentary reform was hardly mentioned during the 2005 general election campaign, but the three main parties all included the subject in their manifestos. Their proposals are summarised below.

Labour: No proposals for significant change; the government has already made the Commons more representative of society by increasing the number of women MPs.

Conservatives: The number of MPs should be reduced by 20% to reflect devolution; English laws should only be voted on by English-based MPs; select committees should be strengthened.

Liberal Democrats: The electoral system should be changed to proportional representation; select committees should be strengthened; a War Powers Act should be introduced to reduce prime minister's power over war and peace.

overmighty executive, it would be even better if a weak government could be induced to make a far-reaching package of reforms, including proportional representation (PR) and a more rigorous Freedom of Information Act that eradicates at least part of the UK's culture of secretive government.

Box 10.10 **Can we do without parliament?**

Recent developments in technology raise the possibility that parliament could be abolished. Instead, individual citizens could vote on legislation from the comfort of their own homes, via their computers. Everyone would have the chance to propose their own laws. This would realise the dreams of theorists (going back to the ancient Greeks) who have felt that representative democracy is an inadequate substitute for the real thing (see Chapter 1).

The idea is tantalising, but only seems realistic in regard to a few vital questions (e.g. UK entry into the euro, which will be subject to referendums). With so many other distractions, few citizens would take the trouble to sift through all the arguments. The informed minority would often be outvoted by people who neither knew nor cared about the issues. The regrettable but inescapable fact is that the increased complexity and scale of government activity, which has helped to bring parliament into disrepute in the democratic age, also makes representative institutions inescapable. A more fruitful question would be: can we devolve more decisions to accountable politicians at local level?

If these reforms were introduced, they would give the Commons a chance to prove that it still has a role to play in monitoring the executive. Despite all their limitations, the committees do seem to have developed something of an *institutional ethos* of their own. Some MPs may well come to regard them as a very acceptable alternative to the old career path, which in almost every case failed to lead to Downing Street. As senior committee members they could expect the kind of media exposure that politicians seem to crave, without any of the decision-making responsibilities that plague ministers. Traditionalists, who think that the main business of politics should be conducted in the Commons' chamber, would be upset, as they have been even by the limited changes to date (see Box 10.11). But the development would merely reflect the fact that the real action moved elsewhere a long time ago. MPs who were not committee members would probably benefit. A critical report by a powerful and independent committee could reduce some of the stigma attaching to any backbencher brave enough to rebel.

While the proposals are promising enough on paper, however, in practice they run up against the difficulties we looked at earlier. Institutions are heavily dependent on the people who operate them. Reform on these lines presupposes that the majority of MPs really *want* to stand up to the executive. But it is much more common for candidates to run for election in the hope of filling a ministerial office sooner rather than later. The idea that the Commons is full of principled people, chafing against the discipline of the whips, is a romantic mirage, at least at present. There are 46 select committees at present, including the Modernisation Committee (see Box 10.12). As the number of committees increases, it might be difficult to find members with the enthusiasm and free time to keep all of them going. An even more disheartening thought is that backbench MPs have been involved in recent scandals no less than ministers. Pinning one's hopes on them might not be the best way of improving parliament's image.

Box 10.11 Objections to reform of the Commons

Three general criticisms from contrasting perspectives are often levelled at Labour's reforms. They could be summarised as follows:

➤ 'Nothing should be done. Although no one would have designed parliament in its current form, its procedures have evolved over centuries and attempts to "bring it into the twenty-first century" only reveal the present government's contempt for history. So, for example, late-night votes might seem irrational, but they add to the drama of parliamentary business. Beginning work in the morning discriminates against MPs who have not given up other jobs, which keep them in touch with the real world. We should leave the institution alone, and look for other reasons for popular disillusionment with politicians.'

➤ 'Reform is necessary, but Labour has diagnosed the wrong problem. Public discontent is caused mainly by the impression that parliament is powerless. Thus reform must be concentrated on measures which reduce the power of the executive.'

➤ 'Labour has not gone far enough. Public discontent is caused mainly by the distance of politicians from normal life. The ceremonies and rituals of parliament are outdated, the working hours are ridiculous, and the decisions of the elected government can be obstructed in a way that would be intolerable in a well-run business. Thus parliament should be reformed from top to bottom, to reflect the most efficient working practices of the private sector. Nothing should be regarded as sacred, and if the changes make life easier for the government of the day, so much the better.'

Box 10.12 Main House of Commons select committees (March 2005)

Broadcasting	Northern Ireland
Culture, Media and Sport	Office of Deputy Prime Minister
Defence	Procedure
Education and Skills	Public Accounts
Environment, Food and Rural Affairs	Public Administration
Environmental Audit	Regulatory Reform
European Scrutiny	Science and Technology
Foreign Affairs	Scottish Affairs
Health	Standards and Privileges
Home Affairs	Trade and Industry
House of Lords Reform (jointly with Lords)	Transport
Human Rights (jointly with Lords)	Treasury
International Development	Welsh Affairs
Liaison	Work and Pensions
Modernisation	

The House of Lords

Given the present balance of power at Westminster, a cynic would not be surprised that most talk of reform recently has focused on the less powerful upper chamber. In fact, one of the main obstacles to change in the Lords has been the executive's fear that reform might make it *more* relevant, thus reviving its influence.

New Labour included House of Lords reform in its 1997 manifesto, and in January 1999 a White Paper, *Modernising Parliament: Reforming the House of Lords*, duly appeared. This proposed that, after a transitional period, hereditary peers would be denied the right to vote (or even to sit) in the House of Lords. While the existing House had a massive in-built Conservative majority, the aim would be to produce a situation where independent, 'cross-bench' peers would hold the balance of power in the Lords. These non-party peers would in future be appointed by an independent commission, thus reducing the patronage powers of the prime minister.

It was clear even at this early stage that New Labour had a very clear idea of the things it disliked, and the House of Lords Bill was introduced speedily to get rid of the hereditary peers. But its positive proposals were much vaguer. Four options for a reformed chamber were advanced. It could be entirely nominated, directly elected, indirectly elected, or a mixture of all these. After publishing its White Paper the government appointed a royal commission to examine these options. It was headed by the former Conservative minister, Lord Wakeham. Critics claimed that its membership had been carefully chosen to ensure that it ruled out an elected element in the new House.

The government's uncertainty about its ultimate plans gave an opportunity for members of the Lords to suggest their own compromise. An amendment was passed to the House of Lords Bill, allowing 92 hereditary peers to retain their voting rights. This represented a 90% reduction in the hereditary tally since life peerages were introduced in 1958 (see Figure 10.1). Ironically, the deal caused much more fuss among Conservatives than inside the Labour Party. The latter was probably content with a

Figure 10.1 Breakdown of House of Lords membership, 1950 and 1999

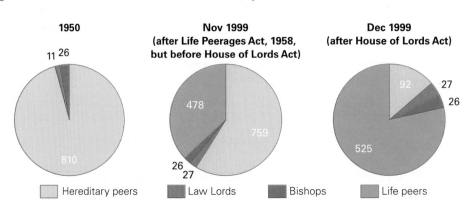

drastic reduction in the hereditary element, despite the fact that the unreformed Lords had been more effective than Labour in resisting Mrs Thatcher's radical reforms in the 1980s.

A half-way House

In fact, the 'interim' House continued to behave much as before, defeating the government in 36 votes in the 1999/2000 session, but ultimately having to back down on most of these issues due to the terms of the Parliament Act (1949). Some of these clashes came on issues like fox hunting and homosexual rights, which lent force to the usual criticisms of a House allegedly full of reactionary old men (even after the reforms, nearly 20% of peers were aged 80 or over). Opposition to the Hunting Bill continued after the 2001 general election, and the measure had to be forced through under the terms of the 1949 Parliament Act. But the Lords also maintained its opposition to the kind of policies it had attacked during the Thatcher years, opposing, for example, Labour's planned privatisation of air traffic control, and standing up for human rights in a prolonged struggle against the Commons over the Prevention of Terrorism Bill (2005). In all, nearly 11,000 amendments to government bills were tabled by the Lords in 1999/2000. At the same time, its committee work increased — in particular, its scrutiny of European legislation was praised widely.

The Wakeham commission finally reported in January 2000. Against expectations, it proposed:

➤ The Lords would consist of 550 members.
➤ Between 65 and 195 members would be elected.
➤ Elected members would serve 15-year terms and could stand for re-election.
➤ The rest of the House of Lords would be appointed by an independent commission.
➤ There would be safeguards to ensure that no single party dominated the House.
➤ A guaranteed proportion of members would be women or members of ethnic minorities.

The Wakeham commission was heavily criticised, both for being too radical and for not going far enough! The government indicated its broad approval, but it set up another committee, made up of members of both Houses, to give the matter further consideration. However, the committee failed to agree even on its terms of reference. At least Wakeham's proposed independent commission was set up, in May 2000. This body went so far as to publish advertisements for 'People's Peers'; more than 3,000 applications were received. But critics regarded this as largely a cosmetic exercise. By September 2003 there were 23 black and Asian peers, marking an advance in social representation. But even if more women and members of ethnic minorities were chosen, it was unlikely that anyone would be appointed to the Lords if they showed much sign of independent thinking.

With the Lords still in limbo, Labour pledged itself to complete the process of reform in its 2001 manifesto. Significantly, though, the measures were given a low priority.

Perhaps the government was hoping that attention would move elsewhere, so that the half-baked 'interim' House would gradually be accepted as a permanent fixture. However, now that the Conservatives had lost the battle over the retention of a strong hereditary element, they felt able to switch to the opposite extreme. Many senior figures within the party argued that a new House should be entirely elected. The Liberal Democrats had already taken this plunge with glee, seeing the reformed chamber as a UK counterpart of the prestigious US Senate.

Thus the reform of the House of Lords, which some might regard as a dry subject fit only for those most obsessed with politics, has become a fascinating political story, full of general points about the UK system of government at the start of the twenty-first century. Before 1997 Labour was able to attack the Lords because its existing shape had no rational justification. Defenders could claim that this made no difference as long as the institution actually worked. But this argument was swept aside on New Labour's early tide of 'modernisation'.

However, Labour's compromises have produced a body which, if anything, has even less to recommend it than the old House of Lords. In February 2003 a series of votes was held on various options for change. The prime minister had let it be known that he favoured a fully appointed House, but this was defeated in the Commons by 78 votes. The result was similar when the Commons considered a 60% elected Lords, but the verdict was much closer on 80% elected (beaten by only three votes) and 100% elected (defeated by 17 votes). All the options that advocated a majority of elected members were crushed in the Lords by more than 200 votes.

In 2004 the responsible minister, Lord Falconer of the Department of Constitutional Affairs, promised that the matter would be resolved once and for all after the next election. In its manifesto Labour pledged to allow another free vote on the final composition of the Lords and to remove the last of the hereditary peers. But it also proposed to reduce the power of the Lords to scrutinise legislation to a maximum of 60 days. This once again betrayed the government's main concern in the whole reform process, which was to prevent the Lords from becoming a more powerful check on the executive.

By contrast, and for understandable reasons, the main opposition parties argued that the Lords should be strengthened. In their 2005 manifestos both the Conservatives and the Liberal Democrats advocated that it should have a strong elected element. Indeed, senior figures in both parties wanted the whole House to be elected. If elected under proportional representation, the eventual outcome of the reform process might be a House of Lords which is actually a closer reflection of the balance of opinion in the UK than the present House of Commons, and thus a serious challenge to the supremacy of the lower House. Even more worryingly for MPs, PR in the Lords might endanger the sacred party system if voters seize the opportunity of choosing well-known candidates from all areas of public life, regardless of party labels.

Devolution and the European dimension

The royal commission on House of Lords reform was explicitly invited to consider changes in the light of other constitutional developments, notably the increasing importance of Europe and the devolution of certain powers to Northern Ireland, Wales and Scotland. These developments are discussed in more detail in Chapters 13 and 14. However, they have had an interesting impact on the debate over the performance of parliament, which we will look at here.

Devolution

To traditionalists, this process has further endangered the prestige of parliament by removing important policy areas from Westminster's control. By contrast, for advocates of reform the move came only just in time, since the unpopularity of much government policy outside England (even before 1979) was bringing parliament into disrepute. New Labour has still to solve the so-called 'West Lothian Question' — the apparent anomaly of Scottish MPs being able to vote on legislation affecting England, while their English counterparts have been deprived of any influence over many areas of policy in Scotland. However, we have seen various instances of UK politicians 'muddling through' and this will probably turn out to be another example.

Europe

Opponents of deeper integration into the European Union believe that on current trends UK sovereignty, represented above all by Westminster, will be destroyed. One of their key arguments concerns *accountability* — the idea that policy is now being decided by people who do not have to defend themselves in the Commons (let alone submit themselves to the judgement of the UK electorate).

But on the basis of our discussion, it would not be too cynical to argue that accountability has been pretty meaningless for many years now. If politicians and the public cannot stir themselves to resist the power of the UK executive, perhaps they might be a bit more active in asserting themselves when decisions are handed down from Brussels.

In fact, the argument is more subtle than this. Although UK ministers like to give the impression that they have nothing to do with the making of EU law, they have a veto in many policy areas. Even when decisions are made by majority votes, they have far more chance of affecting the outcome than ordinary citizens in the UK have of influencing the decisions of, say, the Ministry of Defence.

The reason for ministers' evasion on this point is to disguise the fact that they should be fully accountable to the House of Commons for their conduct in meetings of the European Council of Ministers. This is a conspiracy in which many MPs are happy to cooperate. Since members of the governing party are usually too frightened to hold their own ministers to account on any subject, it suits them to make the public think that 'Europe' holds all the cards. The result, though, is a hardening of Eurosceptic sentiment, and a feeling that since Westminster no longer really matters, our elected politicians are irrelevant egoists, strutting around at public expense. It does not help that ever since the 'Great Debate' of 1972 on membership of the EEC, parliamentary debates on the subject have been characterised by partisan point scoring and emotional outbursts rather than reasoned argument.

Summary

Proposals for reform

➤ There have been numerous ideas for reforming parliament, but the chances of making significant improvements are slim while governments have a vested interest in preventing ordinary MPs from living up to public expectations, and prefer an appointed chamber to an elected House of Lords.

➤ While governments of all parties confine themselves to tinkering with parliamentary procedure, developments such as the growth of 'semi-autonomous' agencies mean that ministers are far less accountable now than at any previous time.

Suggested reading

Allen, G., *The Last Prime Minister: Being Honest About the UK Presidency*, revised edn (Imprint Academic, 2003).

Baldwin, N., 'Reforming the second chamber', *Politics Review*, vol. 11, no. 3, February 2002.

Cowley, P., 'The British MP: not dead yet', *Politics Review*, vol. 12, no. 3, February 2003.

Cowley, P., 'Whips and rebels', *Politics Review*, vol. 14, no. 3, February 2005.

Cowley, P. and Stuart, M., '"Modernising" the House of Commons', *Politics Review*, vol. 12, no. 4, April 2003.

Mitchell, A., 'Backbencher's lament', *Politics Review*, vol. 10, no. 3, February 2001.

Morgan, J. D., 'Teeth for the Commons' watchdogs?', *Politics Review*, vol. 8, no. 4, April 1999.

Norton, P., 'The power of Parliament', *Politics Review*, vol. 14, no. 2, November 2004.

Ridsdill-Smith, C., 'Do we have parliamentary government?', *Politics Review*, vol. 11, no. 1, September 2001.

Rogers, R. and Walters, W., *How Parliament Works* (Longman, 5th edn, 2004).

Wakeham, Lord, 'Lords reform', *Politics Review*, vol. 10, no. 2, November 2000.

Wring, D., 'The fourth estate', *Politics Review*, vol. 14, no.4, April 2005.

Exam focus

Using this chapter and other resources available to you, answer the following questions.

1 Outline the key functions of the House of Commons.

2 Distinguish between ministerial and collective responsibility.

3 What are the main functions of MPs?

4 Outline the functions of the House of Lords.

5 How effectively does parliament perform its role?

6 'The executive has gained power at the expense of the legislature.' How, and why, has this happened?

7 'Reform of the House of Commons has been too limited.' How far do you agree with this view?

8 'The current House of Lords has even less to recommend it than the old House of Lords.' To what extent do you agree?

Chapter 11

The executive

The executive is the branch of government concerned with the formulation and implementation of policy. In the UK system of parliamentary government, all ministers are drawn from parliament and are accountable to it. The prime minister and cabinet are the main institutions within the executive, and their relative importance is a subject for perennial debate. The prime ministerial government thesis holds that the prime minister is the dominant actor, while the cabinet government model contends that the cabinet is still an important constraint on the prime minister. In recent years, proponents of the core executive model have argued that relationships between actors at the centre of government are characterised by dependence.

Key questions answered in this chapter
➤ Where does power lie within the core executive?
➤ What powers does the prime minister have?
➤ What are the constraints on the prime minister's power?
➤ How has Tony Blair strengthened the office of prime minister?
➤ How important are the cabinet and government ministers?
➤ How has the civil service been reformed since 1979?

The role of the prime minister

The prime minister is the head of the government. He or she provides political leadership within the cabinet system and the country at large, chairs the cabinet, appoints ministers and is leader of the majority party in the House of Commons. The office of prime minister emerged in the early eighteenth century with Robert Walpole acknowledged as the first prime minister (1721–42). He commanded majority support in the Commons and cabinet, stamping his imprint on government. The term 'prime minister' became the accepted title for the First Lord of the Treasury. The prime minister's powers (e.g. to appoint ministers and call general elections) are not laid out in statute law, but their parameters emerged gradually. Details of UK prime ministers since the Second World War are given in Table 11.1.

In *The English Constitution* (1867), Walter Bagehot described the prime minister as being *primus inter pares* or 'first among equals' in a system of *cabinet government*. A century later, cabinet minister Richard Crossman

Table 11.1 Postwar UK prime ministers

Prime minister	Period in office	Party
Clement Attlee	1945–51	Labour
Winston Churchill	1951–55	Conservative
Anthony Eden	1955–57	Conservative
Harold Macmillan	1957–63	Conservative
Alec Douglas-Home	1963–64	Conservative
Harold Wilson	1964–70	Labour
Edward Heath	1970–74	Conservative
Harold Wilson	1974–76	Labour
James Callaghan	1976–79	Labour
Margaret Thatcher	1979–90	Conservative
John Major	1990–97	Conservative
Tony Blair	1997–	Labour

argued that this system had been replaced by *prime ministerial government*. The prime minister was the most powerful actor and frequently bypassed the cabinet when taking decisions.

Key terms

> **Cabinet government.** A system of government in which executive power is vested in a cabinet, whose members exercise collective responsibility, rather than in a single office.
> **Core executive.** The organisations and actors who coordinate central government activity, including the prime minister, the cabinet, cabinet committees, the Prime Minister's Office, the Cabinet Office and top civil servants.
> **Prime ministerial government.** The view that the prime minister has become the dominant actor in UK government and is able to bypass the cabinet.

The resources available to the prime minister are considerably greater than those available to other cabinet ministers. They have the potential to invest the prime minister with significant power. However, the resources outlined below do not inevitably produce prime ministerial power, as they are subject to important constraints and may vary according to circumstances. The prime minister's powers and constraints are outlined in Box 11.1, on pages 271–73.

The main resources available to the prime minister are:

> patronage
> authority of the office
> party leadership
> public standing
> policy-making role
> Prime Minister's Office

Patronage

The prime minister is responsible for making a range of appointments to public office. These include government ministers, senior civil servants, life peers, judges, diplomats and senior members of the Church of England. Appointments to the Church, diplomatic service and judiciary are made on expert advice and the prime minister's direct involvement is limited. The power to appoint peers and ministers is more significant.

Prime ministers have long been able to appoint close allies to the House of Lords and thus to ministerial positions. Tony Blair ennobled Lord Irvine and Lord Falconer so that they could become members of his government. The power to nominate life peers has also enabled prime ministers to alter the party balance in the Lords. Blair appointed a large number of Labour peers before embarking on reform of the upper House. An independent Appointments Commission now makes recommendations on non-aligned appointments to the Lords, but Blair has defended his right to nominate Labour members.

Appointing cabinet ministers

The power to appoint and dismiss government ministers, particularly cabinet ministers, gives the prime minister a crucial advantage over colleagues. In theory, prime ministers can create a cabinet in their own image, rewarding supporters and penalising disloyal MPs. The Conservative Party gives its leader a free hand in appointing cabinet ministers. But since 1981, a Labour prime minister forming his or her first cabinet after a spell in opposition must select it from those MPs who had been elected to the shadow cabinet. This tied Blair's hands in 1997 but not in 2001 or 2005.

In practice, the prime minister does not have a free hand. A prime minister is unlikely to overlook senior party figures, some of whom may be rivals for the prime minister's job. John Major's opponents in the 1990 Conservative Party leadership election, Michael Heseltine and Douglas Hurd, were both given cabinet posts. Similarly, John Prescott and Margaret Beckett lost out to Blair in the 1995 Labour leadership contest but were included in his cabinet.

Senior politicians may have claims to office because of their high profile or standing in the party. Some might have sufficient clout to demand a post of their choosing. Gordon Brown provides a striking example. Brown agreed not to stand in the 1995 Labour leadership election to improve Blair's chances of victory. In return, Brown gained assurances that he would become chancellor of the exchequer in a future Labour government and would exercise significant influence over other areas of government policy.

Political balance

Ideological considerations are also important in constructing a government. A cabinet that contains politicians from only one wing of a party may not have the full support of that party; nor will it necessarily question the prime minister's will. Before she established a strong grip on the levers of power, Margaret Thatcher included both economic 'dries' and 'wets' in her cabinet, but took care to give her allies the key positions. In the 1990s, Major ensured that both the pro-European and Eurosceptic wings of his party were represented in the cabinet, but he sought to prevent either from garnering enough strength to challenge his authority directly. Blair's cabinets have contained mainly New Labour politicians, although traditional 'Old' Labour was appeased by the appointment of John Prescott as deputy prime minister.

Finally, the prime minister's choice of ministers is constrained by the talent available in the party. Rising stars should be promoted to give them experience of government. A party that has had a long spell in power, such as the Conservatives in the 1990s, may appear stale and lack sufficient new faces to freshen up the cabinet.

Cabinet reshuffles

Prime ministers can also reshuffle cabinet portfolios. In a reshuffle, some ministers might be moved to another post and others dismissed from the government entirely. This allows the prime minister to promote successful ministers, demote those who have under-achieved and freshen up the team. Ministers whose continued presence might damage the standing of the government can be axed. The prime minister decides the timing of reshuffles, but a sudden resignation may force an unwanted reshuffle.

The power to dismiss cabinet ministers is a blunt weapon that can blow up in the prime minister's face. A botched reshuffle may raise questions about the prime minister's judgement, reveal cabinet divisions and highlight policy failings. This was true of Harold Macmillan's 1962 reshuffle, dubbed the 'night of the long knives', in which he sacked seven cabinet ministers. Thatcher's demotion of Foreign Secretary Sir Geoffrey Howe in 1989 also had damaging consequences for her. Howe's anger eventually boiled over in 1990, when he resigned from the cabinet and launched a withering attack on the prime minister that helped bring about her downfall.

Major was accused of not being ruthless enough with troubled ministers. Norman Lamont survived as chancellor for 9 months after sterling's exit from the exchange rate mechanism (ERM) in 1992. Major too seemed reluctant to sack ministers embroiled in scandal, such as David Mellor. Blair has speedily dismissed ministers whose behaviour was questioned — notably Peter Mandelson, who was twice forced to leave cabinet posts. However, the reorganisation of posts that accompanied Blair's 2003 cabinet reshuffle was criticised widely. Press reports suggested that the refusal of some cabinet ministers to change posts thwarted Blair's initial plans for his 2005 post-election reshuffle.

Authority in the cabinet system

With the post of prime minister comes specific authority within the core executive. The prime minister thus:

➢ chairs cabinet meetings
➢ manages the agenda of cabinet meetings

- directs or influences cabinet discussions
- appoints members of cabinet committees
- decides when to call a general election
- appoints senior civil servants
- organises the structure of government

This authority gives the prime minister a significant advantage over other cabinet ministers. As chair of the cabinet, the prime minister steers discussions and sums up. Skilful prime ministers can use this role to ensure that their favoured position prevails. However, if a group of senior ministers promote an alternative viewpoint, the prime minister may not get his or her way so easily. Poor management of the cabinet by a prime minister who is either too domineering or too indecisive will ultimately weaken the prime minister's authority. An effective prime minister will direct much government policy, but act as coordinator or broker on disputed issues. It is the prime minister's role to direct the government's general strategy, giving a sense of purpose, cohesion and direction.

Agenda setting

The prime minister determines the agenda of cabinet meetings. Potentially difficult issues can be kept off the agenda of the full cabinet and dealt with instead in a cabinet committee or in bilateral discussions with the relevant minister. The prime minister can also exercise control over the information presented to ministers by determining which issues and papers should be brought before cabinet. The prime minister decides upon the chairperson, membership and remit of cabinet committees, where much detailed policy work occurs. Prime ministers can also shape the political agenda by establishing committees to examine issues they wish to promote. But the prime minister is unlikely to take a direct role in proceedings and cannot control all aspects of decision making at this level.

While in office, a prime minister can significantly reshape the structure and top personnel of central government. Government departments might be restructured. Harold Wilson created a short-lived Ministry of Economic Affairs to rival the Treasury in the late 1960s. In 2001, Tony Blair merged responsibility for the environment and agriculture in a new Department for the Environment, Food and Rural Affairs. The prime minister also makes appointments to the top posts in the civil service and can reform the role and organisation of the civil service as a whole.

Party leadership

The prime minister is the leader of the largest party in the House of Commons. A working majority in parliament strengthens the position of the prime minister as it means that he or she is more likely to enjoy the confidence of the Commons and be able to enact the government's policy programme. The executive exerts significant control over the legislative process through, for example, party discipline and the legislative timetable. However, the increased incidence of rebellion by backbench MPs unwilling to follow the party whip on controversial issues suggests that prime ministers cannot regard MPs in their party as 'lobby fodder' who will vote for the government come what may.

Party leadership strengthens the authority of the prime minister and brings him or her extra resources. Labour and Conservative leaders are now both elected by their MPs and party members. This legitimises their position and policy programme. A prime minister is unlikely to face a leadership challenge if he or she won strong support from across the party in a leadership election. The length, cost and complexity of leadership election processes also make the sudden removal of prime ministers by their party less likely.

A party's support for its leader is not unconditional. Margaret Thatcher was forced out of Downing Street when she failed to muster sufficient support from Conservative MPs (and ministers) to win the 1990 Tory leadership contest. Party rules dictated that the leader could face an annual leadership challenge even if he or she were also prime minister. John Major resigned as leader of the Conservative Party — but not as prime minister — in 1995, calling a leadership contest in the hope that this would reassert his authority. Though Major secured a 218–89 vote victory over the Eurosceptic John Redwood (who had resigned from the cabinet to stand against him), one-third of the party failed to support him.

Few prime ministers have enjoyed greater authority within their party than Tony Blair. Blair secured two landslide election victories and reformed Labour's organisation so as to enhance the position of the leader. But more than a hundred Labour MPs opposed Blair's stance on Iraq in early 2003, which again suggested that powerful prime ministers should not take the support of their party for granted.

Box 11.1 The prime minister: powers and constraints

Patronage

Powers of PM

- ➤ appoints ministers
- ➤ reshuffles cabinet
- ➤ allocates cabinet posts
- ➤ dismisses ministers

Constraints

- ➤ claims of senior colleagues for inclusion and specific posts
- ➤ Labour PM required to appoint first cabinet from elected shadow cabinet
- ➤ desirability of ideological balance
- ➤ unintended consequences of botched reshuffles
- ➤ possibility of sacked ministers emerging as rivals for leadership
- ➤ availability of talented backbenchers

Authority in the cabinet system

Powers of PM

➢ chairs cabinet meetings

➢ manages the cabinet agenda

➢ steers, sums up and determines the outcome of cabinet discussions

➢ holds bilateral and informal meetings with key ministers

➢ appoints chairs and members of cabinet committees

➢ restructures central government

Constraints

➢ requires cabinet support on major or controversial issues

➢ senior ministers have authority and may challenge the PM's preferred policy

➢ problems may arise if senior ministers feel they are being ignored

➢ not involved in detailed policy making in cabinet committees

Party leadership

Powers of PM

➢ authority as the leader of a political party

➢ elected by MPs and party members

➢ enjoys a majority in the House of Commons

Constraints

➢ support of party is not unconditional

➢ possibility of backbench rebellions

Public standing

Powers of PM

➢ high public profile

➢ communicator-in-chief for the government

➢ political leader in times of crisis

➢ represents country in international affairs

Constraints

➢ unpopularity with the electorate undermines authority

➢ may become the focus of media criticism

Policy-making role

Powers of PM

➢ directs government policy and sets the agenda

➢ authority to become involved in policy areas of choosing

➢ takes the key role in times of crisis

Constraints

➢ limited time and lack of detailed knowledge

➢ lacks the resources provided by a government department

➢ may be difficult to achieve policy success

Prime Minister's Office

Powers of PM

➤ Prime Minister's Office provides advice and support

➤ better enables PM to direct policy and act as a communicator

➤ appoints special advisers

➤ can reorganise the structure of government

Constraints

➤ Prime Minister's Office has limited resources (staff, funding)

➤ power of other departments, especially the Treasury

Public standing

The prime minister enjoys a high public profile. He or she provides political leadership at home and represents the UK in international affairs. The prime minister has regular discussions with other world leaders and attends formal meetings of heads of government such as European Union summits. Thatcher and Blair made an impact on the world stage in part because they forged a strong relationship with the president of the United States.

The media spotlight has focused more on the prime minister in recent years, with the PM taking on the role of communicator-in-chief for the government, articulating its policy programme and objectives. Blair has formalised this role by holding monthly press conferences and appearing before the House of Commons Liaison Committee. Opinion polls record far higher levels of public recognition of the prime minister than other ministers. High poll ratings strengthen the prime minister's position, for a prime minister who is regarded as effective by a majority of people has greater authority and room for manoeuvre than one who is perceived as weak or out of touch.

Opinion on Margaret Thatcher was divided during her period in office, but she was widely regarded as a determined leader with a clear agenda. This image was politically profitable for much of her premiership, but towards the end she became associated with unpopular policies (e.g. the poll tax) and was regarded as autocratic. Major enjoyed record poll ratings in the 1991 Gulf War, but his popularity fell sharply when his government ran into a series of political problems. Blair enjoyed relatively high poll ratings during his first term, but the war in Iraq damaged his standing. In late 2001, a MORI poll found that more than two thirds of voters were satisfied with Blair's performance as prime minister. By 2003–04, the figure had fallen to less than a third.

Policy-making role

The prime minister does not head a government department and has no specific field to which his or her policy-making role is confined. Instead, prime ministers have licence to get involved in issues across the political spectrum. A prime minister with a strong interest in an issue can give it a central place in the government's programme.

The prime minister is the most important actor when political crises occur. Prime ministers will also take an active interest in economic and foreign policy. The chancellor of the exchequer and foreign secretary are powerful actors in their own right, but the prime minister is likely to play an active role in setting objectives, directing and coordinating policy in these crucial areas.

Success and failure

Thatcher was a hands-on politician who played an active role in many policy fields. Instances of policy success (e.g. the 1982 Falklands War) strengthened her position. But in the case of the poll tax, policy failure undermined her authority. Both Major and Blair chose to play an active role in the Northern Ireland peace process. Blair effectively sidelined the secretary of state for Northern Ireland, Mo Mowlam, in the final stages of the talks that led to the Good Friday Agreement, taking charge of the negotiations himself. Major and Blair also played a key international role in conflict with Iraq. Despite the rapid removal of Saddam Hussein in 2003, the Iraq war undermined Blair's position. His support for the American-led invasion and doubts about the government's case for war raised questions about his judgement and trustworthiness.

Neither Major nor Blair enjoyed the success they hoped for in some domestic areas on which they focused their energies. Major's Citizen's Charter changed the nature of governance in the UK, but it did not bring great political reward. Blair's efforts to improve health and education bore fruit slowly: public spending increased by 40% between 1997 and 2002, but productivity rose by only 14%.

The Prime Minister's Office

The prime minister does not head a government department; nor is there a formal Prime Minister's Department. Within 10 Downing Street, however, lies the Prime Minister's Office, which has grown in importance in the last 20 years. Its staff of 190 contains a mix of career civil servants and special advisers, the latter being political appointees from outside government.

Following its reorganisation in 2001, the Prime Minister's Office consists of three main directorates:
➤ Policy and Government
➤ Communications and Strategy
➤ Government and Public Relations

The Policy and Government Directorate provides the prime minister with policy advice. It offers an alternative source of advice on current issues to that the prime minister receives from his or her ministers. Senior advisers on Europe and foreign affairs are based here. The directorate engages in strategic thinking on the future development of policy and it coordinates the development and implementation of policy across Whitehall.

The Communications and Strategy Directorate handles the presentation of government policy. The Press Office, a unit within this directorate, is responsible for relations with the media. It has grown in importance as the media focus on the prime minister has intensified. Thatcher's press officer, Bernard Ingham, was one of her most important advisers. Alastair Campbell, press officer and then communications director, was an influential member of Blair's inner circle. Overall responsibility for government communications was transferred to a senior civil servant in the Cabinet Office in 2004. This followed criticism of the politicisation of communications and Campbell's resignation in 2003.

The Government and Public Relations Directorate is responsible for the government's relations with the Labour Party and the general public. The former will be of greater significance in Blair's third term given the government's reduced parliamentary majority.

The 2001 reorganisation marked a strengthening of the Prime Minister's Office. Some academics had argued previously that a Prime Minister's Department was needed to direct and coordinate government activity more effectively. Now commentators suggested that Blair's reforms created something akin to a Prime Minister's Department in practice if not in name. The reorganisation also effectively brought about a fusion of the Prime Minister's Office and the Cabinet Office, as a number of units in the latter became directly responsible to the prime minister.

Summary

The role of the prime minister

➤ providing direction for the government
➤ political and policy leadership
➤ making appointments to major public offices
➤ chairing the cabinet and steering its decisions
➤ answering Prime Minister's Questions in the House of Commons
➤ choosing the date of a general election
➤ communicating the government's message
➤ representing the country in international affairs

Prime ministerial leadership style

The structural advantages that the office of prime minister brings its incumbent (authority in the cabinet etc.) are important but not sufficient for an understanding of the location of power within the executive. Power is not static, but dynamic. The context in which a prime minister operates is significant. Policy success and a large parliamentary majority, for example, can strengthen a prime minister's position considerably. A prime minister's leadership style is vital too. Vision and ideology are important here, but the prime minister's relationship with the cabinet as a whole and with senior ministers individually is most significant.

Thatcher as PM

Mrs Thatcher made less use of cabinet than her predecessors. Instead, detailed policy work was increasingly done in cabinet committees or in *bilateral meetings* with the head of a department. Thatcher often began cabinet discussions by announcing the government's policy and kept some issues away from the cabinet. Senior ministers such as Nigel Lawson accused her of paying greater attention to her advisers than to cabinet ministers.

Thatcher resigns as PM, 1990

Early in her premiership, Thatcher's skilful management of the cabinet enabled her to cement her authority at a time when many ministers doubted her policies. Her refusal to bow to pressure to tone down the monetarist budget of 1981 — and her colleagues' unwillingness to flex their muscles seriously — proved decisive. Thatcher was then able to construct a cabinet of ideological allies.

By 1990 though, Thatcher had few loyal allies in the cabinet. Chancellor John Major exploited her relative weakness to persuade Thatcher to agree to UK entry into the ERM — a policy she had previously opposed. Within weeks, Thatcher had failed to win on the first ballot of the Conservative leadership election. She then met her cabinet ministers one by one, but few offered their full support and Thatcher resigned. Economic problems, unpopular policies, cabinet divisions and the Conservative Party's low opinion poll ratings were all factors in Thatcher's downfall. However, Thatcher was in part the author of her own misfortune. By ignoring the concerns of ministers and bypassing cabinet, she had not strengthened her position but weakened it, alienating colleagues whose support she needed. When Thatcher was vulnerable, ministers struck back.

Major as PM

John Major adopted a more collegiate style. Cabinet once again discussed government policy and exercised greater influence over the direction of policy than had been the case under Thatcher. Major has been portrayed as a weak prime minister. He failed to put across a clear vision of what he wanted to achieve, was unable to set the political agenda and appeared overwhelmed by events. But Major recognised the limitations of his authority, managing his cabinet in a way that ensured he stayed in office for over 6 years despite never appearing totally secure. Although he undoubtedly made mistakes, Major could also be tactically astute. He used cabinet meetings to bind both pro-European and Eurosceptic ministers to government policy on Europe. By working closely with senior figures such as Michael Heseltine and Kenneth Clarke, he lessened the chances of a serious rival for his job emerging.

Blair as PM

Seasoned observers of prime ministerial power, such as Peter Hennessy, Dennis Kavanagh and Michael Foley, depict Blair as a more dominant prime minister than Major and even Thatcher. For Hennessy, Blair's is a 'command premiership' while Kavanagh describes Blair's leadership style as 'Napoleonic'. Foley argues that the Blair era offers confirmation of the 'presidentialisation' of the office of prime minister. As well as Blair taking the key decisions in government, the political and media spotlight is focused firmly on the prime minister. Blair is the communicator-in-chief for his government and party, and for the country.

Blair has had little time for cabinet government, preferring to conduct government business through bilateral meetings in which he agrees policy objectives with individual ministers. Key decisions are reached in informal meetings of Blair's inner circle of advisers, a style of government that has been dubbed 'sofa government'. This informality and neglect of the cabinet system was criticised by the former head of the home civil service, Lord Butler, in his report on the use of intelligence on Iraq's weapons of mass destruction (2004). He was 'concerned that the informality and circumscribed character of the government's procedures which we saw in the context of policy-making towards Iraq risks reducing the scope for informed collective political judgement.' The Prime Minister's official spokesperson claimed that the 2005 reorganisation of cabinet committees reflected Blair's desire to involve cabinet ministers in discussion of cross-departmental issues.

The Prime Minister's Office has been strengthened and parts of the Cabinet Office brought within the prime minister's remit. Blair has sought to command swathes of government policy from Downing Street and improve policy coordination and delivery. Numerous task forces and special units have been created to do this, while the number of special advisers has doubled. But devolution, European integration and the decision to grant the Bank of England the power to set interest rates have removed some policy issues from the *core executive* (see p. 291).

In his first two terms in office, Blair enjoyed a number of advantages that eluded Major: large parliamentary majorities, a strong position within his party and a largely quiescent cabinet. But he faced large-scale rebellions by Labour MPs on Iraq, foundation hospitals and tuition fees in his second term, and saw his opinion poll ratings fall. Although Labour won a third term in office in 2005, Labour's reduced majority limited Blair's room for manoeuvre. His announcement that he would step down during his third term also weakened his authority.

Blair and Brown

Despite the prime minister's 'command leadership', the Blair government is unusual for the extent of the chancellor of the exchequer's influence. Referring to Gordon Brown's influence, commentators have talked of a 'dual monarchy', in which both men have their own spheres of influence and 'courts' (i.e. teams of loyal ministers and advisers). The two meet regularly to discuss, and bargain over, policy. Blair has allowed Brown unparalleled influence in policy areas such as pensions, enterprise and welfare-to-work that stretch beyond a chancellor's usual domain. Comprehensive spending reviews allow Brown to shape government priorities in these areas. Brown rather than Blair chairs the Economic Affairs ministerial standing committee. The relationship has not always been smooth. In Labour's

Blair and Brown share a unique relationship in government

second term, it came under severe strain on issues such as foundation hospitals and tuition fees. A dispute over policy 'ownership' also arose over the single currency. Brown's determination that the Treasury should be the ultimate judge of the five economic tests was a crucial factor in the June 2003 decision that Britain was not yet ready to adopt the euro.

Summary

Key features of the Blair premiership

➤ Blair's command leadership
➤ emphasis on policy delivery and 'joined-up government'
➤ strengthening of the Prime Minister's Office and Cabinet Office
➤ growth in the number of special advisers
➤ proliferation of task forces
➤ Blair's strong position in parliament, the Labour Party and the opinion polls
➤ development of the prime minister's role as communicator-in-chief
➤ the influence of Chancellor Gordon Brown

The role of the cabinet

For much of the twentieth century, the UK system of government was described as *cabinet government*. In this model, executive power is vested in a cabinet whose members exercise collective responsibility, rather than in a single office. But the political importance of the cabinet has waned in the modern era. It now plays only a limited role in decision making, as many key policy decisions are made elsewhere in the core executive. However, suggestions (e.g. by Clare Short) that the cabinet has joined the ranks of Bagehot's 'digni-fied institutions' — those that retain a symbolic role but have no real influence — may be premature. As Mrs Thatcher's resignation dramatically illustrated, a prime minister who fails to recognise his or her dependence on the support of senior cabinet colleagues risks losing office.

The *Ministerial Code*, a government handbook on the conduct of business within the cabinet, states that the main business of the cabinet and its ministerial committees is to deal with:

➤ questions that engage the collective responsibility of government because they raise major policy issues or are of critical public importance
➤ matters on which there is an unresolved dispute between government departments

The functions of the full cabinet — the weekly meeting of senior ministers — are as follows:

➤ registering and ratifying decisions taken elsewhere in the cabinet system
➤ discussing major issues
➤ reaching or endorsing final decisions on major issues
➤ receiving reports on important developments
➤ determining government business in parliament
➤ settling disputes between government departments

Registering decisions

The weekly cabinet meeting is formally at the apex of the cabinet system, but many issues are decided at lower levels in ministerial standing committees, in bilateral meetings between the prime minister and a minister or in correspondence between departments. Most decisions are taken in committee and reported to the cabinet as 'done deals'. The cabinet thus acts as a clearing house for policy, registering or ratifying decisions taken elsewhere. If the prime minister and the cabinet minister responsible for the policy in question are agreed, other ministers will have little chance of changing a decision. Ministers are discouraged from reopening issues where a decision has already been reached.

The ability of cabinet to decide policy is constrained by the infrequency of meetings, its size and the detailed nature of much policy. It is impractical for 21 ministers to engage in detailed discussions across a range of issues. Most cabinet ministers are primarily concerned with policy in their department. They have little time to study policy in other departments, lack expertise and may not see the relevant papers. This need not stop ministers offering their opinion on an issue outside their brief, but it curbs their influence. The frequent turnover of ministers may also limit their influence.

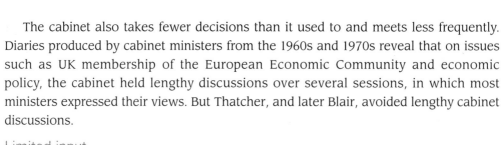

The cabinet also takes fewer decisions than it used to and meets less frequently. Diaries produced by cabinet ministers from the 1960s and 1970s reveal that on issues such as UK membership of the European Economic Community and economic policy, the cabinet held lengthy discussions over several sessions, in which most ministers expressed their views. But Thatcher, and later Blair, avoided lengthy cabinet discussions.

Limited input

Formally, the cabinet remains the supreme decision-making body in UK government. Yet for most areas of government activity, the cabinet is not an important actor in the decision-making process. It may play a more active role in some circumstances, for example when:

- ➢ issues are especially important or sensitive
- ➢ major or unexpected developments require a rapid decision
- ➢ government departments and ministerial committees have been unable to reach agreement

But even when the cabinet does consider major issues, its role is largely advisory. In June 2003, a special cabinet meeting was devoted to the Treasury's verdict on Britain and the euro. Ministers were able to air their views, but in reality the cabinet was merely endorsing a decision — that Britain was not yet ready to adopt the single currency — that had already been taken in bilateral meetings between the prime minister and the chancellor of the exchequer. The Butler Report (2004) noted that the cabinet was briefed on Iraq by the prime minister, foreign secretary or defence secretary on 24 occasions in the year before the war began. But ministers did not have access to key papers. Without these, the report concluded, ministers would not have been able to 'bring their political judgement and experience to bear'.

Ministers can advise and warn, but it is the prime minister who takes the final decision. The prime minister sums up the discussions and announces a verdict. Votes are very rarely taken as they would reveal divisions, while the interests and expertise of departmental ministers differ from issue to issue.

Government policy on important issues is, then, often settled with little or no discussion in the full cabinet. The final decision on the poll tax, for example, was taken by a ministerial committee and discussed in cabinet only briefly. The prime minister may also want to keep a sensitive issue away from cabinet to minimise the possibility of his or her views being challenged. Thatcher did not want open discussion on membership of the ERM. Similarly, only a few senior ministers were consulted about the decision to give operational independence to the Bank of England in 1997.

Reports and discussions

The cabinet hears reports on current developments, allowing ministers to keep abreast of events and policy changes. It also allows ministers to discuss policy and the government's priorities.

Cabinet meetings have a formal agenda, although Blair has proved more likely to stray from the agenda than his predecessors. In the last decade, the cabinet agenda has included the following items as standard:

➤ a report on parliamentary business
➤ a report on economic and home affairs
➤ a report on foreign affairs

In the parliamentary report, the leader of the House of Commons and the leader of the House of Lords outline the following week's business. This reflects the cabinet's formal role in timetabling government bills and ministerial statements. Under Blair, the cabinet is also presented with a plan showing ministerial engagements and announcements. Major added a regular report on European Union developments to the agenda, but Blair dropped it in favour of taking EU issues in reports on domestic or foreign affairs. The cabinet also receives the chancellor of the exchequer's report on the budget — but only on the morning of budget day itself when alterations are impractical.

On domestic and foreign affairs, ministers may wish to clarify or question policy. In so doing they may offer their personal view or that of a department or part of their party. But the cabinet is not a debating society and time for discussion is limited. Only a small number of interventions, usually by senior ministers, will be taken. But blocking discussion of sensitive issues may prove counterproductive for a prime minister, as it allows discontent to fester. It is better to gauge the views of colleagues, assure them that they are being considered and persuade them of the worth of the chosen policy and of cabinet unity.

Court of appeal

It is a working principle of the cabinet system that decisions should, where possible, be reached in ministerial standing committees or bilateral agreements. If an issue cannot be settled at committee level, it will be referred up to the cabinet. Some appeals are relatively straightforward matters of arbitration between the competing claims of departments. Examples include disputes between departments and the Treasury over spending allocations, or where more than one department is striving to be the lead policy actor. The cabinet judges the strength of the cases presented before it and reaches a binding decision.

Appeals to the cabinet are permitted only in special circumstances. Government could not work efficiently if ministers were continually required to wade through complex policy papers and force reluctant departments to give ground. This role as a court of appeal does not always proceed smoothly. In the 1985 Westland affair, the secretary of state for defence, Michael Heseltine, resigned from the cabinet. He was unhappy with Thatcher's ruling that cabinet would not hear his appeal against a ministerial committee decision on the award of a defence contract. The secretary of state for trade and industry, Leon Brittan, was later forced to resign after instructing a civil servant to leak information.

Summary

The role of the cabinet

➤ registering decisions made in cabinet committees

➤ handling political crises

➤ discussing major issues

➤ receiving reports on recent developments

➤ settling disputes between departments

Features of the cabinet

Cabinet membership

The full cabinet consists of the senior ministers in the government. Membership averaged just over 20 in the twentieth century. The wartime cabinets of David Lloyd George (1916–18) and Winston Churchill (1940–45) had fewer than ten members. Edward's Heath cabinet had 18 members — the smallest number in the last 40 years. The number of members of the cabinet who can receive a cabinet minister's salary is currently limited to 22.

The cabinet appointed after Labour's 2005 election victory had 23 members (see Box 11.2). It contained six women, one fewer than the record number of 2001. Baroness Amos is only the second black cabinet minister; Paul Boateng (2001–05) was the first.

Most cabinet ministers are heads of government departments. Departments such as the Treasury, Foreign Office and Home Office have long been represented in cabinet. The lead ministers in spending departments such as health, education and social security have also been fixtures in the cabinet in the postwar period. Other cabinet posts are more recent creations, reflecting organisational change in Whitehall. These include the secretary of state for culture, media and sport (a cabinet post since 1992 when it was known as 'national heritage') and the international development secretary (since 1997). Labour Party chairman Ian McCartney sits in the cabinet — and on a number of ministerial standing committees — as minister without portfolio.

Cabinet ministers must be Members of Parliament, to which they are politically accountable. Most are drawn from the House of Commons. The only exceptions in 2001 were the Lord Chancellor and the leader of the House of Lords, both of whom must be members of the Lords. It is now rare for members of the Lords to hold other cabinet posts, although Baroness Amos was briefly secretary of state for international development in 2003. Secretary of state for constitutional affairs Lord Falconer has retained the title 'Lord Chancellor'.

Cabinet meetings

The frequency and length of cabinet meetings has fallen steadily since the 1950s, when it tended to meet twice per week. Under Blair, the cabinet meets once a week on a

Thursday morning, when parliament is in session. Meetings now last about an hour compared to 2 hours under Major. Some have been over in barely half an hour.

Cabinet meetings are rather formal affairs: there is a fixed seating arrangement; the agenda is settled in advance; items are introduced by departmental ministers; and interventions from senior ministers and relevant departmental ministers are given priority. The prime minister sums up the discussion and votes are rarely taken. Only under Blair have ministers addressed each other by first name rather than official title.

Box 11.2	**The Labour cabinet, May 2005**
Prime Minister, First Lord of the Treasury and Minister for the Civil Service	Tony Blair
Deputy Prime Minister and First Secretary of State	John Prescott
Chancellor of the Exchequer	Gordon Brown
Secretary of State for Foreign and Commonwealth Affairs	Jack Straw
Secretary of State for Work and Pensions	David Blunkett
Secretary of State for Environment, Food and Rural Affairs	Margaret Beckett
Secretary of State for Transport and Secretary of State for Scotland	Alistair Darling
Secretary of State for Defence	John Reid
Lord Privy Seal and Leader of the House of Commons	Geoff Hoon
Secretary of State for Health	Patricia Hewitt
Secretary of State for Culture, Media and Sport	Tessa Jowell
Parliamentary Secretary to the Treasury and Chief Whip	Hilary Armstrong
Secretary of State for the Home Department	Charles Clarke
Secretary of State for Northern Ireland and Secretary of State for Wales	Peter Hain
Minister without Portfolio	Ian McCartney
Leader of the House of Lords and Lord President of the Council	Baroness Amos
Secretary of State for Constitutional Affairs and Lord Chancellor	Lord Falconer of Thoroton
Secretary of State for International Development	Hilary Benn
Secretary of State for Trade and Industry	Alan Johnson
Secretary of State for Education and Skills	Ruth Kelly
Chancellor of the Duchy of Lancaster (Minister for the Cabinet Office)	John Hutton
Chief Secretary to the Treasury	Des Browne
Minister of Communities and Local Government	David Miliband

Note: Three other ministers attend cabinet meetings but are not members of the cabinet — the Chief Whip for the House of Lords (Lord Grocott), the Attorney General (Lord Goldsmith) and the Minister of State for Europe in the Foreign and Commonwealth Office (Douglas Alexander).

Source: **www.number–10.gov.uk**

Cabinet committees

Much decision making in the core executive occurs within cabinet committees. These include:

➢ ministerial standing committees — permanent for the prime minister's term of office
➢ ministerial subcommittees — reporting to a standing committee
➢ ad hoc committees — temporary committees set up to deal with a particular issue
➢ official committees of civil servants — shadowing ministerial committees

Policy decisions are also reached in bilateral meetings between the prime minister and a departmental minister. Tony Blair conducts much government business in this manner.

Ministerial standing committees have considerable autonomy to determine the direction and detail of policy. Only where a final verdict has not been reached will the full cabinet concern itself with the deliberations of a ministerial committee.

The prime minister is responsible for the creation, membership, chairing and terms of reference of cabinet committees. In 2005, Blair chaired a total of 15 committees, including the Anti-Social Behaviour and Public Service Reform Committees. Deputy Prime Minister John Prescott chaired five and deputised on seven (see Table 11.2).

Key committees

The list of cabinet committees was first made public in 1992. The Cabinet Office website now lists the committees, their membership and their terms of reference. The work of cabinet committees falls within four broad spheres:

➢ home and social affairs
➢ economic affairs
➢ overseas and defence policy
➢ legislation

In 2005 Blair reduced the total number of cabinet committees from 61 to 44. Twenty-one of these are ministerial standing committees. Some of the most important, such as the Defence and Overseas Policy Committee and the Domestic Affairs Committee, delegate work to sub-committees.

Ad hoc committees are temporary bodies examining particular issues. Some have a short lifetime; others sit for most of the life of the government. Among the ad hoc committees meeting in 2005 was that on the London Olympic bid. Whereas the members of standing committees are primarily cabinet ministers, subcommittees and ad hoc committees include junior ministers. The Joint Consultative Committee with the Liberal Democrats (set up in 1997 to discuss constitutional reform) was unusual because it included members of another political party.

A 'kitchen cabinet'

Prime ministers periodically hold meetings with small groups of ministers, advisers and officials. In times of crisis, a select group of senior ministers may meet regularly to discuss developments and formulate policy. When this occurs, the group is often dubbed

Table 11.2 Cabinet committees, 2005

Ministerial standing committees and subcommittees (acronym)	Chair	Deputy Chair
Anti-Social Behaviour (ASB)	Prime Minister	Deputy Prime Minister
Asylum and Migration (AM)	Prime Minister	Deputy Prime Minister
Civil Contingencies (CCC)	Home Secretary	
Constitutional Affairs (CA)	Deputy Prime Minister	
Sub-committees:		
Electoral Policy (CA(EP))	Deputy Prime Minister	
Freedom of Information (CA(FoI))	Secretary of State for Constitutional Affairs	
Parliamentary Modernisation (CA(PM))	Leader of House of Commons	
Defence and Overseas Policy (DOP)	Prime Minister	Foreign Secretary
Sub-committees:		
International Terrorism (DOP (IT))	Prime Minister	Home Secretary
Protective Security and Resilience (DOP(IT)PSR))	Home Secretary	
Iraq (DOP(I))	Prime Minister	Foreign Secretary
Conflict Prevention and Reconstruction (DOP(CPR))	Foreign Secretary	Secretary of State for International Development
Domestic Affairs (DA)	Deputy Prime Minister	
Sub-committees:		
Ageing Policy (DA(AP))	Secretary of State for Work and Pensions	
Children's Policy (DA(CP))	Secretary of State for Education and Skills	
Communities (DA(C))	Foreign Secretary	
Legal Affairs (DA(L))	Secretary of State for Constitutional Affairs	
Public Health (DA(PH))	Deputy Prime Minister	
Economic Affairs, Productivity and Competitiveness (EAPC)	Chancellor	
Energy and the Environment (EE)	Prime Minister	Deputy Prime Minister
Sub-committee:		
Sustainable Development in Government (EE(S))	Minister of State for Environment, Food and Rural Affairs	

European Policy (EP)	Foreign Secretary	
European Union Strategy (EUS)	Prime Minister	Foreign Secretary
Housing and Planning (HP)	Prime Minister	Deputy Prime Minister
Legislative Programme (LP)	Leader of House of Commons	
Local and Regional Government (LRG)	Deputy Prime Minister	
Sub-Committee:		
Local Government Strategy and Performance (LRG(P))	Minister for Communities and Local Government	
National Health Service Reform (HSR)	Prime Minister	Deputy Prime Minister
Public Services and Expenditure (PSX)	Chancellor	
Sub-committees:		
Electronic Services (PSX(E))	Chief Secretary	
Public Services Reform	Prime Minister	Deputy Prime Minister
Regulation, Bureaucracy & Risk (RB)	Prime Minister	Chancellor
Sub-committees:		
Panel on Regulatory Accountability (RB(PRA))	Prime Minister	Chancellor / Chancellor of the Duchy of Lancaster
Public Sector Inspection (RB(I))	Chancellor of the Duchy of Lancaster	
Schools Policy (SP)	Prime Minister	Deputy Prime Minister
Science (SI)	Secretary of State for Trade and Industry	
Serious and Organised Crime and Drugs (SOC)	Prime Minister	Deputy Prime Minister
Welfare Reform (WR)	Prime Minister	Chancellor
Restructuring of the European Space and Defence Industry (MISC 5)	Secretary of State for Trade and Industry	
Animal Rights Activists (MISC 13)	Home Secretary	
Universal Banking (MISC 19)	Secretary of State for Work and Pensions	
Olympics (MISC 25)	Foreign Secretary	
London (MISC 26)	Minister for Communities and and Local Government	
Efficiency and Relocation (MISC 30)	Chief Secretary	

Source: www.cabinet-office.gov.uk/cabsec/index/index.htm

a *kitchen cabinet* or *inner cabinet*. No such institution exists officially, although Harold Wilson did create a short-lived inner cabinet in 1968–69 to deal with the sterling crisis. *War cabinets* of senior ministers and defence chiefs were in place during the Falklands War (1982), military action in Kosovo (1999) and the Iraq crisis (2002–03). On 'Black Wednesday', 16 September 1992, John Major held a series of meetings with senior colleagues to decide sterling's fate in the ERM.

Key terms

- ➤ **Bilateral meeting.** A meeting between the prime minister and a departmental minister in which policy is agreed.
- ➤ **Cabinet.** The meeting of senior ministers and heads of government departments. It is formally the key decision-making body in UK government.
- ➤ **Cabinet committees.** Committees appointed by the prime minister to consider aspects of government business. They include standing committees and ad hoc committees.
- ➤ **Kitchen cabinet.** An informal grouping of the prime minister's senior ministerial colleagues and special advisers.

The Cabinet Office

The Cabinet Office was created in 1916 to provide support for the cabinet system. The key unit is the Cabinet Secretariat, which regulates and coordinates cabinet business. It calls meetings, circulates papers, prepares the agenda and writes the minutes of meetings. The secretariat also coordinates policy work on issues that bridge the interests of several departments, and acts as a neutral facilitator in case of disputes between departments.

Although located within the Cabinet Office, the secretariat is directly responsible to the prime minister and to committee chairs. The secretary of the cabinet is the head of the secretariat and of the home civil service. The holder of the post attends cabinet meetings. Gus O'Donnell succeeded Sir Andrew Turnbull in the post in 2005.

The Economic and Domestic Secretariat, the Defence and Overseas Secretariat and the European Secretariat coordinate the work of the cabinet on matters that cross departmental boundaries. Others deal with security issues. The Civil Contingencies Secretariat draws up contingency plans for dealing with domestic threats such as disease or terrorism. The Security and Intelligence Secretariat oversees the intelligence work of the Secret Intelligence Service (MI6) and Security Service (MI5) on international and domestic threats to the security of the UK.

During Blair's second term in office, the Cabinet Office also took a leading role on policy delivery and public service reform. Three units report directly to the prime minister:

- ➤ the Prime Minister's Delivery Unit: ensures that departments meet policy delivery targets set by the centre
- ➤ the Strategy Unit: focuses on longer-term policy and strategy

> the Office for Public Service Reform: takes forward the prime minister's agenda on reform of education, health, transport, etc.

Guidance for ministers

Convention, rather than statute law, governs the work of the cabinet. But authoritative guidance for ministers is contained in a document entitled *The Ministerial Code: A Code of Conduct and Guidance on Procedures for Ministers*. This was made public in 1992 when it was known as *Questions of Procedure for Ministers*. It contains advice on the operation of the cabinet and the relationship between ministers and parliament, the civil service and their constituencies.

Clare Short, who resigned from the Cabinet in opposition to the policy on Iraq, 2003

Legislative and policy proposals to be considered in cabinet committees must receive prior approval from the Treasury and government law officers. If a policy proposal impacts upon the work of another department, the lead minister should seek views on draft proposals. The detailed content of material entering the cabinet system is largely determined in, and by correspondence between, government departments. Each government department is issued with a handbook containing guidance on the production of cabinet papers.

Collective responsibility

The cabinet is theoretically a united body. Ministers are members of the same party and stood on an agreed manifesto at the general election. However, the sense of unity is undermined by departmental and personal rivalries. As well as being members of the government, ministers are heads of government departments, whose interests they fight for in cabinet. Money and influence are scarce resources that ministers must bargain for. Departments provide ministers with authority, policy advice and technical information, so ministers may be tempted to act primarily as departmental chiefs rather than members of a collegiate body.

However, the importance of unity is underlined by the doctrine of *collective responsibility*, which is a key convention governing the behaviour of ministers. It states that all government ministers assume collective responsibility for decisions made in the cabinet and its committees. Once policy has been settled, ministers should support it publicly even if they had opposed aspects of it beforehand. If ministers feel unable to give this support, they should resign — or face dismissal. Resignations on the grounds of political disagreement with government policy include Nigel Lawson (1989), Sir Geoffrey Howe (1990), Robin Cook and Clare Short (both 2003) (see Table 11.3).

If the government is defeated in a vote of confidence in the House of Commons, the convention of collective responsibility obliges the entire government to resign. This is a rare occurrence, the last occasion being the defeat of James Callaghan's Labour government in 1979. Collective responsibility also binds ministers to keep

Table 11.3 Examples of ministerial resignations since 1960 (selected)

Date	Minister	Post	Reason for resignation
1963	John Profumo	Minister of War	*Personal misconduct* (sex scandal) and *political pressure* (lying to House of Commons)
1967	James Callaghan	Chancellor of the Exchequer	*Policy failure* — devaluation of sterling
1972	Reginald Maudling	Home Secretary	*Personal misconduct* — allegations of financial misconduct
1982	Lord Carrington	Foreign Secretary	*Policy failure* — misjudgements before the Argentine invasion of the Falkland Islands
1982	Humphrey Atkins	Lord Privy Seal	*Policy failure* — misjudgements before the Argentine invasion of the Falkland Islands
1982	Richard Luce	Minister of State, Foreign Affairs	*Policy failure* — misjudgements before the Argentine invasion of the Falkland Islands
1983	Cecil Parkinson	Secretary of State for Trade and Industry	*Personal misconduct* — extra-marital affair
1985	Ian Gow	Minister of State, Treasury	*Collective responsibility* — opposed Anglo-Irish Agreement
1986	Michael Heseltine	Secretary of State for Defence	*Collective responsibility* — refused to accept government policy on Westland affair
1986	Leon Brittan	Secretary of State for Trade and Industry	*Political pressure* — leak of letter in Westland affair
1988	Edwina Currie	Under-Secretary of State, Health	*Political pressure* — errors of judgement in salmonella in eggs case
1989	Nigel Lawson	Chancellor of the Exchequer	*Collective responsibility* — disagreed with PM's conduct of economic policy
1990	Nicholas Ridley	Secretary of State for Trade and Industry	*Political pressure* — comments made about Germany
1990	Sir Geoffrey Howe	Leader of the House of Commons	*Collective responsibility* — disagreed with policy on Europe
1992	David Mellor	Secretary of State for National Heritage	*Personal misconduct* — extra-marital affair and personal conduct
1993	Norman Lamont	Chancellor of the Exchequer	*Policy failure* (repercussions of ERM exit) and *personal misconduct* (financial affairs)
1993	Michael Mates	Minister of State, Northern Ireland	*Personal misconduct* — financial affairs
1994	Tim Yeo	Minister of State, Environment	*Personal misconduct* — extra-marital affair
1994	Tim Smith	Minister of State, Northern Ireland	*Personal misconduct* — financial affairs ('cash for questions')

1994	Neil Hamilton	Minister of Corporate Affairs, Board of Trade	*Personal misconduct* — financial affairs ('cash for questions')
1995	Charles Wardle	Minister of State, Home Office	*Collective responsibility* — disagreed with policy on immigration
1995	John Redwood	Secretary of State for Wales	*Collective responsibility* — to challenge John Major in Conservative leadership election
1995	Jonathan Aitken	Chief Secretary to the Treasury	*Political pressure* — ahead of libel trial
1996	David Heathcote-Amory	Paymaster General	*Collective responsibility* — disagreed with PM's policy on Europe
1996	David Willetts	Paymaster General	*Political pressure* — conduct in Standards Committee hearing
1998	Frank Field	Minister for Welfare Reform	*Collective responsibility* — disagreed with PM's policy on welfare reform
1998	Ron Davies	Secretary of State for Wales	*Personal misconduct* — 'moment of madness' on Clapham common
1998	Peter Mandelson	Secretary of State for Trade and Industry	*Personal misconduct* — financial affairs
2000	Peter Kilfoyle	Under-Secretary of State, Defence	*Collective responsibility* — disillusionment with direction of government policy
2001	Peter Mandelson	Secretary of State for Northern Ireland	*Personal misconduct* — role in Hinduja passports affair
2002	Stephen Byers	Secretary of State for Transport	*Political pressure* — disputes in Department for Transport, Local Government and the Regions (DTLR) and policy problems
2002	Estelle Morris	Secretary of State for Education and Skills	*Political pressure* — criticism of her performance and policy problems
2003	Robin Cook	Leader of the House of Commons	*Collective responsibility* — disagreed with PM's position on Iraq
2003	Clare Short	Secretary of State for International Development	*Collective responsibility* — disagreed with PM's position on the reconstruction of Iraq
2003	John Denham	Minister of State, Home Office	*Collective responsibility* — opposed PM's policy on war with Iraq
2003	Lord Hunt	Minister of State, Department of Health	*Collective responsibility* — opposed PM's policy on war with Iraq
2004	Beverley Hughes	Minister of State, Home Office	*Political pressure* — misleading statements over handling of visa applications
2004	David Blunkett	Home Secretary	*Political pressure* — linked to fast-tracked decision on visa application

Note: Callaghan became home secretary in a cabinet reshuffle after resigning as chancellor. Lamont refused the offer of another cabinet post after Major informed him that he was to be removed as chancellor.

cabinet discussions secret. This is to ensure that divisions are not revealed and that sensitive policy information is not made public.

The convention under strain

The convention of collective responsibility has been weakened over the last 30 years. Four main factors account for this:

> **Temporary suspension.** Prime Minister Harold Wilson temporarily suspended the convention in 1975. This was to allow ministers to campaign on different sides of the referendum on UK membership of the European Economic Community. It allowed a government divided over Europe to function collectively on other issues.

> **Leaks.** Disgruntled ministers and their advisers sometimes leak information on cabinet discussions to the media. In the 1990s, the press ran running commentaries on cabinet divisions over Europe. Purportedly verbatim accounts of discussions in the Blair cabinet have been published too, notably in Andrew Rawnsley's book *Servants of the People*. Cabinet discussions have also been made public in diaries and memoirs produced by former cabinet ministers, such as Tony Benn and Robin Cook.

> **Dissent and non-resignation.** Cabinet ministers who oppose important aspects of government policy have survived in office even when their concerns have been public knowledge. 'Wets' in Margaret Thatcher's first cabinet scarcely concealed their opposition to her economic policy. None resigned and Thatcher dismissed them only when her position had been secured. Eurosceptic ministers such as Michael Portillo retained their posts in John Major's cabinet despite their sympathy for the stance taken by backbench Eurosceptic rebels. Clare Short stayed in the cabinet for 2 months following her public criticism of the war on Iraq before resigning.

> **Prime ministerial dominance.** Cabinet ministers who served in the Thatcher and Blair governments have complained that the prime minister has undermined the convention of collective responsibility by ignoring the cabinet. Heseltine, Lawson and Howe all cited Thatcher's contempt for collegiality as a reason for their resignation. Mo Mowlam and Clare Short have complained that Blair does not consult cabinet sufficiently.

The core executive model

Over the last decade, professors Martin Smith and Rod Rhodes have developed the *core executive model*. This aims to provide a more accurate picture of power relations within the cabinet than traditional notions of prime ministerial and cabinet government. In essence, the core executive refers to those organisations and actors which coordinate central government activity. It includes the prime minister and his or her advisers, the cabinet and ministerial committees, coordinating bodies such as the Cabinet Office and Prime Minister's Office, etc. (see Box 11.3 and Figure 11.2).

> **Box 11.3** **The core executive defined**
>
> 'The term "core executive" refers to all those organisations and procedures which coordinate central government policies, and act as final arbiters of conflict between different parts of the government machine. In brief, the core executive is the heart of the machine, covering the complex web of institutions, networks and practices surrounding the prime minister, cabinet, cabinet committees and their official counterparts, less formalised ministerial "clubs" or meetings, bilateral negotiations and interdepartmental committees. It also includes coordinating departments, chiefly the Cabinet Office, the Treasury, the Foreign Office, the law officers and security and intelligence services.'
>
> Source: R. Rhodes, 'From prime ministerial power to core executive', in R. Rhodes (ed.), *Prime Minister, Cabinet and Core Executive* (Macmillan, 1995), p. 12.

Figure 11.2 The core executive

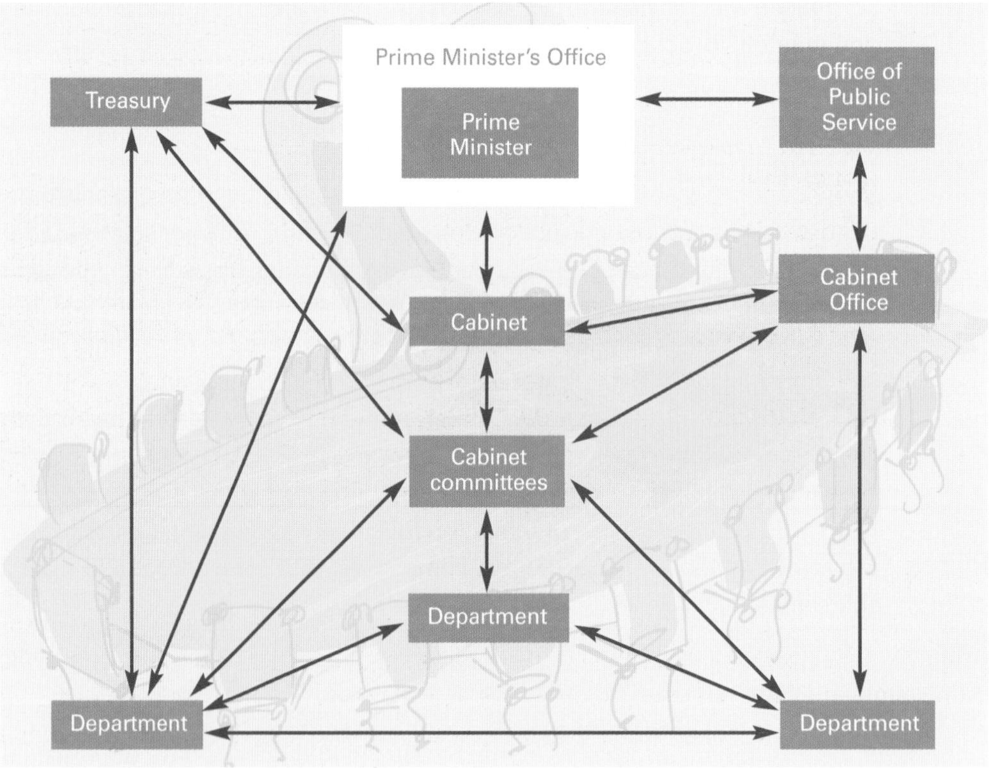

Source: M. Smith, 'The core executive', *Politics Review*, vol. 10, no. 1, September 2000, p. 3.

This approach argues that the debate on whether the UK has either prime ministerial government or cabinet government is flawed. Power is not located inevitably in one institution or the other; instead it is shared between actors who are mutually dependent. The decline in the power of the cabinet does not necessarily mean that the prime minister is dominant. The key actors in the core executive all have resources, but to achieve their goals they need to cooperate and exchange resources with each other. Power is based on dependence, not command. A prime minister needs the support of cabinet ministers and officials to meet his or her objectives. If this cooperation is not forthcoming, success will be difficult to achieve.

The prime minister has considerable resources at his or her disposal. However, the powers of the prime minister are not fixed, but instead depend on a number of variables. These include external factors (e.g. policy success, parliamentary majority and government popularity) and the strategies of resource exchange (e.g. the leadership style) adopted by the prime minister. Cabinet ministers also have resources. Most head a government department, giving them authority and policy knowledge. They may enjoy support within their party and policy success. Departmental civil servants are also significant actors, having detailed knowledge and experience as well as links across the Whitehall network (see Table 11.4).

Martin Smith argues that Margaret Thatcher's downfall was inevitable, given her failure to recognise her dependence on the support of cabinet ministers at a time of wider political difficulties. By contrast, John Major recognised that in difficult times a prime minister needs the support of other actors within the core executive.

Table 11.4 Resources of the prime minister, ministers and officials

Prime minister	Ministers	Officials
Patronage	Political support	Permanence
Authority	Authority	Knowledge
Political support	Department	Time
Party political support	Knowledge	Whitehall network
Electorate	Policy networks	Control of information
Prime Minister's Office	Policy success	Keepers of the constitution
Bilateral policy making		

Source: M. Smith, 'The core executive', *Politics Review*, vol. 10, no. 1, September 2000, p. 3.

The changing core executive

The core executive model recognises that the resources available to the prime minister have increased in recent years. Blair has strengthened the Prime Minister's Office and, for much of his time in Downing Street, has enjoyed a strong position in cabinet, parliament and the Labour Party. However, other developments have made it more difficult for the prime minister to command policy. These include:

➤ the devolution of power to new institutions in Scotland, Wales and Northern Ireland
➤ the continued transfer of policy competences to the European Union
➤ the decision to grant the Bank of England's Monetary Policy Committee the power to set interest rates
➤ the policies of privatisation and the creation of *Next Steps agencies* (see p. 301), which make policy coordination more difficult

Government ministers

There are over a hundred ministers in the UK government. Ministers are allocated positions in government departments (see Table 11.5). Senior ministers hold the rank of *secretary of state*, sit in the cabinet and head government departments. Below them in the hierarchy come the posts of *minister of state* and *parliamentary under-secretary*. These junior ministers are given specific policy roles in a department. In the Home Office there are three ministers of state (responsible for crime reduction and policing; criminal justice; and citizenship and immigration) and four parliamentary under-secretaries.

The main roles performed by ministers are:
- **Policy leadership.** A minister does not have the time or knowledge to play a hands-on role in all detailed policy, but plays an important role in initiation and selection.

Table 11.5 Main government departments, 2004

Government department	No. of civil servants working in department	No. of civil servants working in department and associated Next Steps agencies
Cabinet Office	1,790	2,090
Constitutional Affairs	2,200	11,950
Culture, Media and Sport	510	730
Defence	39,240	91,430
Office of the Deputy Prime Minister	2,780	3,720
Education and Skills	5,130	5,130
Environment, Food and Rural Affairs	6,910	9,690
Foreign and Commonwealth Office	5,910	5,970
Health	2,750	4,180
Home Office	18,780	24,010
International Development	1,780	1,780
Northern Ireland Office	170	170
Trade and Industry	4,960	9,640
Transport	1,900	15,760
Treasury	1,030	1,030
Work and Pensions	19,300	125,170
Customs and Excise*	22,590	22,590
Inland Revenue*	80,110	80,110
Scottish Executive	4,400	12,140
National Assembly for Wales	4,100	4,290

* The Inland Revenue and Customs and Excise operate entirely on Next Steps lines (They were merged and renamed HM Revenue and Customs in 2005).

Note: Figures are for full-time equivalent staff in post at 1 April 2004. They show that 523,580 people worked in the civil service at the time (2% of the UK workforce), of whom 381,260 worked in agencies or units operating on Next Steps lines.

Source: Cabinet Office, civil service statistics, October 2004 (www.civilservice.gov.uk/management_information/statistical_information/statistics/index.asp).

Only a small number of ministers, such as former home secretaries Michael Howard and David Blunkett, have changed their department's policy framework dramatically.

➤ **Representing departmental interests.** Ministers represent the interests of their department in the cabinet and negotiate for funding increases. They represent both the government and their department in meetings of the Council of Ministers of the European Union.

➤ **Departmental management.** Ministers play a strategic role in managing the work of their department, setting objectives and shaping the internal distribution of resources.

➤ **Relations with parliament.** Ministers perform two main roles in parliament. First, they steer a department's legislative proposals (government bills) through parliament. Second, they are accountable to parliament for decisions taken in their department, answering questions on the floor of the House and appearing before select committees.

Individual ministerial responsibility

The convention of *individual ministerial responsibility* states that government ministers are responsible to parliament for the policy of their department and for the conduct of themselves and their civil servants. The convention is not a rigid one, however, and confusion exists as to when a minister should be obliged to resign. Fortunate ministers choose when to step down and leave on their own terms. Other ministerial resignations of the last 40 years fall into five main categories, but in practice there may be some overlap (see Table 11.3 on pp. 289–290):

➤ **Mistakes made within departments.** A clear example of a minister carrying the can for mistakes made by his civil servants was the 1954 resignation of the agriculture minister, Sir Thomas Dugdale. He resigned when mistakes made in the Crichel Down case came to light. Such cases are rare. It is much easier to find cases (e.g. on 'arms to Iraq' and BSE) where ministers survived despite mistakes in their departments being brought to light.

➤ **Policy failure.** Ministerial resignations following policy failure include those of Chancellor James Callaghan after the 1967 devaluation of sterling and that of Foreign Secretary Lord Carrington and two junior ministers after the 1982 Argentine invasion of the Falklands. Other ministers have survived policy failure. Norman Lamont did not resign as chancellor when sterling left the ERM in 1992.

➤ **Political pressure.** This category is looser than those immediately above and below, as it covers resignations that are not primarily attributable to a single policy problem or scandal. Instead they result from a period of sustained pressure from parliament, the party or the press about a minister's performance in office. Examples include the resignations of Stephen Byers and Estelle Morris in 2002. The failure of Beverley Hughes and David Blunkett to provide full and accurate information to parliament and the public led to their resignations in 2004.

➢ **Personal misconduct.** A number of ministers were forced to resign in the 1990s following revelations of personal misconduct. Grounds for resignation have included allegations of financial impropriety (e.g. Peter Mandelson) and sex scandals (e.g. David Mellor). In such cases, the minister's position becomes untenable if he or she is subject to a lengthy press campaign and loses the support of the prime minister.

➢ **Collective responsibility.** As noted earlier, resignations of cabinet ministers such as Robin Cook resulted from the convention of collective responsibility, which states that ministers should resign if they cannot accept key government policies. Ministers often claim to have taken a principled stand in these cases, but the reality is often one of messy disagreements with the prime minister.

Accountability to parliament

Ministers have a duty to give parliament 'as full information as possible' and 'not to deceive or mislead parliament and the public'. Ministers have not always lived up to these principles. The 1996 Scott Report on the sales of arms to Iraq chronicled a number of occasions on which ministers misled parliament about changes in government policy. However, no minister resigned as the government argued that ministers are only culpable if they 'knowingly' mislead parliament; they cannot be held accountable for things that happen in their departments that they do not know about.

Beverley Hughes and David Blunkett resigned in 2004 after failing to provide full information to parliament and the media. Immigration minister Hughes stood down after admitting that she unwittingly gave a 'misleading impression' to MPs on checks on migrants from eastern Europe. Blunkett was alleged to have requested that a visa application by a nanny employed by his ex-lover be fast-tracked. Blunkett denied that he had acted improperly and an independent inquiry found no conclusive evidence. But Blunkett resigned when the head of the inquiry, Sir Alan Budd, indicated that he had discovered a 'chain of events' linking the Home Secretary to the speeding up of the application.

The reform of the civil service has also had implications for the convention of individual ministerial responsibility. In 1995 Home Secretary Michael Howard dismissed Derek Lewis, the chief executive of the Prison Service, holding him ultimately responsible for a series of prisoner escapes.

Key terms

➢ **Collective responsibility.** The convention that all members of the government are collectively responsible for government policy. Ministers who oppose a key element of government policy should resign.

➢ **Individual ministerial responsibility.** The convention that ministers are responsible to parliament for the policy of their department, the actions of officials within it, and their own personal conduct.

The civil service

Government departments are staffed by civil servants: that is, officials appointed by the Crown. Civil servant posts range from junior clerks to senior policy mandarins who advise ministers. Four principles have traditionally applied to the civil service:

- ➤ **Impartiality.** Civil servants serve the Crown, not the government or a political party. They are expected to be impartial and not to become involved in overtly political tasks.
- ➤ **Anonymity.** Civil servants are anonymous — individual civil servants should not be identified publicly as the source of policy advice. They also sign the Official Secrets Act. Civil servants are only held directly accountable to parliament in special circumstances.
- ➤ **Permanence.** Civil servants stay in their posts when a government leaves office. As impartial officials, they are expected to serve governments of different political persuasions during their career.
- ➤ **Meritocracy**. The civil service is staffed by generalists, recruited through competitive examinations, rather than people with professional expertise.

These principles have come under strain in recent years. The role of *special advisers* (see p. 298) may have adverse implications for civil service impartiality. A series of arguments arose, for example, in the Department of Transport, Local Government and the Regions in 2001–02 between the secretary of state Stephen Byers, his media adviser Jo Moore and Martin Sixsmith, the civil servant in charge of the department's communications. The dispute ultimately cost all three their jobs.

Jo Moore, 2002

Cases in which civil servants have leaked information have also raised questions about impartiality. David Shayler was jailed for 6 months in 2002 for breaking the Official Secrets Act by leaking sensitive information about the activities of the intelligence service, MI5. In 2004 the British consul in Romania, James Cameron, exposed anomalies in issuing visas to applicants from eastern Europe. The ensuing controversy led to the resignation of the immigration minister, Beverley Hughes. Both 'whistleblowers' claimed that they were acting in the public interest.

Ministers have shown a willingness to allow civil servants to be blamed for misjudgements made by government departments. The secretary of state for defence, Geoff Hoon, told the Hutton Inquiry that he did not know about, and was not responsible for, the decision to identify Dr David Kelly as the source of briefings made to BBC journalist Andrew Gilligan on Iraq's weapons of mass destruction. Kelly, a civil servant working in the Ministry of Defence, committed suicide in 2003 having been subjected to intense pressure by government, parliament and the media.

The Hutton Inquiry cast light on the workings of Whitehall by publishing numerous government documents on its website. The Freedom of Information Act has also brought about the release of documents containing policy advice by civil servants.

The boundary between legitimate civil service tasks and political tasks is sometimes blurred. Since the 1990s, civil servants have been asked to present information on the government's policy achievements. This may be interpreted as providing justification for policy rather than simply reporting it. Meanwhile, some appointments and promotions to the top rank of the civil service appear to have been made, in part at least, on political rather than purely meritocratic grounds.

Recruitment

The 1854 Northcote-Trevelyan Report established a method of recruiting civil servants that remained largely unchanged for 150 years. Civil servants would be generalists recruited on merit through open competitive examination.

The social characteristics of the top ranks of the civil service changed little over the next century. Top civil servants were almost all white, middle-class men who had a public school and/or Oxbridge education. Recent efforts to increase diversity in the higher echelons of the civil service have slowly borne fruit. Women make up a majority of civil servants, but are more likely to hold lowly positions. In 2004 women made up only 28% of the Senior Civil Service and ethnic minorities 3%. Many chief executives of Next Steps agencies (see p. 301) are now recruited from the private sector.

The size of the civil service fell from 732,000 in 1979 to 500,000 in 1997, when the Conservatives left office. After a further reduction, the figure rose to 554,000 in 2004. Following the publication of the Gershon Report (2004) on efficiency savings, the government announced that 104,000 civil service posts would be cut. A further 20,000 would be moved from London to the English regions. But more specialists in areas such as IT, finance, management and communications would be recruited.

Special advisers

Special advisers are not career civil servants, but political appointments made by government ministers. They tend to provide ministers with either policy advice or media liaison. The latter are known as *spin doctors*. The increased number of advisers and their perceived influence has caused controversy. In 2004, there were 87 special advisers working in Whitehall — 29 of them working directly for the prime minister. This compared to 38 under John Major, three of whom worked for the prime minister. Two of Blair's most prominent advisers, his chief of staff Jonathan Powell (1997–) and his communications director Alastair Campbell (1997–2003), were appointed as temporary civil servants and given the power to issue instructions to civil servants. A number of senior civil servants, including the permanent secretary to the Treasury, Sir Terry Burns, left the civil service, reportedly concerned by the role of special advisers.

Civil service standards

The Neill Committee on Standards in Public Life (2000) concluded that the increased number of special advisers had not brought a politicisation of the civil service. It did, however, recommend a limit on numbers and a code of conduct for special advisers. The Commons Select Committee on Public Administration (2001) felt that special advisers need not threaten the civil service, but recommended new mechanisms for funding and accountability.

In 1995, the Nolan Committee set out seven principles of public life that officeholders should follow:

> ➤ selflessness — acting in the public interest, not for personal gain
> ➤ integrity — avoiding inappropriate financial relationships
> ➤ objectivity — appointments and contracts to be awarded on merit
> ➤ accountability — open to scrutiny
> ➤ openness — disclosing information when the public interest demands
> ➤ honesty — declaring private interests
> ➤ leadership — promoting these principles by example

A *Civil Service Code* came into force in 1996 based on proposals from the House of Commons Treasury and Civil Service Select Committee. It sets out the duties of civil servants, although critics felt that it did not spell out fully the respective responsibilities of ministers and civil servants. The 1996 Scott Report on 'arms to Iraq' then found that civil servants had assisted government ministers in misleading parliament about a change in policy on defence orders. No ministers or senior civil servants resigned.

The government produced a draft Civil Service Bill in 2004. It proposed some limits on the powers of special advisers: they would not be permitted to authorise spending, issue orders to civil servants or discharge statutory powers. The Commons Public Administration Committee, which produced its own draft bill, sought a greater role for the civil service commissioners in protecting civil service neutrality. But the government is unwilling to expand their current role of ensuring that appointments are made on merit.

Key terms

> ➤ **Civil servant.** An official employed in a civil capacity by the Crown.
> ➤ **Special adviser.** A temporary political appointment made by a government minister.

The role of the civil service

The civil service has a number of functions within the core executive.

Policy advice

Civil servants provide policy advice to ministers. In doing so, they may have a number of advantages over ministers, such as experience, expertise and access to information (see Table 11.4 on p. 293). Although bound to provide impartial advice, civil servants can define which policy options are practicable, affordable and so on. Government departments may not, then, be passive actors in the policy process, as it is difficult to separate purely administrative work from that with a political element.

Concerns that senior civil servants had too great an influence on the policy process were frequently aired in the 1970s and 1980s. Politicians like Tony Benn complained that civil servants had frustrated his policies when he was a minister. The BBC television comedy *Yes Minister* depicted a Whitehall mandarin manipulating his hapless ministerial boss. But by the late 1990s, ministers appeared to have tilted the balance back in their favour. Rather than simply relying on advice from officials, they employed special advisers while many civil servants were engaged in more mundane activities.

Policy consultation

Civil servants are expected to consult with, and seek information from, a range of interested actors when formulating policy options. Government departments may thus build up a close relationship with interest groups in their policy sphere. So the Department of Transport will have regular communications with a range of transport groups, including the car industry, oil companies, road users and environmental groups.

Concerns arise if some groups have a privileged relationship with a government department. For many years, the Ministry of Agriculture, Fisheries and Food (MAFF) was accused of being sympathetic to the interests of producers (the farmers), but less amenable to the interests of consumers. Cases such as salmonella in eggs, BSE in cattle and the 2001 foot-and-mouth epidemic raised serious questions about MAFF's record. In 2001 MAFF was replaced by a new Department for the Environment, Food and Rural Affairs, which was expected to take fuller account of the interests of consumers and the environment as well as those of producers.

Policy implementation

The civil service is involved in all stages of the policy process, from searching for policy options, to drawing up legislative proposals and on to the implementation of new laws. Since the mid-1980s, much of the policy implementation role of the civil service has been carried out by Next Steps agencies working at arm's length from their parent department. Whitehall monitors the policy delivery records of these agencies.

Departmental administration

Civil servants are responsible for the day-to-day administration of their departments (see Table 11.5 on p. 294). Since the civil service reforms of the 1990s, senior civil servants have taken on greater managerial responsibility within departments and Next Steps agencies (e.g. meeting targets and financial management).

Reforms under the Conservatives, 1979–97

The principles under which the civil service operated in the early 1980s were not greatly different from those of the 1880s. Reform attempts had made only a limited impact.

Harold Wilson, himself a former civil servant, had sought to modernise central government in the 1960s. He reorganised government departments and established the post of ombudsman to handle citizens' grievances with civil servants. Wilson also set up a major review of the role and structure of the civil service. The Fulton Report (1968) duly recommended changes to recruitment and training, sharper long-term planning and a new Civil Service Department to manage the civil service. The reforms produced little, however: a Civil Service Department was created, but then abolished by Margaret Thatcher.

Influenced by New Right ideology, Thatcher viewed the civil service as inefficient, badly managed and unresponsive. She and John Major introduced reforms that transformed the civil service. In the early 1980s, Lord Rayner's Efficiency Unit was created to find savings. The Financial Management Initiative (1982) then brought an efficiency drive.

Next Steps reforms

The pivotal changes followed the 1988 'Next Steps' report — properly called *Implementing Management in Government: The Next Steps* — which followed a study by businessman Sir Robin Ibbs. The civil service lacked innovation and was not providing quality advice or policy delivery. It was too large to be managed as a single organisation. The reforms that followed separated the policy-making and policy-implementation roles of the civil service. Government departments continued to provide policy advice. But policy implementation and the delivery of public services were transferred to newly created executive agencies (many of which are known as *Next Steps agencies*). They

Table 11.6 Examples of Next Steps agencies

Parent department	Next Steps agency	Staff numbers
Department for Constitutional Affairs	Court Service	9,420
	HM Land Registry	7,930
Ministry of Defence	Army Training and Recruitment Agency	3,920
	Defence Procurement Agency	3,790
	Ministry of Defence Police	6,010
Home Office	Forensic Science Services	2,450
	HM Prison Service	45,280
	UK Passport Services	2,450
Department of Trade and Industry	Companies House	1,110
Department of Transport	Driver and Vehicle Licensing Agency	6,000
	Driving Standards Agency	2,130
	Highways Agency	1,930
HM Treasury	Office for National Statistics	3,450
Department of Work and Pensions	Child Support Agency	10,570
	Jobcentre Plus	76,760
	Pension Service	17,790

Source: Cabinet Office, civil service statistics, October 2004 (www.civilservice.gov.uk/management_information/statistical_information/statistics/index.asp).

are staffed by civil servants, but are headed by a specially appointed chief executive who is responsible for the day-to-day running of the agency. Framework agreements spell out the relationship between government department and agency.

A variety of Next Steps agencies have been created (see Table 11.6). There were 88 Next Steps agencies in 2002. The largest were Jobcentre Plus (76,000 staff) and the Prison Service (45,000). Three-quarters of civil servants work in Next Steps agencies or departments such as the HM Revenue and Customs that operate along Next Steps lines.

Next Steps agencies were given greater freedom to manage their funds and alter pay and conditions in the 1990s. Some agencies and departments (e.g. HMSO) were privatised following the 1993 'prior options' programme. The reforms produced examples of greater efficiency and improved service. Waiting times for driving licences, now issued by the Driver and Vehicle Licensing Agency, fell. But problems were also apparent — those in the Passport Agency, the Prison Service and the Child Support Agency attracted public attention. In the case of the last two, ministerial involvement was strengthened as a result of the problems.

Market-testing

Reform of the civil service continued under John Major. The 1991 White Paper, *Competing for Quality*, extended market-testing. Compulsory competitive tendering was extended to central government. This meant that the activities of government departments and Next Steps agencies had to be opened up to tender to see if the private sector could provide services more efficiently. Some tasks were thus contracted out to the private sector. By 1995, over £2 billion of activities had been market-tested. The Private Finance Initiative (PFI) was set up in 1992 to bring the private sector into large public sector capital spending projects. It was relaunched as Public–Private Partnerships (PPPs) under the Blair government and used to fund information technology and building projects.

The 1994 White Paper, *The Civil Service: Continuity and Change*, devolved financial responsibility to Whitehall departments and restructured senior positions in the civil service. In 1996 a group of some 3,800 top civil servants (less than 1% of the total) were given a new status — the senior civil service — and placed on personal contracts with flexible salaries.

Key terms

> **Compulsory competitive tendering.** The policy that public bodies are compelled to open up contracts to provide services to outside bodies.

> **Executive agency.** An agency performing a government policy delivery function that is subordinate to, but not controlled by, a government department.

> **Market-testing.** The policy that activities provided by public bodies such as government departments should be subject to tests for efficiency, including outside bids to provide services.

> **Privatisation.** The transfer of state-owned assets to the private sector, often through the sale of shares.
> **Public–private partnership.** An initiative to bring private sector finance into the provision of public sector functions.

The Citizen's Charter

The Citizen's Charter was launched in 1991 to promote quality, choice, standards and value in the provision of public service. The methods it specified for achieving these goals were familiar ones: privatisation, contracting out the publication of performance targets and standards, and mechanisms for dealing with complaints. The original document provided the framework, but a series of specific service charters (e.g. the Patient's Charter and the Parent's Charter) set out the ways in which the National Health Service and schools, for example, would be regulated. Hospitals were obliged to publish detailed information on their services (e.g. waiting lists for various treatments), they were set performance targets and their progress towards these was monitored. Critics argued that the criteria used to draw up hospital waiting lists and school league tables were too crude, but the information was published widely and public service providers were given extra impetus to improve performance.

Summary

Reforms under the Conservatives, 1979–97

Key themes:

> efficiency — cost cutting and job losses
> agencies — the creation of semi-autonomous Next Steps agencies
> markets — the market-testing of civil service activities
> privatisation — the transfer of some civil service tasks to the private sector
> management — the introduction of private sector management techniques
> regulation — the monitoring of performance targets

Labour and the civil service

Civil service reform was not a priority for a Labour government committed to radical change elsewhere in the UK state. It adopted a pragmatic approach, accepting most of the Conservative reforms and promising further improvements. The 1999 White Paper, *Modernising Government*, signalled that Labour's priorities for the civil service would be public service delivery, coordination, innovation, and diversity. By 2004, Blair was looking to a smaller core with a clearer sense of purpose, greater recruitment from the private sector and more effective leadership within departments. Civil service numbers would be cut by up to 100,000 after 5 years of increased employment.

Box 11.4 **Blair's seven challenges for the civil service**

1 Implement constitutional reform in a way that preserves a unified civil service and
   ensures an effective working relationship between UK government and the devolved
   administrations.

2 Integrate the European Union dimension into policy making in government departments.

3 Improve public services so that they are more innovative and responsive to users, and
   delivered in an efficient and joined-up way.

4 Create a more innovative culture in the civil service.

5 Improve collaborative working across organisational boundaries.

6 Manage the civil service so that it is equipped to meet these challenges.

7 Think strategically about future priorities.

Source: adapted from R. Pyper, 'The civil service under Blair', *Politics Review*, vol. 9, no. 3, February 2000, p. 4, Box 4.

Among the main developments since 1997 have been the following.

Service First

This was the name given to the relaunched Citizen's Charter. There are strong similarities between Service First and its predecessor, although Labour's programme does place greater emphasis on public consultation. A People's Panel of 5,000 citizens was created to gather feedback on public services.

Best Value

Labour's 'Better Quality Services' initiative replaced market-testing with Best Value. Again the change was not as dramatic as the alteration in title might suggest. Best Value modified the principles behind market-testing. Units are expected to identify the best value supplier of a service, but they are not obliged to set up a compulsory competitive tendering process if they can satisfy various government bodies (e.g. the Cabinet Office and Treasury) that their reasons are sound.

Labour has sought to build on the previous government's efforts to improve management practices and service delivery. It has expanded the use of *benchmarking* (i.e. the identification of best practice as a model for others to follow), performance indicators and public service agreements. Public–Private Partnerships replaced the Private Finance Initiative, but the use of private funding to provide public goods has been a source of controversy within the Labour Party.

'Joined-up government'

Concerned by the fragmented nature of policy making at the centre, the Blair government has sought to improve policy coordination and to give Downing Street a greater role in directing policy and monitoring its implementation. It established numerous policy *task forces* to bring together government departments and outside advisers. Units charged with policy planning and delivery were set up within the Cabinet Office.

The Treasury oversees departmental spending plans over a 3-year cycle through the Comprehensive Spending Review. The Cabinet Office and Treasury also monitor departments' success in meeting their delivery targets, which are set out in public service agreements.

Devolution

The devolution of power to new institutions in Scotland, Wales and Northern Ireland has significant implications for the civil service. In theory it remains a unified body. But whereas a single civil service once worked for the UK government, some civil servants now work for devolved institutions while others serve central government. The transfer of policy functions from Whitehall to devolved institutions required new guidelines on policy responsibility and coordination. A series of *Concordats* between UK government departments and the devolved institutions were drawn up, specifying these new working relationships.

Summary

Labour's vision for the civil service
➢ a smaller core civil service providing strategic advice
➢ 'joined-up government' with better coordination of policy and services that cut across departments
➢ more recruitment from the private sector, flexible pay and fast-track promotions
➢ greater use of information technology
➢ more women and ethnic minorities in the senior civil service

Reform concerns

The speed and radicalism of the reform of the civil service since the 1980s brought concerns. Some commentators argued that the reforms undermined the traditional principles of impartiality, anonymity and permanence. Their concerns cover:
➢ **Fragmentation.** The separation of the policy advice and service delivery functions of the civil service has brought fragmentation and resulting problems of effective control and coordination.
➢ **Inappropriate business practices.** Critics of the managerial reforms argue that market forces and private sector management practices have limited value for the civil service. What works for a private company will not necessarily work for a government department. Public–Private Partnerships create long-term financial costs for the state. Critics also fear that changes to working practices have undermined the public service ethos of the civil service.
➢ **Accountability.** The creation of Next Steps agencies has blurred the lines of accountability within government departments. It is not clear whether agency chief

executives or government ministers should be held ultimately responsible for policy failures. Ministers have used this confusion to avoid being held accountable for problems. Contracting-out has also had implications for accountability, as evidenced by problems in the Passport Agency and Immigration Service. These resulted from problems with a contract to supply computer software.

➤ **Politicisation.** The Thatcher, Major and Blair governments have been criticised for exerting too much political pressure on the civil service. The use of special advisers, the public relations role that civil servants have played in promoting government policy, and promotions based in part on political considerations are said to have undermined the impartiality of the civil service.

Suggested reading

Butcher, T., 'The civil service under New Labour', *Politics Review*, vol. 11, no. 3, February 2002.

Foley, M., *The British Presidency* (Manchester University Press, 2000).

Garnett, M., 'A feeling of resignation', *Politics Review*, vol. 13, no. 3, February 2004.

Garnett, M., 'Still first among equals?', *Politics Review*, vol. 14, no. 4, April 2005.

Hennessy, P., *The Prime Minister: The Office and its Holders since 1945* (Penguin, 2001).

Kavanagh, D., 'Tony Blair as prime minister', *Politics Review*, vol. 11, no. 1, September 2001.

Kavanagh, D. and Seldon, A., *The Powers behind the Prime Minister* (HarperCollins, 2001).

Magee, E. and Garnett, M., 'Is cabinet government dead?', *Politics Review*, vol. 12, no. 1, September 2002.

Pyper, R., 'The civil service under Blair', *Politics Review*, vol. 9, no. 3, February 2000.

Pyper, R., 'Politics and the civil service', *Politics Review*, vol. 15, no. 1, September 2005.

Smith, M., *The Core Executive in Britain* (Macmillan, 1999).

Smith, M., 'The core executive', *Politics Review*, vol. 10, no. 1, September 2000.

Thomas, G., 'The prime minister and cabinet', *Politics Review*, vol. 11, no. 4, April 2002.

Turner, A., 'Is there a Prime Minister's Department?', *Politics Review*, vol. 12, no. 3, February 2003.

Websites

10 Downing Street: www.number-10.gov.uk

Cabinet Office (includes information on the cabinet and the civil service): www.cabinet-office.gov.uk

Civil service (official site on the civil service): www.civilservice.gov.uk

Directgov (official directory with links to central government sites): www.direct.gov.uk

'How to be a Civil Servant' (site produced by author and civil servant Martin Stanley): www.civilservant.org.uk

UK government (provides links to government departments, etc.): www.ukonline.gov.uk

Exam focus

Using this chapter and other resources available to you, answer the following questions.

1   Do the resources available to the prime minister invest him with 'significant power'? Give reasons for your answer.

2   How far do you agree with the view that changes to the Prime Minister's Office under Tony Blair have created a Prime Minister's Department?

3   Compare the leadership styles of Thatcher, Major and Blair as prime ministers.

4   What is the role of the cabinet?

5   How far do you agree with the view that cabinet government is dead?

6   What is collective cabinet responsibility?

7   To what extent has the convention of collective responsibility been weakened?

8   Discuss the extent to which the core executive model provides 'a more accurate picture of power relations within the cabinet than traditional notions of prime ministerial or cabinet government'.

9   Under what circumstances and why have ministers resigned because of the convention of individual ministerial responsibility?

10 In what ways have the three principles of impartiality, anonymity and permanence of the civil service been under strain in recent years?

11 To what extent has the civil service been politicised in recent years?

12 Outline the role of the civil service within the core executive.

13 Evaluate the reforms of the civil service under the Conservatives between 1979 and 1997.

14 'A mixture of continuity and change.' How far is this an accurate description of the Blair government's approach to the civil service?

Chapter  12

Rights, the judiciary and the law

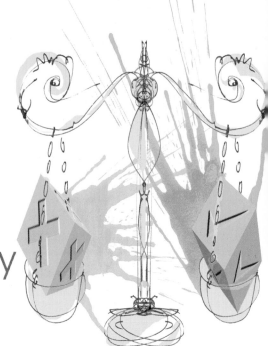

Until fairly recently it was possible to regard the role of the judiciary as an issue of secondary importance to students of UK politics. Even before the passage of the Human Rights Act (1998), this view was becoming untenable. Judges have always played an active constitutional role, and in previous centuries their decisions have widened the scope of civil liberties in Britain. But now they are expected, as part of their regular routine, to rule on the actions of government servants and to declare whether legislation passed by elected representatives is compatible with the European Convention on Human Rights (1951). Their role is becoming increasingly controversial, and critics from a variety of political standpoints are beginning to question whether unelected judges should enjoy so much political influence. This chapter explains the key developments of recent years, and explores the leading criticisms.

Key questions answered in this chapter

➤ What are the means by which citizens' grievances are redressed in the UK?
➤ What has been the impact of the Human Rights Act?
➤ How far are the UK's judges independent?
➤ How effective is the UK judicial system in protecting freedom?
➤ Are the UK's judges neutral?

Judicial independence and impartiality

The case for the prosecution

A consistent theme of this book has been the extent to which the unwritten constitution of the United Kingdom concentrates power in relatively few hands. Some liberal democracies, such as the United States and Germany, have institutions designed to protect their citizens against the possibility of dictatorship. In the UK, by contrast, these constitutional 'checks and balances' are informal, and have developed in an unplanned fashion over the centuries.

This contrast can be summed up by saying that, while there is a *separation of power* in countries like the USA, in the UK there is a fusion of power (see Chapter 10). The UK judicial system is an excellent illustration of this phenomenon. Liberal constitutional theorists have placed special emphasis on the need to place the power to make law, and the duty of applying it to individual cases, in different hands. Yet in the UK, the head of the judiciary, the Lord Chancellor, must be a member of the legislature and is appointed by the prime minister (see Box 12.1). In addition, the Lord Chancellor appoints judges and normally chairs some key government committees as well as sitting in cabinet and presiding over the House of Lords. When the Lord Chancellor has been a close personal friend of the prime minister — as in the cases of Lord Irvine and Lord Falconer, who successively held the post under Tony Blair — the judiciary seemed particularly subordinate to the executive.

Box 12.1 **The British judicial system** (prior to reforms announced in June 2003)

Key personnel

Lord Chancellor — head of the judiciary; appointed by the prime minister.

Attorney-General — the government's barrister; represents the state in cases where the government is involved; usually an MP; appointed by the prime minister.

Solicitor-General — the government's solicitor outside Scotland; usually an MP; appointed by the prime minister.

Solicitor-General for Scotland — usually an MP; appointed by the prime minister.

Lord Chief Justice — heads the Court of Appeal (criminal division); assigns judges to preside over cases; appointed by the Lord Chancellor.

Master of the Rolls — heads the Court of Appeal (civil division); appointed by the Lord Chancellor.

Law Lords (Lords of Appeal in Ordinary) — 12 members of the House of Lords who act as the final court of appeal in the UK.

Magistrates — mainly part-time, unpaid officials who adjudicate on minor offences; around 30,000 in the UK; appointed by committees of local 'worthies'.

Key institutions

High Court — deals with most complicated and important cases, under senior judges.

Court of Appeal — hears appeals arising from previous decisions in other courts (in practice, people rarely appeal against convictions in magistrates' courts); criminal division headed by the Lord Chief Justice.

Crown Courts — adjudicate on serious offences; 90 of them in the UK; under 'circuit' (junior) judges.

Magistrates' courts — deal with minor offences; more than 700 of them throughout the UK.

In theory, at least, this arrangement seemed to provide all the necessary components of what one recent long-serving Lord Chancellor, Lord Hailsham (1970–74, 1979–87), described in 1976 as an 'elective dictatorship'. He argued that a prime minister with a healthy parliamentary majority could pass any legislation that he or she liked. They could be confident that the resulting laws would be upheld in the courts because judges in the UK have nothing like the powers of the US Supreme Court (see Box 12.2). Hailsham felt that, in the UK, liberties could only survive because of cultural restraints that prevented politicians from abusing power. As a Conservative writing during a controversial period of Labour government, he felt that these restraints were disappearing.

Hailsham's intervention was a striking illustration of the delicate relationship in the UK between politics and the law. To his critics, he was trumpeting his concern for the constitution only in order to score a party-political point. As such, far from warning people about a worrying trend, he was himself a symptom of it!

In fact, when Hailsham became Lord Chancellor again in Margaret Thatcher's first government, he acted like most of his predecessors by defending the independence of the judiciary. But after 1979 it was the turn of left-leaning campaigners, notably members of the pressure group Charter 88, to press the case for reform. The most common argument was for a codified constitution with a US-style Bill of Rights, to defend the individual from an over-mighty government.

Lord Hailsham, pictured in 1995

Box 12.2 The US judiciary

The Supreme Court presides over the US judicial system. This body has the ability to rule that certain laws are unconstitutional, and therefore null and void. The president appoints its members, but only when there is a vacancy, so that a majority at any time is usually made up of people who were appointed under previous administrations. The appointments have to be approved by both Houses of Congress (the legislature), thus illustrating the operation of the US separation of powers.

The case for the defence

For others, the fact that both the left and the right opposed the existing system, depending on which party was in power, seemed in itself a reasonable argument for keeping things just as they were. Those who defended the unwritten UK constitution under Labour and Conservative administrations also argued that, even if the theoretical safeguards against dictatorship were brittle, in practice they worked quite satisfactorily. They were confident that the culture of independence generated by the UK judiciary guarantees freedom and rights more securely than a written constitution. They argued that a British citizen who feels unfairly dealt with can always hope to have his or her grievances redressed. The Lord Chancellor might be a political appointee, but by convention the occupant of the post has always been an experienced lawyer (like Hailsham himself), who instinctively puts the law above other considerations. So, for example, when appointing judges he or she consults other lawyers, and chooses people because of their abilities rather than their political allegiance.

According to this positive view of the judiciary, citizens in the UK have traditionally been guaranteed the *impartial* administration of justice by independent experts who, in the last resort, would rather quarrel with politicians than lose their reputation among other lawyers. It might be true that parliament will sometimes pass unfair laws under governments of any colour. But far from having to worry about the presence of a senior lawyer in the highest ranks of the government, citizens should be grateful for it. The Lord Chancellor could always be trusted to speak up for traditional liberties in cabinet discussions.

This final point provides an interesting perspective on the relationship between law and democracy. It portrays unelected lawyers as more reliable than politicians as defenders of liberty and rights. There is actually some historical support for this view. For example, in the seventeenth and eighteenth centuries, the judiciary often defended citizens against arbitrary arrest and upheld the right of *habeas corpus*, which ensures that people in prison can demand to have their cases heard in front of a jury. Moreover, this was a period when judges depended far more on political favour than they do today. The debate about trial by jury has revived in recent years, with the senior judges firmly supporting this traditional right against Labour and Conservative politicians.

As we shall see, however, in the late twentieth century it became increasingly difficult to defend what seemed to be a privileged and unrepresentative profession, and campaigners claimed that it was no longer (if it had ever been) an adequate guardian of fundamental 'human rights'. A common theme for reformers was the need to incorporate the European Convention on Human Rights (1951) into UK law. This seemed to be long overdue because the UK had agreed to the convention when it was first drawn up by the Council of Europe. (This institution should not be confused with the European Economic Communities, which subsequently became the European Union.)

Key terms
➤ **Fusion of powers.** A feature of UK government in which the three branches of government (the *executive*, the *legislature* and the *judiciary*) do not operate independently of each other.
➤ **Judiciary.** The branch of government responsible for the interpretation and enforcement of laws through the courts.
➤ **Redress of grievances.** A remedy for a citizen's complaint about an administrative action taken by any publicly funded body.

Summary

Judicial independence and impartiality
➤ Liberal democratic theory suggests that freedom depends on judicial independence from the executive, and that citizens must have confidence that any grievances against government decisions can be redressed.
➤ In the UK the judiciary has been tied closely to the executive through the political role of the Lord Chancellor, who is head of the judiciary.

Rights in the UK

As we saw in Chapter 7, the language of *rights* is a key element of liberal ideology. In liberal democracies like the UK, the judicial system has been regarded as the ultimate protector of citizens' rights. This position was reinforced in 1998, when the New Labour government passed the Human Rights Act, which incorporated the European Convention on Human Rights into UK law. To critics and supporters alike, this development marked a revolution in the relationship between law and politics in the UK, promising a far more active role for the judiciary in future and paving the way for further reforms to bring the UK closer to other liberal democracies.

Natural rights

Most of us are familiar with the language of rights, but we tend to be rather inconsistent when we use it and few of us have much idea of where it came from. In fact, it was originally used by certain religious thinkers, such as John Locke (see Box 12.3), who built their moral theories around the idea of *natural rights*, given to us all by God. For example, if I have a God-given right to form my own religious opinions and to speak out in their favour, it follows that everyone else has a *duty* (or *obligation*) to respect this. But I cannot be sure that everyone will obey God's intentions. Government is therefore necessary to ensure that my rights are protected, and that those who fail to respect them are properly punished. On this view, instead of *restricting* freedom, a system of law, administered impartially, should be its strongest guarantee.

> **Box 12.3** **John Locke and natural rights**
>
> In the context of the modern UK, the Englishman John Locke (1632–1704) is the most important figure in the debate over rights. Locke believed that the original condition of society was a 'state of nature', inhabited by individuals who possessed God-given rights to 'life, liberty and property'. He felt that human beings were essentially rational and good, but that disputes could still arise between them. In their own self-interest, the individuals in the state of nature freely agreed to establish a government to protect their rights.
>
> Locke had no historical evidence for this argument. His purpose was to justify the maximum amount of freedom, while ensuring that everyone who infringed upon 'natural rights' was punished. If a government failed to carry out its task of protecting such rights, he argued that ultimately the people had the right to rebel against it.
>
> Locke's ideas had a powerful influence over the Founding Fathers of the US constitution, who held 'life, liberty and the pursuit of happiness' to be 'inalienable' rights. Unlike the USA, the United Kingdom lacks a codified constitution, and its own Bill of Rights (1689) refers to parliament rather than to individual citizens. Yet the impact of Locke's thinking is felt no less strongly in the UK. The European concept of rights, by contrast, envisages a more positive role for the state.

Human rights

Despite its religious origin, the language of rights was easily transferred into an era when belief was less common. The only difference is that we are accustomed to talk about *human rights*, rather than natural ones. Whether we believe in a divine creator or think that we arrived on this planet as the result of a curious accident, we can still argue that human beings deserve equal treatment by virtue of their humanity. (Of course, the animal rights lobby extends this principle much further.) Essentially, though, people who believe in human rights share John Locke's belief that such rights exist *independently* of government (see Box 12.3). They are regarded as an external standard by which governments can (or rather *should*) be judged.

To some thinkers (particularly traditional conservatives: see Chapter 7) the idea of an inflexible system of rights is a recipe for constant political instability. Until recently, the concept found little favour among lawyers in Britain. One highly influential British legal authority, the utilitarian Jeremy Bentham (1748–1832), went so far as to describe talk of natural rights as 'nonsense upon stilts'. For Bentham and his disciples, the language of rights was nothing more than a pompous way of expressing a personal preference. In other words, when someone claims that something is a 'right', they are really saying that in their opinion it *should* be reflected in law. But others are perfectly entitled to disagree — and because of changing circumstances our preferences can be different from one day to the next. In these arguments, talk of 'rights' can be worse than confusing. It raises the temperature and encourages people to take direct action rather than coolly discussing the facts.

If the language of rights is potentially dangerous 'nonsense', what should replace it? The utilitarians thought that moral debates should be decided by what appears to be a more simple principle. If someone proposes a reform of the law, would the change lead to an improvement in the overall level of happiness? If so, the change should be made. If they so desired, people could then talk of having won a new 'right' under the law — a *civil* or a *legal* right. But, for utilitarians, that is the only way in which the language of rights can make any sense at all.

Civil rights

In the UK nowadays, we often do talk about rights as Locke did — that is, as if they held good at all times and in all circumstances, regardless of man-made laws. As well as regularly appealing to concepts like the right to life and the right to privacy, we often express the same ideas in terms of 'freedoms', such as freedom of speech (which is really the right to speak out without external restraint). But the traditional way of looking at rights in the UK can be regarded as a sort of mixture of Locke and Bentham. Over the centuries, general propositions concerning rights have been established in UK law. We are so used to enjoying these rights that we might come to regard them as 'natural'. Actually it would be more in keeping with the facts to describe them as *civil rights* or *civil liberties* because we enjoy them as a result of man-made laws and precedents that can be suspended in emergencies. Traditionally, Britons have associated 'rights' with those actions which are not prohibited specifically by law (see Box 12.4).

Box 12.4 **Casanova on the English**

'The Englishman, fortified by the rights which the law confers upon him, and only allowing himself to do what the laws do not forbid, is brusque, inexorable, and rude.'

Casanova, 1763.

In other words, citizens of liberal democracies tend to accept that rights depend on governments, whereas thinkers like Locke denied this. For Example, freedom of speech is not always protected in the UK. Since the 1960s declarations that seem likely to incite racial hatred have been subject to legal penalties, and the Conservative government of Margaret Thatcher prevented broadcasters from transmitting the voices of people speaking on behalf of terrorist organisations like the Provisional IRA.

This qualified view of rights can be summarised as a belief in general principles that ought to apply, all things being equal, because they have stood the test of time and become an integral part of the UK's political culture. If we look back to our discussion of political ideologies in Chapter 7, we can see that this pragmatic, flexible approach has much in common with the tradition of British conservatism. In particular, it betrays a suspicion of abstract principle, and a ready preference for the tried and trusted.

It might be argued, in fact, that the judicial system in Britain as a whole has tended to reflect the conservative (rather than a Conservative Party) outlook. This is not just because its senior figures tend to be middle-aged or elderly people who have risen slowly within the profession. Judges feel bound by *precedent*: that is, when reaching a decision they refer back to previous similar cases. Their behaviour reflects the view of the conservative philosopher Edmund Burke (1729–97) that, instead of relying on their own opinions, people should depend on the accumulated wisdom of many generations.

Significantly, Burke himself was trained in the law, like many senior UK politicians. Barristers have traditionally been the best-represented profession in the House of Commons (see Box 12.5), with the result that lawyers go to court to argue over laws made for them by other lawyers! This also reflects a general increase in the number of British lawyers. Between 1962 and 2002 the number of solicitors rose from 20,000 to 87,000.

Box 12.5 Senior British politicians with a legal background

David Lloyd George (solicitor; prime minister, 1916–22)

Margaret Thatcher (barrister; prime minister, 1979–90)

Kenneth Clarke (barrister; chancellor of the exchequer, 1993–97)

Tony Blair (barrister; prime minister, 1997–)

Michael Howard (barrister; leader of the opposition, 2003–05)

The Human Rights Act

As we have seen, the UK was a signatory to the European Convention on Human Rights in 1951. But until the Human Rights Act (1998) came into force, a UK citizen seeking redress under the convention had to appeal to the European Court of Human Rights at Strasbourg. They were first allowed to do this in 1966. By 1998 this court had ruled against the UK government 38 times, out of around a hundred cases (see Box 12.6).

Box 12.6 Important cases at the European Court of Human Rights (ECHR)

1979: the UK government amended the law governing contempt of court, after the ECHR ruled that an injunction against a *Sunday Times* article infringed freedom of expression.

1982: an ECHR ruling led the UK government to outlaw corporal punishment in all state schools.

1990: the 'Factortame' case. The ECHR ruled that the Merchant Shipping Act (1988) was contrary to EU legislation and should be suspended.

1995: the ECHR found that UK soldiers who shot and killed three IRA terrorists in Gibraltar had acted with unreasonable force.

1999: the ECHR found that the home secretary, Jack Straw, had no right to alter the term of detention imposed on the two boys who killed the toddler James Bulger.

Our discussion of the British attitude to rights helps to explain the delay in incorporating the convention into UK law. From a conservative perspective, the convention reads like a wish list that would be appropriate only in a perfect world. The judiciary is flexible enough to allow that rights might be guaranteed by different laws in different places. But if we accept that the world is not perfect, why bother with an idealistic declaration of rights in the first place?

The convention subtly revived the traditional UK view of rights, too. Instead of being defined *negatively* — that is, referring to things that are not prohibited by law — the convention introduces a more *positive* perspective, making it much more difficult for governments to introduce new prohibitions. There could hardly be a more serious challenge to the traditional view that the UK parliament is the country's sovereign law-making body.

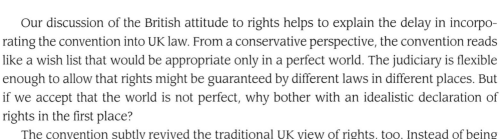

Box 12.7 Lord Lester on law making

'According to conventional wisdom, it is undemocratic for the non-elected judiciary to act as law makers. It is also inappropriate, because judges are ill-equipped by their narrow origins, training and professional experience, and by the very nature of the judicial process itself, to make laws.'

Lord Lester, QC, 1993.

Another important reason for caution, though, is illustrated by Lord Lester's remark quoted in Box 12.7. 'Conventional wisdom' has indeed suggested that judges should stick to the task of *applying* laws in individual cases. But the terms of the Human Rights Act (see Box 12.8) suggest a much more active role for the judiciary. Most importantly, the act allows judges to declare that legislation passed by parliament is incompatible with human rights. In the USA, the Supreme Court can rule that a particular piece of legislation is unconstitutional, thus making it null and void. Under the Human Rights Act, UK governments can ignore judicial rulings if they wish, so the act lacks the force of the Bill of Rights which is enshrined in the US constitution. But in practice the government will usually have to respond. Once a judge has found that a law conflicts with the terms of the convention, a precedent will have been set for other judges to follow in future cases.

Dictators in wigs?

When the Human Rights Act came into force fully in 2000, it was not clear how far-reaching its effects would be. In February 2001 the Lord Chancellor, Lord Irvine, claimed that the European Convention on Human Rights had proved perfectly compatible with exisiting UK law, and that the fears of the critics had been confounded. However, it was not long before the real implications of the act began to emerge and to affect a wide range of political and social issues.

An early test of the Human Rights Act came in February 2003, when the High Court ruled against a government decision to restrict the social security benefits of

Box 12.8 Human Rights Act (1998)

The main provisions of the Human Rights Act were:
➤ right to personal liberty and security
➤ right to life
➤ prohibition of torture
➤ right to a fair trial
➤ right to privacy and family life

asylum seekers who had not registered a claim immediately. The home secretary, David Blunkett, responded angrily, saying that he was 'fed up with having to deal with a situation where parliament debates issues and the judges overturn them'. The *Daily Mail* published an article denouncing judges as 'dictators in wigs'.

In turn, the Lord Chief Justice, Lord Woolf, retorted that the judiciary was not usurping the functions of parliament. Since parliament had passed the Human Rights Act, the judges had to apply it just like any other law. He pointed out that the European Convention on Human Rights merely gave a codified form to rights that had been long established in the UK. But he noted with regret that, until the passage of the act, UK citizens had 'to rely primarily on the self-restraint of the government of the day for the protection of human rights values'.

The government had already signalled deep misgivings about the operation of the act. In the aftermath of the terrorist attacks in the USA in September 2001, the UK government withdrew from the fifth clause of the convention, covering the right of detained people to a trial. In the new situation, with secret terrorist cells apparently operating throughout Europe, it looked as if the government's need to treat certain criminal suspects outside the terms of the convention would continue indefinitely. In the face of public misgivings about asylum seekers, in January 2003 Prime Minister Blair indicated that the government was also reviewing Clause Three, which prevents states from sending refugees back to countries where they face the threat of ill treatment. It seemed possible, indeed, that the UK government would be forced by circumstances to repeal legislation that it had heartily endorsed when it was in opposition.

In December 2004 the Law Lords rejected the government's treatment of nine terrorist suspects held without trial in Belmarsh Prison by a majority of 8 to 1. The technical reason for the judgement was that the government had introduced a distinction between foreign nationals and British subjects to the existing law covering suspected individuals. Foreign detainees would normally have been deported, but it was felt that their lives might have been in danger if they were sent back to their countries of origin.

The government claimed that the suspects could not be charged in court, either, because the evidence produced against them might put intelligence sources at risk. As a result, until the Law Lords intervened there was a chance that the suspects would be kept in prison indefinitely, contrary to fundamental ideas about British freedom.

The ruling forced the home secretary, Charles Clarke, to draw up new legislation, which was strongly opposed by the House of Lords and amended before being passed in March 2005. As a result of the new laws, the foreign detainees were then released under new 'control orders', so that their activities could be closely monitored.

You are advised to follow cases brought under the Human Rights Act, in order to judge its impact for yourself, particularly in the aftermath of the July 2005 terrorist outrages in London, which will place the new culture of rights under additional strain. Interestingly, it seems that the act has encouraged judges to uphold more actively the right to privacy against media intrusion, as in the high-profile cases of Catherine Zeta-Jones and the disc-jockey Sara Cox (2003). This development might improve the relationship between the judiciary and politicians who are protective of their private lives — but only at the expense of making the tabloid press into new enemies for the judges.

Judicial review

Even before the human rights legislation was passed there were clear signs of increasing *judicial activism* in the UK, and whether the act is repealed or not, this trend looks set to continue. Significantly, judges were prominent among those who had argued for years that the European Convention on Human Rights should be incorporated into domestic law; and they were beginning to take a closer interest in ministerial decisions. Given the traditional reluctance of the judiciary in the UK to trespass on the territory of politicians, the enthusiasm for the convention is a strong indication that the legal profession has become increasingly alarmed at the growing power of the UK government.

One important factor in encouraging this new judicial activism is the marked increase in *delegated* power over the last 100 years. Government has become much more complicated, taking responsibility in more and more fields of activity. Ideally, parliament should lay down detailed provisions to guide a minister in making decisions. But if they covered more than a small fraction of possible cases, Acts of Parliament would become hopelessly long and complicated. So legislation often identifies areas in which ministers can use their *discretion*, and this is open to challenge.

When citizens feel that a minister has abused or exceeded the powers laid down by statute, they can ask for leave to apply for a *judicial review* of a decision. If the application is successful, High Court judges rule on the case. If the wording of the relevant legislation does not apply directly or conclusively to the case in question, the judges can interpret parliament's intention at the time that it was passed.

In practice, the majority of MPs are usually too busy to read bills very carefully — or have to obey the party whip regardless of their personal opinions. So although the judges can read the record of parliamentary debates to gain an impression of opinion at the time, almost invariably they have to fall back on *their own* view of what parliament 'must' have meant. In practice, this means that they are comparing the minister's action to what any reasonable person would have done in the same circumstances — and, like most people, they tend to regard themselves as 'reasonable'. So unelected judges end up comparing their personal judgement to that of the minister in question.

Once judges become more active in evaluating ministerial decisions, it is easy to see how the process can accelerate. Citizens hear about cases in which a decision has been overruled, so they are more likely to appeal for a judicial review of their own grievances. MPs, faced with increasingly complex bills, are tempted to leave vague clauses unchanged, expecting the judges to resolve any problems in the working of the legislation. The judges themselves will begin to feel that, instead of being an unusual occurrence, the process of review is part of their normal routine. When other members of their profession overrule ministers in controversial cases, they will be more ready to follow their example. Finally, the type of person appointed to high judicial posts may begin to change, from the old 'conservative' type of judge to more energetic (and, perhaps, outspoken) characters.

Expansion of judicial review

The effect of these factors has been clear over the past two decades, even before the passage of the Human Rights Act. Over the last two decades there has been a steep rise in the number of requests for judicial review of ministerial decisions. Although many of the cases concern just two areas — immigration and housing — the increase suggests that people regard the courts as a more effective means of redress than tribunals or *ombudsmen* (see Box 12.9).

Box 12.9 **Other ways of redressing grievances**

While most attention has focused on the growth of judicial review, this way of redressing grievances is unattainable for most citizens. Often cases will only be heard if they are backed by a well-resourced pressure group, with the money and expertise to argue the case.

However, other avenues are open to a citizen who believes that he or she has been the victim of faulty administration:

➤ *Administrative tribunals* are public bodies that rule on disputes between citizens and the state. There are over 100 different types of tribunal, covering a range of issues including social security, education, immigration and complaints of unfair dismissal. The Leggatt Report (2001) recommended reforms to the system, pointing out that while some bodies heard more than 100,000 cases per year, others were virtually inactive. Even though the tribunals were supposed to make it easier for aggrieved citizens to win a hearing, Leggatt found that they still left much to be desired in this respect.

➤ *Ombudsmen* are charged with investigating complaints of maladministration, passed on to them via MPs. The title itself is Swedish, and literally means 'grievance-man'. Since 1967, when a single UK ombudsman was appointed, the system has been extended. There are now similar officials for Northern Ireland, Scotland and Wales; for the National Health Service; for local administration; for housing associations; and for the Prison Service.

> ➤ Although the *Citizen's Charter* (introduced in 1991) did not in itself provide new means for the redress of grievances, it set standards of service for public sector bodies and publicised the various ways in which citizens could register complaints.
> ➤ Citizens can always approach their *Members of Parliament* for help. A letter from an MP will almost always win a respectful hearing from a government agency.

Political controversy

Although it would be wrong to jump to dramatic conclusions, it is clear that recent developments have drawn judges into political controversies far more than used to be the case. For example, in 1977 the Court of Appeal ruled that the Labour government had acted illegally in preventing Tameside Education Authority from cancelling plans to introduce comprehensive secondary education. But the real shift towards judicial activism began in the following decade, and accelerated in the 1990s (see Box 12.10).

Box 12.10 The rise of judicial activism before the Human Rights Act

1981: ruled that the government was wrong to reduce the rate support grant to local authorities.

1981: ruled that the Greater London Council's policy of reducing fares for public transport infringed the rule that the system should be economically sustainable.

1984: ruled that the government was not exceeding its powers in banning trade unions from a key intelligence-gathering facility (GCHQ), but that citizens appealing against decisions taken on the grounds of 'national security' could apply for judicial reviews.

1993: ruled that the home secretary was wrong to order the deportation of an asylum seeker from Zaïre.

1994: ruled that the foreign secretary had exceeded his powers in granting £234 million towards the construction of the Pergau Dam in Malaysia.

1995: ruled that the new system of compensation payments for criminal injuries was unlawful.

Judges have also been called in to head controversial inquiries. In 1981 the home secretary asked Lord Scarman to investigate inner-city rioting; in 1994 Lord Justice Nolan was appointed head of a committee to examine standards in public life; in 1996 Justice Scott reported on the sale of arms to Iraq in breach of the government's own guidelines; and in 2003 Lord Hutton presided over a controversial inquiry into the death of the government weapons expert, Dr David Kelly. In all of these cases, except the last, the findings were embarrassing to the elected governments. At the same time, the legal community was trying to resist attempts to reform its own practices. After a protracted struggle, the Conservatives allowed solicitors to be heard in court, which was previously the exclusive right of barristers, and the legal aid budget, which provides funds for citizens who lack the resources to pursue legal actions, was 'capped'. The election of the New Labour government in May 1997 has not produced a noticeable thaw in relations, and successive home secretaries have had decisions struck out by judicial reviews. Apart from controversies over the treatment of terrorist suspects, in February 2005 the High Court even allowed a judicial review of a government consultative White Paper, suggesting that in future decisions could be subject to review even before they were taken!

Key terms

> **Civil rights/civil liberties.** Freedoms possessed by a country's citizens that are guaranteed in law, with corresponding obligations imposed on government for their observance.

> **Natural/human rights.** Claims to fundamental freedoms advanced by citizens, whether or not they are guaranteed in the law of a particular country.

Summary

Rights in the UK

> In recent years, UK judges have become more willing to question government decisions, and the European Court of Human Rights has also made important critical rulings.
> The passage of the Human Rights Act gives UK judges more power to rule against government actions.
> There are several other ways in which citizens can obtain redress, but they are open to criticism for being costly, time consuming and intimidating for the average citizen.

Judicial neutrality

The most effective defence of the UK's judicial system, then, is that the institutions work because of the integrity and independent outlook of the people who operate them. In summary, the main points of this argument are as follows:

> British judges have always protected the rights of the citizen.
> Although the Lord Chancellor is a politician appointed by the prime minister, he or she is a member of a proud profession and is acutely aware of its sensitivities.
> While the supporters of a written constitution might deplore the way in which it has developed, a system has evolved in the UK through which citizens can be confident of having their grievances redressed. The Human Rights Act merely reinforces freedoms that had never been seriously challenged.

Are judges neutral?

The legal profession has not escaped the general mood of misgivings about the UK's institutions, and the demand for 'modernisation'. In part, this has arisen from a series of well-publicised *miscarriages of justice*, when, after much delay, convicted prisoners have had their appeals upheld (see Box 12.11 overleaf).

> **Box 12.11 Recent 'miscarriages of justice'**
>
> **1990:** release of the 'Guildford Four', convicted of an IRA bombing in 1975.
>
> **1991:** release of the 'Birmingham Six', convicted of IRA bombings in 1974.
>
> **1997:** release of the 'Bridgewater Three', convicted of the murder of a newspaper boy in 1978.
>
> **2001:** release of Stephen Downing, who had been in prison for 27 years after making a murder confession that he subsequently retracted.
>
> **2003:** release of Angela Cannings, jailed for life for allegedly killing her two baby sons.

In their own defence, judges can argue that these wrongful convictions arose from misleading evidence presented by the police or witnesses. Yet the feeling remained that senior members of the judiciary shared the prejudices that had led to the convictions.

Other, rather different cases reinforced this impression. For example, the judge of the libel action brought by the former Conservative MP Jeffrey Archer in 1987 paid a lyrical tribute to the 'fragrant' and 'radiant' qualities of the plaintiff's wife in his summing-up (by contrast, the main witness for the defence was a prostitute). While lapses of this kind are unusual, critics pointed to the fact that, as a general rule, defendants from ethnic minorities tend to receive heavier sentences than their white counterparts, and that the whole system was hostile to rape victims.

To the working class and unemployed — in fact, to anyone ill versed in the rituals of the establishment — the whole court procedure seems alien. Since the time of the Taff Vale case (1901) and the Osborne Judgement (1910), judges have always seemed hostile to trade unions. These early examples of judicial activism ruled respectively that employers could sue unions for compensation arising from industrial disputes, and that unions could not use funds for political purposes. After the anti-union legislation passed by the Thatcher governments of the early 1980s, judges could argue that they had no alternative but to uphold parliament's laws, whether they liked them or not. But wherever the law needed judicial interpretation, the rights of property seemed to be preferred to the right to strike. In a case of 1986, for example, the print union SOGAT was held to have breached a new law against the picketing of premises not directly involved in a dispute. But the company in question was an offshoot of News International, which published Conservative-supporting newspapers and was the main target of the industrial action.

For all the occasions on which the judges have embarrassed the government of the day, there have also been cases when they were obviously avoiding a hornet's nest. In 1999, for example, the House of Lords set aside its previous ruling that the former dictator of Chile, Augusto Pinochet, could be extradited to Spain to face allegations of torture. The grounds were that the first hearing had been tainted by the presence of one Law Lord, Hoffman, who had failed to declare his links with the human rights pressure group Amnesty International, a party to the case. If applied more generally, this principle would prevent many judges from presiding over criminal cases — many have shared membership of 'freemason' organisations with policemen whose evidence they are supposed to hear impartially. It could also be argued that it was a good thing that at least one senior UK judge had a strong commitment to human rights.

Are judges representative?

Critics of the judicial system in the UK claim that its defenders have missed the main point. Examples such as the treatment of trade unions might not prove any party-political bias. But whether or not those who preside over the UK's courts vote for a particular party, they cannot be *neutral* because they almost invariably belong to those social groups that are least likely to fall foul of the law. At all levels, the judiciary are members of the 'establishment' (see Box 12.12). As such, it is no surprise that the most senior figures are male, white and Oxbridge educated. Among magistrates at the bottom of the pyramid, representation by gender is roughly equal. In 2003 only 9 out of 107 High Court judges were women. There was only one representative of the ethnic minorities. More than 80% had attended either Oxford or Cambridge University. The Labour government was anxious to make the judiciary more representative in terms of gender and ethnicity, but it is likely that senior judges will continue to be middle class in social origin.

Box 12.12 Anthony Sampson on the judicial system

'The Law is the most striking example of a profession which has become trapped in its conservatism and mystique. Its proud independence and remoteness have given it magnificent strength as a bastion of liberty and justice; but have also made it totally unsusceptible to pressures of change.'

Anthony Sampson, *The New Anatomy of Britain* (1965), p. 162.

In any case, it can be argued that the senior judiciary merely *reflects* the existing power imbalances in society, and cannot be blamed for them. Equality of opportunity is being reinforced in other walks of life, and hopefully this will soon be reflected in the legal profession. But it will take time, and a purge of white, middle-class males who have always done their duty would be a contradiction of the very natural justice that the judiciary at its best is supposed to represent. Besides, the vast majority of cases are heard by magistrates, who are more representative of the population than the top judges.

A more ingenious argument (not often advanced in public) is that, in a society where money can ensure the best education, the high social status of the judiciary actually makes them more impartial. If they were more 'representative', they might be even more likely to discriminate against minority groups (see Box 12.13). Whatever the rights and wrongs of the public schools, this argument runs, well-educated people are best placed to appraise the facts of a case, rather than being blinded by irrelevancies like the class or colour of the defendants. Finally, as we have seen in other chapters, the elitist response to complaints about the judiciary would be that *any* society at a given time will be ruled by an elite, so the fact that the British judiciary reflects more general structures of power is simply unavoidable.

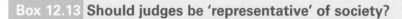

Box 12.13 Should judges be 'representative' of society?

Nowadays it seems difficult to resist the argument that an institution that is not representative of society needs reform. But in the case of the legal system, would this not lead to surprising conclusions? Might it allow one to argue that we should have a few teenagers, or even convicted criminals, among our High Court judges?

If the judiciary really can be made more 'representative' and the law made more accessible to ordinary citizens, would it lose some of the respect in which it has been held?

The last Lord Chancellor?

Perhaps the main obstacle for the judiciary in its attempts to defend its position is its image. As a symbol of an outdated institution, the Lord Chancellor could hardly be bettered, since his most public role is to perform elaborate rituals at the opening of parliament, decked out in his robes and his wig. It did not help that Tony Blair's first appointment to the post was the man who had been head of chambers to himself (and his wife Cherie) during his own legal career. Lord Irvine of Lairg compounded the problem by using public money for redecorating his official apartment at a cost to the taxpayer of £650,000.

Even before Lord Irvine became embroiled in controversy, the proponents of reform had singled out the office of Lord Chancellor for criticism. They argued that his roles should be split:

➤ Judicial appointments should be made by an independent committee.
➤ The (non-political) Lord Chief Justice should take over as head of the judiciary.
➤ The Lord Chancellor's Department (which has grown significantly in recent years) should be replaced by a Ministry of Justice, headed by a minister drawn from the House of Commons rather than the Lords. The House of Lords is expected to be less willing than the Commons to hold ministers to account even after the process of reform is complete (see Chapter 10).

It was argued that reform along these lines had become vital. Since the passage of the Human Rights Act, which will result in a steady stream of legal challenges to ministerial decisions, it is more important than ever that senior judges are seen to be independent of the executive. Ironically, it could even be argued that the post of Lord Chancellor was incompatible with the terms of the act. In 1999 the European Court of Human Rights ruled that the bailiff of Guernsey could not judge cases that involved government decisions, because this would contravene Article 6 of the European Convention. In February 2003 the Council of Europe, which gave birth to the European Convention on Human Rights, debated a resolution suggesting that the Lord Chancellor should no longer sit as a judge.

Until June 2003 most commentators assumed that Lord Irvine would retain most of his powers until he decided to retire, probably at the time of the next election. He seemed willing to give up the right to choose 'Queen's Councillors' (QCs), the elite among barristers. But this role had little or no constitutional significance.

So it was a major surprise when in the cabinet reshuffle of June 2003 Lord Irvine stepped down from his post. His replacement, Lord Falconer of Thoroton, was a trusted friend of the prime minister just as Irvine had been. But although Falconer retained the title of Lord Chancellor, this was understood to be only a formality while the necessary legislation was passed to reform the old system. In time, Falconer would give up the right to appoint judges, who would now be selected by an independent Judicial Appointments Commission. He would also relinquish the status of head of the judiciary. He would not himself sit in the capacity of a judge, and he only put on his robes to preside over the House of Lords on the understanding that a replacement would soon be elected by his fellow peers. His real duties would be performed as secretary of state for a new Department of Constitutional Affairs, which would oversee constitutional reforms and conduct a thorough reform of the legal system.

Lord Falconer of Thoroton

The reshuffle was attacked by the government's critics as a piece of instant improvisation rather than a considered move. Most unusually, Tony Blair was required by the Speaker of the Commons to make a statement on his changes. The position of Lord Chancellor was the oldest government office, dating back to 605 AD. It seemed rash to announce its abolition without full consultation. The most logical replacement for the Lord Chancellor's Department would have been a fully-fledged Ministry of Justice, but it was rumoured that this had been vetoed by the home secretary (at that time, David Blunkett). Overall, the incident was widely interpreted as a sign that the Blair government would always be keen to take radical action on constitutional matters, to compensate its left-wing supporters for having retained most of the domestic policies of Conservative governments of the 1980s and 1990s. It could certainly be accused of taking action without thinking through the likely consequences.

After prolonged debate, the House of Lords insisted that the title of Lord Chancellor should remain, much to the annoyance of the government. But the rest of the proposals will go ahead, which in theory ought to remove some of the constitutional anomalies associated with the fusion of powers. The judiciary will be much more independent of the executive, although the prime minister will retain some influence in the selection of judges because he or she will choose the members of the Judicial Appointments Commission. In another key change, the highest legal body in the land will no longer be the Lords of Appeal in Ordinary (see Box 12.1 on p. 309), but a new 'supreme court', consisting of peers who will no longer sit as a committee of the House of Lords. However, this plan has been delayed because of the lack of a suitable building to house the supreme court.

Radicals will argue that an independent judiciary and the Human Rights Act represent important elements in a new settlement which could eventually leave the UK with a system of government broadly similar to the United States, complete with a fully codified constitution and a president who is no longer responsible to the elected legislature. This would tally with recent changes in the executive branch of government (see Chapter 11). In other constitutional fields, though — notably reform of the House of Lords (see Chapter 10) — the Blair government seemed to act in accordance with its own convenience, rather than following a logical blueprint for change. Whatever happens in the next few years, further changes are likely. Those who take a special interest in constitutional matters will be fully occupied in the years ahead.

Summary

Judicial neutrality

➤ As a result of the increased power of the law, demand is growing for a judiciary that enjoys greater constitutional independence.

➤ While judges are becoming more active and powerful, they are still unrepresentative of ordinary people.

➤ By June 2003 the position of the Lord Chancellor was ripe for reform, as Britain moved slowly towards a written constitution with a separation of powers.

Suggested reading

Banner, C., Beloff, A. and Deane, A., *Off With Their Wigs! Judicial Revolution in Modern Britain* (Imprint Academic, 2003).

Garnett, M., 'Judges versus politicians', *Politics Review*, vol. 14, no.1, September 2004.

Ridsdall-Smith, C., 'Citizenship and the Human Rights Act', *Politics Review*, vol. 10, no. 4, April 2001.

Roberts, H., 'The last Lord Chancellor', *Politics Review*, vol. 13, no.4, April 2004.

Woodhouse, D., 'The office of Lord Chancellor', *Politics Review*, vol. 11, no. 3, February 2002.

Websites

Details of the court system in England and Wales and recent judgements:
www.hmcourts-service.gov.uk

Department of Constitutional Affairs: www.dca.gov.uk

Human Rights Unit: www.humanrights.gov.uk

Exam focus

Using this chapter and other resources available to you, answer the following questions.

1 If there is a fusion of powers in the UK, how can there be judicial independence?
2 What civil rights do UK citizens have?
3 How effectively are these civil rights protected?
4 Why has it taken so long to incorporate the European Convention on Human Rights into UK law?
5 Outline the main provisions of the Human Rights Act.
6 Has the Human Rights Act created 'dictators in wigs'? Give reasons for your answer.
7 What is judicial review and what impact has the Human Rights Act had on it?
8 In what other ways may citizens seek redress of grievances?
9 Are judges neutral? Give reasons for your answer.
10 To what extent do you agree with the view that the reforms announced in June 2003 put the relationship between executive, legislature and judiciary on a modern footing?

Chapter 13

Devolution

The United Kingdom is a multinational state of four nations: England, Scotland, Wales and Northern Ireland. For much of the postwar period, the UK was one of the most centralised states in western Europe. Labour's 1997 general election victory, however, brought major changes to the territorial politics of the UK as power was devolved to new institutions in Scotland, Wales and Northern Ireland. Devolution has affected significantly the politics of these nations and the UK political system as a whole.

Key questions answered in this chapter
➤ How were the nations of the UK governed before devolution?
➤ Why did demands for devolution emerge?
➤ What powers do the devolved bodies in Scotland, Wales and Northern Ireland have?
➤ Why has the situation in Northern Ireland proved especially difficult?
➤ What are the main implications of devolution for UK politics?

The United Kingdom

The official title of the British state is the 'United Kingdom of Great Britain and Northern Ireland'. Great Britain is the largest of the British Isles and consists of three nations: England, Scotland and Wales. The six counties that make up Northern Ireland stayed in the Union when the rest of the island of Ireland formed the Irish Free State in 1922.

England is the largest of the UK's four nations, with a population of 49 million (83.5% of the total UK population). It is also the wealthiest of the four nations and provides the UK's capital city, London. Scotland has a population of 5 million, Wales almost 3 million and Northern Ireland just 1.6 million people.

Britishness is an umbrella identity that provides a common bond between the peoples of the UK, but which enables them to retain their distinctive national (i.e. English, Welsh, Scottish and Northern Irish) identities (see Table 13.1). British identity has been built around symbols of the UK state such as the monarchy, the Westminster Parliament and the National Health Service. Until the second half of the twentieth century, the British Empire was also an important element in British identity. Since devolution, the number of people seeing themselves as primarily Scottish or English rather than British has increased.

Table 13.1 National identity in England and Scotland (%)

Identity	1997	2000
England		
English, not British	17	19
More English than British	15	14
Equally English and British	37	34
More British than English	11	14
British, not English	3	6
Scotland		
Scottish, not British	23	37
More Scottish than British	38	31
Equally Scottish and British	27	21
More British than Scottish	4	3
British, not Scottish	4	4
Other	2	–

Note: respondents in England and Scotland were asked to choose how they would describe themselves from among the options presented above.
Source: J. Curtice and B. Seyd, 'Is devolution strengthening or weakening the UK?', in A. Park et al. (eds), *British Social Attitudes: The 18th Report* (Sage, 2001), p. 236.

Wales and Scotland

The nations of the UK joined a Union with England at different times and in different circumstances. Wales entered a Union with England in 1536 when England completed its conquest of the principality and thereafter governed it from London. But Wales retained elements of its distinctive culture despite Anglicisation. The 2001 census found that 28% of people in Wales had one or more skills in the Welsh language.

The crowns of England and Scotland were united in 1603 when King James VI of Scotland succeeded to the English throne as King James I. Scotland remained an independent state with its own parliament until the Act of Union (1707). This was an international treaty between Scotland and England by which Scotland joined the Union. It included a number of guarantees about Scotland's position in the Union. Scotland retained its legal system, education system and local government. The Scottish Parliament was abolished and Scotland sent MPs to Westminster instead. Scottish identity continues to draw upon the history of independent statehood and a robust civil society. Only 1% of the population of Scotland are Gaelic speakers.

Ireland and Northern Ireland

After centuries of English and Scottish settlement, Ireland joined the Union in 1800 through an Act of Union. The Union was a troubled one, with the 'Irish Question' becoming one of the longest running and most difficult issues in UK politics. By the 1880s, Irish Nationalists dominated Ireland's representation at Westminster. The Liberal Party looked to Home Rule to solve the Irish Question, but three Home Rule

Bills (1886, 1893 and 1913) fell in the House of Lords. The 1916 Easter Rising in Dublin, crushed by British troops, showed the strength of Irish nationalist feeling.

Negotiations between the UK government and Irish republicans led to the Government of Ireland Act (1920). This became effective in 1921 when Ireland was partitioned and the Irish Free State (a dominion within the Commonwealth) was created by the Anglo-Irish Treaty. The Irish Free State became the Republic of Ireland (an independent state) in 1949. Six counties in the north of Ireland where there was a Protestant majority exercised their right to remain part of the UK, becoming Northern Ireland. For the next 50 years, Northern Ireland was governed by a devolved parliament at Stormont, which was controlled by unionists.

Unitary or union state?

A unitary state

Prior to devolution, the United Kingdom was usually described as a *unitary state*. A unitary state is a centralised state in which political power is located at the centre in national institutions. They exhibit a high degree of centralisation and homogeneity — all parts of the state are governed in the same way. In the UK, the doctrine of *parliamentary sovereignty* means that Westminster can make law on any subject of its choosing, and this law cannot be overturned by any higher institution. Aside from the Stormont Parliament (1922–72) in Northern Ireland, the regions of the UK did not have their own parliaments.

The centralisation apparent in a unitary state contrasts with the division of powers that characterises *federal* systems. In federal states such as the USA and Germany, power is divided between the national government (the federal government) and regional (i.e. state) governments. The constitutions of federal states allocate policy competences to the different tiers and give the states protected status.

A union state

Not all political scientists accepted the description of the UK as a unitary state. Professor James Mitchell contended that the term did not reflect the character of the multinational UK. He preferred to describe the UK as a *union state*. In a union state, important political and cultural differences remain after union has occurred. The different parts of the union will also have joined under different circumstances, as in the UK. Although there is a relatively high degree of administrative standardisation, political differences persist in the way parts of the state are governed. In the UK, then, Scotland retained its own legal system and local government, while power was devolved to the Stormont Parliament in Northern Ireland. British identity was a unifying force, but Scottish and Welsh identities survived union with England.

Legislative devolution (i.e. the creation of a separate parliament with legislative powers) existed in Northern Ireland in the Stormont period. *Administrative devolution* was the norm in Scotland and Wales: that is, special arrangements were made to take account of Scottish and Welsh distinctiveness, but power was concentrated at the centre. These arrangements included:

> territorial ministries in UK central government
> special procedures for Scottish and Welsh business at Westminster
> a preferential formula — the *Barnett formula* — for public spending, which gave Scotland and Wales more funds per head of population than England

Territorial ministries

The Scottish Office was established as a government department in 1885 and the Welsh Office in 1964. These territorial ministries were responsible for a range of government activities (e.g. agriculture, education, health, local government) in their respective nations. A secretary of state headed the ministry and sat in the UK cabinet. Territorial ministries had two main functions:

> to represent the interests of their nation in UK central government
> to implement the policies of the UK government in their nation

The Scottish Office was both a lobbyist for Scottish interests in Whitehall and an agent for the UK government in Scotland. By the late 1990s, it tended to be seen as an agent for the Conservative government (e.g. on the poll tax), rather than an effective lobbyist for Scotland. The territorial ministries played a reactive role in policy making rather than an innovative one, partly because the secretaries of state for Scotland and Wales were junior cabinet posts with limited political clout.

Committees at Westminster

A Scottish Grand Committee and a Welsh Grand Committee were established in the House of Commons to discuss matters in those countries. They contained all MPs representing Scottish and Welsh constituencies respectively. Special standing committees also dealt with Scottish and Welsh legislation. Departmental select committees on Scottish affairs and Welsh affairs were created in 1979. On the floor of the House, time was set aside for questions to ministers from the Scottish Office and Welsh Office. Finally, Scotland and Wales were over-represented in the Commons, having more MPs per head of population than England.

Key terms

> **Devolution.** The transfer of political power from central government to subnational government.
> **Federalism.** The sharing of power, enshrined in a constitution, between national (federal) and regional (state) authorities.
> **Union state.** A state in which there are cultural differences and where, despite a strong centre, different parts of the state are governed in slightly different ways.
> **Unitary state.** A homogeneous state in which power is concentrated at the political centre and all parts of the state are governed in the same way.

Sub-state nationalism

Demands for legislative devolution have a long history in UK politics. In the early twentieth century, the 'Irish Question' prompted brief interest in 'Home Rule all round', under which the nations of the UK would have their own parliaments in a federal union. Celtic nationalism increased with the formation of the Welsh nationalist party Plaid Cymru (1925), the National Party of Scotland (1928) and the Scottish Party (1932). The latter two merged in 1934, forming the Scottish Nationalist Party (SNP). The nationalist parties campaigned for independence and promoted their national cultures. But cultural issues also provoked internal divisions, notably in Plaid Cymru, where some members emphasised Welsh language issues while others sought a broader focus.

Breakthrough at Westminster

The 1960s and 1970s brought electoral breakthroughs for the nationalist parties. They benefited from dissatisfaction with the constitution and the two main parties, plus a revival of Scottish and Welsh nationhood. Plaid Cymru won its first seat at Westminster in the 1966 Carmarthen by-election. The SNP had held Motherwell briefly in 1945 but returned to prominence with a 1967 by-election victory in Hamilton. In the October 1974 election, the SNP won 30.4% of the vote and 11 seats; Plaid Cymru scored 10.8% and won 3 seats.

The Conservatives, Labour and devolution

The nationalists' success posed difficult questions for Labour and the Conservatives. The Conservatives reacted in 1968 by supporting a Scottish Assembly. But this policy was not implemented by the Heath government of 1970–74, which introduced local government reform instead. Margaret Thatcher reversed the party's support for legislative devolution.

Historically, Labour had focused on class politics and opposed nationalism, but it now saw its electoral dominance in Scotland and Wales threatened by the SNP and Plaid Cymru. Two broad camps developed in the party:

➢ opponents of devolution, who feared that it would undermine the equitable provision of public services and make the break-up of the UK more likely
➢ supporters of devolution, who argued that it would cement support for Labour in its heartlands and reduce the appeal of the nationalist agenda

The 1979 devolution referendums

Support for devolution grew in the Labour Party, although it remained a divisive issue. The Callaghan government (1976–79) introduced bills to establish legislative assemblies in Scotland and Wales. The legislation would not come into force, however, unless the proposed assemblies were supported in referendums in Wales and Scotland. An amendment stipulated that the Scottish Assembly must gain the support of 40% of the total Scottish electorate.

The 1979 Welsh referendum produced a decisive 'no', as just 20% of those who voted backed an assembly. In Scotland the result was much closer: 51.6% of those who voted supported devolution, but the 40% threshold was not reached as only 32.8% of the electorate had voted 'yes'. The devolution proposal was defeated. The Labour government soon fell and was replaced by a Conservative administration opposed to devolution.

Devolution gains momentum

Demands for legislative devolution gathered momentum from the late 1980s. They were fuelled by the four consecutive election victories won by the Conservatives, despite their low (and declining) support in Scotland and Wales. A further concentration of power in Whitehall and the perceived insensitivity of the Thatcher government to Scottish distinctiveness also increased support for devolution. John Major's administration sought to bolster support for the Union by giving the Scottish Office limited new powers, but this did not turn the pro-devolution tide.

Crucial to the prospects of devolution was Labour's conversion to the cause, particularly during the leadership of John Smith (a Scot) from 1992 to 1995. For Labour, devolution was the optimal way of preserving the Union and part of a wider programme of constitutional reform. It advocated a Scottish Parliament with legislative and tax-raising powers. Labour politicians were important movers in an unofficial Scottish Constitutional Convention set up in 1989 to develop a blueprint for a Scottish Parliament. Liberal Democrats and representatives from Scottish civil society also took part, but the Conservatives and the SNP did not. The convention's final proposals (1995) formed the basis of the 1997 devolution White Paper.

The 1997 general election

In its 1997 general election manifesto, Labour pledged to:

> hold referendums on devolution in Scotland and Wales
> establish a Scottish Parliament with legislative and tax-varying powers
> establish a Welsh Assembly with secondary legislative powers

The Liberal Democrats also proposed a Scottish Parliament, while the SNP (and, to a lesser extent, Plaid Cymru) continued to argue for independence. The Conservatives were the only major party opposed to devolution. They warned that devolution was a slippery slope to independence. By producing constitutional problems such as the 'West Lothian Question' (see pp. 351–52), it would make independence seem a more viable option. But the Tories were defeated heavily, failing to win a single seat in either Scotland or Wales. After the devolution referendums, the party dropped its policy of principled opposition to devolution.

The 1997 devolution referendums

After its election victory, the Labour government issued White Papers on devolution to Scotland (*Scotland's Parliament*) and Wales (*A Voice for Wales*), then held devolution referendums in September 1997.

Scotland

The two-question Scottish devolution referendum asked voters whether they supported (1) a Scottish Parliament and (2) tax-varying powers for the parliament.

Both questions were answered with decisive 'yes' votes. On the first question, 74.3% supported a Scottish Parliament while 25.7% voted 'no'. There was a majority for the parliament in all 12 local authority areas. 63.5% supported tax-varying powers with 36.5% opposed. Two local authority areas — Dumfries and Galloway, and Orkney — registered a majority against tax-varying powers. The double 'yes' and a 60% turnout gave the parliament added legitimacy.

The convincing outcome resulted from a number of factors:

> the establishment of cross-party support for devolution since the late 1980s
> the development of popular support for devolution in the preceding decade
> the popularity of the newly elected Labour government
> the effective 'yes' campaign run by Labour, the Liberals and the SNP, plus the cross-party 'Scotland Forward' group
> the relatively weak 'no' campaign run by the 'Think Twice' group, but associated with an unpopular Conservative Party

Wales

The Welsh devolution referendum asked voters if they supported a National Assembly for Wales. The result was very close: 50.3% voted 'yes' and 49.7% 'no'. The 'yes' majority was just 6,721 votes or 0.6% of those who voted. Only 50.1% of the electorate voted, meaning that only a quarter of people in Wales had actively supported an assembly.

Wales was divided on the issue geographically. Eleven of the 22 local authority areas voted in favour of devolution and 11 against. The areas voting 'no' were, with the exception of Pembrokeshire, located in the east and had closer connections with England than areas voting 'yes', which were located in west Wales and had more Welsh speakers.

The close result and low turnout denied the assembly the legitimacy bestowed upon its Scottish counterpart. However, even the narrow 'yes' marked a substantial turnaround from the 20% support recorded in 1979.

The 'yes' vote was smaller than in Scotland for a number of reasons:

> There was no stable cross-party consensus in favour of devolution and Labour was divided on the issue.
> There was no popular consensus in support of devolution.
> Wales was geographically divided on the issue: as well as the east–west split, some voters in north Wales feared that south Wales would predominate.
> A low-key referendum campaign inspired little interest.
> The assembly would have few powers.

The devolved institutions in Scotland and Wales

Labour's huge parliamentary majority and the referendum 'yes' votes ensured a relatively smooth passage for the bills establishing devolved institutions in Scotland and Wales. They began their work after the first elections to the new bodies were held in May 1999.

Devolution has been asymmetric. Rather than following a standard blueprint, each of the devolved institutions has different powers and distinctive features. The Scottish Parliament has *legislative powers* (the power to make laws) and *tax-raising powers*. The Welsh Assembly is weaker, having only *executive powers* — the power to implement laws made at Westminster or to issue secondary legislation within the existing legal framework.

The Scottish Parliament

The Scottish Parliament contains 129 members (MSPs), elected by the additional member system. Seventy-three MSPs (57% of the total) are elected in single-member constituencies on a first-past-the-post basis. The remaining 56 MSPs (43%) are *additional members* chosen from party lists. They are elected in eight multi-member regional constituencies, each of which elects seven additional members using the d'Hondt method of proportional representation (see Chapter 3). Elections are held every 4 years. The parliament moved from its temporary home on the Mound to a new (and expensive) building in Holyrood in 2004.

Legislative powers

The Scottish Parliament has primary legislative powers in a wide range of policy areas. The areas in which it has law-making authority include law and order, health, education, transport, the environment and economic development (see Box 13.1 overleaf). The Westminster Parliament no longer makes law for Scotland on these matters.

Under the Scotland Act (1998), the legislative powers of the Scottish Parliament are constrained in a number of ways. The act states that Westminster remains sovereign in all matters, but has chosen to exercise its sovereignty by devolving legislative responsibility to a Scottish Parliament without diminishing its own powers. Westminster retains the right to override the Scottish Parliament in areas where legislative powers have been devolved. The Westminster Parliament also retains the right to abolish the Scottish Parliament, although an attempt to do so would prove hugely controversial.

The 1998 act also lists a number of policy areas in which the Scottish Parliament has no legislative authority. These *reserved powers* are the sole responsibility of the Westminster Parliament. They include economic policy, the UK constitution, foreign policy and relations with the European Union (see Box 13.2 overleaf). Finally, the Scottish Parliament has made use of the *Sewel motion* procedure, which allows Westminster to legislate on issues that are technically devolved to the Scottish Parliament.

Box 13.1 Powers of the devolved administrations

Scottish Parliament

➢ Law and home affairs
➢ Economic development (including industry, administration of EU Structural Funds, inward investment and tourism)
➢ Agriculture, fisheries and forestry
➢ Education and training
➢ Local government
➢ Health
➢ Social work
➢ Housing
➢ Environment
➢ Transport
➢ Culture and sport
➢ Research and statistics
➢ Tax-varying power: three pence in the pound

National Assembly for Wales

➢ Economic development (including industry, administration of EU Structural Funds, inward investment and tourism)
➢ Agriculture, fisheries and forestry
➢ Education and training
➢ Local government
➢ Health
➢ Social work
➢ Housing
➢ Environment
➢ Transport
➢ Culture, the Welsh language and sport

Northern Ireland Assembly

➢ Economic development (including industry, administration of EU Structural Funds, inward investment and tourism)
➢ Agriculture, fisheries and forestry
➢ Education and training
➢ Local government
➢ Health and social services
➢ Housing
➢ Environment
➢ Transport
➢ Planning
➢ Sport and the arts
➢ Tourism

Box 13.2 Reserved powers: policy areas 'reserved' to Westminster

Constitution of the UK

Defence and national security

Foreign policy, including relations with the European Union

Fiscal, economic and monetary systems

Common market for UK goods and services

Employment legislation

Social security

Transport safety and regulation

Some areas of health (e.g. abortion, medicine)

Media and culture

Protection of borders

The Scottish Executive

The Scottish Executive is responsible for drawing up policy proposals and implementing legislation passed by the Scottish Parliament. The first minister — usually the leader of the largest party in parliament — heads the executive and appoints the executive cabinet. The cabinet appointed after the 2003 elections had 11 members, seven of whom headed executive departments. The overall number of ministers was cut from 20 to 18. Ministers exercise statutory powers, issuing secondary legislation and making public appointments. They are accountable to the Scottish Parliament.

The devolved bodies are funded by a block grant from the UK Treasury. This totalled £21 billion in 2005. The executive and parliament decide how this money will be allocated. The size of the grant is determined by the *Barnett formula*. This is an automatic formula agreed in 1978, by which public spending is allocated to Scotland, Wales and Northern Ireland, based on spending levels in England. The Scottish Parliament also has tax-varying powers: it can raise or lower the rate of income tax in Scotland by up to 3% (i.e. three pence in the pound). It also decides the basis of local taxation in Scotland.

The National Assembly for Wales

The National Assembly for Wales, which is commonly known as the 'Welsh Assembly', consists of 60 directly elected Assembly Members (AMs). It is elected using the additional member system. Forty of the 60 members are elected in single-member constituencies by first-past-the-post. The other 20 AMs are elected in five multi-member constituencies, each sending four additional members to the assembly. These list or 'top-up' seats are allocated using the d'Hondt rule (see Chapter 3). Elections are held at fixed 4-year terms. The new assembly building in Cardiff Bay was opened in 2004.

The Welsh Assembly is weaker than the Scottish Parliament, as it has only executive and secondary legislative powers. It determines how legislation passed by Westminster on a range of Welsh issues should be implemented. It can, for example, pass secondary legislation to flesh out acts of the Westminster Parliament. If Westminster leaves significant scope for interpretation, the assembly can play an important role in determining policy in Wales.

The Government of Wales Act (1998) specified the policy areas in which the assembly has executive power. They include education, health, transport, the environment and economic development (see Box 13.1 on p. 336). Like the Scottish Parliament, it also oversees the role of quangos. Funding is provided by a block grant from the UK Treasury (£11 billion in 2005) determined by the Barnett formula. The assembly decides how to spend this money, but it does not have tax-varying powers.

The Assembly Government

The Welsh Assembly Government formulates and implements policy. Originally called the Administration of the National Assembly for Wales, it was renamed in 2001. The first minister (initially known as First Secretary of the Assembly) heads the Assembly Government and appoints cabinet ministers. The nine-member cabinet includes eight departmental ministers. The first minister is normally the leader of the largest party in the assembly.

Summary

The devolved institutions in Scotland and Wales

➢ The Scottish Parliament has legislative and tax-varying powers.

➢ The National Assembly for Wales has executive powers only.

➢ Certain powers are 'reserved' to Westminster, which remains sovereign.

➢ Both devolved assemblies are elected by the additional member system.

➢ The devolved administrations are led by a first minister, who appoints cabinet members.

Elections to the devolved assemblies

No party won an overall majority in the first elections to the devolved assemblies in Scotland and Wales in 1999. Labour won 56 seats in Scotland and agreed a joint programme with the Liberal Democrats, who won 17 seats. Labour leader Donald Dewar became first minister with the Liberal Democrat leader, Jim Wallace, as deputy first minister. The Liberal Democrats took three other cabinet seats. The SNP won 35 seats (28 of them list seats). The Conservatives failed to take any constituency seat but won 18 list seats.

In Wales, Labour won 28 seats in the 1999 assembly election. Alun Michael formed a minority administration. His successor, Rhodri Morgan, negotiated a Labour/Liberal Democrat partnership in 2000. Plaid Cymru were the second-placed party with 17 seats.

In the 2003 elections, Labour maintained its position as the largest party in both nations. In Scotland, both Labour and the SNP lost seats, while two minor parties, the Scottish Greens and the Scottish Socialist Party, gained ground (see Table 13.2). Labour and the Liberal Democrats again formed a coalition government, but with a majority of just 5. In Wales, Labour improved its position, winning 30 seats (see Table 13.3). It held exactly half the seats in the assembly, but Rhodri Morgan opted to govern alone rather than renew his deal with the Liberal Democrats. With the presiding officer and his deputy being a Plaid Cymru member and Independent respectively, Labour had a technical majority. This disappeared in 2005 when Labour AM Peter Law left the party to sit as an independent.

Table 13.2 Elections to the Scottish Parliament, 2003

| | Constituency contests | | Regional lists | | |
	Share of vote (%)	Seats won	Share of vote (%)	Seats won	Total seats
Conservative	16.6 (+1.1)	3 (+3)	15.5 (+0.1)	15 (–3)	18 (+0)
Labour	34.6 (–4.1)	46 (–7)	29.3 (–4.3)	4 (+1)	50 (–6)
Lib Dem	15.4 (+1.2)	13 (+1)	11.8 (–0.6)	4 (–1)	17 (+0)
SNP	23.8 (–5.1)	9 (+2)	20.9 (–6.5)	18 (–10)	27 (–8)
Green	0.0 (+0.0)	0 (+0)	6.9 (+3.3)	7 (+6)	7 (+6)
Scottish Socialist	6.2 (+5.2)	0 (+0)	6.7 (+4.7)	6 (+5)	6 (+5)
Others	3.4 (+1.7)	2 (+1)	8.9 (+3.3)	2 (+0)	4 (+3)

Turnout: constituency seats: 49.4% (–8.8), regional lists: 49.4% (–8.7)
Note: figures in brackets refer to change since 1999.
Source: the Electoral Commision, www.electoralcommision.gov.uk

Table 13.3 Elections to the National Assembly for Wales, 2003

| | Constituency contests | | Regional lists | | |
	Share of vote (%)	Seats won	Share of vote (%)	Seats won	Total seats
Conservative	20.4 (+4.5)	1 (+0)	19.2 (+2.9)	10 (+2)	11 (+2)
Labour	39.5 (+1.9)	30 (+3)	36.6 (+1.2)	0 (–1)	30 (+2)
Lib Dem	14.1 (+0.7)	3 (+0)	12.7 (+0.3)	3 (+0)	6 (+0)
Plaid Cymru	21.2 (–7.2)	5 (–4)	19.7 (–10.6)	7 (–1)	12 (–5)
Others	4.8 (+0.1)	1 (+1)	11.8 (+6.2)	0 (+0)	1 (+1)

Turnout: constituency seats: 38.2% (–7.7) regional lists: 38.1% (–7.8).
Note: figures in brackets refer to change since 1999.

Devolution has raised difficult questions for each of the main parties. Labour previously dominated Scottish and Welsh politics but since devolution has had to share power in Edinburgh and (for a period) Cardiff. The Conservatives have sought to establish their

Scottish and Welsh credentials by distancing themselves from the UK party but their electoral fortunes have not improved greatly. The Liberal Democrats presented themselves as the 'real alternative' to Labour in the 2005 general election but are in coalition with Labour at Holyrood.

The pro-independence rationale of the SNP and Plaid Cymru is less suited to a post-devolution environment in which the devolved assemblies enjoy significant autonomy. Alex Salmond became SNP leader for a second time in 2004 while Plaid Cymru had three joint leaders after 2003 — a party president, a leader at Westminster and one in the assembly. With their share of the vote in decline, neither party looks likely to enter government.

Devolution in action

Post-devolution politics has normalised since 1999 as the devolved administrations have bedded down.

A new politics in Scotland?

The Scottish Parliament began its work against a backdrop of strong popular support and optimism that devolution would usher in a 'new politics'. Politics in Scotland appeared more consensual and inclusive than the adversarial politics characteristic of Westminster. The first Labour/Liberal Democrat coalition operated smoothly. Most MSPs had no experience of Westminster and the parliament encouraged consultation on legislative proposals.

Scotland had three first ministers in the first three years of devolution. Donald Dewar died in October 2000. Henry McLeish MSP won the Scottish Labour leadership election and became first minister. He resigned in November 2001 following controversy over payments he received from the lease of a constituency office while an MP at Westminster. Jack McConnell MSP was then elected unopposed as Labour leader and became first minister.

Devolution has enabled the Scottish Parliament and executive to adopt policies that differ from those pursued by the UK government in England. The introduction of free long-term personal care for the elderly is one example of this (see Box 13.3). The executive has also declined to follow UK government policy on tuition fees and foundation hospitals.

Jack McConnell

Since 2003, tensions within the Labour/Liberal Democrat coalition have been more apparent. Labour MSPs have been unhappy about some policies pushed through by the Liberal Democrats, notably STV for local elections. Some Liberal Democrat MSPs believe that coalition undermines the party's ability to establish a distinctive message.

Box 13.3 Examples of differential policy

Scotland

➢ Free long-term personal care for the elderly

➢ Abolition of tuition fees for university students

➢ Abolition of fox hunting

➢ Abolition of ban on 'promoting homosexuality' in schools (i.e. repeal of Scottish equivalent of 'Section 28')

➢ Abolition of feudal system of land tenure

➢ Three-year pay settlement for teachers

➢ Freedom of Information Act (2002) with fewer restrictions than the UK version

➢ STV for local government elections (from 2007)

➢ Proposed ban on smoking in public

Wales

➢ Abolition of school league tables

➢ Abolition of tests for 7, 11 and 14 year olds

➢ Creation of 22 local health boards

➢ Piloting of new Welsh baccalaureate in 19 schools and colleges

➢ Freeze on prescription charges and free prescriptions for 18–25-year-olds

➢ Free bus travel for pensioners

➢ Free school milk for children under 7

➢ Establishment of Children's Commissioner

Northern Ireland

➢ Abolition of school league tables

➢ Free fares for the elderly

➢ New package for student finance

➢ Establishment of Children's Commissioner

Devolution remains the preferred constitutional option of the Scottish electorate. But by 2003 fewer than one in five believed that the Scottish Parliament had most influence over Scottish life. Critics complained that the parliament often aped decisions taken in London. A stagnant economy and controversy over the cost of the Holyrood building contributed to the erosion of early optimism and a fall in turnout to 49% at the 2003 elections.

Towards a stronger Welsh Assembly?

Alun Michael's period as leader of a minority Labour administration did little to improve the standing of the Welsh Assembly. Michael had only won the 1999 Welsh Labour leadership election after heavy-handed intervention by the London party machine. A dispute over the release of EU funding damaged his position further and he resigned in February 2000. Rhodri Morgan won the subsequent leadership contest and

negotiated a partnership agreement with the Liberal Democrats 8 months later. The new coalition was proactive, introducing differential policies such as the abolition of school league tables and a reduction in prescription charges. But policy shortcomings were also apparent, notably an increase in hospital waiting lists.

The coalition ended when Labour opted to govern alone after the 2003 election. Turnout fell to 38%, but support for devolution had increased since the 1997 referendum. In 2004, an independent commission set up by the assembly to examine whether its powers should be increased issued the Richard Report. This

Rhodri Morgan

proposed that the assembly be given primary legislative powers in those policy areas where it currently exercised executive powers. It also recommended an increase in the size of the assembly (to 80 members) and replacing the AMS electoral system with STV. Neither the assembly government nor the UK government accepted the proposals on primary legislative powers or STV. The UK government revealed plans to widen the assembly's secondary legislative powers (e.g. by giving it greater discretion to tailor Westminster legislation to its needs) in the 2005 White Paper 'Better Governance for Wales'.

Summary

Devolution in action

➤ Labour/Liberal Democrat coalitions took power in Scotland (from 1999) and Wales (2000–03).
➤ Both administrations have introduced policies that differ from those that the UK government has put in place for England.
➤ Political problems brought about the resignation of a first minister in both Scotland and Wales.

Devolution in Northern Ireland

The Stormont Parliament

From 1922 to 1972, the Stormont Parliament and executive was responsible for the government of Northern Ireland. The Stormont regime was dominated by unionist politicians, who represented the Protestant majority and pursued policies that discriminated against the Catholic minority. The civil rights movement and the Provisional Irish Republican Army (IRA) took up Catholic grievances in the 1960s. British troops were sent to the province in 1969, but as 'the Troubles' escalated, Edward Heath's Conservative

'A place apart'

British governments have treated Northern Ireland as a 'place apart' in UK territorial politics. Special circumstances applied to Northern Ireland:

- **Conditional status.** Northern Ireland's status as a part of the UK is conditional on a majority of the population wishing to remain in the UK. At present, a majority supports the constitutional status quo. The UK government, meanwhile, depicts itself as a neutral broker in the search for a peaceful solution, claiming that it has 'no selfish strategic or economic interest' in Northern Ireland.
- **Separate administration.** Northern Ireland has been governed differently. From 1922 to 1972, it was the only part of the UK that had its own parliament with legislative and executive powers. After 1972, under direct rule, the secretary of state for Northern Ireland had greater powers than the secretaries of state for Scotland and Wales. Policy was made through Orders in Council rather than primary legislation at Westminster. Devolution in Northern Ireland has also been distinctive, as it is designed to ensure that the main unionist and nationalist parties share power.
- **The 'Irish dimension'.** Since the 1980s, the UK government and the government of the Republic of Ireland have worked together to find a peaceful settlement in Northern Ireland. The Anglo-Irish Agreement (1985) gave the republic a formal role in the search for a settlement.
- **Ethnic conflict.** The main political divide in Northern Ireland is that between unionists and nationalists. Unionists want Northern Ireland to remain part of the UK and would prefer a majoritarian rather than power-sharing system of devolution. Nationalists favour constitutional change, such as a united Ireland or a greater role for the Irish Republic in the affairs of Northern Ireland (see Table 13.4). This is an ethnic divide: unionists identify with the British state and tend to be Protestant whereas

Table 13.4 Preferred long-term policy for Northern Ireland (%)

	Protestant	Catholic	All
Remain part of the United Kingdom	85	24	59
Reunification with the rest of Ireland	5	47	22
Independent Northern Ireland	6	15	11
Other/Don't know	4	15	9

Source: Northern Ireland Life and Times Survey 2004, www.ark.ac.uk/nilt/2004/Political_Attitudes/NIRELAND.html

343

nationalists identify themselves as Irish and tend to be Catholic. Catholics made up 40% of the Northern Ireland population in 2001. Ethnic conflict colours everyday life in Northern Ireland: unionists and nationalists tend to live in different areas, attend different schools and socialise with people from their own community. Each community attaches great importance to history and symbols (e.g. flags and marches).

➢ **Distinctive party system.** Ethnic divisions shape Northern Irish politics. Elections are contested between unionist and nationalist parties, the main electoral issue being the constitutional status of Northern Ireland. But differences do exist within both the unionist and nationalist blocs. Under David Trimble (1995–2005), the Ulster Unionist Party (UUP) has supported the Good Friday Agreement (see the next section) while Ian Paisley's Democratic Unionist Party (DUP) opposed key parts of it. The Social Democratic and Labour Party (SDLP) has sought closer links with the Republic of Ireland through constitutional means. Sinn Fein, a republican party led by Gerry Adams, has close associations with the IRA, whose armed struggle it supported. Labour and the Liberal Democrats do not field candidates in Northern Ireland. The Northern Ireland Conservative Party has limited links with the London party and has had little success. The main UK parties have also tried to keep the Northern Ireland issue out of mainstream British politics and have adopted a broadly bipartisan position supportive of power-sharing devolution.

➢ **Security.** The terrorist campaigns of republican and loyalist paramilitary organisations posed particular security problems. The British Army and the Royal Ulster Constabulary (RUC), now the Police Service of Northern Ireland, have been in the front line in the fight against terrorism. The IRA was on ceasefire for much of the period since 1995 and ended its armed campaign in 2005. But the breakaway Real IRA (which killed 29 people in the Omagh bombing) and some loyalist groups have continued to wage terror campaigns. Sectarian violence between people of different religious faiths is a problem too.

The Good Friday Agreement

Negotiations aimed at securing a peaceful settlement to the conflict in Northern Ireland made slow progress in the 1990s. They finally bore fruit with the Good Friday Agreement of 1998 (the 'Belfast Agreement'). It established a 108-member Northern Ireland Assembly, elected by the single transferable vote (STV) system (see Chapter 3). The assembly has primary legislative power in a range of policy areas, although certain policies are reserved to Westminster (see Boxes 13.1 and 13.2 on pp. 336 and 337 respectively). Some measures require cross-community support from both unionist and nationalist parties.

Sinn Fein's Martin McGuinness and Gerry Adams outside 10 Downing Street

Executive functions are discharged by the Northern Ireland Executive, which is headed by a first minister and deputy first minister. The first minister is the leader of the largest party in the assembly, while the deputy first minister is drawn from the second largest party. The executive also includes an executive committee of ministers who head departments (see Table 13.5). Ministerial posts are allocated on a proportional basis according to party strength in the assembly.

Table 13.5 The Northern Ireland Executive Committee, 2002

Post	Minister	Party
First Minister	David Trimble	UUP
Deputy First Minister	Mark Durkan	SDLP
Minister of Enterprise, Trade and Investment	Reg Empey	UUP
Minister of Culture, Arts and Leisure	Michael McGimpsey	UUP
Minister of Environment	Dermot Nesbitt	UUP
Minister of Finance and Personnel	Sean Farren	SDLP
Minister for Employment and Learning	Carmel Hanna	SDLP
Minister of Agriculture and Rural Development	Brid Rodgers	SDLP
Minister for Social Development	Nigel Dodds	DUP
Minister for Regional Development	Peter Robinson	DUP
Minister of Health, Social Services and Public Safety	Bairbre de Brún	SF
Minister of Education	Martin McGuinness	SF

Other provisions

The agreement established three other bodies:

➤ a North–South Ministerial Council, in which the Northern Ireland administration and the Republic of Ireland government cooperate on cross-border issues
➤ a British–Irish Council, in which the UK and Irish governments, and the devolved administrations in Scotland, Wales, Northern Ireland, plus the Isle of Man and Jersey, exchange policy ideas
➤ a British–Irish Intergovernmental Conference, in which the UK and Irish governments discuss the situation in Northern Ireland

The agreement also required the UK and Irish governments to amend their constitutions to clarify the status of Northern Ireland. Within Northern Ireland, an independent commission on policing was established. This reformed and renamed the RUC. Provision was made for the early release of prisoners, and parties pledged to use their best endeavours to bring about the decommissioning of weapons held by paramilitary groups.

Northern Ireland devolution in action

The Good Friday Agreement was approved in referendums in Northern Ireland and the Republic of Ireland in 1998. The Northern Ireland referendum produced 71% support for

Table 13.6 Elections to the Northern Ireland Assembly, 1998 and 2003

Party	1998		2003	
	First preference vote (%)	Seats won	First preference vote (%)	Seats won
Unionist				
Ulster Unionist Party	21.3	28	22.7	27
Democratic Unionist Party	18.1	20	25.7	30
Progressive Unionist Party	2.6	2	1.2	1
United Kingdom Unionist Party	4.5	5	0.8	1
Other unionists	2.9	3	0.5	0
Nationalist				
Social Democratic and Labour Party	22.0	24	17.0	18
Sinn Fein	17.7	18	23.5	24
Others				
Alliance Party	6.5	6	3.7	6
Women's coalition	1.6	2	0.8	0
Independent (West Tyrone)	–	–	0.9	1

Source: the Electoral Commision, www.electoralcommision.gov.uk

the agreement on a high turnout of 81%. A slim majority of unionists and a large majority of nationalists backed it.

The first elections to the assembly were held in 1998 (see Table 13.6). Pro-agreement parties won 80 of the 108 assembly seats. The UUP was the largest party with 28 seats. The DUP, which opposed much of the agreement, won 20 seats. The SDLP (24 seats) was the largest nationalist party, although the Sinn Fein vote increased, giving it 18 seats. There was a pro-agreement majority within the assembly, but this was soon eroded when some UUP members ended their support for it, given the absence of IRA decommissioning.

UUP leader David Trimble became first minister and the SDLP's Seamus Mallon deputy first minister. New SDLP leader Mark Durkan replaced Mallon in 2001. The UUP and SDLP had four cabinet posts each, and the DUP and Sinn Fein two each (see Table 13.5) Power was devolved to the assembly in December 1999. It then launched some policy initiatives, e.g. abolishing school league tables (see Box 13.3).

But devolution has been dogged by problems over police reform, prisoner releases and, primarily, a lack of progress towards full decommissioning of IRA arms. The UK government suspended the devolved institutions on several occasions, reimposing direct rule. The assembly and executive have been suspended since October 2002.

Unionist support for the agreement has fallen significantly. A majority of unionist voters now oppose it, believing that too many concessions have been made to the republican movement. The IRA put some weapons 'beyond use' but did not decommission its arms fully. It also remained engaged in paramilitary and criminal activities. It was hoped that the agreement would encourage unionists and nationalists to work together. But the failure to implement it fully increased mutual suspicion while sectarian tensions between the two communities remained.

The 'hollowing out' of the pro-agreement centre has been evident in the changing fortunes of the Northern Ireland parties. The UUP has suffered serious divisions: Trimble faced numerous leadership challenges, three UUP assembly members defected to the DUP in 2003 and the Orange Order severed its ties with the party. Trimble stood down after his election defeat in 2005. The anti-agreement DUP has overtaken the UUP as the main representative of the unionist community. It was the largest party in the 2003 assembly elections, which were held while the assembly was suspended (see Table 13.6). The DUP then won nine seats to the UUP's one in the 2005 general election. Sinn Fein has similarly overtaken the SDLP. Support for the non-sectarian Alliance party has also fallen.

All parties support a form of devolution and propose some reworking of the agreement, but finding common ground is far from easy. The prospects of cooperation between the DUP and Sinn Fein are unpromising. But the IRA's 2005 announcement that it was ending its armed struggle offered new hope, though unionists reacted with caution. The British and Irish governments remain committed to the agreement, believing that it offers the best chance for a stable, peaceful settlement. Other options — a united Ireland, joint British–Irish authority, or the integration of Northern Ireland into the UK — enjoy little cross-community support.

Summary

Devolution in Northern Ireland

➢ The assembly is elected by STV.
➢ Some legislation requires cross-community support in the assembly.
➢ The executive is a power-sharing body in which four main parties are represented.
➢ The executive is headed by a first minister and deputy first minister.
➢ The secretary of state for Northern Ireland retains important powers on security and the search for a peaceful settlement.
➢ The assembly and executive have been suspended since 2002 when direct rule was reimposed.

Devolution and UK politics

It is not only in Scotland, Wales and Northern Ireland that the impact of devolution has been felt. Devolution has already had a significant impact on the UK constitution and UK politics. The impact of devolution will be examined in a number of areas:

> a quasi-federal UK
> differential policy
> intergovernmental relations
> Whitehall
> Westminster
> funding
> elections and parties
> moves towards regional government in England

A quasi-federal UK

The UK no longer fits the classic definition of a unitary state, namely a state in which power is concentrated at the political centre and all parts of the state are governed in the same way. Nor has it become a federal state, in which power is constitutionally divided between autonomous institutions.

Commentators have instead described the new territorial settlement as 'quasi-federal'. This recognises that the post-devolution UK does have some federal-type features. So the acts creating the devolved institutions set out a formal division of powers between the UK government and new bodies in Scotland, Wales and Northern Ireland. New arrangements have also been put in place to handle intergovernmental relations (i.e. relations between the UK government and the devolved administrations).

Parliamentary sovereignty

The legislation creating the devolved institutions stated that Westminster remains the ultimate legislative authority in the UK. Clear limits were placed on the activities of the new bodies: they could not, for example, vote themselves new powers. Policy areas such as relations with the EU and economic policy are 'reserved' to Westminster. Parliamentary sovereignty also means that Westminster has the right to overrule policy made by the devolved institutions, or even to abolish the institutions.

Differential policy

The devolved administrations in Scotland, Wales and Northern Ireland have implemented policies that differ from those pursued by the UK government in England (see Box 13.3). Differences have been most apparent in health and education. On the former, the Scottish Executive introduced free long-term personal care for the elderly while the Welsh Assembly has provided free prescriptions for the young and elderly and frozen charges for other age groups. Up-front tuition fees were abolished in Scotland and school league tables were scrapped in Scotland and Wales.

Some commentators view policy divergence as a natural and welcome consequence of devolution. The devolved administrations have responded to the particular concerns of their electorates. They have also acted as 'policy laboratories', trying out new approaches that can then be applied elsewhere. A children's commissioner for England was thus appointed after the success of this approach in Wales. Foxhunting was abolished in Scotland before England and the same pattern is expected for a ban on smoking in public places.

However, policy divergence undermines an underlying principle of the welfare state, namely that people should be treated equally regardless of where they live. Scottish students studying in Scotland will pay neither the university tuition fees levied from their counterparts in English universities nor the charges facing English students studying in Scotland. The devolved assemblies have had to fund students studying in England or home universities. Patients in Wales get cheaper prescriptions than those in England but face longer waits for hospital treatment. However, concerns about 'postcode lotteries' in healthcare in England reveal that cases like these result from the decentralisation of the welfare state rather than simply devolution.

The extent of policy divergence can be exaggerated. In most areas, there is little difference between policy regimes in Scotland, Wales and England. Indeed, supporters of devolution have complained about the willingness of the devolved administrations to adopt frameworks determined by the Labour government in London.

Multi-level governance

The UK has moved away from a model of centralised government to one of multi-level governance. Central government remains the single most important actor, but it does not monopolise decision making as a number of bodies operating at different levels have policy competences. These include subnational institutions (e.g. devolved administrations and the Mayor of London) and, at a supranational level, the European Union.

Intergovernmental relations

Devolution has required new mechanisms to handle the relationship between the UK government and the devolved administrations: that is, intergovernmental relations within the UK. These procedures serve a number of purposes:

➤ promoting policy cooperation in areas where policy competences are shared. An example is social inclusion, where the UK government is responsible for social security but devolved bodies make policy on employment and training.

➤ developing an agreed UK single negotiating position in the European Union on issues where the devolved assemblies have competence (e.g. regional funding)

➤ sharing ideas and policy experiences

➤ resolving disputes between the devolved administrations and central government

New procedures

A number of formal institutions and processes have been put in place to deal with intergovernmental relations.

➤ **Concordats.** Concordats set out the rules governing the relationship between various UK government departments and the devolved administrations. The most important document is the Cabinet Office 'Memorandum of Understanding and Supplementary Agreements', which was issued in 1999 and revised in 2001. It spells out procedures on matters such as relations with outside bodies (including the EU) and the sharing of information. The European Union plays an important policy-making role in many areas now handled by the devolved administrations, but relations with the EU are a 'reserved power'. The Concordats spell out that the UK government will consult the devolved administrations on policy in the EU, but that once the UK government's negotiating line has been settled, the devolved bodies are bound by it.

➤ **Joint Ministerial Committee (JMC).** This provides an arena for discussions between ministers from the UK government and those from the devolved administrations on policy in devolved matters. They may also be called upon to resolve policy disputes, although only as a last resort when problems have not been ironed out at an earlier stage (e.g. in working groups). The JMC meets in plenary and sectoral sessions. *Plenary sessions* are annual meetings attended by the UK prime minister and the leaders of the devolved administrations. *Sectoral sessions* discuss policy in particular fields and are attended by relevant departmental ministers from the UK government and devolved bodies. Sectoral meetings have been held on poverty and health. The UK government is the lead actor in JMC meetings.

➤ **Judicial Committee of the Privy Council.** This is the final arbiter in cases where legal disputes about the competences of the devolved administrations arise. It takes a binding decision on whether the UK government or a devolved body has legal responsibility for a policy area if this is not made clear in existing legislation. It has only been called upon to issue judgements in a handful of cases.

➤ **British–Irish Council.** This body was set up under the Good Friday Agreement to promote cooperation and an exchange of ideas in selected devolved policy areas (e.g. the environment). Its members are the British and Irish governments, and the devolved administrations in Scotland, Wales, Northern Ireland, plus the Isle of Man and Jersey.

Whitehall

Once the devolved administrations began operating, the territorial ministries in Whitehall were renamed the Scotland Office and the Wales Office. Most civil servants who worked in the territorial ministries were transferred to the devolved institutions. The Scotland Office and the Wales Office lost their executive functions: they were no longer responsible for formulating and implementing policy. As the Welsh Assembly does not enjoy legislative power, the Wales Office played an important role in drawing up Westminster legislation on Welsh issues and coordinating relations between the UK government and the assembly.

The Scotland Office and the Wales Office ceased to exist as separate departments in 2003. They became part of a new Department for Constitutional Affairs, which had responsibility for the devolution settlement as a whole. However, the Northern Ireland Office remained a separate department while the Office of the Deputy Prime Minister handled devolution to the English regions. The Department for Constitutional Affairs included a junior minister responsible for Scottish affairs and one for Welsh affairs, but they reported to the secretary of state for Scotland and the secretary of state for Wales rather than to the secretary of state for constitutional affairs.

Cabinet posts

The posts of secretary of state for Scotland and secretary of state for Wales remained as cabinet positions in their own right until June 2003. In the reshuffle of that month, the posts were combined with other cabinet portfolios. Secretary of state for transport Alistair Darling also became secretary of state for Scotland while Peter Hain was both leader of the House of Commons and secretary of state for Wales. The government argued that, with devolution bedded down, the limited workload of the territorial ministries no longer justified separate cabinet posts. But the reshuffle had been carried out with insufficient thought on how the new arrangements would work.

The office of secretary of state for Northern Ireland was untouched. It is regarded as more important than those for Scotland and Wales as the office holder acts as a broker in negotiations with the Northern Ireland political parties and is responsible for security policy. If the devolved institutions in Northern Ireland were suspended, the Northern Ireland Office would regain responsibility for the execution of policy. In 2005, Hain became secretary of state for Northern Ireland and retained the post of secretary of state for Wales.

Since devolution, a number of government departments spend much of their time on policy for England. This was particularly true of the Department of Local Government, Transport and the Regions until 2002. It was then split and responsibility for the English regions was transferred to the Office of the Deputy Prime Minister.

Westminster

Devolution has required procedural change at Westminster. The Westminster Parliament no longer handles devolved matters. MPs have thus been prevented, for example, from asking the secretary of state for Scotland questions on matters that are now the sole responsibility of the Scottish Parliament. The membership of departmental select committees has not changed substantially, but the remit of the three select committees dealing with Scottish, Welsh and Northern Ireland affairs has been adapted. The Standing Committee on Regional Affairs has been revived and serves as a forum for discussions on the English regions.

The 'West Lothian Question'

The 'West Lothian Question' asks why MPs representing Scottish constituencies at Westminster should be permitted to vote on purely English matters (e.g. local government in England), when English MPs have no say over matters devolved to the Scottish Parliament. The question was raised by Tam Dalyell (MP for West Lothian) in the 1970s and has yet to be fully answered. The situation is complicated further by Westminster's primary legislative role on policies relating to Wales.

The West Lothian Question came to the fore in 2003–04 when the votes of Scottish MPs were crucial in securing government victories on one bill establishing foundation hospitals and another providing for differential university tuition fees in England. A majority of MPs representing English constituencies opposed both measures. Conservatives complained of a 'constitutional outrage' but Scottish MPs who voted (both for and against) argued that both bills contained measures relating to Scotland. The introduction of tuition fees for English universities would also have an impact on Scottish universities and Scottish students.

The issue is likely to emerge again in Labour's third term, given its reduced parliamentary majority. The Conservatives are also unhappy that they won more votes in England than Labour in the 2005 election, but got fewer seats.

The main solutions to the West Lothian Question are as follows:

➤ The number of Scottish MPs should be reduced, ending the over-representation of Scotland at Westminster. This occurred at the 2005 general election when the number of Scottish MPs was reduced from 79 to 59. The size of the Scottish Parliament was unaltered. This means that constituency boundaries for Westminster and Holyrood elections differ.

➤ MPs representing Scottish constituencies should be barred from voting on legislation on English matters (e.g. health or education in England). The speaker would designate certain bills (or clauses) as 'English only' or 'English and Welsh' only. This 'English votes for English laws' position is supported by the Conservatives but has been rejected by the Labour government.

➤ Elected assemblies with some executive functions should be created in the English regions. This was the position of the Labour government until the 'no' vote in the 2004 referendum in the northeast of England.

None of these is unproblematic — the 'answers' may create more problems than the 'question'. There have always been anomalies in the UK constitution: there was no 'Belfast Question' when Northern Irish MPs voted on English matters after power was devolved to Stormont.

The appointment of John Reid, MP for Hamilton North and Belshill, as secretary of state for health in June 2003 caused some controversy. Reid was responsible for health policy in England and Wales, but not Scotland where the Scottish Parliament had legislative competence. He introduced legislation on foundation hospitals in England, a policy that the Scottish executive was not pursuing and which would therefore not affect his own constituents. Reid left the post in a 2004 cabinet reshuffle.

In Scotland, meanwhile, there has been some questioning of the use of Sewel motions, under which the Scottish Parliament allows Westminster to legislate on devolved matters. This mechanism had been used on 61 occasions between 1999 and 2005. It was not used just on technical matters but on issues such as same-sex marriages and the building of 'super casinos'.

Funding

The devolved administrations are funded by block grants from the UK Treasury, the size of which is settled by the Barnett formula. This formula, agreed in 1978, determines public spending levels in Scotland, Wales and Northern Ireland in relation to levels in England, using a series of calculations that take account of social differences. Under the Barnett formula, Scotland, Wales and Northern Ireland receive more public spending per head of population than England. Total public expenditure per head in Scotland in 2005 was £7,786 compared to £7,312 in Wales, £8,566 in Northern Ireland and £6,376 in England. Critics (including some English Conservative MPs and the Mayor of London, Ken Livingstone) claim that this amounts to an English subsidy of the other nations of the UK. Opinion polls offer only limited evidence of English discontent. The UK government has no immediate plans to change the Barnett formula radically.

The Scottish Parliament's tax-varying power has not yet been utilised. Should it decide to raise income tax by the maximum 3% to pay for higher public spending, this would only bring in some £500 million (compared to the bloc grant of £21 million). Support for greater financial powers has grown on both the left and the right of the Scottish political spectrum.

Elections and parties

Party systems in Scotland and Wales were distinctive before devolution because of the performance of nationalist parties and the decline of Conservative support. Devolution has cemented further the distinctive nature of the Scottish and Welsh party systems. Both are genuinely multiparty systems, in which four parties score over 10% of the vote. The AMS electoral system has ensured that the distribution of seats reflects voting behaviour more accurately. Following the 2003 elections, the Scottish Parliament contained MSPs from seven parties and three independent members. Four electoral systems will be in use in Scotland by 2007: FPTP for Westminster elections, AMS for the Scottish Parliament, STV for local elections and the regional list system for European Parliament elections.

Differential voting

Differential voting patterns have developed too. Electors voted in different ways in the 1999 and 2003 elections to the Scottish parliament and Welsh assembly than they did in the 1997 and 2001 general elections. Support for Labour was lower in the elections to the devolved assemblies than it had been in the preceding general elections. The SNP and Plaid Cymru have fared better in elections to the devolved assemblies but their support has declined since 1999. Overall, the centre left is in a stronger position in Scotland and Wales than in England.

Campaigns

The Scottish and Welsh Labour, Conservative and Liberal Democrat parties have enjoyed more autonomy since devolution. They now determine their own priorities, select their own candidates and organise their election campaigns with less interference from the

UK party headquarters in London. The desire of the Scottish and Welsh parties to put some distance between themselves and their UK parent parties also increases the likelihood of differential policies emerging across the Union.

Key terms

> **Barnett formula.** A formula by which relative levels of public spending in England, Scotland, Wales and Northern Ireland are determined.
> **Intergovernmental relations.** Relations between the UK government and devolved administrations.
> **Multi-level governance.** Subnational, national and supranational institutions all have policy competences.
> **West Lothian Question.** Why should Scottish MPs be able to vote on English matters when English MPs cannot vote on matters devolved to the Scottish Parliament?

England after devolution

The English dimension of devolution has still to be addressed fully. A number of questions about the status of England in the post-devolution UK have been posed. These include voting on English legislation at Westminster, funding arrangements and the representation of English interests in the UK government. The UK government and Westminster Parliament continue to make policy for England on issues such as education, health and local government that have been devolved to new bodies in Scotland, Wales and Northern Ireland.

English identity has undergone an intellectual revival (seen in the recent vogue for books on 'Englishness') and a popular resurgence (evidenced in the increased visibility of the St George flag). Surveys show that more people in England now describe themselves as 'English rather than British' than was the case before devolution (see Table 13.1 on p. 329). However, this has not (yet?) brought the nationalist backlash against the post-devolution settlement that some commentators predicted. The English have accepted Scottish and Welsh devolution with minimal fuss and do not support English regional assemblies or an English Parliament in any great numbers.

Regional Development Agencies

The Labour Party has proposed the transfer of limited powers to the English regions since the mid-1990s, but divisions in the party and the relatively low profile of the issue have slowed progress.

In 1999, the Blair government established Regional Development Agencies (RDAs) in the eight English regions (see Figure 13.1). Another was established for London. These promote economic development, investment, employment, skills and sustainable development within their region. They are required to draw up a regional economic strategy and are accountable to ministers. RDAs have limited budgets (totalling £2 billion) provided by the centre and have little scope for policy autonomy — they have neither revenue-raising nor legislative powers.

Figure 13.1 The English regions and their population (2001)

Scotland

North-east (2,515,442)

North-west (6,729,764)

Yorkshire and the Humber (4,964,833)

English regions

East Midlands (4,172,174)

West Midlands (5,267,308)

East of England (5,388,140)

Wales

London (7,172,091)

Southeast (8,000,645)

Southwest (4,928,434)

Regional Chambers (also known as 'assemblies') in the eight regions outside London act as regional planning bodies and are involved in the production of regional sustainable development frameworks. Seventy per cent of members are local councillors; the other 30% are drawn from sectors such as education, business and trade unions.

Labour's 1997 election manifesto stated that elected regional assemblies would be created in those English regions where public support for an assembly was confirmed in a referendum. The assemblies would have limited powers. However, no action was taken during Labour's first term when the focus shifted to directly elected mayors in English cities. The creation of the Greater London Assembly and Mayor of London does not count as devolution, as local authorities rather than central government previously held the powers they now exercise.

Elected assemblies

The White Paper, *Your Region, Your Choice* (2002) detailed Labour's proposals. Regional assemblies would have 25–35 members elected by AMS. They would take over the executive functions of the RDAs and other regional bodies. Funding would be via an HM Treasury block grant.

Elected assemblies would be established only if (1) wholly unitary local government was instituted in the region and (2) an assembly was approved in a referendum. The first such referendum took place in the northeast in November 2004. A long-running campaign for a northeast assembly had drawn support from local businesses, trade unions and politicians. A government consultation exercise had also suggested that popular support for devolution was higher there than elsewhere in England. But the referendum produced a 78% 'no' on a turnout of 48%. Reasons for the decisive rejection of the assembly include:

➢ the potential cost to local taxpayers of the assembly
➢ opposition to the creation of another tier of politicians and bureaucrats
➢ doubts about the usefulness of the assembly given its limited powers
➢ unease among local politicians about the creation of unitary authorities
➢ the inability of the 'yes' campaign to translate a strong regional identity into support for an assembly

The 'no' vote signalled the end of the road (in the medium-term at least) for Labour's plans for elected regional assemblies. Referendums planned for the northwest and Yorkshire and the Humber were abandoned. Support for assemblies was highly unlikely in areas lacking a strong regional identity. The 2005 Labour manifesto made no mention of elected assemblies; instead it proposed to give greater powers to RDAs and regional chambers, and to press for more elected mayors. Regionalisation is set to continue but without significant democratisation.

Some Conservative MPs have suggested that an English Parliament should be created to legislate on English matters, leaving Westminster to handle UK economic policy, foreign policy, etc. However, this idea has received little political support.

Summary

Devolution and UK politics

The impact of devolution on UK politics has been apparent in:

➢ the emergence of a quasi-federal UK

➤ differential policy
➤ new mechanisms for intergovernmental relations
➤ changes in UK central government
➤ changes at Westminster
➤ questions about funding
➤ the emergence of differential party systems and voting patterns
➤ moves towards regional government in England

Audit and future prospects

Four years on from devolution, the new territorial settlement appears more stable than might have been expected. Conservative warnings at the 1997 election of the break-up of the UK now seem far-fetched. The post-devolution settlement is asymmetric: the devolved administrations do not conform to one model, but have different powers and procedures. The devolved administrations have bedded in, although each has faced difficulties. There have been no major confrontations between the new bodies and the UK government.

Alternatives

The prospects of an alternative model of territorial management emerging in the UK have receded. There looks to be no going back to the pre-1999 system of administrative devolution for Scotland and Wales. But, as former secretary of state for Wales Ron Davies noted, 'devolution is a process, not an event'. Changes to the Scottish Parliament's electoral system have been proposed. Following the Richard Report a strengthening of the Welsh Assembly is likely. A reworking of aspects of the Good Friday Agreement may be required if devolution is to be restored in Northern Ireland.

Independence for Scotland and Wales also seems less likely. Opinion polls suggest that popular support for independence has fallen, although a significant minority of Scots are in favour. Nationalist parties seem unlikely to gain power in either country. However, the number of people identifying themselves as 'primarily British' has declined, while the number describing themselves as Scottish, Welsh or English has grown.

Federalism may appear to offer a more coherent system than asymmetric devolution. In a federal UK, Westminster might act as a federal parliament, handling issues such as the UK economy, constitution and foreign policy, while 'domestic' issues such as health and education are devolved to assemblies with equal powers in England, Scotland, Wales and Northern Ireland. This might resolve some of the anomalies of the post-devolution settlement, but it raises other problems. A major obstacle to federalism is England's dominance within the Union: England is by far the most populous and wealthy part of the UK.

Future challenges

The quasi-federal settlement that has emerged since 1997 is not trouble-free. A number of unanswered questions remain, and tensions within the UK may become more pressing. Despite the creation of the Department for Constitutional Affairs, strategic management by central government of the post-devolution settlement has not been as effective as it might have. The 'no' vote in the northeast referendum has forced a government rethink on regional government in England. The West Lothian Question reared its head in 2003–04 and may become more acute given Labour's reduced parliamentary majority. The electoral advances of the DUP and Sinn Fein have reduced the chances of an early restoration of the assembly and executive.

Major disputes between the devolved assemblies and the UK government have been avoided to date. Reasons for the smooth transition include pragmatic adaptation by politicians and civil servants, plus the fact that Labour has been in power in London, Edinburgh and Cardiff. There have been some tensions (e.g. members of the Welsh Assembly have been frustrated by their limited power). Difficulties may not be resolved so readily should a Conservative government take power at Westminster or nationalists gain the balance of power in Scotland or Wales.

Suggested reading

Bogdanor, V., *Devolution in the United Kingdom* (Opus, 2001).

Bradbury, J., '2003 Welsh Assembly elections: Labour reclaims power', *Politics Review*, vol. 13, no. 2, November 2003.

Denver, D., 'The devolution project', *Politics Review*, vol. 11, no. 1, September 2001.

Denver, D., '2003 Scottish Parliament elections: messages for unpopular parties', *Politics Review*, vol. 13, no. 2, November 2003.

Jeffrey, C., 'Devolution: a fractured project', *Politics Review*, vol. 14, no. 4, April 2005.

Mitchell, J., 'Reviving the union state? The devolution debate in Scotland', *Politics Review*, vol. 5, no. 3, February 1996.

Pilkington, C., *Devolution in Britain Today* (Manchester University Press, 2002).

Tonge, J., 'The only show in town?', *Politics Review*, vol. 13, no. 1, September 2003.

Websites

Constitution Unit: www.ucl.ac.uk/constitution-unit/

National Assembly for Wales: www.wales.gov.uk/index.htm

Northern Ireland Assembly: www.ni-assembly.gov.uk/index.htm

Northern Ireland Executive: www.nics.gov.uk

Office of the Deputy Prime Minister: www.odpm.gov.uk (responsible for UK government policy on the English regions)

Scottish Executive: www.scotland.gov.uk

Scottish Parliament: www.scottish.parliament.uk

Exam focus

Using this chapter and other resources available to you, answer the following questions.

1 Distinguish between devolution and federalism.
2 Is the UK a unitary or a union state? Give reasons for your answer.
3 Distinguish between legislative and administrative devolution.
4 Why did demands for Scottish and Welsh devolution gather momentum from the 1980s onwards?
5 Explain the decisive 'yes' vote in the 1997 Scottish devolution referendum.
6 Why was the Welsh devolution referendum vote less decisive than the Scottish vote?
7 What are the powers of the Scottish Parliament?
8 What are the powers of the National Assembly for Wales?
9 Why does the Welsh Assembly have less power than the Scottish Parliament?
10 How successful have the coalition administrations been in Scotland and Wales?
11 Explain how devolution in Scotland differs from devolution in Wales.
12 In what ways is Northern Ireland 'a place apart'?
13 Outline the main changes resulting from the Good Friday Agreement.
14 Why have the Northern Ireland Assembly and Executive been suspended on a number of occasions?
15 Present the case for regional assemblies in England.
16 Discuss the impact of devolution on the UK constitution and UK politics.

Chapter 14

The United Kingdom and the European Union

The United Kingdom joined the European Economic Community — later to become the European Union (EU) — in 1973. Since then, the EU has enlarged further and taken on more policy responsibility. Membership of the EU has had a significant impact on the political system of the UK, and the UK's relationship with the EU is a major issue in contemporary politics.

Key questions answered in this chapter
➤ How has the EU developed?
➤ What powers do the major EU institutions have?
➤ What have been the policies of UK governments towards the EU?
➤ How has EU membership affected the UK's political system?

The development of the European Union

The origins of the European Union lie in the aftermath of the Second World War (1939–45) when six west European states sought closer economic cooperation (see Box 14.1). The lead actors were France, Germany, Italy, Belgium, the Netherlands and Luxembourg ('the Six'). The Schuman Plan (1950) proposed a European Coal and Steel Community (ECSC). Set up in 1952, this was a supranational body with its own policy-making authority and budget, and a body of law that took priority over national law. It differed from inter-governmental bodies in which states cooperated voluntarily and could veto proposals.

Box 14.1 The development of the European Union

1950: Schuman Plan proposes a European Coal and Steel Community (ECSC).

1952: ECSC is created.

1957: Treaty of Rome establishing the European Economic Community (EEC) is signed by Belgium, France, Germany, Italy, Luxembourg and the Netherlands.

1958: EEC comes into operation.

1960: Seven states, including the UK, set up the European Free Trade Association (EFTA).

1961: UK applies for EEC membership (vetoed by France in 1963).

1962: Common Agricultural Policy (CAP) is agreed.

1965: Merger Treaty establishes the European Community (EC).

1967: UK reapplies for EEC membership — again vetoed by France.

1968: Customs union completed.

1973: UK, Ireland and Denmark join the EC.

1974: European Council established.

1979: European Monetary System established; first direct elections to the European Parliament.

1981: Greece joins the EC.

1985: Single European Act agreed at Luxembourg European Council (comes into force in 1987), paving the way for a single European market.

1986: Spain and Portugal join the EC.

1989: Delors Report on economic and monetary union (EMU); collapse of communist regimes in eastern Europe.

1990: German unification.

1991: Treaty on European Union agreed at Maastricht — sets out a timetable for EMU.

1992: Deadline for completion of the single European market; UK and Italy leave the exchange rate mechanism.

1993: European Union (EU) is established as the Maastricht Treaty comes into force.

1994–96: Central and east European states apply to join the EU.

1995: Austria, Finland and Sweden join the EU, which now has 15 members.

1997: Amsterdam Treaty agreed (entered into force in 1999).

1999: Stage III of EMU begins with 11 member states; Santer Commission resigns.

2000: Treaty of Nice agreed (entered into force in 2003).

2001: Greece joins the euro zone.

2002: Euro notes and coins come into circulation in 12 of the 15 EU member states.

2004: Ten new member states join the EU— Cyprus, Czech Republic, Estonia, Hungary, Latvia, Lithuania, Malta, Poland, Slovakia and Slovenia; EU Constitutional Treaty agreed.

2005: EU Constitutional Treaty rejected in referendums in France and the Netherlands.

The European Economic Community

In 1957 the Six signed the treaties of Rome establishing the European Economic Community (EEC) and the European Atomic Energy Community (EURATOM). They began operating in 1958. The EEC was a supranational organisation with its own institutions and budget. The Six agreed a Common Agricultural Policy (CAP) in 1962 and in 1968 completed a customs union by removing internal tariff barriers and establishing a common external tariff. The 1965 Merger Treaty brought together the ECSC, EEC and EURATOM institutions to form the European Community (EC).

The pace of integration slowed in the mid-1960s as the French president, Charles de Gaulle, blocked proposals to strengthen the EC's supranational elements. De Gaulle also vetoed UK membership twice. The 1970s brought only limited policy advances. The most significant was the creation of the European Monetary System in 1979. Central to this was the exchange rate mechanism (ERM), a currency grid in which the values of EC currencies were fixed against each other. The EC expanded to nine members when the UK, Ireland and Denmark joined in 1973. Three further states joined in the 1980s: Greece (1981), Spain and Portugal (both 1986).

The Single European Act

The mid-1980s brought a revival of European integration. The Single European Act (SEA), a major amendment to the treaties of Rome, was agreed in 1985 and came into effect in 1987. It brought about institutional reform, notably an increase in the use of *qualified majority voting* (QMV) and a strengthening of the European Parliament. The extension of QMV meant that individual states would be unable to veto key pieces of single market legislation.

The centrepiece of the SEA was the creation of a single European market (the 'internal market') by the end of 1992. The single market is 'an area without internal frontiers in which the free movement of goods, services, persons and capital is ensured'. Barriers to achieving this fell into three main categories:

- *Physical barriers*: customs checks at borders were removed.
- *Technical barriers*: under a system of 'mutual recognition', goods that met minimum standards in one member state could be freely traded in another. Professional qualifications would be accepted across the EC.
- *Fiscal barriers*: new procedures for VAT were introduced.

Most of these targets were met by the deadline successfully, although some problems remain. The single market programme also led to a greater EC role in social policy, with the European Commission looking to protect the rights of workers. It also prompted calls for *economic and monetary union* (EMU).

The Maastricht Treaty

The single market, the end of the Cold War (1989) and the reunification of Germany (1990) gave the integration process new impetus. France, Germany and the European

Commission pushed for further political union and EMU, but the UK opposed them.

The 'Maastricht Treaty', properly known as the Treaty on European Union, was agreed in 1991 and came into force in 1993. Its key elements were:

- the creation of the European Union, which comprised three pillars: the existing EC; an inter-governmental pillar on Common Foreign and Security Policy (CFSP); and an intergovernmental pillar on Justice and Home Affairs (JHA)
- a blueprint for economic and monetary union, with a single currency to be established by 1999 at the latest for member states meeting specified targets (*convergence criteria*)
- an extension of QMV and a strengthening of the European Parliament
- the principle of subsidiarity, by which the EU should act only where member states are unable to do so effectively

The UK government won two crucial exemptions:

- An opt-out from Stage III of EMU, meaning that the UK did not have to join the single currency. The UK Parliament could decide whether to participate at a future date.
- Non-participation in a Social Agreement, signed by the other 11 EC member states, which extended cooperation in social policy. This was often referred to as an opt-out from the 'Social Chapter'.

Danish voters rejected the treaty in a referendum in 1992, but a 'yes' vote was secured in a second vote and the treaty came into force in 1993. But commentators talked of a *democratic deficit* in the EU. There was limited popular support for further integration and EU institutions appeared unaccountable. The turmoil in the ERM in 1992 (when the UK and Italy left) and 1993 (when the bands of permitted currency fluctuation were widened) raised doubts about the viability of EMU too.

The EU recovered and spent the remainder of the 1990s engaged in both 'deepening' (further integration) and 'widening' (enlargement). The two main projects were:

- economic and monetary union
- eastward enlargement

Economic and monetary union

The Maastricht Treaty set out three stages to EMU:

- Stage I: the completion of the single market.
- Stage II: greater economic coordination and the creation of the European Monetary Institute (the forerunner of the European Central Bank).
- Stage III: the creation of the European Central Bank (ECB), the irrevocable fixing of exchange rates and the replacement of national currencies with the single currency (the euro).

Stage III would begin in 1999 for those states which met the convergence criteria specified in the treaty. These were: low inflation, low interest rates, sound public finances (levels of government debt) and membership of the ERM. Eleven member states — Austria, Belgium, Finland, France, Germany, Ireland, Italy, Luxembourg, the Netherlands, Spain and Portugal — formed the 'first wave' of states joining the single currency on 1 January 1999. The UK, Denmark and Sweden opted out. Greece did not meet the criteria for entry in 1999, but joined in 2001. Euro notes and coins entered circulation on 1 January 2002; national currencies ceased to be legal tender the following month.

In Stage III of EMU, decisions on interest rates are taken by the independent European Central Bank. The Stability and Growth Pact ensures budgetary discipline, providing surveillance of national economic performance and possible sanctions against EMU states that fail to reduce excessive deficits. Finance ministers of the euro zone states meet in the 'Euro-12' committee, but the Ecofin Council remains the main decision-making body on economic issues.

EMU brings a number of benefits, including an end to exchange rate uncertainty and the elimination of transaction costs on cross-border trade. But it also involves a loss of monetary sovereignty. The ECB sets interest rates for the euro zone as a whole. Problems will arise should one area suffer adverse economic conditions. Governments of states experiencing such difficulties would, under EMU rules, not be able to respond by altering interest rates or increasing spending dramatically.

Eastward enlargement

Three states — Austria, Finland and Sweden — joined the EU in 1995. But the path to the most difficult enlargement of the EU began in the mid-1990s when 12 states, predominantly from eastern Europe, applied for membership. These states had been under communist control and Soviet influence during the Cold War. They were only slowly developing into liberal democratic political systems with functioning market economies — key criteria for EU membership. Each state would also have to adopt existing Community law in its entirety on entry. This would require years of political, economic and administrative reform.

But the EU would also have to reform itself. The Common Agricultural Policy (CAP) and EU regional policy would have to be overhauled, as would the institutions of the EU.

Ten of the applicant states joined the EU on 1 May 2004 (see Figure 14.1). They were Cyprus, the Czech Republic, Estonia, Hungary, Latvia, Lithuania, Malta, Poland, Slovakia and Slovenia. Bulgaria and Romania are scheduled to join in 2007. The EU agreed in 2004 that accession negotiations with Turkey, which applied for membership in 1987, could begin. They could, though, take a decade to reach fruition.

The Amsterdam Treaty

The Amsterdam Treaty was agreed in 1997. The main changes it introduced were as follows:

= founder members (1958)
= members joining 1973–95 (date of joining)
= members joining in 2004
= applicants scheduled to join in 2007
= candidate countries

Finland
1995

Sweden
1995

Estonia

Latvia

Lithuania

Ireland
1973

United
Kingdom
1973

Denmark
1973

Netherlands

Poland

Belgium

Germany

Luxembourg

Czech
Republic

Slovakia

France

Austria
1995

Hungary

Slovenia

Croatia

Romania

Portugal
1986

Spain
1986

Italy

Bulgaria

Black Sea

Mediterranean Sea

Greece
1981

Turkey

Malta

Cyprus

Figure 14.1 The European Union

- The establishment of an 'area of freedom, security and justice' in which supranational procedures applied. The UK could opt out of policies in this area.
- The incorporation of legislation on border control issues (e.g. police cooperation) previously agreed by the 13-member Schengen Group into Community law. The UK was not a member of the Schengen Group, but could opt into these laws.
- The creation of the post of CFSP high representative and a new planning unit.
- New flexibility clauses that allow a majority of member states to pursue further integration (subject to certain safeguards) without the need for all states to participate.

However, member states failed to agree on how to reform EU institutions and the key decisions were postponed. Agreement was reached finally during bruising negotiations at the Nice European Council in 2000.

The Nice Treaty

The Nice Treaty came into force in 2003. The main changes introduced by the treaty are as follows:

➤ A qualified majority vote requires a specified number of votes, which are reweighted according to population and approval by a majority of member states.
➤ The European Commission comprises one national per member state. Once the EU reaches 27 members, there will be fewer commissioners than member states.
➤ A new distribution of seats in the European Parliament.
➤ A European Security and Defence Policy (ESDP) will be developed. The aim is for the EU to develop a common defence policy and the capacity for autonomous military action.

Many member states were unhappy with the Nice Treaty. Preparations for further treaty change got underway with the formation of a Convention on the Future of Europe. It produced a draft constitution that was then discussed by member states who agreed the EU Constitutional Treaty (commonly known as the 'EU constitution' or 'European constitution') at the 2004 Dublin European Council. Its main provisions are:

➤ a full-time president for the European Council, serving a term of 2 years 6 months
➤ a 'team presidency' system for the Council of Ministers
➤ a 'dual majority' system of QMV requiring the support of 55% of member states representing 65% of the EU's population
➤ a further extension of QMV
➤ a smaller College of Commissioners
➤ the end of the three pillar structure, though special arrangements remain for CFSP and JHA
➤ a clearer definition of EU competences
➤ the incorporation of the Charter of Fundamental Rights into the treaty
➤ an EU foreign affairs minister

The EU constitution cannot come until force unless approved by all member states. Voters in France and the Netherlands voted against the EU Constitution in referendums in 2005. This effectively killed off the constitution in its current form.

Key terms

➤ **Democratic deficit.** The argument that the transfer of powers from national governments to the EU has eroded the accountability of decision-makers and the control exercised over them by citizens.
➤ **Economic and monetary union.** The creation of a single currency, central bank and single monetary policy.

> **Enlargement.** The expansion of the EU to include new member states.
> **Euro zone.** The 12 states that have adopted the single currency.
> **Integration.** The process of coordinating the activities of different states through common institutions and policies.
> **Intergovernmentalism.** Concerning an international organisation in which national governments have primacy in decision making.
> **Subsidiarity.** The idea that decisions should be taken as close as possible to the citizens.
> **Supranationalism.** Concerning an international body such as the EU which contains institutions with independent authority, taking decisions that are binding upon member states.

Institutions of the European Union

The institutional architecture of the European Union is unique. It includes both *intergovernmental* bodies, in which national governments meet (the Council of Ministers and European Council), and *supranational* bodies with their own authority (the European Commission, European Parliament and European Court of Justice). The balance of power between the institutions has changed over time and remains fluid, although national governments tend to be the most powerful actors.

The European Commission

The European Commission is the executive body of the European Union. It is based in Brussels. As a supranational body, it acts in the general interest of the EU and is independent of member states. The president of the commission and the College of Commissioners are its political face. But the commission also acts as a civil service for the EU, employing some 22,000 officials — far smaller than most national bureaucracies.

José Manuel Barroso, President of the European Commision

Structure

> **The commission president.** The commission president is nominated by national governments acting in the European Council. Until the Treaty of Nice came into force, the president was appointed by a unanimous vote. Now only a qualified majority is required. The European Council's nominee must be approved by a vote in the European Parliament. The president and other commissioners serve a 5-year term. The president allocates portfolios within the College of Commissioners, can reshuffle posts and may demand the resignation of a commissioner. He provides leadership within the commission, but needs support from member states to play a leading role within the EU. Jacques Delors (1985–94) was the most influential president of recent years (see Table 14.1 overleaf).

Table 14.1 Presidents of the European Commission

Term of office	President	Member state
1958–67	Walter Hallstein	West Germany
1967–70	Jean Rey	Belgium
1970–72	Franco Maria Malfatti	Italy
1972	Sicco Mansholt	Netherlands
1973–77	François-Xavier Ortoli	France
1977–81	Roy Jenkins	United Kingdom
1981–85	Gaston Thorn	Luxembourg
1985–95	Jacques Delors	France
1995–99	Jacques Santer	Luxembourg
1999–2004	Romano Prodi	Italy
2004–09	José Manuel Barroso	Portugal

➤ **The College of Commissioners.** The 25 commissioners meet in the college to finalise legislative proposals and discuss developments. Commissioners are nominated by national governments but are not national representatives: they must swear an oath of independence. The European Parliament votes to approve the college as a whole, but not individual commissioners. Each commissioner is given a portfolio covering an area of EU activity (see Table 14.2). Prior to the 2004 enlargement, the college consisted of 20 commissioners. The five largest states — Germany, France, the UK, Italy and Spain — had two commissioners and the remaining states one each. Now each member state nominates one commissioner. The proposed EU constitution would reduce the number of commissioners to 18 by 2014, requiring a new system to rotate posts.
➤ **Directorates-General.** Commission officials work within Directorates-General that handle specified policy areas. There are currently 23 Directorates-General.

Functions and powers

The commission has a number of powers:
➤ It has the sole right to initiate draft legislation in most areas of EU activity.
➤ It executes and administers EU legislation and programmes.
➤ It administers EU expenditure and collects revenue.
➤ It acts as a 'guardian of the treaties', ensuring that Community law is applied properly.
➤ It represents the EU on the world stage, notably in international trade negotiations.

The commission has both a bureaucratic and a political role. Much of its work involves technical and administrative tasks similar to those performed by a national civil service. But it relies on national bureaucracies to monitor the implementation of Community law and on the Court of Justice to punish transgressors.

Table 14.2 The Barroso Commission, 2004–09

Commissioner	Member state	Portfolio
José Manuel Barroso	Portugal	President
Margot Wallström	Sweden	Vice-president, institutional relations and communications
Günter Verheugen	Germany	Vice-president, enterprise and industry
Jacques Barrot	France	Vice-president, transport
Sii Kallas	Estonia	Vice-president, administrative affairs, audit and anti-fraud
Franco Frattini	Italy	Vice-president, justice and home affairs
Vivianne Reding	Luxembourg	Information, society and media
Stavros Dimas	Greece	Environment
Joaquin Almunia	Spain	Economic and monetary affairs
Danuta Hübner	Poland	Regional policy
Joe Borg	Malta	Fisheries and maritime affairs
Dalia Grybauskaité	Lithuania	Financial programming and budget
Janez Potocnik	Slovenia	Science and research
Ján Figel'	Slovakia	Education, training, culture and multilingualism
Markos Kyprianou	Cyprus	Health and consumer protection
Olli Rehn	Finland	Enlargement
Louis Michel	Belgium	Development and humanitarian aid
László Kovács	Hungary	Taxation and customs union
Neelie Kroes	Netherlands	Competition
Mariann Fischer Boel	Denmark	Agriculture and rural development
Benita Ferrero-Waldner	Austria	External relations and European neighbourhood policy
Charlie McCreevy	Ireland	Internal market and services
Vladimír Spidla	Czech Republic	Employment, social affairs and equal opportunities
Peter Mandelson	United Kingdom	Trade
Andris Piebalgs	Latvia	Energy

The commission played a significant agenda-setting role under Delors. But its standing was damaged by the allegations of nepotism and fraud that led to the resignation *en masse* of the Santer Commission in 1999. Romano Prodi and José Manuel Barroso played a low-key role in EU affairs.

The Council of Ministers
The Council of Ministers is the main decision-making body of the EU. Since the Maastricht Treaty, it is formally known as the 'Council of the European Union', but it is

still frequently referred to as the Council of Ministers. Based in Brussels, the council is the institution in which government ministers from the member states take decisions on EU legislation. It is thus the scene of intensive bargaining and negotiation. The council consists of nine sectoral councils that handle specific areas of EU activity. The most important councils, which meet on a monthly basis, are as follows:

> General Affairs and External Relations — made up of national foreign ministers, dealing with foreign affairs and particularly sensitive general issues
> Economic and Finance Affairs (Ecofin) — made up of national finance ministers
> Agriculture and Fisheries — dealing with the largest area of EU expenditure

Much preparatory work is done by national delegations, each headed by a permanent representative. They hold weekly meetings in COREPER (the Committee of Permanent Representatives), a body that takes decisions on technical issues.

Table 14.3 Rotation of the presidency of the Council of Ministers and European Council (provisional)

Year	January–June	July–December
2005	Luxembourg	United Kingdom
2006	Austria	Finland
2007	Germany	Portugal
2008	Slovenia	France
2009	Czech Rep.	Sweden
2010	Spain	Belgium
2011	Hungary	Poland
2012	Denmark	Cyprus
2013	Ireland	Lithuania
2014	Greece	Italy
2015	Latvia	Luxembourg
2016	Netherlands	Slovakia
2017	Malta	United Kingdom
2018	Estonia	Bulgaria
2019	Austria	Romania
2020	Finland	—

Member states take it in turns to hold the presidency of the Council of Ministers for a 6-monthly term (see Table 14.3). The state holding the presidency hosts and chairs council meetings, acts as spokesperson for the EU and shapes the agenda of the council. But the presidency would be criticised if it pushed its own interests at the expense of consensus. The EU constitution would create a 'team presidency' system in which groups of three states share the presidency for a period of 18 months.

Functions and powers

The council has a number of functions:

> It is the EU's legislative body, although it shares legislative power with the European Parliament on many issues and legislative proposals emanate from the commission.
> It takes the key decisions in the CFSP and JHA intergovernmental pillars.
> It coordinates the broad economic policies of member states.

Voting in the council

Many decisions in the council are taken by consensus, but votes are held regularly. Voting procedures vary from policy to policy. There are three main procedures:

> **Unanimity.** Here a proposal will fail if at least one member state vetoes it (an abstention does not count as a veto). Unanimity is now only required for major policies or those of a sensitive nature.
> **Simple majority.** This applies to a limited number of technical decisions.
> **Qualified majority voting (QMV).** QMV now applies to many areas of EC activity. Each member state is allocated a set number of votes roughly according to its population (see Table 14.4 overleaf). Under arrangements introduced by the Nice Treaty, proposals require (1) a qualified majority of 232 votes out of 321 (72.3%) and (2) support from a majority of member states. In addition, a member state may request that the qualified majority represents at least 62% of the EU's total population. The EU constitution would replace weighted votes with a 'double majority' system in 2009. It defines a qualified majority as at least 55% of member states plus at least 65% of the EU population. A blocking minority would require at least four states.

The European Council

Set up in 1974, the European Council is the meeting place of the heads of government (and, in the case of France and Finland, heads of state) and foreign ministers of EU member states. The commission president and vice-presidents attend too. It is a political rather than legislative body.

The European Council meets at least twice per year, in June and December. Additional meetings are held frequently and are sometimes devoted to particular issues (e.g. employment). Meetings are chaired by the state holding the presidency of the Council of Ministers. When (or if) the EU constitution comes into force, the presidency will be held by an individual elected by the European Council. These summits are major events and often determine the development of the EU.

The functions of the European Council include:

> discussing key issues in the EU and in international affairs
> setting the agenda and political direction for the EU
> making key decisions on foreign policy and the economic situation in the EU
> launching new policy initiatives and agreeing treaty changes

The European Council has established itself as the EU's key strategic body, enhancing the power of member states and reducing the political influence of the commission.

The European Parliament

The European Parliament (EP) is the only directly elected institution of the EU. The first direct elections were held in 1979. They take place at fixed 5-year intervals: the last were held in May 2004. Each state uses a version of proportional representation.

Citizens vote for candidates from national parties. But in the parliament, MEPs sit in political groupings based on ideology rather than nationality. The centre-right European People's Party and European Democrats have formed the largest grouping since 1999.

Table 14.4 EU member states and future member states

Member state	Population (millions)	QMV votes, 2004–09	Seats in EP, 2004–09
Germany	82.5	29	99
France	59.9	29	78
United Kingdom	59.6	29	78
Italy	57.9	29	78
Spain	42.3	27	54
Poland	38.2	27	54
Netherlands	16.3	13	27
Greece	11.0	12	24
Portugal	10.5	12	24
Belgium	10.4	12	24
Czech Republic	10.2	12	24
Hungary	10.1	12	24
Sweden	9.0	10	19
Austria	8.1	10	18
Denmark	5.4	7	14
Slovakia	5.4	7	14
Finland	5.2	7	14
Ireland	4.0	7	13
Lithuania	3.5	7	12
Latvia	2.3	4	9
Slovenia	2.0	4	7
Estonia	1.4	4	6
Cyprus	0.7	4	6
Luxembourg	0.5	4	6
Malta	0.4	3	5
Total	456.8	321	732
QMV majority	–	232	–
States joining in 2007			
Romania	21.8	14	35
Bulgaria	7.8	10	18
Total in 2007	486.4	345	785
QMV majority	–	255	–

Turnout in EP elections is lower than for general elections. Turnout across the EU fell to a low of 45.7% in 2004. But it rose from 24% to 38.5% in the UK because of postal voting and greater interest in the campaign.

The EP consists of 732 MEPs with seats allocated to member states roughly according to their population. The EU constitution would set a maximum of 750 seats from 2009.

The EP has three locations: Strasbourg (where most plenary sessions are held), Brussels (where committee meetings are held) and Luxembourg (where the secretariat is based).

Functions and powers

The European Parliament has a number of powers:

- **Legislative power.** The EP shares legislative power with the Council of Ministers, but it cannot initiate legislation. The parliament's influence varies according to the legislative process being used. There are three main legislative routes for EU legislation:
  - **Assent procedure.** The EP holds a simple majority vote. This is used to approve the accession of new members.
  - **Consultation procedure.** The EP is asked for its opinion on a legislative proposal, but the council and commission are not obliged to take account of it.
  - **Co-decision procedure.** The EP's power is greatest here, as it can both amend and block proposed legislation. This is now used for many areas of activity.
- **Budgetary authority.** The EP shares budgetary authority with the Council of Ministers and can influence EU spending. The parliament can request amendments to the draft budget and can veto the final budget. A parliamentary committee then monitors spending.
- **Democratic supervision.** The EP oversees the activities of the European Commission. The parliament approves the nomination of the commission president and commissioners, and can censure the commission. Its investigations of financial mismanagement brought about the resignation of the Santer Commission in 1999. In 2004, the EP forced the withdrawal of two nominees. It also scrutinises commission activities by questioning commissioners, examining reports and monitoring the commission's actions. Members of the Council of Ministers are also questioned in the parliament.

Although the powers of the European Parliament have increased over the last decade, it does not enjoy the authority or legitimacy of national parliaments.

The European Court of Justice

The European Court of Justice (ECJ), located in Luxembourg, is the EU's judicial body. The court consists of 25 judges, one from each member state. Many cases are heard by only 3 or 5 judges. The ECJ upholds Community law, ensuring that it is applied uniformly and effectively. The court decides cases under Community law involving member states, EU institutions, businesses and individuals. National courts can ask the ECJ for a preliminary ruling on a matter of Community law. ECJ decisions have had an important impact on the

European Union, extending the EU's policy role and strengthening its institutions. The workload of the court has increased dramatically.

The European Court of Human Rights in Strasbourg is associated with the Council of Europe, not the EU.

Other institutions

Aside from these major EU institutions, there are a number of other EU bodies. Some are specialised agencies with important powers in a narrow policy field; others are relatively weak advisory bodies. Worthy of note are:

- the European Central Bank (located in Frankfurt) — sets interest rates for the euro zone
- the European Court of Auditors (Luxembourg) — financial watchdog overseeing EU accounts
- the European Investment Bank (Luxembourg) — issues loans to industry and regions
- Europol (the Hague) — promotes cooperation between national police forces
- the Committee of the Regions (Brussels) — advisory body made up of regional representatives
- the Economic and Social Committee (Brussels) — advisory body representing business and trade union interests

Summary

Institutions of the European Union

- European Commission: the EU's executive body with political and bureaucratic functions.
- Council of Ministers: the EU's main decision-making body and meeting place for ministers from member states.
- European Council: meetings of heads of state and government that determine the EU's political direction.
- European Parliament: a directly elected body sharing legislative power with the Council of Ministers.
- European Court of Justice: the judicial body of the EU, upholding Community law.

Key terms

- **Co-decision.** A legislative procedure in which the Council of Ministers and European Parliament share legislative power.
- **Community law.** The laws of the European Union, contained primarily in treaties and secondary legislation.
- **Qualified majority voting.** A voting arrangement in which proposals must win a set number of votes to be approved. Votes are allocated to states according to their population.
- **Unanimity.** A voting arrangement in which states can veto proposals.

What sort of organisation is the EU?

The EU is not easy to classify. It has some of the characteristics of an international organisation and some of the characteristics of a federal state, but cannot be accurately described as either. Classic international organisations (e.g. the United Nations) and regional trade bodies (e.g. the North American Free Trade Area) are intergovernmental bodies in which nation states are the primary decision-makers. States cooperate voluntarily and retain the right to veto decisions they oppose: in other words, they retain sovereignty. But the EU has an important supranational element: the commission has independent authority and Community law is binding upon member states. States cede or pool sovereignty when joining the EU.

Federalism

Federalism is a political system in which the constitution divides power between two autonomous tiers of government: a federal (i.e. national) government and state (i.e. subnational) governments. Federalist ideas inspired the pioneers of European integration in the postwar period, while some commentators also speak of the contemporary EU in terms of federalism. The term 'federalism' is, however, used differently in the UK — where it is associated with the creation of a supranational EU 'superstate' — than in continental Europe, where it refers to a constitutional sharing of power between the EU and its member states.

The EU has some of the features of a federal system:
- The EU treaties set out the powers held by different levels of government.
- EU law has primacy over national law.
- It has authority in many areas of public policy, including trade, monetary policy and agriculture.
- It has its own budget.
- It has its own currency, the euro.
- The European Commission negotiates trade treaties on behalf of member states.
- EU citizens are directly represented in the European Parliament.

To be a fully-fledged federal system, the EU would have to be equivalent to a federal government, while the governments of member states would only have powers equivalent to regional governments. This is not the case:
- The member states retain their own identities and distinctive political systems.
- Citizens identify with their nation states primarily, while European identity is weak.
- Except for the EP, the EU's major institutions derive their authority from national governments. The European Council and Council of Ministers are run by national governments; the leading actors in the European Commission and Court of Justice are also appointed by them.
- The EU does not have substantial authority over taxation, health, foreign policy or defence policy.

Multi-level governance

Many academics now describe the EU as a system of multi-level governance, in which a range of actors are involved in decision making. National governments remain the most important actors. They have authority in the major policy areas and are the key players in big decisions in the EU (e.g. treaty changes and CFSP). But national governments do not monopolise decision making. Supranational actors such as the commission have their own authority and are the most important actors in technical areas of policy (e.g. single market rules). Subnational governments such as the Scottish Executive also have policy-making powers.

Key terms

> **Federalism.** A political system in which power is constitutionally divided between federal and state (regional) authorities.
> **Multi-level governance.** A system of decision making in which subnational, national and supranational institutions all have policy competences.

UK membership of the European Union

The UK did not join the EEC at the outset, as the government feared the loss of sovereignty that would result from membership. British policy-makers saw the UK operating in 'three circles' in world affairs: the Commonwealth, the 'special relationship' with the United States of America, and intergovernmental cooperation in Europe. The UK also supported free trade rather than a customs union and joined the European Free Trade Association (EFTA) in 1960.

Edward Heath signs the EEC Accession Treaty, 1972

Membership applications

Harold Macmillan's Conservative government applied for EEC membership in 1961. The change in policy was due to:

> the declining political and trade importance of the Commonwealth
> the UK's declining influence in world affairs, illustrated by the 1956 Suez crisis
> the successful development of the EEC, which prompted fears that the UK would be left behind
> pressure for UK entry from the US government

The UK still did not support supranationalism, but hoped to defend its sovereignty from within the EEC. But French president de Gaulle vetoed the application in 1963 and did so again in 1967 when Labour prime minister Harold Wilson applied for entry.

Membership negotiations proved successful under Edward Heath's Conservative government. The issue caused divisions in both main parties, but Heath secured parliamentary backing for entry when 69 rebel Labour MPs voted with the government. The UK finally joined the EEC on 1 January 1973. In 1975, the Labour government called a referendum on UK membership. It produced a two-to-one vote in favour of continued membership.

The Thatcher governments, 1979–90

In its early years, Mrs Thatcher's Conservative government sought to reduce UK contributions to the EEC budget and reform the CAP. It then became a leading supporter of the single European market, which dovetailed with the Thatcherite commitment to free markets. But in the late 1980s, Thatcher was a staunch opponent of further European integration, particularly the Social Charter and plans for EMU. Divisions on Europe emerged at cabinet level. Concerns about Thatcher's views on Europe — expressed memorably in her 1988 Bruges speech — and the UK's isolation in the EC contributed to her downfall in 1990.

The Major governments, 1990–97

John Major had been instrumental in taking the UK into the ERM in the final weeks of Thatcher's premiership. He promised a more cooperative approach than his predecessor and presented the Maastricht Treaty as a good deal for the UK. The UK could opt out of EMU, would not be involved in new areas of EC social policy and had ensured that cooperation on foreign policy and immigration was placed on an intergovernmental footing.

But Eurosceptics argued that Maastricht meant an unacceptable loss of sovereignty and wanted the government to signal that it would not join EMU. Sterling's forced exit from the ERM in 1992 fuelled Eurosceptic opposition to EMU. As Eurosceptic feeling intensified in the Conservative Party, Major had to force the Maastricht Treaty through parliament. He refused to rule out UK entry into EMU, sticking by his non-committal 'wait and see' policy, under which no decision would be made until just before the launch of Stage III of EMU.

Government policy became more Eurosceptic in other ways. Major threatened to veto further treaty change and pursued a policy of 'non-cooperation' after the EU banned UK beef exports during the BSE crisis. He also wanted to see a more flexible Europe in which states could opt out of new EU policy activity. The prime minister struggled to hold the Eurosceptic and pro-European wings of his party together. These divisions contributed to a heavy Conservative defeat in the 1997 general election.

The Blair governments, 1997–

Weeks after coming to power, the Blair government agreed the Amsterdam Treaty. It signed the Social Chapter and helped frame an EU employment strategy that sought to balance labour market flexibility with effective social protection. At Amsterdam, Nice, and in negotiations on the EU constitution, Blair accepted a limited extension of QMV but was determined to preserve unanimity (i.e. the national veto) on issues of 'vital national interest', such as taxation, treaty change and defence. He presented the constitution as a 'tidying up exercise' that set clear limits on the EU's powers and strengthened the position of large member states.

At Amsterdam, the government maintained UK opposition to supranational authority in tax, foreign and defence policy. But war in Kosovo persuaded Blair that the EU had to develop a more effective defence and security role. The government first reached agreement with France and then supported the Nice Treaty's provision for the creation of a European Security and Defence Policy. The EU would deploy rapid reaction forces in conflict prevention and crisis management situations where NATO chose not to act. However, divisions between member states during the 2003 Iraq crisis damaged hopes that the EU would develop a common policy.

The UK gained opt-outs in the Amsterdam Treaty that enabled it to maintain border controls, but has exercised its right to opt-in to Schengen legislation on cooperation on crime. The Blair governments have supported EU action on organised crime, illegal immigration and asylum.

Labour and the euro

In October 1997, Chancellor Gordon Brown announced that the UK would not join the single currency during Labour's first term in office. But the government supported UK membership of the euro zone if the economic conditions were right. Labour had no constitutional objection to entry, but it would hold a referendum to approve any Cabinet decision to join. Brown set five 'economic tests' against which entry would be judged:

➤ *sustainable convergence* between the UK economy and those of the euro zone
➤ sufficient economic *flexibility*
➤ the impact on *investment* in the UK
➤ the impact on *financial services*
➤ the impact on *employment*

Detailed targets were not specified, allowing Brown and Blair to take account of the bigger political picture too. Ahead of the 2001 election, Blair indicated that a decision on whether the economic tests had been met would be made by June 2003. If the verdict was positive and a referendum voted 'yes' to entry, the changeover to the euro could be achieved within a couple of years. However, differences between Blair and Brown on the circumstances and timing of entry were reported widely. Brown was cautious about the impact of membership on the UK economy, while Blair saw EMU entry as important for full engagement in the EU.

In June 2003, Brown duly announced that the cabinet had agreed that Britain was not yet ready to adopt the euro. The Treasury released 18 studies on the euro, concluding that only one of the five economic tests (financial services) had been met. The chancellor claimed that Labour was committed to future entry and announced further measures to bring about sustainable convergence and economic flexibility. But during the 2005 election campaign, Blair and Brown hinted that euro entry in Labour's third term was unlikely.

The UK: an 'awkward partner'

Professor Stephen George has described the UK as an 'awkward partner' within the EU. This does not imply that it is the only country to oppose further integration or fight for its national interest. But a combination of circumstances makes the UK less enthusiastic about integration than most other member states.

Facets of UK 'awkwardness' include the following:

- **A distinctive history and culture.** The UK's historical development differs from that of continental European states. It has tended to have a global outlook and a close relationship with the USA, and it has not experienced the major political upheavals seen in other European states. The UK joined the EEC in 1973, 15 years after it was created.

- **Wariness of further integration.** UK governments have tended to be less enthusiastic about (and often hostile to) proposals for further integration. Rather than having a long-term vision, they have often acted pragmatically. The UK has supported intergovernmental cooperation rather than extensive supranational authority, and a single market rather than EMU. Key to UK concerns is the importance attached to the defence of national sovereignty.

- **Limited influence in EU negotiations.** The UK has often been unable to steer the evolution of the EU decisively. On policies such as EMU, UK governments have not set the agenda but have reacted to proposals emanating from other states, and have attempted to slow the pace of integration or to limit its impact on UK sovereignty. The UK has regularly been in a minority of states opposed to change and has not developed durable alliances with other states to rival the Franco-German alliance. However, the UK has been highly influential on some issues, notably the single market.

- **Weak elite consensus.** The UK does not have the strong consensus among the governing elite that exists in many other EU member states on the benefits of integration. Instead, Labour and the Conservatives have often taken adversarial positions on Europe, with one adopting a sceptical position to counter the pro-European position of the other. The issue of 'Europe' has also caused divisions within the two main parties which have then forced party leaders to seek compromises between pro-Europeans and Eurosceptics.

- **Limited popular support.** Levels of public support for EU membership and further integration have been lower in the UK than in most other member states. Sovereignty issues dominate the UK debate, while a Eurosceptic press has fuelled negative perceptions of the EU. Euroscepticism has become more significant in party politics, given its prominence in the Conservative Party and the rise of the United Kingdom Independence Party (UKIP).

Summary

The UK: an 'awkward partner'
- distinctive history and culture
- late entry into the EEC
- support for intergovernmentalism and opposition to a federal Europe
- limited influence on the evolution of the EU
- inability to construct lasting coalitions of support in EU negotiations
- divisions within UK political parties
- relatively low levels of popular support for further integration
- influence of Eurosceptics (e.g. newspapers)

UK politics and the EU

Membership of the EU has had a significant impact upon the UK political system. The EU is the main actor in many areas of public policy (see Table 14.5). Much legislation in policy fields such as agriculture and the standards of goods and services emanates from the EU. Government departments and local authorities implement these laws, while the UK courts enforce them by hearing cases under Community law.

Sovereignty

The precise meaning of sovereignty is disputed, but an institution is generally understood to be sovereign if it has final legislative authority and can act without undue external constraint. The term 'sovereignty' is used in different ways in the debates on Europe. For example:
- *national sovereignty* — the idea that final decision-making authority should reside in the nation state, with the national government determining law for its own territory
- *parliamentary sovereignty* — the doctrine that the Westminster Parliament is the supreme legislative body in the UK
- *popular sovereignty* — the idea that the electorate should choose decision-makers
- *economic sovereignty* — the idea that national governments should have the authority to determine economic and monetary policy

The Eurosceptic perspective

Eurosceptics and pro-Europeans offer different interpretations of the nature of sovereignty and the implications of EU membership. Eurosceptics tend to define sovereignty in absolute terms, seeing it as ultimate decision-making authority. They argue that the supranational EU has undermined UK sovereignty:

Table 14.5 Policy competences (selected) of the EU and its member states

Areas where the EU has most authority	Areas where the EU and national governments share authority	Areas where national governments have most authority
Agriculture	Employment	Tax
Fisheries	Regional policy	Defence
Trade	Energy	Criminal law
Internal market	Social issues	Citizenship law
Monetary policy (in euro zone)	Relations with non-EU countries	Electoral law
Competition policy	Overseas aid	Health care
Consumer protection		Education
Working conditions		Local transport
Environment		Broadcasting

> Community law has primacy over national law, meaning that UK law can be overturned.
> The UK has lost its right of veto in policy areas where qualified majority voting applies.
> The EU acts in areas such as monetary policy, immigration and foreign policy that are crucial to national life.
> Parliament and the electorate have little opportunity to hold EU decision-makers (particularly the European Commission, the ECJ and the ECB) accountable for their actions.

Eurosceptics differ on how 'lost' sovereignty can be regained. Some favour UK opt-outs on policies such as EMU, while others would like to renegotiate the treaties so that some EU powers (e.g. on agriculture) are returned to national governments. Others view withdrawal from the EU as the optimal means of restoring sovereignty.

The pro-European perspective

Pro-Europeans reject claims that EU membership has had negative consequences for UK sovereignty. Instead of viewing sovereignty as a legal concept concerned with ultimate law-making authority, they define sovereignty in terms of effective influence and a practical capacity to act. The UK has not lost sovereignty; rather it has 'pooled' or shared it with other EU member states. EU membership has, they argue, enhanced UK sovereignty:

> By pooling sovereignty, the UK has achieved policy objectives, such as the single European market, which it could not have done alone.
> Globalisation means that no state can act fully independently on issues such as the environment, economic policy and immigration.
> The UK has more international clout as a member of a strong European Union.

Parliamentary sovereignty

The doctrine of parliamentary sovereignty is central to the UK constitution. It makes three claims:

> Legislation made by parliament cannot be overturned by any higher authority.
> Parliament can legislate on any subject of its choosing.
> No parliament can bind its successors.

But Community law has primacy. In cases of conflict between national law and Community law, the latter takes priority. The European Communities Act (1972) gave future Community law legal force in the UK and denied effectiveness to national legislation that conflicts with it. This was illustrated in the 1990 *Factortame* case. The Merchant Shipping Act (1988) had prevented non-British citizens from registering boats as British in order to qualify for the UK's quota under the Common Fisheries Policy. But the House of Lords, following a ruling from the ECJ, decided that the act was incompatible with Community law and stated that it should be 'disapplied'.

This would appear to undermine parliamentary sovereignty, as parliament cannot legislate on any subject of its choosing, and legislation made by parliament can be overturned by another authority. However, we cannot say that parliamentary sovereignty is now meaningless: parliament still retains ultimate legislative authority, as it has the right to withdraw from the EU by repealing the European Communities Act (1972).

Key terms

> **Eurosceptic.** Concerned about the extension of supranational authority in the EU and hostile to further integration.
> **Globalisation.** The process by which states across the world become more inter-dependent and interconnected. This is apparent in trade, international organisations, global communications, etc.
> **National sovereignty.** Ultimate decision-making authority is located in the nation state.
> **Parliamentary sovereignty.** Parliament is the supreme law-making body.
> **Pro-European.** Supportive of further European integration and a leading role for the UK in the EU.

Policy making

Within central government, the lead actors in developing UK policy towards the EU are the prime minister, the Cabinet Office and the Foreign Office. The prime minister shapes the key objectives of UK policy and attends European Council meetings. In this respect, EU membership has strengthened the position of the prime minister. But the divisions on European policy that were evident with Conservative cabinets in the 1980s and 1990s undermined the authority of Margaret Thatcher and John Major.

Within the cabinet system, ministerial standing committees on European Union strategy and foreign affairs undertake detailed policy work. The European Secretariat, based in the Cabinet Office, coordinates policy so that all departments fall in line with the agreed negotiating position. A European adviser is based in the Prime Minister's Office. The Foreign Office coordinates UK policy towards the EU and takes the lead role in EU negotiations. The foreign secretary attends meetings of the Council of Ministers and European Council. The Treasury is the lead department on policy on EMU and oversees EU-related spending.

Government departments

There is an EU dimension to the work of most government departments. The Department of Trade and Industry, for example, spends most of its time dealing with EU policy. Most departments have established European units to coordinate EU policy. They are also involved in negotiations with other member states. In addition, ministers represent departmental interests in the Council of Ministers. Departments are also responsible for implementing much EU legislation. UK pressure groups have stepped up their lobbying of EU institutions, too.

Subnational government

Local government is responsible for implementing a large proportion of EU legislation. Some UK local authorities have also benefited from the money available to poorer regions through the EU Structural Funds. Many UK local authorities have established offices in Brussels to lobby for funding, while some have members on the EU Committee of the Regions.

The EU has a policy role in many of the areas (e.g. agriculture and the environment) devolved to the Scottish Parliament, Welsh Assembly and Northern Ireland Assembly. But responsibility for the UK's relations with the EU is 'reserved' to the UK Parliament. The devolved administrations are consulted on UK policy in the EU. Once the UK government's single negotiating line has been settled, they are bound by it.

UK political parties and Europe

The UK's role in the EU has become a major issue in contemporary politics, and it is one that political parties have found difficult to handle. The issue of 'Europe' is a complex one in the UK party system. The reasons for this include changes in the positions of the main parties, internal divisions and the problems of exploiting the issue for electoral advantage.

Policy change

The two main parties have changed their positions on Europe radically. The Conservatives were the more pro-European of the two from the 1960s to late 1980s. They first applied for membership (1961), achieved EEC entry (1973) and agreed the Single European Act (1985). But Euroscepticism escalated after Maastricht and became the dominant creed of the Conservative Party after 1997.

Labour has changed its position on a number of occasions, partly because of internal divisions. It opposed EEC membership in 1961, applied for entry in 1967, then opposed the membership terms agreed by the Conservatives in 1971–72. Labour called for withdrawal from the EC in its 1983 manifesto. A pro-European conversion began in the late 1980s when Labour supported EC social policy. Under Blair, Labour favours joining the single currency and has agreed to further integration.

Internal divisions

The most pronounced differences on Europe have often been found within the two main parties rather than between them. These internal divisions have created difficulties for the party leaders. If they adopt a firmly pro-European or Eurosceptic position, they risk exposing serious divisions and rebellions. To avoid this, leaders have tried to strike compromise positions that are acceptable to many MPs, but which do not fully satisfy either wing of the party. Major's 'wait and see' policy on EMU was a classic example.

Conservative divisions

In the 1960s and 1970s, most Conservative MPs supported EC membership. But a significant number on the right of the party (e.g. Enoch Powell) were 'anti-marketeers', who opposed the loss of sovereignty that membership involved. Divisions re-emerged in the 1990s when Europe became the main fault-line in the party. Eurosceptic MPs challenged Major's European policy. Many previously pragmatic MPs became Eurosceptic, as they felt that Maastricht and EMU meant an unacceptable loss of sovereignty and ran counter to Thatcherite economic policy.

In the 1992–97 parliament, Europe provoked the most serious dissent in the recent history of the Conservative Party. The ratification of the Maastricht Treaty saw large, well-organised rebellions (totalling 51 MPs or 20% of the party on one vote). Nine MPs later lost the party whip for disobeying the government on a vote on EU funding. Major also struggled to contain divisions in his cabinet between pro-Europeans (e.g. Kenneth Clarke and Michael Heseltine) and Eurosceptics (e.g. Michael Portillo and Michael Howard).

In opposition, the party leadership and policies have been Eurosceptic. Dissent from pro-Europeans is relatively muted, but some hardline Eurosceptics have called for withdrawal from the EU.

Labour divisions

Serious divisions occurred in the Labour Party during the 1970s and early 1980s. Many Labour MPs opposed EC membership, but the leadership broadly supported it. To limit the damage, Labour leader Harold Wilson focused on the details rather than the principle of EC membership, but 69 Labour MPs defied the whips and voted for entry. Cabinet ministers took opposing sides in the 1975 referendum. The policy of withdrawal from the EC was an important factor in the defection of pro-European Labour MPs to the breakaway Social Democratic Party in 1981.

Labour's switch to a pro-European position since the late 1980s has been relatively smooth, although 66 Labour MPs voted against the Maastricht Treaty. Blair's support for eventual UK membership of the single currency has not provoked serious revolts within the party. The promise of a referendum and failure to meet the five economic tests has hidden the scale of Euroscepticism within the party. Some 30 Labour MPs were expected to oppose the EU constitution; more would oppose EMU entry.

Party competition

Debates on Europe have often been characterised by *adversarial politics*, in which the two main parties take opposing positions. The first-past-the-post electoral system and the two-party system encourage this adversarial style. This partisanship has sometimes resulted from pronounced differences between the parties, as was the case in the 1983 and 2001 elections. On other occasions, the parties have broadly agreed on the benefits of membership of an intergovernmental EU, but have differed on particular policies. For example, the Conservative and Labour leaderships broadly supported the Maastricht Treaty, but Labour voted against it because the government had not signed the Social Chapter.

The parties and Europe

As the differences between the economic policies of the Conservatives and New Labour narrowed in the 1990s, Europe emerged as an area of disagreement. At the 1997 general election, Labour criticised the Conservatives for being isolated and ineffectual in the EU. Blair claimed that Labour would better protect UK interests and be more influential. The Conservatives accused Labour of being willing to surrender UK sovereignty by giving up the veto and joining the euro. Labour would sign the Social Chapter, while the Tories continued to oppose it. But both parties supported continued membership of an enlarged intergovernmental EU.

The Conservatives in opposition

The differences between the main parties have become more pronounced since 1997 because the Conservatives adopted a more Eurosceptic position. William Hague ruled out UK participation in the single currency for two Parliaments; under Iain Duncan Smith and Michael Howard the position hardened further as they unconditionally opposed euro entry.

The Conservatives oppose the EU constitution, arguing that it gives greater power to the EU in areas such as immigration, home affairs and foreign policy. They would like to renegotiate the EU treaties to create a more flexible Europe, in which member states could opt out of new policies, and to reduce the power of the EU's supranational institutions. They also support the repatriation of some EU competences to national governments (e.g. fisheries). Were the Conservatives to win power, their policies suggest significant changes in the relationship between the UK and the EU — though it is far from certain that they could persuade other member states to support their proposals.

The issue of Europe appeared a potential vote winner for the Conservatives in the 1997 and 2001 elections. Conservative policy on UK membership of the euro was more popular with voters than Labour's position. But the Conservatives did not reap significant electoral rewards. In 1997, Conservative divisions on Europe put voters off, while 1 million voters supported Eurosceptic fringe parties (the Referendum Party and UKIP).

Europe was the number one issue in the 2001 Conservative election campaign. But it did not figure prominently among the concerns of voters (it was ranked eleventh). Opposition to the euro did bring limited electoral gains for the Conservatives: they won support back from the Eurosceptic parties. However, it did not win them enough support from target voters. Hague's 'keep the pound' message was most popular with elderly voters and those without university degrees. But for many younger and professional voters, it reinforced the caricature of the Conservatives as extreme and 'out of touch'.

Europe barely featured in the Conservatives' 2005 general election campaign, in part because Blair had already promised a referendum on the EU constitution. Unsurprisingly, the issue had a higher profile in the 2004 European Parliament elections. UKIP won 16% of the vote then but fares less well in general elections, when voters look at a range of issues and are less inclined to cast a protest vote. (UKIP wants the UK to leave the EU.)

Summary

UK political parties and Europe

- Labour and the Conservatives have changed positions on European integration.
- Labour was hostile to European integration but is now supportive; the Conservatives were pro-European but are now Eurosceptic.
- Both main parties have experienced internal divisions on Europe.
- Europe was a major issue in the 2001 general election when the main parties took opposing positions, but did not feature prominently in 2005.
- The 'keep the pound' campaign did not win the Conservatives sufficient votes to affect the election outcome significantly.

Public opinion

The Labour government has proposed holding two referendums on European issues: one on the euro (should the cabinet recommend UK entry) and one on the EU constitution. The latter was expected to take place in 2006 but was abandoned after 'no' votes in France and the Netherlands in 2005. The timing of a referendum on the euro is uncertain: the cabinet declared in 2003 that the five economic tests for membership had not been met. This situation is unlikely to change in the short term.

Cross-party campaigns

Should they occur, the EU constitution referendum — and a future EMU referendum — would be contested by cross-party campaign groups. The 'yes' campaign would include many Labour MPs, the Liberal Democrats and some pro-European Conservative MPs. The 'no' campaign would largely consist of Conservative MPs but would also include Labour Eurosceptics. Both sides would use people from outside Westminster politics (e.g. business leaders, trade unionists and celebrities) to publicise their cause. Each of the campaign groups would be able to spend up to £5 million during the campaign. Public support for the EU and the euro is lower in the UK than in most other member states. A plurality of voters would vote to stay in the EU if a referendum on this issue were held (see Table 14.6). But opinion polls suggest that two thirds of British voters are against joining the euro. A majority also oppose the EU constitution: Blair's decision to hold a referendum on this looks like a dangerous gamble. The 'yes' camp would face an uphill challenge, though an effective campaign might persuade some voters to change their minds. The EU has negative connotations for many UK citizens and these are reinforced by the populist Euroscepticism of much of the tabloid press.

Table 14.6 British public opinion and EU membership

Question: If there was a referendum now on whether Britain should stay in or get out of the European Union, how would you vote?		
Year	Stay in (%)	Get out (%)
1977	47	42
1980	26	65
1983	36	55
1987	48	39
1990	62	28
1991	60	29
1992	52	35
1993	46	39
1994	52	36
1996	44	40
1997	49	35
1998	47	40
1999	51	41
2000	49	44
2001	48	43
2003	49	41

source: www.mori.com/europe

Suggested reading

Blair, A., *The European Union since 1945* (Longman, 2005).

Denver, D., 'European Parliament elections 2004', *Politics Review*, vol. 14, no. 2, November 2004.

Geddes, A., *The European Union and British Politics* (Palgrave, 2004).

Lynch, P., 'British Politics and Europe', *Politics Review*, vol. 13, no. 4, April 2004.

McCormick, J., *Understanding the European Union*, 3rd edn (Palgrave, 2005).

Watts, D. and Pilkington, C., *Britain in the European Union Today*, 3rd edn (Manchester University Press, 2005).

Websites

Britain in Europe campaign group: www.britainineurope.org.uk

European Commission: http://europa.eu.int/comm/index_en.htm

European Parliament: http://www.europarl.eu.int/home/default_en.htm

European Union (includes information on the history, institutions and policies of the EU, plus links to thousands of official documents): http://europa.eu.int/index_en.htm

European Union constitution (includes a guide to the EU constitution, plus the full text): http://europa.eu.int/constitution/index_en.htm

Foreign and Commonwealth Office (the 'Britain and the EU' section has information on UK policy in the EU): www.fco.gov.uk

The No Campaign: www.nocampaign.com

Exam focus

Using this chapter and other resources available to you, answer the following questions.

1 Why did the pace of European integration slow in the mid-1960s?

2 In what ways did the Single European Act contribute to the revival of European integration?

3 Outline the main elements of the Maastricht Treaty.

4 Discuss the impact of the Maastricht Treaty on members of the EU, particularly the UK.

5 Outline the main changes brought about by the Amsterdam and Nice treaties.

6 Discuss the impact of the Amsterdam and Nice treaties on EU member states, particularly the UK.

7 What are the powers of the main institutions of the EU?

8 Distinguish between intergovernmentalism and supranationalism.

9 What is qualified majority voting?

10 To what extent is the EU a federal system?

11 Is multi-level governance a better description of how the EU operates? Give reasons for your answer.

12 Why did the UK not join the EEC at the outset?

13 Why did the UK change its mind and apply for membership in 1961?

14 The UK has been described as an 'awkward partner'. In what ways has the UK been an 'awkward partner', and why?

15 Discuss the impact of EU membership on (a) UK sovereignty, and (b) parliamentary sovereignty.

16 In what ways have the Conservative and Labour parties changed their positions on Europe?

17 'The differences within the Conservative and Labour parties are greater than the differences between them.' To what extent do you agree with this view?

18 To what extent is there a democratic deficit in EU institutions and how might this deficit be addressed?

Index

A

B

C